AGAINST THE DEATH PENALTY

This edited volume brings together leading scholars on the death penalty within international, regional and municipal law. It considers the intrinsic elements of both the promotion and demise of the punishment around the world, and provides analysis which contributes to the evolving abolitionist discourse. The volume is divided into three general themes. Part I: Regional Conspectus and Analysis, considers the current developments within the United Nations, the Council of Europe, the African Commission, and the Commonwealth Caribbean, and engages with the emergence of regional norms promoting collective restriction and renunciation of the punishment. In Part II: Perspectives and Questions for Retentionist Countries, the United States, China, South Korea and Taiwan are investigated, and the iniquities of contemporary capital judicial systems are revealed. Emphasis is placed on the issues of transparency of municipal jurisdictions, the jurisprudence on the 'death row phenomenon' and the changing nature of public opinion. The book concludes with Part III: Overview of Abolition Strategies and Alternatives to the Death Penalty, where the arguments used to scrutinize the death penalty are surveyed and critiqued, and a detailed analysis of possible replacement sanctions is provided.

The physical confrontation between the sovereign
and the condemned man must end.
Michel Foucault, *Discipline and Punish: The Birth of the Prison* (1979)

Against the Death Penalty
International Initiatives and Implications

Edited by

JON YORKE
University of Surrey, UK

Routledge
Taylor & Francis Group
LONDON AND NEW YORK

First published 2008 by Ashgate Publishing

Published 2016 by Routledge
2 Park Square, Milton Park, Abingdon, Oxon OX14 4RN
605 Third Avenue, New York, NY 10017

Routledge is an imprint of the Taylor & Francis Group, an informa business

British Library Cataloguing in Publication Data
Against the death penalty : international initiatives and
implications. - (Law, justice and power series)
1. Capital punishment
I. Yorke, Jon
364.6'6

Library of Congress Cataloging-in-Publication Data
Yorke, Jon.
Against the death penalty : international initiatives and implications / by Jon Yorke.
p. cm.
Includes index.
ISBN 978-0-7546-7413-9 (alk. paper)
1. Capital punishment. 2. Life imprisonment. I. Title.

K5104.Y67 2008
345'.0773--dc22

2008026235

ISBN 13: 978-0-7546-7413-9 (hbk)

Contents

List of Figures

List of Contributors

Sangmin Bae is Assistant Professor of Political Science at Northeastern Illinois University. Her current research focuses on the impact of international human rights norms on domestic policy change. Her previous research on the death penalty has appeared in *The International Journal of Human Rights*, *Human Rights Review*, *Asian Affairs*, *International Politics*, and in Austin Sarat and Christian Boulanger (ed) *The Cultural Lives of Capital Punishment: Comparative Perspectives* (Stanford University Press, 2005). In her book, *When the State No Longer Kills: International Human Rights Norms and Abolition of Capital Punishment* (SUNY Press, 2007), she addresses the role of political leadership and domestic political institutions in helping explain why some countries comply with international norms against the death penalty while others do not.

Lilian Chenwi, is a Senior Researcher in the Socio-Economic Rights Project of the Community Law Centre, at the University of the Western Cape, South Africa. She has worked for a range of academic research institutions in the human rights field. She has assisted in various capacities in the editing of scholarly journals in human rights law, and has a record of publications on socio-economic rights, as well as on the death penalty in Africa, including the leading publication, *Towards the Abolition of the Death Penalty in Africa: A Human Rights Perspective* (Pretoria: Pretoria University Law Press, 2007).

Richard C. Dieter is an attorney of New York City. He has been the Executive Director of the Death Penalty Information Center in Washington, DC since 1992. The Center is a non-profit organisation serving the public and the media with analysis and information on issues concerning capital punishment. The Center prepares in-depth reports, issues press releases, and conducts briefings for journalists and others working on this issue. Mr. Dieter has worked for many years on issues related to human rights and the death penalty, including work as the director of the Community for Creative Non-violence's pre-trial release program, the founder of the Alderson Hospitality House for visitors to the women's federal prison in Alderson, West Virginia, and the founder of the Quixote Center's death penalty project. He has given numerous speeches at universities and is frequently quoted in the major newspapers around the country. He has testified about the death penalty before numerous state legislatures and has prepared reports for the U. S. House Judiciary Subcommittee on Civil and Constitutional Rights. He has authored articles on the death penalty for both magazines and scholarly journals.

Lina Gyllensten is a Research Associate at the Centre for Capital Punishment Studies, School of Law, University of Westminster, London. She is responsible for the Humane Advocacy Programme, the Centre's Occasional Papers Series and monitoring and research on the death penalty in the former British Commonwealth Caribbean and Asia. Lina is also currently managing the CCPS Internship Programme.

Peter Hodgkinson, OBE, is Director of the Centre for Capital Punishment Studies, School of Law, University of Westminster, London. He is an advisor to the Council of Europe, and was a founding member of the British Foreign Secretary's Death Penalty Panel. He has authored a number of publications on the death penalty including Peter Hodgkinson and Andrew Rutherford (ed) *Capital Punishment: Global issues and prospects* (Waterside Press, 1996); Hodgkinson, et al, *Capital Punishment in the USA*, UK Parliamentary Human Rights Group, 1996 and Hodgkinson and William Schabas (ed) *Capital Punishment: strategies for abolition* (Cambridge: Cambridge University Press, 2004); 'Capital Punishment – The families of homicide victim and the condemned', *Death Penalty. Beyond Abolition,* and 'Alternatives to the death penalty – The United Kingdom experience' in *Death Penalty. Beyond Abolition* (Strasbourg: Council of Europe, 2004).

Roger Hood, CBE, QC (Hon), PhD, DCL. FBA is Professor Emeritus of Criminology at the University of Oxford and Emeritus Fellow of All Souls College. From 1973 to 2003 he was Director of the Oxford Centre for Criminological Research. He has held research and teaching posts at the LSE, University of Durham, the Cambridge Institute of Criminology and Oxford, and is a visiting professor at the University of Virginia Law School, Adjunct Professor at the City University Law School Hong Kong, and Guest Professor at the College of Criminal Law, Beijing Normal University. In 1986 he received the Sellin-Glueck Award of the American Society of Criminology for 'Distinguished International Contributions to Criminology'. He has been a consultant to the United Nations, responsible for preparing the Secretary-General's quinquennial reports on the status of the death penalty worldwide. Among his books are: *Key Issues In Criminology* (with R. F. Sparks 1970); *A History of English Criminal Law: The Emergence of Penal Policy* (with Sir Leon Radzinowicz 1986); *Race and Sentencing* (1992); *The Death Penalty: a Worldwide Perspective* (4th ed. With Carolyn Hoyle 2008); and *A Fair Hearing? Ethnic Minorities in the Criminal Courts* (with Stephen Shute and Florence Seemungal (2005).

Seema Kandelia is a Research Fellow at the Centre for Capital Punishment Studies, and teaches in the School of Law, University of Westminster. She has written widely on the death penalty including, *Incestuous Rape and the Death Penalty in the Philippines: psychological and legal implications*, Philippine Law Journal, Vol. 80, No. 4, June 2006.

Julian Killingley is Professor of American Public Law at Birmingham City University. His current research focuses on due process in American capital trial procedure and the US Supreme Court's Eighth Amendment jurisprudence. His previous research on the death penalty has included contributions to amicus curiae briefs before the US Supreme Court filed on behalf of the Bar of England and Wales Human Rights Committee and the Law Society of England and Wales. In 2005 he received a certificate of appreciation from the National Association of Criminal Defense Lawyers for outstanding service for his work in connection with the NACDL's amicus curiae brief in *Deck v. Missouri*. He has authored three reports for the Foreign & Commonwealth Office on executive clemency and executions of juvenile and mentally retarded defendants in the United States (Amicus, 2007).

Nicola Macbean is the founding director of The Rights Practice, an independent NGO which works with local partners to help realise international human rights standards. The organisation currently works primarily in China with projects including strengthening the defence in death penalty cases, promoting access to justice in rural areas and combating torture and ill-treatment through the development of monitoring mechanisms for places of detention. Nicola also consults occasionally for the UN Office of the High Commissioner for Human Rights on its technical cooperation programme with China and has conducted research for the Foreign Office on the death penalty in the Kyrgyz Republic. Nicola was previously Director of the Great Britain-China Centre. She has a degree in social anthropology from the University of Cambridge and a Masters in economics and educational planning from the Institute of Education. Nicola has also studied at the Chinese University of Hong Kong and Fudan University Shanghai and speaks Chinese. She hopes to complete an LLM in human rights at Birkbeck College in October 2008.

Jane Marriott is a Lecturer in Law at the University of Surrey School of Law, whose research embraces issues in American Constitutional Law and contemporary Jurisprudence. She has published on comparative constitutional law, prisoners' rights and constitutional issues arising out of attempts to regulate campaign finance.

William A. Schabas, OC, MRIA, is Professor of Human Rights Law, National University of Ireland, Galway, and Director, Irish Center for Human Rights. He is also the Global Legal Scholar, University of Warwick School of Law, and a Visiting Professor of Queen's University Belfast School of Law. He has published extensively on the death penalty in international law, including *The Abolition of the Death Penalty in International Law*, 3rd ed (Cambridge: Cambridge University Press, 2002).

Rachael Stokes is the Research and Publications Manager at Penal Reform International (PRI). She is also a National Council member of the World

Development Movement (WDM). Prior to joining PRI in 2006, she has worked for a number of UK and international organisations, including Victim Support and Christian Aid. She graduated from the University of Edinburgh with an MA in Social Anthropology and from the University of East Anglia with an MA in Social Development.

Quincy Whitaker, is a barrister who practises in criminal justice related human rights law from Doughty Street Chambers, London. Her practice encompasses all aspects of the criminal justice process from trial litigation to obtaining civil redress for unlawful State actions, domestic and international, including representing defendants at the Special Court for Sierra Leone and the ICTY. She has provided human rights training in the UK for senior police officers, the Foreign office and lawyers in private practice and on behalf of the Council of Europe and the Bar Human Rights Committee abroad. She acted as a consultant in the field of criminal justice in transitional societies for the Department for International Development in Kosovo capacity building with local defence lawyers on case work and Advocacy and HR Law training. She has extensive experience of constitutional death penalty litigation in the Commonwealth Caribbean at the Privy Council and domestically in the Caribbean. She is currently teaching LLM students on the Death Penalty, Prohibition on Torture, Fair Trial rights and Access to Justice on the Human Rights and the Developing World course at the LSE, and is joint author of *Criminal Justice, Police Powers and Human Right*s (Blackstones, 2001).

Jon Yorke, is Lecturer in Law at the University of Surrey School of Law, and a member of the Surrey European Law Unit (SELU). He has worked on death penalty projects in the United States and Africa, and currently researches on the Council of Europe and European Union strategies against the death penalty. He was a consultant for the British Institute of International and Comparative Law, Commonwealth Africa death penalty project, between 2003–5, and is a former committee member and journal editor of the *Amicus Journal* for the UK death penalty charity *Amicus*. He has published widely on the death penalty including in the *European Law Review* and the *International and Comparative Law Quarterly*.

Preface

In his 1848 Preface to *A Treatise on Death Punishments*, François Guizot wrote, 'I think the present time is favourable for … attacking the use of capital punishment' (Guizot 1848, 249). A survey of the history of anti-death penalty discourse reveals a consistent lineage of optimistic voices arguing against the imposition of the punishment: and as such, in each generation, the 'present time' was thought favourable for attack. From the great oratory of Diodotus in 427 BCE, who against Cleon's call for the execution of the Mytilenians for revolting against Athens, asked, '[i]f we are sensible people, we shall see that the question is not so much whether they are guilty as whether we are making the right decision for ourselves' (Thucydides 1972, 219). Diodotus was making a principled argument against the punishment which was grounded in whether the punishment was 'right' for the Athenians. His position could be seen as a pre-liberal statement rendering the punishment 'illegitimate', and also, perhaps, the vast scholarship available to us today which renounces any claim to the death penalty's special deterrent quality can be seen as emanating from Diodotus when he argued:

> One of Cleon's chief points is that to inflict the death penalty will be useful to us in the future as a means of deterring other cities from revolt; but I, who am just as concerned as he is with the future, am quite convinced that this is not so … [w]e must not, therefore, come to the wrong conclusions through having too much confidence in the effectiveness of capital punishment (*ibid* 219, 221).

In 63 BCE, Cicero spoke in defence of Gaius Babirius. His passion for the campaign against the death penalty was clearly demonstrated, and he argued that honour should be bestowed upon his fellow Roman abolitionists when he stated:

> Nothing in the world could give me greater satisfaction than the knowledge that I myself, during this present consulship of mine, had succeeded in expelling the executioner from the forum … But instead the glory belongs in the first place, citizens, to our ancestors who, at the time when they drove out the kings, expunged every trace of their cruel ways from among the Roman people that had now become free. And, secondly, the credit belongs to a whole host of courageous men – the men who were determined that this freedom of yours should not be tainted by barbarous punishments, but should instead rely on the very leniency of its laws for its protection (Cicero 1990, 273).

Such 'courageous men' presented their arguments, sometimes at the expense of their own lives, against the all powerful sovereigns, and the abolitionist mantel had been passed down the generations. Particular significance for the modern day movement must be given to the great work of the Enlightenment humanists Cesare Beccaria and Voltaire, and the utilitarian position provided by Jeremy Bentham. In many ways, their work can be seen as a moulding of the ancient arguments to provide a humanistic, ethical, political and philosophical position.

Each generation has to be reminded of the vicissitudes of this 'barbarous punishment' and consequentially, the governments of the world have become more sympathetic to the genealogy of these cogent claims (see Megivern 1997). In our postmodern period, the scholarship, judgeship and campaigning of *inter alia* Hugo Bedau, Austin Sarat, William Schabas, Franklin Zimring, Roger Hood, Albie Sachs, Arthur Chaskalson, William Brennan, Thurgood Marshall, and Eric Prokosch, has sought to take a stand against the retentionist claim. It is significant that the anti-death penalty chorus is continuously de-legitimising the sovereign arguments of the 'right' to impose the punishment, and also, operating to dismantle the 'power' to execute.

This vast historical discourse can be seen as intrinsically contributing to a unique epoch of global penal history when on 18 December 2007, the very first United Nations General Assembly resolution to renounce the death penalty was adopted.[1] Point two of the resolution '[*c*]*alls upon* all states that still maintain the death penalty to … (d) Establish a moratorium on executions with a view to abolishing the death penalty'. The collective campaigns in the United Nations, by the abolitionist governments, the European Union, the Council of Europe, and various nongovernmental organisations, such as Hands Off Cain and Amnesty International, finally brought about this historical United Nations decision. It was a moment of jubilation for the global anti-death penalty community.

Roger Hood, in his Introduction to this book, and William Schabas, in Chapter 2, outline this resolution. However, both note points of caution. They state that there is still a way to go before witnessing global removal, as the General Assembly was not unanimous on the resolution. A careful reading of the resolution reveals that it should be interpreted as providing *part* of a pedagogical instruction for sovereign states on contemporary global penological standards. The resolution's value is demonstrated through its creation of a global 'norm' identifying that the punishment is no longer to be accepted as a legitimate aspect of sovereign rule. Also, the resolution is a reminder to those states which have removed the punishment that this abstention is to be continued.

All the contributors to this book provide a valuable engagement, in various ways, with the abolitionist pedagogy and they demonstrate that an educative process is still required. Perhaps the most poignant example for this need in our recent history was the execution of Saddam Hussein on 30 December 2006. The verbal condemnations by the international community, including the United Nations and the European Union, were powerless to prevent him being hanged. Hence, the global abolitionist trend and the General Assembly resolution, must be juxtaposed against the 'utter fiasco' (Scharf 2007, 259) of the former Iraqi leader's

1 Moratorium on the use of the death penalty, UN Resolution, A/C.3/62/L.29.

execution.[2] Indeed, Renate Wohlwend, the former *rapporteur* to the Committee on Legal Affairs and Human Rights, of the Parliamentary Assembly of the Council of Europe, noted '[r]ight now, the scandalously blunderous way in which Saddam Hussein and his henchmen were executed in Iraq provides an excellent prompt to demand an end to executions, once and for all' (Wohlwend 2007).

To heed to Wohlwend's call the international movement to abolish the death penalty must demonstrate that the international and municipal laws which remove, or call for removal, fundamentally provide a paradigmatic platform from which a multi-disciplinary discourse, of *inter alia*, political philosophy, criminology, sociology, culture, religion, ethics, feminism, anthropology and history, can be used to combat a sovereign's *will* to impose the punishment. The execution of Saddam Hussein demonstrates that the anti-death penalty discourse has not yet reached its threshold. However, the current situation may be read in that although it has not yet *severed* the sovereign power and right of application, it is getting very close to a universal *suspension.* This book engages with the continuous need to demonstrate that the world should do without the repugnant punishment of death.

Jon Yorke
Guildford
Summer, 2008

References

Boulander, M. (2007), 'Can the Iraqi Special Tribunal sentence Saddam Hussein to death?', *Journal of International Criminal Justice*, 463.
Cicero (1990) *Murder Trials* (London: Penguin).
Doebbler, C. F. J. (2007), 'An intentionally unfair trial', *Journal of International Criminal Justice*, 264.
Guizot, M. F. (1848), *A Treatise on Death Punishments*, in *ibid*, *General History of Civilisation in Europe: From the Fall of the Roman Empire Till the French Revolution* (Edingurgh: William and Robert Chambers Press).
Megivern, J. J. (1997), *The Death Penalty: An Historical and Theological Survey* (New Jersey: Paulist Press).
Scharf, M. P. (2007), 'The Iraqi high tribunal: a viable experiment in international justice?' *Journal of International Criminal Justice*, 258.
Thucydides (1972), *History of the Peloponnesian War* (London: Penguin).
Wohlwend, R. (2007), 'Full text of Speech delivered by Renate Wohlwend (Liechtenstein/EPP/CD) on the occasion of the 3rd World Congress against the Death Penalty', February, Paris.

2 On the arguments surrounding the execution of Saddam Hussein, see also Doebbler 2007; Bohlander 2007; and Zolo 2004.

Zolo, D. (2004), 'The Iraqi special tribunal: back to the Nuremberg paradigm?' *Journal of International Criminal Justice*, 313.

Acknowledgements

As a law student in 1996 and 1997, I worked with state and federal public defenders in Oklahoma on capital cases, and the experience which I gained through working with the passionate lawyers, meeting local 'Sooners' and visiting clients on H-Unit (Oklahoma's death row in McAlester) made a life-long impression on me, and revealed the importance of the continued need for arguing that the state is not justified in imposing capital punishment. The 'Okie' lawyers which impacted my life were Hoss Parvizian, Brian Lester Dupler, Randall Coyne and Vicki Werneke, and I am eternally grateful to them for showing me the fruits of passionate, determined, lawyering, against violence imposed by the state.

I also want to thank a woman whose name I never knew. At a candle light vigil in front of the Oklahoma State Capitol Building in Oklahoma City, as one of our clients was executed over in H-Unit, she squeezed my hand and said 'thank you for coming from England to care'. From this moment the importance of the arguments against the death penalty continually encompassing an international element became very real to me. It was on those marble steps under the Corinthian pediment of the grand building that the seedlings for this book were planted.

I gladly give wholehearted thanks to everyone who contributed to this book. But I must thank Julian Killingly first. He sent me to work in Oklahoma and his erudite and enthusiastic teaching on the death penalty in the United States put me, and many other students since, on this path. I owe a great debt to Julian. Roger Hood and William Schabas have provided invaluable scholarship calling for the ending of this repugnant punishment and their work can be seen as directly contributing to its modern day demise. Both Sangmin Bae and Nicola Macbean's work in Asia is extremely important for the reduction of the death penalty in this region. As is Lilian Chenwi's scholarship on Africa and the African Commission, and the litigation undertaken by Quincy Whitaker in the Judicial Committee of the Privy Council is directly responsible for preventing executions in the Caribbean. Jane Marriott has intricately contributed to the debates in the United States, and Richard Dieter and the Death Penalty Information Center, provide a remarkably generative service for the whole of the capital defence community within the United States. Peter Hodgkinson, Seema Kandelia and Lina Gyllensten at the Centre of Capital Punishment Studies, have formulated a fundamentally important pedagogical environment for worldwide studies concerning the death penalty, and they provide invaluable advice to NGOs and international organisations such as the Council of Europe. Finally, but certainly, not least, Rachael Stokes and Penal Reform International, are shining the light forward to demonstrate what the next challenge will be for the abolitionist community – this being the alternative punishment to the death penalty. Many, many, thanks to you all.

My personal work and research on the death penalty has been enriched by past colleagues at Warwick Law School. I am extremely grateful to Andrew Williams for his continued encouragement, academic guidance, and entering into a dialogue with me on the axiomatic vicissitudes of classifying the punishment. Also thanks to Professors Upendra Baxi, Istvan Pogeny, and Jackie Hodgson, and to Ralf Rogowski, Sammy Adelman, and Dallal Stevens. I really appreciate the support of Professor Rosalind Malcolm, the Head of Surrey Law School, and my colleagues at Surrey who have engaged with me in a dialogue of the death penalty, Christina Eckes, Leslie Blake, Theodore Konstadinidies, Susan Breau, Tim Sinnamon, Miriam Goldby, and Jane Marriott. Also thanks to Professor Mark Olssen, from the Politics Department, University of Surrey, and to Viv Boon, Centre for Culture and Media studies, University of Surrey, for their theoretical discussions on the death penalty. Thanks also to the participants of the Surrey European Law Unit (SELU) seminar series, 2007–8, for their discussions at the presentation of a paper which formed my chapter in this book.

Many thanks also to the remarkable UK death penalty charity, *Amicus*. I am no longer with you in body, but am in thought. I have benefitted so much from the conversions on the death penalty with Michael Mansfield QC, Rupert Skilbeck, Joanne Cross, Sophie Garner, Claire Jenkins, Jane Officer, Louise Maclynn, Patrick Moran, Anthony Solomou, Courtenay Barklem, and with Stephen Hellman, my former co-editor on the *Amicus Journal*.

I want to give special thanks to Professor Austin Sarat, firstly, for agreeing to publish this book within Ashgate's *Law, Justice and Power Series*, but secondly, and more importantly, for his extremely impressive, erudite, and instructive scholarship on the death penalty both within the United States and internationally. Austin's voice for the anti-death penalty campaign is an extremely pure and important one. He is passionately guiding us, and in many aspects of critical studies on the death penalty, he is our beacon. Many thanks also to Eric Levy, who recently joined Ashgate's US publishing arm, and to Gemma Lowle and Petra Jones, for providing encouraging comments and skilful editorial judgment.

My final, and most important, thanks, go to my family. I hope that they already know how much I love them, but I guess it is always nice to be told. My wonderful mother, Elizabeth and father, David, and brother Aaron, and recently, nephew, Cameron, and my grandparents, Laura and Stanley. My precious and dear wife, Marelize, deserves all that I can give in this life. Thank you for your love and may all your dreams come true.

List of Abbreviations

ABA	American Bar Association
ACHPR	African Commission on Human and Peoples' Rights
ACHR	American Convention on Human Rights
ADPAN	Anti-Death Penalty Asia Network
African Charter	African Charter on Human and Peoples' Rights
CCHR	Caribbean Centre for Human Rights
CCPS	Centre for Capital Punishment Studies
DPIC	Death Penalty Information Center
ECHR	European Convention on Human Rights (Convention for the Protection of Human Rights and Fundamental Freedoms)
ECtHR	European Court of Human Rights
ECPM	Ensemble Contre la Peine de Mort
ECPTIDT	European Council of Prevention of Torture and Inhuman or Degrading Treatment
ICCPR	International Covenant on Civil and Political Rights
IV	International Victimology
LDF	Legal Defence Fund
LWOP	Life without parole
LWP	Life with parole
MORI	Market and Opinion Research International
NAACP	National Association for the Advancement of Coloured People
NGO	Nongovernmental Organisation
NHRC	National Human Rights Commission
OAU	Organisation of African Unity
PACE	Parliamentary Assembly of the Council of Europe
PCRAJ	Presidential Commission on the Reform of the Administration of Justice in Nigeria
PRI	Penal Reform International
RCCP	Royal Commission on Capital Punishment
RCICP	Report of the Commission of Inquiry on Capital Punishment
SCCP	Select Committee on Capital Punishment
SPLA	Sudan People Liberation Army
TAEDP	Taiwan Alliance to End the Death Penalty
UDHR	Universal Declaration of Human Rights
UNCPCJB	United Nations Crime Prevention and Criminal Justice Branch
UNHRC	United Nations Human Rights Committee
UNODC	United Nations Office for Drugs and Crime
VSP	Victim Support Programme
WSV	World Society of Victimology

Chapter 1
Introduction

Roger Hood

Against the Death Penalty: International Initiatives and Implications appears just as the movement to abolish the death penalty worldwide has entered a new and challenging phase. It was marked, as William Schabas points out, by the resolution passed in favour of a world-wide moratorium on executions pending abolition of capital punishment at the plenary session of the United Nations General Assembly in December 2007. A large majority of countries (104) voted in favour, 29 abstained and only 54 stood out against it. This success was, of course, a reflection of the great strides made in persuading countries to abandon the death penalty over the past 20 years. At the end of December 1988, 35 countries had abolished the death penalty completely and a further 17 for all 'ordinary' crimes in peacetime: 28 per cent of the 180 countries recognised by the UN. One hundred and one countries (56%) were 'actively' retentionist, in that they had carried out at least one judicial execution within the past 10 years. Yet on the 1st January 2008 – a day marked by the complete abolition of capital punishment in Uzbekistan – only 50 of 195 countries were 'actively retentionist': just over a quarter of independent nations of the world. Furthermore, 102 of 112 countries that had abolished capital punishment had done so for all crimes, in all circumstances, in peacetime, under threat of war or during military conflict. A further 44 had not executed anyone for at least 10 years or had declared a moratorium. Of these, Amnesty International declares 33 to be truly 'abolitionist in practice': the death penalty remaining on their statute books but with no intention of it ever leading to an execution. Put simply, the vote at the UN was a foregone conclusion if all abolitionist and non-executing countries pulled together.

However, before abolitionist euphoria takes hold, some realism and caution is in order. On the positive side: only one abolitionist country (Solomon Islands) voted against the resolution at the plenary meeting, and only three abstained (Bhutan, Djibouti and Liberia). The 'yes' votes included Uzbekistan, which was on the cusp of abolition, Burundi, a country on the brink of becoming abolitionist *de facto* (the last execution occurred in 1997) and 11 other abolitionist *de facto* countries. Furthermore, nine of the 50 'actively retentionist' countries abstained: Cuba, Equatorial Guinea, Guinea, Lebanon, Sierra Leone, and perhaps most significantly Belarus, United Arab Emirates and Vietnam.

On the other hand, of the 33 countries listed by Amnesty International as abolitionist in practice, only 10 voted for the resolution,[1] 14 abstained and 8 voted against. Among another 11 countries that had not executed anyone for at least 10 years or had declared a moratorium, only one (Tajikistan) voted in favour, 8 voted against and 2 abstained. Thus, 16 (36%) of the 44 countries classified by the UN as abolitionist *de facto* voted against the resolution. It is clear, therefore, that if the object is to secure a *commitment* to abolition there still remains a substantial number of countries to influence. Altogether 83 of the 187 countries that voted (44%) did not support the call for a 'moratorium on executions with a view to abolishing the death penalty'.

One of the most persistent arguments put forward during previous attempts to get a moratorium resolution endorsed at the United Nations was again brought up in 2007 by several retentionist countries. Namely, that it was a matter for the sovereignty of each independent country, that there was no international consensus that capital punishment is a human rights violation, and that attempts by (largely) western powers to press this agenda on other countries amounted to a sort of cultural imperialism – indeed, a lack of respect for the history and culture of other regions and nations.[2] The challenge, which this valuable book identifies, is how to overcome the final hurdle to achieve abolition everywhere, a goal first promulgated by the United Nations in 1971. Several essays identify the 'sovereignty problem' as a fundamental and perpetual issue that must be confronted. This vital question is addressed in a scholarly paper by the book's editor Jon Yorke. He describes how the original signatories to Protocol No 6 to the European Convention on Human Rights had, in reality, voluntarily *suspended* their sovereign right to carry out capital punishment. He thus warns against complacently assuming that, because countries have entered into an international covenant to abolish the death penalty, there could never be any conditions under which they might reintroduce it. Indeed, he reminds readers of the recent pressures to reinstate it in Poland. Thus the human rights arguments against it need to be constantly bolstered and re-affirmed. Indeed, Jon Yorke argues that 'the key to maintaining the European moral sentimentality against the punishment is to ensure that the scholarship on the punishment does not disappear when the punishment disappears'.

It is true, of course, as Peter Hodgkinson, Seema Kandelia and Lina Gyllensten emphasise in their wide-ranging contribution, that abolitionists cannot be satisfied with moratoria on executions, for far too many countries and states in the United States have resumed executions after long periods of abstention. Jon Yorke is absolutely right to point out, as does Lilian Chenwi in her revealing essay on the situation facing the African Commission on Human Rights, and Peter Hodgkinson

1 Algeria, Benin, Burkina Faso, Congo (Brazzaville), Gabon, Madagascar, Mali, Nauru, Russian Federation and Sri Lanka.

2 See General Assembly GA/10678, 18 December 2007, 'General Assembly Adopts landmark Text Calling for Moratorium on Death Penalty' <http://www.un.org/News/Press/docs/2007/ga10678.doc.htm>. Also, Hood and Hoyle, 2008, 32–35.

and colleagues, as well as Quincy Whitaker in relation to the Commonwealth Caribbean, that many states see international law, as regards the death penalty, as a threat to their sovereignty over law enforcement polices, and therefore to be resisted. It is for this reason that Lilian Chenwi calls for the adoption of an African Protocol banning the death penalty, because 'African States believe that international human rights instruments do not always address the unique problems of the continent'. It may well be true that African states will sign-up more readily to a home-inspired protocol, but it is not clear in what ways the wording of a protocol for Africa to abolish capital punishment could differ significantly from the wording of the internationally agreed Protocol No. 2 to the International Covenant on Civil and Political Rights (ICCPR). Thus, while Sangmin Bae notes that the Bangkok Declaration on Human Rights of 1993 insisted on the 'significance of national and regional peculiarities and various historical, cultural and religious backgrounds' because 'the universalist perspective of human rights does not properly acknowledge and respect cultural variation', she tells a different story in describing the abolitionist movement in South Korea (which has just become abolitionist de facto) and Taiwan (where executions have declined to zero). The 'two most prominent rationale' for abolition in both South Korea and Taiwan, she writes, have been the universal principle of the right to life and the desire of these states 'driven by both moral and political considerations, to comply with international human rights standards so that they can become "beacon[s] of human rights throughout the region"'.

The world wide abolition of capital punishment will not be achieved until states recognise that, whatever sovereign powers they hold over citizens, the right to kill their criminal captives is not, and can never be, one of them. The fact that since the 1960s only four countries (Gambia, Nepal, Papua New Guinea and Philippines) have reinstated capital punishment and that the only one of them to carry out executions (the Philippines) subsequently abolished it again, as did Nepal, gives grounds for optimism. The ceding of sovereignty on this matter by so many countries, embodied by nearly all of them in international treatise and\or their constitutions, is really a recognition that abolition is intended to be permanent. Indeed, experience shows that, as time passes by, the demand for its return withers away as it becomes no longer a culturally acceptable punishment – a relic of less civilised times.

One path along which abolition can proceed, as William Schabas emphasises in his illuminating account of the role of the United Nations, is through development of the *Safeguards guaranteeing the rights of those facing the death penalty*, first promulgated in 1984 and subsequently expanded in 1989 and 1996 following UN surveys of the use of capital punishment. These have had the effect not only of drawing attention to the procedural safeguards embodied in the ICCPR but have identified categories of offender for whom capital punishment has been deemed an inappropriate penalty in all circumstances, notably juveniles and those with learning difficulties (encapsulated in the now old-fashioned and stigmatic term 'mentally retarded or extremely limited mental competence'). The report on the

UN Seventh Quinquennial Survey in 2004 suggested that persons suffering from any kind of mental illness should be added to this list. If international agreement could be reached on this, and procedures and trained personnel made available to enforce it, the number of persons executed worldwide would undoubtedly decline steeply and capital punishment would be further marginalised.

Several contributors discuss how far, through legal challenges and legislative processes, the death penalty can be whittled away, notably Julian Killingley, in his lively essay on how far the abolitionist movement can be taken in the United States through 'imaginative application' of the Eighth Amendment to the Constitution, rather than hoping for 'outright *de jure* prescription'. Jane Marriott focuses on the question of how likely it is that this can be achieved through attacking the 'death row phenomenon'. The Safeguards already lay down that capital punishment where it exists shall be carried out 'so as to inflict the minimum possible suffering' and that the Standard Minimum Rules for the Treatment of Prisoners' should be applied so as 'to keep to a minimum the suffering of prisoners under sentence of death and to avoid an exacerbation of such suffering'. Readers will recall the eloquence of Lord Griffiths in giving judgment in 1993 to limit the time between conviction and execution to five years in *Pratt and Morgan v Attorney General for Jamaica*: 'There is an instinctive revulsion against the prospect of hanging a man after he has been held under sentence of death for many years ... we regard it as an inhuman act to keep a man facing the agony of execution over a long period of time'.

As William Schabas notes, during the 1990s the UN Special Rapporteur on extra-judicial, summary or arbitrary executions (as did the Human Rights Committee) drew back from arguing that the 'death row phenomenon' is contrary to international norms governing the imposition of the death penalty for fear that it might be counterproductive, simply leading to the curtailment of other vital rights, namely the right to appeal to domestic and international courts and the exercise of clemency. This is the nub of the argument put forward by Jane Marriott for not going down this road as a means of attempting abolition by the 'back door'. Although I am not sympathetic to all her arguments, she has undoubtedly performed a valuable service in bringing this question so boldly to the fore. It surely deserves to be more thoroughly debated than it has been in the past. I am confident that at some point there will be universal recognition that it is impossible to avoid lengthy cruel and degrading suspension of execution in a system that lives up to the due process safeguards embodied in the ICCPR and wishes at all costs to avoid the execution of the innocent. As Richard Dieter points out, the 'innocence problem' is the issue most likely to undermine support for the death penalty in America, for 'an overwhelming 69 per cent of the public believes that [any possible] reforms will not eliminate all wrongful convictions'. The death row phenomenon is an inevitable consequence of the irresolvable tensions that accompany capital punishment and has become one of the worst human rights violations that it systematically perpetrates.

The question of what standards should apply – universal or local – in assessing whether there has been a breach of human rights emerges also in Quincy Whitaker's interesting critique of the role of Judicial Committee of the Privy Council (JCPC), as the court of final appeal, for countries in the Commonwealth Caribbean. She berates the Board for its failure all too often to interpret constitutional principles in the context of the development of human rights law. Among her other examples she roundly criticises the JCPC for accepting that the appalling conditions under which prisoners were held on death row in Trinidad could not, given the resources of that country, be expected to match the 'civilised' standards of first-world countries: 'The excusing of appalling conditions on the basis that they emanate from a third world country is … an attitude which may bear the hallmarks of the first world imperialism that the Board was trying to avoid'. Thus, she argues persuasively for constitutional and human rights standards to be regarded as universal 'minima which regulate the lawfulness of state conduct irrespective of which country they operate in'.

Nicola Macbean discusses with great authority the 'growing rights consciousness and the development of a legal ideology' in China. Here the debate at present is mostly about the pace of change and centres on what China must do if it is to comply with the standards it must adopt in order to ratify the ICCPR. But here too, as she reports, 'there has recently been a high level of concern following news of coerced confessions and wrongful executions'. The return of the power to review death sentences to the Supreme People's Court resulted from a recognition that the probability of receiving an immediate death sentence varied enormously across the country and that some standards and guidelines were necessary both to control the rate of executions and to make the system more equitable in order to present 'an image of a state that executes only when absolutely necessary'. The message from China is that international dialogue does not have to be so confrontational that it produces a 'backlash' against abolition. Indeed, even though China voted against the resolution at the General Assembly in December 2007, there appears now to be no ideological opposition to abolition being the goal to strive for.

Should worldwide abolition be achieved, the question remains: What penalty or penalties should replace capital punishment? And here abolitionists are, and will increasingly be, forced to continue their struggle to protect human beings from cruel and degrading punishment or treatment. It is fitting therefore that this book should end with a bold essay on life imprisonment without the possibility of parole. As Rachael Stokes, reminds us, one in four life sentenced prisoners in the USA is ineligible for parole and certainly not all those serving such a sentence would have been executed. She rightly calls for the development of internationally agreed human rights standards as regards the nature of imprisonment so that 'those reprieved from death row are not fated to an alternative that is equivalent to or worse than their original sentence'. The penalty of a lifetime behind bars without, from the outset, any hope of earning release through redemption, must surely not to be allowed to become the epitaph of the crusade against capital punishment.

References

Hood, R. and Hoyle, C. (2008), *The Death Penalty. A Worldwide Perspective.* Oxford: Oxford University Press, 4th edition.

PART I
REGIONAL CONSPECTUS AND ANALYSIS

Chapter 2
The United Nations and Abolition of the Death Penalty

William A. Schabas

As diplomats were labouring in San Francisco to create the United Nations in 1945, a parallel exercise was underway in London to establish the first international tribunal for the prosecution of serious violations of international law. The institution that resulted, the International Military Tribunal, which sat in Nuremberg and tried several of the Nazi leaders, was a creation of the four 'great' powers, and was independent of the United Nations. Nevertheless, the principles established at Nuremberg were endorsed by the United Nations General Assembly at its first session, in December 1946.[1] Only a few weeks earlier, the Tribunal had completed its work with the execution by hanging of eleven leading Nazis.[2] Although the General Assembly of the United Nations did not then speak specifically to the use of capital punishment for the punishment of Nazi war criminals, the matter was, at the time, entirely uncontroversial. A report on the death penalty prepared by the Secretariat of the United Nations more than thirty years later noted that 'the post-war years were not conducive to allowing Member States to come to an unequivocal position on the issue. Some countries with a long abolitionist tradition argued for barring the death penalty during times of war, while other members proposed an exception for offenders guilty of crimes against mankind'.[3]

Not quite half a century later, the United Nations Security Council established two international criminal tribunals, to deal with atrocities committed in the former Yugoslavia and Rwanda.[4] In at least one major respect, the new institutions contrasted with their ancestor at Nuremberg: the tribunals could only impose terms of imprisonment.[5] During the Security Council debate on the *Statute of the International Criminal Tribunal for Rwanda*, the representative of New

1 GA Res. 95(I).

2 *Agreement for the Prosecution and Punishment of Major War Criminals of the European Axis, and Establishing the Charter of the International Military Tribunal (I.M.T.)*, annex (1951) 82 UNTS 279, art. 27.

3 UN Doc. A/CONF.87/9, para. 4.

4 UN Doc. S/RES/827 (1993); UN Doc. S/RES/955 (1994).

5 *Statute of the International Criminal Tribunal for the former Yugoslavia*, UN Doc. S/RES/827 (1993), annex, art. 24(1); *Statute of the International Criminal Tribunal for Rwanda*, UN Doc. S/RES/955 (1994), annex, art. 23(1). See also: *Statute of the Special*

Zealand stated that '[f]or over three decades the United Nations has been trying progressively to eliminate the death penalty. It would be entirely unacceptable – and a dreadful step backwards – to introduce it here'.[6] Indeed, over the forty-nine years since the beginning of the United Nations, world opinion and national practice with respect to capital punishment had shifted dramatically, and this was reflected in the policy of the organisation. This chapter endeavours to chart the evolution of the death penalty debate within the United Nations.

Standard Setting: The Universal Declaration of Human Rights and the International Covenant on Civil and Political Rights

The *Charter of the United Nations*, adopted in San Francisco in June 1945, provided several references to human rights, and declared that 'promoting and encouraging respect for human rights and for fundamental freedoms for all without distinction as to race, sex, language, or religion' was among the purposes of the United Nations.[7] To the dismay of many, however, the major powers reneged on earlier commitments to include a declaration of human rights within the *Charter* itself (Lauren 2003). The compromise at San Francisco was to make ample reference to human rights in the *Charter* but to postpone adoption of anything substantive. In early 1947, the Commission on Human Rights began work on two documents, a general declaration of human rights principles of a non-binding nature and a full-blown treaty or 'covenant' to which States could adhere if they so decided. Three years later, on 10 December 1948, the United Nations General Assembly adopted the *Universal Declaration on Human Rights*.[8] Work on the proposed covenant took considerably longer, and a final text was only adopted in 1966.[9] Important debates about capital punishment figured in the preparation of both instruments, principally within the context of discussion about the 'right to life'.

The issue of capital punishment was debated at considerable length by the Commission on Human Rights and the General Assembly in the course of adoption of the *Universal Declaration of Human Rights*, during 1947 and 1948. This was the first significant consideration of the death penalty within the United Nations. In its final version, article 3 of the *Universal Declaration* states: 'Everyone has the right to life, liberty and security of person'. However, the original draft of this provision, prepared by John P. Humphrey in early 1947, recognised a right to life that 'can be denied only to persons who have been convicted under general

Court for Sierra Leone, art. 19(1); *Statute of the Special Tribunal for Lebanon*, UN Doc. S/RES/1757 (2007), Attachment, 11, art. 24(1).

6 *ibid.*, p. 5.

7 *Charter of the United Nations*, TS 67 (1946), Cmd. 7015, P. (1946-7) XXV 1, 145 BSP 805.

8 *Universal Declaration of Human Rights*, GA Res. 217 A (III) UN Doc. A/810.

9 GA Res. 44/128.

law of some crime to which the death penalty is attached'.[10] Eleanor Roosevelt, who chaired the Drafting Committee of the Commission on Human Rights, cited movement underway in some states to abolish the death penalty, and suggested that it might be better not to make any explicit mention of capital punishment as an exception to the right to life.[11] René Cassin reworked Humphrey's draft and removed the reference to the death penalty.[12]

Although Cassin's proposal found its way, virtually unchanged, into the final version of the *Universal Declaration,* when the text was being studied by the Third Committee of the General Assembly in late 1948 there was an important debate about the death penalty. The Soviet Union proposed an amendment calling for abolition of the death penalty in peacetime.[13] In the ensuing debate, nary a voice was raised to defend the use of capital punishment in peacetime, although some delegates conceded that their governments had not yet abolished the death penalty.[14] Many participants in the debate said only that the proposal was inopportune[15] or premature.[16] The United Kingdom representative said that its inclusion in the declaration might make it difficult for some states to accept,[17] and a number of delegates said they would abstain in the vote for this reason.[18]

Several Latin American delegates were unhappy with the Soviet amendment because it did not go far enough. They were opposed to the death penalty entirely, even in wartime. Costa Rica's delegation said it would abstain from voting on the Soviet amendment because it restricted abolition to times of peace.[19] The Venezuelan delegate said he could not support the Soviet proposal on the death penalty, because it implied that such punishment was legal in times of war, and this was contrary to his country's laws.[20] He said that he would have been able to vote in favour of the proposal, if it had envisaged the complete abolition of the death penalty.[21] Uruguay's delegate proposed an amendment aimed at total abolition,

10 UN Doc. E/CN.4/AC.1/3; reprinted in UN Doc. E/CN.4/21, Annex A.

11 UN Doc. E/CN.4/AC.1/SR.2, 10.

12 UN Doc. E/CN.4/AC.1/W.2/Rev.1; UN Doc. E/CN.4/AC.1/W.2/Rev.2.

13 UN Doc. A/C.3/265.

14 e.g., Belgium: UN Doc. A/C.3/SR.103, 9 (Belgium). Although Belgium had not actually carried out executions since the nineteenth century, with a few exceptions following the Second World War, it did not formally abolish capital punishment until the 1990s, and Belgian courts continued to pronounce death sentences until that time.

15 UN Doc. A/C.3/SR.105, 5; Norway (UN Doc. A/C.3/SR.104, 12); Pakistan (UN Doc. A/C.3/SR.105, 8); Haiti (UN Doc. A/C.3/SR.105, 2); New Zealand (UN Doc. A/C.3/SR.105, 10); Australia (UN Doc. A/C.3/SR.103, 2); Turkey (UN Doc. A/C.3/SR.103, 11).

16 UN Doc. A/C.3/SR.102, 4–5.

17 *ibid.*, 9.

18 Pakistan: UN Doc. A/C.3/SR.105, 8; Peru: UN Doc. A/C.3/SR.104, 10.

19 UN Doc. A/C.3/SR.105, 6.

20 UN Doc. A/C.3/SR.102, 10–11.

21 UN Doc. A/C.3/SR.104, 10.

although it was never put to a vote.[22] The Soviet amendment was defeated, on a roll call vote, by twenty one votes to nine, with eighteen abstentions.[23] Uruguay actually voted against the amendment, and other proponents of abolition abstained. The United Kingdom delegate expressed the view that the vote on the Soviet proposal aimed at abolition could in no way be interpreted as a vote for or against capital punishment.[24]

After adoption of the *Universal Declaration*, work proceeded in the Commission on Human Rights and subsequently in the Third Committee of the General Assembly on the more detailed provisions of the proposed covenant. With respect to the death penalty, the result was article 6 of the *International Covenant on Civil and Political Rights*, the final text of which was agreed by the Third Committee in 1957.[25] Article 6 of the *Covenant* states as a general principle that nobody shall be deprived arbitrarily of the right to life, but goes on to recognise capital punishment explicitly as an exception or limitation on the right to life.[26] Article 6(2) of the *Covenant* declares:

> In countries which have not abolished the death penalty, sentence of death may be imposed only for the most serious crimes in accordance with the law in force at the time of the commission of the crime and not contrary to the provisions of the present Covenant and to the Convention on the Prevention and Punishment of the Crime of Genocide. This penalty can only be carried out pursuant to a final judgment rendered by a competent court.[27]

The provision goes on to state that anyone sentenced to death is entitled to seek amnesty, pardon or commutation of sentence, and to prohibit the death penalty for persons under eighteen at the time of commission of the crime (see Schabas and Sax 2006)[28] and for pregnant women. A final paragraph, really more programmatic

---

22 UN Doc. A/C.3/274/Rev.1.

23 UN Doc. A/C.3/SR.107, 6. *In favour*: Byelorussian Soviet Socialist Republic, Cuba, Czechoslovakia, Dominican Republic, Mexico, Poland, Ukrainian Soviet Socialist Republic, Union of Soviet Socialist Republics, Yugoslavia. *Against*: Afghanistan, Australia, Brazil, Canada, Chile, China, France, Greece, Guatemala, Haiti, Luxembourg, Panama, Philippines, Siam, Syria, Turkey, Union of South Africa, United Kingdom, United States of America, Uruguay, Yemen. *Abstained*: Argentina, Belgium, Burma, Costa Rica, Denmark, Ecuador, Egypt, Ethiopia, Honduras, India, Lebanon, Netherlands, New Zealand, Norway, Peru, Saudi Arabia, Sweden, Venezuela.

24 UN Doc. A/C.3/SR.103, 12.

25 UN Doc. A/C.3/SR.820, para. 27.

26 *International Covenant on Civil and Political Rights* (1976) 999 UNTS 171, art. 6.

27 *ibid.*, art. 6(2).

28 *ibid.*, art. 6(5). The *Convention on the Rights of the Child*, GA Res. 44/25, annex, art. 37(a), adopted by the General Assembly in 1989, also prohibits execution for crimes committed under the age of eighteen. It has been ratified by 192 countries, and signed but

than normative, proclaims: 'Nothing in this article shall be invoked to delay or to prevent the abolition of capital punishment by any State Party to the present Covenant'.[29] This was the marker placed in article 6 by abolitionist States. There is a tension between paragraphs (2) and (6) of article 6. It is a relationship that testifies to a conservative reality in terms of State practice, at the time the text was adopted, but at the same time it manifests a progressive vision. The 1957 text remained unchanged in the final version of the *Covenant*, which was adopted by the United Nations General Assembly in 1966, and which entered into force a decade later.

The *Covenant* is currently ratified by approximately 155 States, and its principles are therefore approaching near-universal acceptance. In accordance with dynamic principles of treaty interpretation, the meaning given to article 6 has evolved considerably since its adoption. The primary body charged with implementation of the *Covenant*, the Human Rights Committee, has recently taken the view that the prohibition on arbitrary deprivation of the right to life, affirmed in article 6(1) of the *Covenant*, means that the death penalty is fundamentally incompatible with the right to life. The exception, set out in article 6(2), is to be applied narrowly and can only be invoked by States that still retain capital punishment. The inevitable conclusion is that States that have abolished the death penalty are permanently foreclosed from reinstating it.[30] Moreover, they cannot participate indirectly in its implementation by, for example, extraditing or otherwise transferring individuals to places where they might be at risk of execution.[31]

Positioning the Issue on the United Nations Agenda

Although the issue of capital punishment had been debated as part of United Nations standard-setting in the area of human rights, it was far from obvious, in the early years of the organisation, that the death penalty should be part of the organisation's regular agenda. Some States took the view that this was solely an issue of domestic criminal law, with no claim to the organisation's activity. They invoked, in this respect, article 2(7) of the *Charter of the United Nations*; 'Nothing contained in the present Charter shall authorise the United Nations to intervene in matters which are essentially within the domestic jurisdiction of any state'. Thus, merely positioning capital punishment as an issue with which the United Nations should be concerned, outside the context of human rights standard-setting, was no small accomplishment.

---

not ratified by the United States of America. On the relevant provision, see, Schabas and Sax 2006.

29 *ibid.*, art. 6(6).

30 *Piandong et al.* v. *Philippines* (no. 869/1999), UN Doc. CCPR/C/70/D/869/1999, para. 7.4.

31 *Judge* v. *Canada* (No. 829/1998), UN Doc. CCPR/C/78/D/829/1998.

The 1957 debate in the Third Committee of the General Assembly during adoption of article 6 of the *International Covenant on Civil and Political Rights* had the consequence of stimulating abolitionist States to further action. In 1959, Austria, Ceylon, Ecuador, Sweden, Venezuela, and Uruguay proposed a resolution in the General Assembly inviting the Economic and Social Council to begin a study on the question of capital punishment.[32] These countries managed to rally support from a spectrum of United Nations Member States, including Ghana, India, Israel, Japan, Pakistan, the Philippines and the United Kingdom. The proposed study was to be based on the relevant provisions of the *Universal Declaration of Human Rights* and on article 6 of the draft covenant.[33] Pursuant to a resolution adopted by the General Assembly, Marc Ancel, an eminent French jurist and Director of the Criminal Science Section of the Institute of Comparative Law in Paris, was engaged to prepare the study.[34] Discussing the consequences of abolition and the issue of deterrence, Ancel observed that 'all the information available appears to confirm that such a removal [of the death penalty] has, in fact, never been followed by a notable rise in the incidence of the crime no longer punishable with death' (Ancel 1962, 54). According to Ancel, the 'modern tendency' was towards a discretionary and not a mandatory death penalty, the latter being used only in exceptional cases, such as capital murder or crimes against the external security of the state (Ancel 1962, 12). Ancel also concluded that most legal systems protected juveniles and pregnant women from the death penalty and that, in practice, a stay of execution for pregnant women nearly always led to commutation of the sentence (Ancel 1962, 13, 25).

A resolution proposed in the 1968 session of the Commission on Human Rights noted, in its preamble, that 'the major trend among experts and practitioners in the field is towards the abolition of capital punishment', and affirmed a number of safeguards respecting appeal, pardon and reprieve, and delay of execution until the exhaustion of such procedures.[35] During the brief discussion in the Commission on Human Rights,[36] some voices opposed the mention of a general trend towards abolition, agreeing however with the idea that there was a trend to reducing the number and categories of offences.[37] There were also objections to what one delegate termed the 'pejorative nuance' that states that had not abolished the death penalty were in breach of article 3 of the *Universal Declaration of Human Rights*.[38]

---

32 UN Doc. A/C.3/L.767. The idea of such a study had originally been suggested by Sweden, during the 1957 debate on article 6 of the draft *Civil Rights Covenant*: UN Doc. A/C.3/SR.813.

33 UN Doc. A/4250, para. 55.

34 GA Res. 1396(XIV), by fifty-seven to zero, with twenty-two abstentions, UN Doc. A/SR.841.

35 UN Doc. E/4475, UN Doc. UN Doc. E/CN.4/972, 134–136, 162–164.

36 UN Doc. E/4475, UN Doc. UN Doc. E/CN.4/972, 265–269.

37 France, India, Poland, Union of Soviet Socialist Republics.

38 UN Doc. E/CN.4/SR.990, 267.

The United States supported the resolution, noting a trend in its country towards reducing the number of executions and the federal government's contemplation of abolition of the death penalty.[39] After Sweden toned down the draft resolution slightly, it was adopted by the Commission.[40]

In 1971, the Secretary-General prepared a note on information received from member states on the subject of the death penalty which in effect updated the Ancel report, and a subsequent one by Norval Morris (Morris 1967).[41] The note was submitted to the Economic and Social Council, together with a draft resolution reminding states of the principle of progressive restriction of the number of offences for which capital punishment should be imposed, and of the desirability of full abolition.[42] Operative paragraph 3 of the draft stated that the 'main objective to be pursued is that of progressively restricting the number of offences for which capital punishment might be imposed with a view to total abolition of this punishment in all countries, so that the right to life, provided for in article 3 of the *Universal Declaration* may be fully guaranteed'. During debate in the Social Committee of the Economic and Social Council, the sponsors agreed to change the term 'total abolition' to 'desirability of abolishing'.[43] The resolution was adopted in the Economic and Social Council by fourteen votes to zero with six abstentions.[44] After addition of an operative paragraph requesting the Secretary-General to prepare a separate report on practices and statutory rules which may govern the right to petition for pardon, commutation, or reprieve, the resolution[45] was adopted by the General Assembly, with a lone negative vote, Saudi Arabia, and a large number of abstentions.[46]

39 *ibid.*, 266.

40 *ibid.*, by nineteen votes to none, with three abstentions.

41 UN Doc. E/4947, UN Doc. ST/SOA/SD/9, U.N. Doc. ST/SOA/SD/10.

42 UN Doc. E/AC.7/L.578, proposed by Italy, Norway, United Kingdom, Uruguay. Amendments were proposed by the Soviet Union: UN Doc. E/AC.7/L.579.

43 UN Doc. E/4993, para. 6.

44 ESC Res. 1574(L); UN Doc. E/SR.1769.

45 U.N. Doc. A/C.3/L.1908, sponsored by Austria, Costa Rica, Italy, Netherlands, New Zealand, Norway, Sweden, United Kingdom, Uruguay, Venezuela.

46 GA Res. 2857(XXVI), UN Doc. A/PV.2027, by fifty-nine votes to one, with fifty-four abstentions. In the Third Committee, a separate vote was taken on the term 'total abolition' in the first preambular paragraph, UN Doc. A/C.3/SR.1905, para. 69, and it was retained by twenty-four votes to eight, with sixty-one abstentions. A separate vote was taken on the term 'total abolition' in operative paragraph four, UN Doc. A/C.3/SR.1905, para. 69, and it was retained by twenty-three votes to nine, with sixty-two abstentions. The request for a new report from the Secretary-General was also accepted on a separate vote, UN Doc. A/C.3/SR.1905, §69, adopted by thirty-three votes to none, with sixty-two abstentions. In the Third Committee, the resolution was adopted, UN Doc. A/C.3/SR.1905, para. 69, by thirty-three votes to none, with sixty-two abstentions.

The Secretary-General's report on capital punishment was presented to the Economic and Social Council in February 1973.[47] Citing article 3 of the *Universal Declaration of Human Rights* and suggesting it implied limitation and abolition of the death penalty,[48] the report observed that 'the United Nations has gradually shifted from the position of a neutral observer concerned about, but not committed on, the issue of capital punishment to a position favouring the eventual abolition of the death penalty'.[49] The Economic and Social Council called on the Secretary-General to prepare similar reports every five years.[50] It also asked the Committee on Crime Prevention and Control and the United Nations Social Defence Research Institute to study the Secretary-General's report and propose appropriate areas for further scientific examination (see Leone 1987).[51] The resolution, 'with a view to the desirability of abolishing this punishment in all countries', reaffirmed that progressive restriction of capital offences was the main objective to be pursued. Indonesia suggested deletion of the phrase 'in all countries' from this paragraph,[52] and this was accepted on a separate vote.[53]

In 1975, the Economic and Social Council reaffirmed the commitment to progressive restriction and the desirability of abolition.[54] It requested the United Nations Committee on Crime Prevention and Control, with the cooperation of the United Nations Social Defence Research Institute, to study appropriate ways of analysing existing trends towards the restriction of the number of capital offences. The resolution also asked the Secretary-General to proceed with a report on practices and statutory rules which might govern the right to petition for pardon, commutation, or reprieve, and to include this information in its next report, due in 1980.[55]

At the General Assembly session of 1977, a draft resolution on capital punishment adopted the formulation of several earlier Economic and Social Council resolutions, affirming that the main objective in the field of capital punishment was progressive restriction of the number of offences for which it might be imposed,

47 UN Doc. E/5242 and Add.1. See also UN Doc. E/AC.57/12 and Corr.1, paras. 1–6; UN Doc. E/AC.57/18.

48 UN Doc. E/5242, para. 11.

49 *ibid.*, para. 16.

50 UN Doc. E/5298.

51 UN Doc. E/AC.7/L.624, sponsored by Italy, Austria, Finland, the Netherlands, New Zealand, Sweden and Venezuela. For the Secretary-General's communication with the Committee on Crime Prevention and Control, see UN Doc. E/AC.3/18. On the work of the Social Defence Research Institute.

52 UN Doc. E/AC.7/L.624/Rev.2.

53 UN Doc. E/5298, para. 16, by twenty-five votes to ten, with seven abstentions.

54 UN Doc. E/AC.7/L.678/Rev.1, sponsored by Italy, Austria, Ecuador, Norway, the Netherlands and Venezuela.

55 ESC Res. 1930(LVIII), UN Doc. E/SR.1948, by twenty-seven votes to zero with nine abstentions. See also: UN Doc. A/10003, paras. 296–302.

with the desirability of overall abolition.[56] It urged Member States to cooperate with the Secretary-General in providing information for his five-year study and called upon the 1980 United Nations Congress on the Prevention of Crime and the Treatment of Offenders to consider the matter. The General Assembly undertook to consider the question of capital punishment at its 1980 session, which would follow the Congress by a few weeks, 'with high priority'.[57]

The Congress was held from 25 August to 5 September 1980, in Caracas. At the Congress, more time was devoted to the issue of capital punishment than to any other question.[58] The report of Committee II noted that many delegations representing countries which still retained capital punishment 'expressed their interest in the attainment of its abolition as a possible final goal'.[59] But there were also strong voices raised in support of the death penalty, something which had not previously featured in United Nations debates on the subject.[60] A draft resolution called for restriction and eventual abolition of the death penalty and added that abolition would be 'a significant contribution to the strengthening of human rights, in particular the right to life'.[61] States retaining the death penalty were invited to respect the terms of articles 6 and 14 of the *Civil Rights Covenant*, which codified 'generally accepted international human rights standards'. A controversial provision urged states which had not abolished capital punishment to 'consider establishing a moratorium in its application, or creating other conditions under which capital punishment is not imposed or is not executed, so as to permit those States to study the effects of abolition on a provisional basis'.

Egypt challenged the draft resolution with an 'amendment', which added preambular paragraphs stressing the importance of general deterrence in providing for penalties, including capital punishment, and referred to 'the importance of providing for capital punishment in order to instil the necessary fear in the hearts of people...'.[62] Faced with stiff opposition and inadequate time to complete the discussions, the sponsors withdrew the revised draft resolution.[63] For abolitionists,

56 UN Doc. A/C.3/32/L.21, sponsored by Austria, Costa Rica, Denmark, Ecuador, Finland, Honduras, Italy, Netherlands, New Zealand, Norway, Portugal, Senegal, Sweden, Venezuela. See also UN Doc. A/C.3/32/SR.40, paras. 46–47.

57 GA Res. 32/61. UN Doc. A/PV.98, adopted without a vote. In the Third Committee: UN Doc. A/C.3/SR.49, para. 35.

58 See comments of the Chief, Crime Prevention and Criminal Justice Branch, UN Doc. A/C.3/35/SR.74, para. 40.

59 UN Doc. A/CONF.87/14/Rev.1, para. 98.

60 *ibid.*, paras. 99–100.

61 UN Doc. A/CONF.87/C.1/L.1. Sponsored by Austria, Ecuador, the Federal Republic of Germany, Sweden. It was revised following informal discussions (UN Doc. A/CONF.87/14/Rev.1, para. 111; UN Doc. A/CONF.87/C.1/L.1/Rev.1). The resolution is reproduced as an Annex to the Congress Report (UN Doc. A/CONF.87/14/Rev.1, 58–60).

62 UN Doc. A/CONF.87/C.1/L.9. The amendment is reproduced as an Annex to UN Doc. A/CONF.87/14/Rev.1, 60.

63 UN Doc. A/CONF.87/14/Rev.1, para. 111.

the results of the desultory discussion were disappointing, although, had the resolution proceeded to a vote and been defeated, the movement might have been seriously set back.[64]

The debates at the 1980 Congress were in many ways the culmination of an evolution that had begun in 1957, when the General Assembly adopted article 6 of the *Covenant*. Progressively, the debate on capital punishment had advanced from one of neutral studies, in the 1959 General Assembly resolution, to calls for the restriction of the death penalty and suggestions that abolition was the only view consistent with modern scientific thought, in the late 1960s and throughout the 1970s. A technique of reporting on the subject had been developed, and it seemed to discern a trend towards abolition. The time was now ripe to take the debate a step further. Although the Congress failed to adopt a resolution on the issue of capital punishment that expressed the goal of 'further restriction in the application of capital punishment',[65] in its report it 'took note' of the draft resolution and agreed that it should be considered further by United Nations legislative bodies (United Nations 1983, 781, 783).[66] The immediate result was the preparation of 'safeguards' concerning use of the death penalty, aimed at those countries that still retained capital punishment.

The 'Safeguards'

In 1981 the General Assembly assigned the Committee on Crime Prevention and Control to examine how to delineate summary execution from 'legitimate' capital punishment in accordance with article 6 of the *International Covenant on Civil and Political Rights*.[67] The Secretary-General subsequently prepared a report on summary and arbitrary executions,[68] based on a questionnaire sent to Member States, and in 1982 the Committee on Crime Prevention and Control issued a series of draft 'guidelines' or 'safeguards' that were to be respected where the death penalty was being imposed.[69] According to the draft, capital punishment could only be imposed for the most serious crimes, in accordance with the law in

64 Later that year a draft resolution in the General Assembly was aimed at the same moratorium on the death penalty that had failed in Caracas (UN Doc. A/C.3/35/L.67, sponsored by Austria, Costa Rica, Denmark, Ecuador, Federal Republic of Germany, Italy, Norway, Panama, Papua New Guinea, Portugal, Spain, Sweden, Venezuela). It was criticised for reviving the Caracas debate, and effectively shelved by procedural motions from two retentionist states, Morocco and India: UN Doc. A/C.3/35/SR.76, UN Doc. A/C.3/35/SR.84.

65 UN Doc. A/CONF.87/C.1/L.1.

66 UN Doc. A/CONF.87/14/Rev. 1.

67 GA Res. 36/22.

68 UN Doc. E/AC.57/1982/4 and Add.1.

69 UN Doc. E/CN.5/1983/2, chap. I, sect. A, para. 1, draft resolution I; also chap. V, para. 174.

force at the time of commission of the crime, and not for crimes committed while under eighteen or by pregnant women, and always pursuant to a final judgment by a competent court, for which legal assistance should be available at all stages of the proceedings. The death penalty must be suspended pending any appeal or proceedings relating to pardon or commutation, there must be a right to appeal and a right to apply for pardon or commutation, and there must be the possibility of seeking amnesty, pardon, or commutation at all stages.

The United Nations Secretariat proposed a number of changes to the text. It suggested expanding the guideline referring to 'the most serious crimes', mentioning that the scope of this term be limited to intentional lethal offences and that it exclude political offences.[70] On the guideline prohibiting the death penalty for juveniles and pregnant women, the report urged the addition of new mothers and persons over seventy years of age,[71] groups that had not been included in article 6(5) of the *Covenant* but that appeared in other instruments drafted subsequently.[72] Returning to an old proposal,[73] the Secretary General recommended a temporary stay of the death penalty, following sentencing, that could vary from two to six months.[74] The Secretary-General also urged that the guidelines specify that an appeal procedure be automatic in capital cases.[75]

The Committee adopted the 'Safeguards Guaranteeing Protection of the Rights of those Facing the Death Penalty' at its March 1984 session, proposing they be entrenched in an Economic and Social Council resolution.[76] Many of the changes suggested by the Secretary-General were accepted, but the Committee made some innovations of its own. For example, in article 1, providing that the death penalty

70 UN Doc. E/AC.57/1984/16, para. 43: '...it being understood that their scope should be limited to intentional lethal ofences. Accordingly, it should be excluded for offences which are considred to be of a merely political nature, or for cases in which the political nature of the offence exceeds its criminal aspects'.

71 UN Doc. E/AC.57/1984/16, para. 49.

72 The elderly, in article 4(5) of the *American Convention on Human Rights* (1979) 1144 UNTS 123, OASTS 36, adopted in 1969; 'mothers having dependent children' in article 76(3) of *Protocol Additional I to the 1949 Geneva Conventions and Relating to The Protection of Victims of International Armed Conflicts* (1979) 1125 UNTS 3, adopted in 1977; 'mothers of young children' in article 6(4) of *Protocol Additional II to the 1949 Geneva Conventions and Relating to The Protection of Victims of Non-International Armed Conflicts* (1979) 1125 UNTS 609, adopted in 1977.

73 GA Res. 2393(XXIII), art. 1(b).

74 UN Doc. E/AC.57/1984/16, para. 55: '...and in any case, not until a specific minimum period of time has elapsed, ranging on average betrween two and six months, and established in accordance with the legal practice and social circumstances of each non-abolitionist country, after all the legal remedies in capital proceedings have been exhausted and taking into account the physical and mental health condition of the condemned person'.

75 UN Doc. E/AC.57/1984/16, para. 87.

76 'Draft resolution VII', UN Doc. E/1984/16, UN Doc. E/AC.57/1984/18.

could only be imposed for 'the most serious crimes', the Committee welcomed the suggestion that it refer to crimes with lethal consequences but added a rather large loophole with the addition of the phrase 'or other extremely grave consequences'.[77] Article 2 essentially provided for the rule against retroactive imposition of the death penalty and for the benefit of the lesser penalty where the law has been changed.

Other significant additions to restrictions on the use of capital punishment that had not previously figured in the debates about standard-setting included article 4, dealing with the burden of proof in capital cases. It declared that capital punishment could not be imposed unless there was 'clear and convincing evidence leaving no room for an alternative explanation of the facts'. Article 6 of the Safeguards took up the suggestion of the Secretary-General that appeals should be mandatory (see Strafer 1983; Urofsky 1984; White 1991, 164–185).[78] Article 9 added that capital punishment should be carried out so as to inflict the minimum possible suffering, a point which had previously received little attention in the international law debate on the death penalty.[79]

After adoption by the Committee, the Safeguards were submitted to the Economic and Social Council. There were concerns that they might appear to legitimise capital punishment, and an amendment from staunchly abolitionist states replaced, in article 3, the more neutral phrase 'not to be interpreted as affecting the consideration of the question of the abolition or retention of capital punishment' with the abolition-leaning 'not to be invoked to delay or to prevent the abolition of capital punishment'.[80] In the Council, an oral amendment proposed by the United States calling for reinstatement of the original article 3 was rejected.[81] The phrase '[i]n countries which have not abolished the death penalty,' borrowed from article

77 According to Nigel Rodley, who attended the meeting as an observer for Amnesty International, the term 'or other extremely grave' was added upon the representations of a member of the Committee, who said that some acts, such as provision of secret information to an enemy in wartime, could result in large scale loss of life, although the lethal results of the offence might not easily be proven (see Rodley 1987, 174).

78 Several cases in the United States courts have raised the problem of persons condemned to death who refuse to exhaust their appeals, in effect welcoming execution and renouncing to any right of appeal, even if the right is mandatory. See: *Gilmore* v. *Utah*, 429 U.S. 1012 (1976); *Commonwealth* v. *McKenna*, 476 Pa. 428, 383 A.2d 174 (1978); *Lenhard as next friend of Bishop* v. *Wolf*, 100 S.Ct. 3 (1979); *Betty Evans, as next friend of John Evans* v. *Bennett*, 440 U.S. 1301 (1979).

79 See: *General Comment No. 20(44)*, UN Doc. CCPR/C/21/Rev.1/Add.3, para. 6; *Ng* v. *Canada* (No. 469/1991), UN Doc. CCPR/C/49/D/469/1991, UN Doc. A/49/40, Vol. II, 189.

80 UN Doc. E/1984/C.2/L.8, sponsored by Austria, Costa Rica, Italy, Netherlands, Sweden, Uruguay. The amendment was adopted by twenty-nine votes to one, with seventeen abstentions.

81 UN Doc. E/1984/SR.21, para. 22, by twenty-three votes to six, with sixteen abstentions.

6(2) of the *Covenant*, was added at the beginning of paragraph 1 of the Safeguards. Its value is twofold, recalling that abolition is the goal and suggesting that states which have already abolished the death penalty may not revive it.

After adoption by the Economic and Social Council,[82] the Safeguards were endorsed by the General Assembly[83] and by the Seventh United Nations Congress on the Prevention of Crime and the Treatment of Offenders, held in Milan in 1985,[84] which called in a resolution for their widespread dissemination and implementation.[85]

The Safeguards may be said to constitute an authoritative development of the content of article 3 of the *Universal Declaration of Human Rights*. Because of the circumstances of their adoption and the importance of their subject matter, it is also arguable that they constitute a statement of norms of customary international law, a sort of common denominator of acceptable behaviour applicable even to States that have not ratified the *International Covenant on Civil and Political Rights*.[86] In its consideration of State reports as part of the new universal periodic review, it is likely that the United Nations Human Rights Council, which replaced the Commission on Human Rights in 2006, will rely upon the 'Safeguards' when dealing with States for whom the treaty norms are not directly applicable.

Subsequent resolutions have effected minor improvements to the Safeguards. In 1988, building upon a study of the death penalty by criminologist Roger Hood (Hood 1989),[87] the Committee on Crime Prevention and Control adopted a resolution dealing with implementation of the Safeguards that expanded upon their content. The resolution declared that not only must there be adequate assistance of counsel, as found in article 5 of the Safeguards, but also this must go 'above and beyond the protection afforded in non-capital cases'.[88] The resolution also stated that a maximum age should be established above which the death penalty cannot be imposed or carried out.[89] However, the 1988 resolution did not set a specific

82 ESC Res. 1984/50, adopted without a vote.

83 GA Res. 39/118, UN Doc. A/PV.101, para. 79, without a vote.

84 UN Doc. A/CONF.121/22/Rev.1, 83–84, 131–132.

85 UN Doc. A/CONF.121/C.1/L.9, sponsored by Austria, Denmark, France, Greece, India, Italy, Norway, Uruguay and Yugoslavia. Adopted by consensus at the fifteenth meeting of Committee I, UN Doc. A/CONF.121/22/Rev.1, para. 195; adopted by the Congress at its fourteenth plenary meeting, UN Doc. A/CONF.121/22/Rev.1, para. 214. The resolution adopted at the Congress had been drafted at the Varenna preparatory meeting for the Congress, held in 1984: UN Doc. A/CONF.121/IPM/3, para. 61–68. A Secretariat note on capital punishment had been submitted to the Varenna meeting: UN Doc. A/CONF.121/CRP.2.

86 'Capital punishment and implementation of the safeguards guaranteeing protection of the rights of those facing the death penalty', UN Doc. E/2005/3.

87 UN Doc. E/AC.57/1988/CRP.7. See: E/1988/20, para. 72.

88 UN Doc. E/1988/20, UN Doc. E/AC.57/1988/17, 28-29. Draft resolution E/AC.57/1988/L.19, art. 1(a).

89 *ibid.*, art. 1(c).

age, as had been proposed, unsuccessfully, in 1984. The 1984 'Safeguards' had excluded the insane from the death penalty; the 1988 resolution added 'persons suffering from mental retardation or extremely limited mental competence'.[90] The change in emphasis was due to developments in Washington, where the issue of execution of the mentally disabled was before the Supreme Court at the time.[91] The new resolution, entitled 'Implementation of the Safeguards Guaranteeing Protection of the Rights of Those Facing the Death Penalty', was adopted by the Economic and Social Council.[92]

The Second Optional Protocol to the International Covenant on Civil and Political Rights

The late 1970s were very much of a turning point within the international debate on capital punishment. Amnesty International took on the issue as one of its core campaigns. An important international conference, held in Stockholm, built momentum for abolition. The result of these developments was a series of initiatives in both regional organisations, such as the Council of Europe, and in the United Nations itself. Development of the Safeguards was one manifestation. But of perhaps more enduring importance was the effort to enhance the *International Covenant on Civil and Political Rights* by in a sense correcting its original compromise on the death penalty, which is reflected in article 6. Here, the idea was to devise a subsidiary treaty or 'protocol' that would amend or repeal the references to capital punishment, making the instrument truly abolitionist. A similar effort undertaken in Strasbourg led to the adoption, in 1983, of *Protocol No. 6 to the European Convention on Human Rights*.[93]

The first universal treaty abolishing the death penalty was submitted in draft form to the United Nations General Assembly at its 1980 session. Annexed to a draft resolution was the 'Second Optional Protocol to the International Covenant on Civil and Political Rights'.[94] There was no preamble, although space had been left to add some paragraphs later. Of the nine operative paragraphs in the protocol, article 1 quickly established the substance:

90 *ibid.*, art. 1(d).

91 *Penry* v. *Lynaugh*, 492 US 302, 331, 109 SCt 2934, 2953, 106 LEd.2d 256 (1989). Subsequently reversed: *Atkins* v. *Virginia*, 122 SCt 2242 (2002).

92 ESC Res. 1989/64, adopted without a vote.

93 *Protocol No. 6 to the Convention for the Protection of Human Rights and Fundamental Freedoms Concerning the Abolition of the Death Penalty*, ETS No. 114.

94 UN Doc. A/C.3/35/L.75. Submitted by Austria, Costa Rica, Dominican Republic, Federal Republic of Germany, Italy, Portugal, Sweden. Another draft resolution, UN Doc. A/C.3/35/L.80, dealt with summary executions.

> *Article 1*
>
> 1. Each State party shall abolish the death penalty in its territory and shall no longer foresee the use of it against any individual subject to its jurisdiction nor impose nor execute it.
>
> 2. The death penalty shall not be re-established in States that have abolished it.

Article 2 provided that article 1 would be regarded as an additional article to the *International Covenant on Civil and Political Rights* 'as between the States parties'. Furthermore it stated that no derogation whatsoever could be permitted from article 1. The remainder of the draft dealt with such matters as communications to the Human Rights Committee and the formalities of signature, ratification, or accession, federal states, and coming into force. The sponsors of the draft protocol advanced with considerable caution, admitting that their proposal was 'breaking new ground' and that it might be years before any action was taken. Their real goal, they said, was for the Secretary-General to take note of the proposal and seek information from member states, with a view to a more thorough discussion the following year.[95]

The General Assembly decided to seek further submissions from member states, with a view to a full debate on the subject in the 1982 session.[96] Sixteen governments replied to the Secretary-General, with the responses being almost equally divided between abolitionist and retentionist states.[97] In 1982, the General Assembly assigned the issue to the Commission on Human Rights.[98] It, in turn, transmitted the draft second protocol to its Sub-Commission on Prevention of Discrimination and Protection of Minorities.[99] At its August 1984 session, the Sub-Commission assigned Belgian academic Marc Bossuyt to prepare an analysis of the question.[100] Bossuyt's 1987 report to the Sub-Commission[101] included a review of the international law provisions dealing with the death penalty, the decisions of the Human Rights Committee under the *Optional Protocol to the International Covenant on Civil and Political Rights*, the periodic reports submitted to the Committee pursuant to article 40 of the *International Covenant on Civil and Political Rights*, the comments of the Committee on those reports, and the case law of the Inter-American Commission and Court of Human Rights.[102]

95 UN Doc. A/C.3/35/SR.74, para. 56.

96 U.N.Doc. A/C.3/36/L.33/Rev.1, sponsored by Austria, Costa Rica, Dominican Republic, Ecuador, Federal Republic of Germany, Italy, Netherlands, Nicaragua, Norway, Panama, Peru, Portugal, Sweden, Uruguay.

97 See: UN Doc. E/CN.4/Sub.2/1987/20, para. 83.

98 GA Res. 37/192, UN Doc. A/37/PV.111.

99 CHR Res. 1984/19, UN Doc. E/1984/14.

100 S.-CHR Res. 1984/7, UN Doc. E/CN.4/Sub.2/1984/L.8, UN Doc. E/CN.4/1985/3.

101 UN Doc. E/CN.4/Sub.2/1987/20.

102 UN Doc. E/1985/43.

Bossuyt's analysis and revised draft protocol were accepted by the Sub-Commission and transmitted to the Commission on Human Rights on 1 September 1988.[103] The draft was approved by the Commission[104] and the Economic and Social Council[105] early the following year and then submitted to the General Assembly at its forty-fourth session in the autumn of 1989. The *Second Optional Protocol to the International Covenant on Civil and Political Rights, Aiming at the Abolition of the Death Penalty* was adopted by the General Assembly on 29 December 1989, with fifty-nine votes in favour, twenty-six votes against and forty-eight abstentions.[106] The numbers were such that supporters of capital punishment might well have blocked adoption using procedural gambits. Perhaps they were simply not sufficiently organised. Possibly, also, adoption was influenced by the heady atmosphere that accompanied the end of the Cold War, and that seemed to inaugurate a new era for the promotion of human rights by the United Nations. The *Second Optional Protocol* entered into force on 11 July 1991, following its tenth ratification. As of 1 September 2007, it had obtained 60 ratifications.[107]

The 1989 session of the United Nations General Assembly was the scene of another important initiative respecting capital punishment, the adoption of the *Convention on the Rights of the Child.* Article 6(5) of the *International Covenant on Civil and Political Rights* prohibits execution of persons for crimes committed while under the age of eighteen. The norm also appears in the 'Safeguards Guaranteeing the Rights of Those Facing the Death Penalty'. This prohibition on execution of individuals for crimes committed while under the age of eighteen is reaffirmed in article 37(a) of the *Convention on the Rights of the Child.*[108] Because the *Convention* has attained near-universal ratification, there is a strong claim that the norms it sets out are customary in nature. Following a 2005 judgment of the Supreme Court of the United States, the practice of execution for juvenile offenders appears to have been totally eradicated, with the possible exception of Iran. The Committee on the Rights of the Child has said it is 'seriously disturbed' at the application of the death penalty for crimes committed under the age of eighteen by the Iranian authorities.[109] In 2007, the special *rapporteur* on summary, arbitrary and extrajudicial executions said that Iran was the only country in the world from which he continued to receive credible reports of juvenile executions (United Nations 2007a, 63).

---

103 S-CHR Decision 1988/22, UN Doc. E/CN.4/Sub.2/1987/28.

104 CHR Res. 1985/25, UN Doc. E/1989/20, 83–84.

105 ESC Res. 1989/139.

106 GA Res. 44/128, UN Doc. A/44/824, UN Doc. A/44/PV.82, 11.

107 When this figure is combined with the ratifications of the abolitionist instruments of the Council of Europe and Organisation of American States, a total of 80 States are bound to abolition of the death penalty by international treaty.

108 *Convention on the Rights of the Child*, GA Res. 44/25, annex.

109 UN Doc. CRC/C/15/Add.123, para, 29; UN Doc. CRC/C/SR.617, paras. 46–47.

As Momentum Grows, the Opponents Mobilise

In 1989 Amnesty International published a seminal study, *When the State Kills*, that offered a statistical portrait of capital punishment in the modern world (Amnesty International 1989). It showed that 70 States had abolished capital punishment, either in law or in practice, while 100 still retained it. Many in the latter category only used capital punishment occasionally. Perhaps of greatest importance, the statistics showed an unmistakable trend towards universal abolition. Each year, two to three countries abolished capital punishment. There was only isolated evidence of movement in the other direction. Nevertheless, three of the five permanent members of the Security Council, Russia, China and the United States, made generous use of the death penalty. A fourth, France, had held its last execution barely a decade earlier, and had only abolished capital punishment in 1981. The fifth, the United Kingdom, had not executed anyone since 1964, but its Conservative Party government led by Margaret Thatcher was profoundly negative about efforts to advance an abolitionist agenda at the international level.

Alongside this somewhat precarious situation, there was an increasingly active caucus of Islamic states within the United Nations, who espoused a reactionary interpretation of Islamic law and maintained that capital punishment was actually required by their religion (see Schabas 2000a). As a result, while the abolitionist agenda continued to advance throughout the 1990s and into the twenty-first century, debates were increasingly rancorous and difficult.

At the 1990 Congress on the Prevention of Crime and the Treatment of Offenders, held in Havana, a resolution on capital punishment was proposed that returned to the idea of a moratorium on the death penalty, 'at least on a three year basis'.[110] Promoted by the Italian delegation, the resolution was adopted in Committee by forty votes to twenty-one, with sixteen abstentions,[111] but was rejected in plenary session because it failed to obtain a two-thirds majority (Clarke 1990, 518–519).[112] The issue of capital punishment was absent from the agenda of the 1995 Congress, held in Cairo.

In 1994, Italy attempted to take the issue to a new level, proposing a resolution in the United Nations General Assembly that called for a moratorium on the death penalty.[113] Italy's efforts began with a request addressed to the Office of the Presidency of the General Assembly that the item 'capital punishment' be added to

110 UN Doc. A/CONF.144/C.2/L.7, as amended orally.

111 UN Doc. A/CONF.144/28/Rev. 1, para. 350.

112 UN Doc. A/CONF.144/28/Rev. 1, para. 358.

113 UN Doc. A/49/234 and Add. 1 and Add.2 (1994), later revised by UN Doc. A/C.3/49/L.32/Rev.1 (1994). The resolution originated from a newly-formed non-governmental organisation, 'Hands Off Cain – the International League for Abolition of the Death Penalty Before the Year 2000', which had obtained the support of the Italian Parliament for the draft resolution.

the agenda. Pakistan opposed modification of the agenda to include the item.[114] The representative of Sudan described capital punishment as 'a divine right according to some religions, in particular Islam'.[115]

A series of preambular paragraphs referred to earlier General Assembly resolutions on the death penalty, the 1984 'Safeguards', relevant provisions, in the *Universal Declaration of Human Rights*, the *International Covenant on Civil and Political Rights* and the *Convention on the Rights of the Child*, the Statutes of the *ad hoc* criminal tribunals for the former Yugoslavia and Rwanda, and the draft statute of the proposed International Criminal Court. The first of three operative paragraphs invited States that still maintain the death penalty to comply with their obligations under the *International Covenant* and the *Convention on the Rights of the Child*, and in particular to exclude pregnant women and juveniles from execution. The second paragraph invited states which had not abolished the death penalty to consider the progressive restriction of the number of offences for which the death penalty may be imposed, and to exclude the insane from capital punishment. The final paragraph 'encourage[d] states which have not yet abolished the death penalty to consider the opportunity of instituting a moratorium on pending executions with a view to ensuring that the principle that no state should dispose of the life of any human being be affirmed in every part of the world by the year 2000'.

Italy eventually obtained forty-nine co-sponsors for the resolution.[116] During debate in the Third Committee of the General Assembly, Singapore took the initiative in attacking the draft resolution. According to Singapore's representative, 'it strongly opposed efforts by certain States to use the United Nations to impose their own values and system of justice on other countries'. He added that it was evident, from the wording of the *International Covenant on Civil and Political Rights*, that no universal consensus held capital punishment to be contrary to international law.[117]

Singapore initially attempted to block the resolution by proposing a 'no action' motion, which is often an effective procedural technique to block such initiatives. This attempt was rejected, sixty-five States voting in favour to seventy-four against, with twenty abstentions. Singapore then proposed an 'amendment' that in effect distorted the original purpose of the resolution, by adding the following

---

114 UN Doc. A/BUR/49/SR.6, para. 2.

115 UN Doc. A/BUR/49/SR.5, para. 13.

116 Andorra, Argentina, Australia, Austria, Belgium, Bolivia, Cambodia, Cape Verde, Chile, Colombia, Costa Rica, Cyprus, Czech Republic, Denmark, Dominican Republic, Ecuador, El Salvador, Finland, France, Germany, Greece, Haiti, Honduras, Hungary, Iceland, Ireland, Liechtenstein, Luxembourg, Malta, Marshall Islands, Micronesia, Monaco, New Zealand, Nicaragua, Norway, Panama, Paraguay, Portugal, Romania, San Marino, São Tomé and Príncipe, Slovak Republic, Solomon Islands, Spain, Sweden, Uruguay, Vanuatu and Venezuela.

117 UN Doc. A/C.3/49/SR.33, paras. 23–27.

preambular paragraph: 'Affirming the sovereign right of states to determine the legal measures and penalties which are appropriate in their societies to combat serious crimes effectively'.[118] In order to save the resolution, Italy then modified its original text by incorporating the Singapore amendment, while at the same time adding a reference to the *Charter of the United Nations* and to international law, aimed at making Singapore's reactionary appeal to 'state sovereignty' subject to some recognition of international norms.[119] By a close vote, seventy-one to sixty-five, with twenty-one abstentions, Singapore's amendment was adopted. The amendment made the resulting text unacceptable to many abolitionist States. Italy continued to support the resolution, even with the Singapore amendment, but most of its co-sponsors had deserted the camp and abstained in the final vote (a total of seventy-four States abstained). The remainder, essentially retentionist states, tended to divide: thirty-six voted in favour and forty-four voted against.[120]

While the debate was underway in the Third Committee of the General Assembly, a dispute erupted within the Security Council about the death penalty in the course of creation of the International Criminal Tribunal for Rwanda. The draft statute excluded the death penalty as a possible sanction for crimes of genocide, war crimes and grave breaches of international humanitarian law concerning non-international armed conflicts.[121] The draft statute was modelled on a similar instrument adopted by the Security Council in May, 1993, creating the *ad hoc* tribunal for the former Yugoslavia.[122] The provision excluding the death penalty in the case of the Yugoslav tribunal does not appear to have provoked any controversy whatsoever. The draft statute for a permanent International Criminal Court, proposed in 1994 by the International Law Commission, also excluded any use of the death penalty.[123]

Rwanda, which by pure chance was itself a member of the Security Council at the time, opposed the prohibition on capital punishment. It claimed there would be a fundamental injustice in exposing criminals tried by its domestic courts with execution if those tried by the international tribunal – presumably the masterminds of the genocide – would only be subject to life imprisonment, while those prosecuted by the country's national courts would be liable to execution.[124] 'Since it is foreseeable that the Tribunal will be dealing with suspects who devised, planned and organised the genocide, these may escape capital punishment whereas those who simply carried out their plans would be subjected to the harshness of

118 UN Doc. A/C.3/49/L.73.

119 UN Doc. A/C.3/49/L.74.

120 UN Doc. A/C.3/49/SR.61.

121 *Statute of the International Tribunal for Rwanda*, UN Doc. S/RES/955 (1994) annex, art. 23(1).

122 *Statute of the International Tribunal for the Former Yugoslavia*, UN Doc. S/RES/827 (1993), annex, art. 24(1).

123 UN Doc. A/49/10 (1994), art. 47.

124 UN Doc. S/PV.3453, 16.

this sentence', said Rwanda's representative. 'That situation is not conducive to national reconciliation in Rwanda'.[125]

Eventually, when the International Criminal Tribunal for Rwanda offered to transfer some of its backlog of cases back to Rwanda for trial by national jurisdictions, Rwanda promised the death penalty would not be applicable in such cases.[126] Some months later, it took its position to its logical conclusion, and abolished capital punishment throughout the country (United Nations 2007b). Thus, the insistence by the Security Council that the International Criminal Tribunal refrain from capital punishment ultimately promoted abolition within the country itself.

It took a few years for the abolitionists to regroup after the 1994 setback in the General Assembly. A resolution was adopted at the fifth session of the Commission on Crime Prevention and Criminal Justice in 1996, following up on the quinquennial report of the Secretary-General.[127] The resolution was subsequently endorsed later that year by the Economic and Social Council.[128] In March 1997, a resolution on capital punishment was presented to the annual session of the Commission on Human Rights.[129] The resolution welcomed the exclusion of capital punishment from the statutes of the *ad hoc* international criminal tribunals, took note of the Human Rights Committee's General Comment noting that article 6 of the *International Covenant on Civil and Political Rights* refers to abolition of the death penalty in terms which strongly suggest that abolition is desirable, and said the Commission was '[c]onvinced that abolition of the death penalty contributes to the enhancement of human dignity and to the progressive development of human rights'. It called upon States parties to the *Covenant* that had not yet ratified or acceded to the *Second Optional Protocol* to consider doing so, urged States that still maintain the death penalty to comply fully with their international treaty obligations on the subject to observe the Safeguards guaranteeing protection of the rights of those facing the death penalty, to progressively to restrict the number of offences for which the death penalty may be imposed and to make available to the public information on imposition of the death penalty. It 'called upon' such

125 *ibid.*

126 UN Doc. S/PV.5594, 31; UN Doc. S/PV.5697, 15.

127 UN Doc. E/CN.15/1996/19.

128 UN Doc. E/RES/1996/15.

129 In addition to the annual resolutions, which began in 1997, the Commission on Human Rights has also condemned the manner in which the death penalty is used in its geographic or country resolutions. For example, in 1998 it expressed its concern that use of the death penalty by military tribunals in the Democratic Republic of Congo as being contrary to the provisions of the *International Covenant on Civil and Political Rights*. See: CHR Res. 1998/61, para. 2(b)(ii); also CHR Res. 1999/56, para. 2(b)(iv). Similarly, on death row conditions in Burundi: CHR Res. 1998/82, para. 12; on lapidation and public executions, and the scope of crimes for which the death penalty is imposed in Iran: CHR Res. 1998/80, para. 3(a) (j); CHR Res. 1999/13, para. 4(b); on arbitrary imposition of capital punishment in Iraq: CHR Res. 1999/14, para. 2(b).

States 'to consider suspending executions, with a view to completely abolishing the death penalty'.[130] The resolution was adopted by a roll-call vote of twenty-seven votes to eleven, with fourteen abstentions.[131]

The subject returned to the agenda of the Commission on Human Rights the following year.[132] The call for a moratorium was worded somewhat more robustly, 'urging' States that still maintain the death penalty '[t]o establish a moratorium on executions, with a view to completely abolishing the death penalty'.[133] The results of the voting were about the same: twenty-six to thirteen, with twelve abstentions, once again on a roll-call vote. Reacting to this development, fifty-one States filed a letter with the president of the Commission on Human Rights, on 31 March 1998, asserting that there was no international consensus calling for abolition of the death penalty, citing differences linked to religion and judicial systems in various countries.[134] The successful resolution in the Commission may also have helped provoke efforts a few months later to make the issue of the death penalty a 'deal breaker' during the Rome Diplomatic Conference where the *Statute of the International Criminal Court* was adopted (Schabas 2000b).

The 1999 resolution in the Commission on Human Rights was proposed by the fifteen-member European Union.[135] The preamble of the 1999 resolution 'welcomed' the exclusion of capital punishment from the *Rome Statute*, a jab at the retentionist States who, at the Rome Diplomatic Conference, had negotiated ambiguous statements that might suggest the *Statute* was neutral on the subject. The draft resolution went considerably further than the 1997 and 1998 version, calling upon States that still maintain the death penalty not to impose it 'for non-violent financial crimes or for non-violent religious practice or expression of conscience' or 'on a person suffering from any form or mental disorder', and '[n]ot to execute any person as long as any related legal procedure, at international or at national level, is pending'. The draft resolution also urged States not to enter any reservations to article 6 of the *Covenant*, and to withdraw any existing reservations (at the time, the only State with reservations to article 6 was the United States of

130 UN Doc. E/CN.4/1997/L.40.

131 Retentionist states later complained to the Economic and Social Council: UN Doc. E/CN.4/1997/L.20, UN Doc. E/1997/196.

132 UN Doc. E/CN.4/1998/L.12.

133 'The question of the death penalty', E/CN.4/RES/1998/8.

134 UN Doc. E/CN.4/1998/156. It was signed by: Algeria, Antigua and Barbuda, Bahamas, Bahrein, Bangladesh, Barbados, Bhutan, Brunei Darussalam, Burundi, China, Congo, Egypt, Ghana, Guyana, Indonesia, Iran, Iraq, Jamaica, Japan, Jordan, Kuwait, Lesotho, Lebanon, Liberia, Libya, Malaysia, Malawi, Maldives, Mauritania, Mongolia, Myanmar, Nigeria, Oman, Philippines, Qatar, Rwanda, St. Kitts and Nevis, St. Lucia, St. Vincent and the Grenadines, Saudi Arabia, Singapore, Sudan, Swaziland, Syria, Tadjikistan, Tanzania, Trinidad and Tobago, United Arab Emirates, Vietnam, Yemen, Zimbabwe.

135 UN Doc. E/CN.4/1999/L.91. There were seventy-two cosponsors of the 1999 resolution, compared with sixty-five in 1998.

America).[136] The addition of a reference to extradition, and a request for States to reserve explicitly the right to refuse extradition in the absence of effective assurances that the death penalty would not be carried out, drove Canada, at least temporarily, off the list of the resolution's sponsors.[137] Compromise language was ultimately developed that managed to woo Canada back to the camp of those supporting the resolution. It was adopted in the final days of the Commission's annual session, on 28 April 1999, by a roll call vote of thirty votes to eleven, with twelve abstentions.[138]

The European Union was emboldened by this success in the Commission, and developed a strategy to conquer the General Assembly, where efforts had failed in 1994. Finland held the European Union presidency, and to it fell the initiative to submit the proposal. The Finnish delegation's draft, circulated on 7 October 1999, called on States to apply international safeguards in the application of death sentences, urged ratification of the *Second Optional Protocol* by States parties to the *International Covenant on Civil and Political Rights*, progressive restriction of the death penalty and establishment of a moratorium, all with a view to complete abolition.[139]

Opposition mobilised, with Egypt and Singapore – both of them subject to international criticism for death penalty practice[140] – in the lead. As in the past, the strategy was not to vote down the resolution but rather to use so-called 'wrecking amendments' to make it unpalatable for the abolitionists. Two draft amendments were tabled, adding language stating that the death penalty was not prohibited under international law, as there is no global consensus on the issue, invoking article 2(7) of the *Charter of the United Nations*, asserting that capital punishment is primarily a criminal justice issue, not a human rights one, 'in the context of the rights of victims and the community to live in peace', and recalling that not all rules are suitable for application in all places at all times because of diversity of socio-legal and economic conditions in each country.[141]

136 UN Doc. E/CN.4/1999/L.91.

137 UN Doc. E/CN.4/1999/SR.58, para. 40.

138 CHR Res. 1999/61. See: UN Doc. E/CN.4/1999/SR.58, paras. 61–62. A separate vote was held on paragraphs 3(f), 4(b) and 5, adopted by twenty-seven to thirteen with thirteen abstentions.

139 UN Doc. A/C.3/54/L.8.

140 On Singapore: UN Doc. E/CN.4/1997/60/Add.1, para. 438; on Egypt: UN Doc. E/CN.4/1999/39, para. 57.

141 On Singapore: UN Doc. E/CN.4/1997/60/Add.1, para. 438; on Egypt: UN Doc. E/CN.4/1999/39, para. 57; UN Docs. A/C.3/54/L.31 and A/C.3/54/L.32. These amending principles were signed by Afghanistan, Algeria, Antigua and Barbuda, Bahamas, Bahrain, Bangladesh, Barbados, Belize, Benin, Botswana, Brunei, Burkina Faso, Burundi, Cameroon, Chad, China, Comoros, Cuba, North Korea, Congo, Dominica, Egypt, Equatorial Guinea, Eritrea, Ethiopia, Gabon, Ghana, Guatemala, Guyana, India, Indonesia, Iran, Jamaica, Japan, Jordan, Kazakhstan, Kenya, Kuwait, Kyrgyzstan, Laos, Lebanon, Lesotho, Liberia, Libya, Malawi, Malaysia, Maldives, Mauritania, Mongolia, Morocco, Myanmar, Niger, Nigeria,

Humiliated, the European Union decided to withdraw the resolution rather than see it transformed beyond recognition. Speaking to the European Parliament some time afterwards, Commissioner Chris Patten said it had been necessary 'to freeze our resolution on the death penalty or risk the passing of a resolution that would have incorporated wholly unacceptable arguments that asserted that human rights are not universally applicable and valid' (Patten 2000a). He explained that 'following intensive negotiation, we decided at last year's General Assembly in November that no resolution was better than a fatally flawed text, and that therefore the EU should not pursue its initiative in UNGA'. Patten said that 'hardline retentionists' now seem resigned to resolutions in the Commission on Human Rights, but that they will continue to resist strongly any efforts to secure a General Assembly resolution. 'This would lead to further divisive debate', he noted. Consequently, the European Union has decided 'it would not be either advisable or timely to table a resolution on the death penalty' at the 2000 session of the General Assembly (Patten 2000b).

Any nervousness that the setback in the General Assembly would ricochet on what had become a tradition in the Commission on Human Rights, with its progressively more exigent annual resolutions, proved to be misplaced. In 2000, the Commission resolution was adopted by twenty-seven votes to thirteen, with twelve abstentions, essentially comparable to the voting pattern in the previous three years (Dennis 2001, 214).[142] It welcomed the fact that many countries were in fact applying a moratorium on executions, repeating the principles of the 1999 resolution. In 2001, the result was twenty-seven votes to eighteen, with seven abstentions. The number in favour was essentially comparable to results over the previous four resolutions, but the number against was the highest ever.[143] The resolution repeated its request to the Secretary-General to prepare annual updates to the quinquennial reports, a practice since the first Commission resolution in 1997. The resolution 'welcomed' a resolution adopted the previous August by the Sub-Commission on the Promotion and Protection of Human Rights, that had described the prohibition of juvenile executions as a norm of customary international law.[144] At the Commission's final working session, in 2005, the death penalty resolution was the strongest ever adopted. It called for states to abolish the death penalty completely and, in the meantime, to establish a moratorium on executions. Those that retain the death penalty were requested to progressively restrict the number

Oman, Pakistan, Philippines, Qatar, South Korea, Rwanda, St. Kitts Nevis and Anguilla, St. Lucia, St. Vincent and Grenadines, Saudi Arabia, Sierra Leone, Somalia, Sudan, Surinam, Swaziland, Syria, Tajikistan, Thailand, Togo, Trinidad and Tobago, Tunisia, Uganda, United Arab Emirates, Tanzania, Uzbekistan, Vietnam, Yemen, Yugoslavia, Zambia, Zimbabwe and Turkey.

142 UN Doc. E/CN.4/RES/2000/65.

143 UN Doc. E/CN.4/RES/2001/68, based on UN Doc. E/CN.4/2000/L.93. For the vote, see: UN Doc. E/CN.4/2001/SR.78, paras. 17–18.

144 UN Doc. E/CN.4/Sub.2/RES/2000/17. The resolution is discussed below.

of offences for which the death penalty may be imposed and, at the least, not to extend its application to crimes to which it did not apply. They were also to ensure also that the notion of 'most serious crimes' does not go beyond intentional crimes with lethal or extremely grave consequences and that the death penalty is not imposed for non-violent acts such as financial crimes, religious practice or expression of conscience and sexual relations between consenting adults, nor as a mandatory sentence. The resolution, which was adopted by twenty-six votes to eighteen, with seven abstentions, garnered the largest number of co-sponsors since the process had begun, in 1997.[145]

The Commission on Human Rights, where the first discussion on capital punishment within the United Nations had taken place in 1947, was dissolved in 2006 and replaced by the Human Rights Council.[146] A resolution on capital punishment has yet to appear on the agenda of the body. Because the composition of the Council is somewhat different than that of the Commission, the pattern in the earlier body cannot be mechanically transposed. Nevertheless, if members of the Council vote in the same way that they did in the Commission, a death penalty resolution would almost certainly succeed. There was a brief discussion of the death penalty at the March 2007 session of the Council. On that occasion, one sign of evolution was a statement by the representative of China, La Yifan, who said: 'The death penalty's scope of application was to be reviewed shortly, and it was expected that this scope would be reduced, with the final aim of abolishment' (United Nations 2007c, 9).

Initiatives aimed at restriction and abolition of the death penalty have also arisen in other United Nations organs. In 1999, the United Nations Sub-Commission on the Promotion and Protection of Human Rights adopted a resolution condemning 'unequivocally the imposition and execution of the death penalty on those aged under eighteen at the time of the commission of the offence' (United Nations, 1999a). At the same session, the Sub-Commission also adopted a resolution expressing concern at denunciation of human rights treaties, referring specifically to the death-penalty related denunciation of the *Optional Protocol to the International Covenant on Civil and Political Rights* by Trinidad and Tobago and by Guyana.[147] The Sub-Commission returned to the issue in 2000, this time managing to adopt a resolution by consensus. The resolution claimed that execution for juvenile offences was contrary to customary international law. It adopted a draft decision for the Commission on Human Rights stating 'that international law concerning the imposition of the death penalty in relation to juveniles clearly establishes that the imposition of the death penalty on persons aged under 18 years at the time of the offence is in contravention of customary international law'.[148]

145 UN Doc. E/CN.4//RES/2005/59.

146 UN Doc. A/RES/60/251.

147 SCHR Res. 1999/5.

148 UN Doc. E/CN.4/Sub.2/RES/2000/17, para. 6.

Much of the human rights monitoring work of the United Nations is carried out by special *rapporteurs* and similar institutions known generically as special procedures. Capital punishment issues have been addressed by several of the thematic *rapporteurs*, including the special *rapporteur* on violence against women (United Nations 1998a), on religious intolerance[149] and on independence of judges.[150] The Working Group on Arbitrary Detention has also considered death penalty cases.[151] Similarly, concerns about the death penalty have been expressed by the geographic *rapporteurs* with respect to Nigeria,[152] Democratic Republic of Congo,[153] Myanmar,[154] Sudan,[155] Iraq,[156] Burundi[157] and the former-Yugoslavia,[158] as well as by the special representative on Iran (United Nations 1997a, 19–21, 65; 1998b 4, 27–29). But the special *rapporteur* on Equatorial Guinea, noting that capital sentences imposed for murder had no political connotation, said that there was no violation of international law and that it did not fall within his mandate to issue opinions about the application of capital punishment.[159]

The mechanism with particular responsibility for capital punishment is the special *rapporteur* on extrajudicial, summary and arbitrary executions. The position of special *rapporteur* on summary and arbitrary executions was created by the Economic and Social Council in 1982,[160] on the recommendation of the Commission on Human Rights.[161] Addition of the word 'extrajudicial' to the title, in 1992, signalled adoption of a broader approach to the mandate, and implied this to include the subject of capital punishment (see United Nations 1993, 42–68).[162] The Commission on Human Rights has specifically charged the special *rapporteur* with 'monitor[ing of] the implementation of international standards, including safeguards and restrictions, relating to the imposition of capital punishment'.[163] On a regular basis, the special *rapporteur* protests the non-respect of international standards concerning implementation of the death penalty (United Nations 2005, 19(a)). The special *rapporteur* has also made visits, to countries such as the United

149 UN Doc. E/CN.4/1998/6, para. 62(A).

150 UN Doc. E/CN.4/1998/39, paras. 96, 122, 170.

151 UN Doc. E/CN.4/1998/44/Add.1, para. 5; UN Doc. E/CN.4/1998/44/Add.2, para. 33.

152 UN Doc. E/CN.4/1998/62, paras. 31, 81, 91, 109(g) and (x).

153 UN Doc. E/CN.4/1998/65, paras. 102, 126.

154 UN Doc. E/CN.4/1998/70, para. 24.

155 UN Doc. E/CN.4/1998/66, paras. 7, 8, 9, 10, 11, 16

156 UN Doc. E/CN.4/1998/67, paras. 1–5, 12, 18, 32, 34, 37.

157 UN Doc. E/CN.4/1998/72, paras. 45–46.

158 UN Doc. E/CN.4/1998/13, paras. 72–75, 159–160; UN Doc. E/CN.4/1998/15, paras. 16, 17, 19, 38.

159 UN Doc. E/CN.4/1998/73, para. 43.

160 ESC Res. 1982/35.

161 CHR Res. 1982/29.

162 CHR Res. 1992/72, ESC Res. 1992/242.

163 UN Doc. E/CN.4/RES/2000/31; UN Doc. E/CN.4/RES/2003/53.

States (United Nations 1998c) and Jamaica (United Nations 2004, 21), with the purpose of monitoring death penalty practice.

The special *rapporteur* on extrajudicial, summary and arbitrary executions has made certain authoritative statements about the interpretation of article 6 of the *International Covenant*, and other applicable norms. In annual reports to the Commission on Human Rights, the special *rapporteur* has expressed the view that 'given that the loss of life is irreparable ... the abolition of capital punishment is most desirable in order fully to respect the right to life', adding that 'where there is a fundamental right to life, there is no right to capital punishment'.[164] According to the special *rapporteur*, the extension of capital punishment to new crimes is contrary to article 6 of the *Covenant* (United Nations 1997b, 176). The special *rapporteur* has complained that laws that reverse the onus of proof upon a person found in possession of a substantial quantity of narcotic drugs, requiring that person to negative charges of trafficking in dangerous drugs, may violate not only the presumption of innocence but also the right to life in capital cases (United Nations 1995, 212; 1997b, 306–307, 436, 438). Transparency in its application is required, and this dictates the availability of accurate statistics in States where capital punishment is still practiced (United Nations 2005, 57–59). The special *rapporteur* has also complained about the practice of public executions in some countries (United Nations 2004, 53). The special *rapporteur* has said that 'the death penalty should be abolished for economic and drug-related crimes' (United Nations 1997b, 473; 2007) and that it should never be mandatory as punishment for a specific offence (United Nations 2005, 63–64; 2007, 54–62). But the special *rapporteur* has been hesitant to argue that the 'death row phenomenon' is contrary to international norms, expressing concern that this might encourage governments to carry out executions more rapidly (United Nations 1994, 682; 1995, 382).

The High Commissioner on Human Rights, who is the primary executive officer within the United Nations with responsibility for human rights, opposes capital punishment and regularly calls for its suspension, for a moratorium and for abolition.[165] A representative of the High Commissioner has noted that considering the death penalty within the United Nations exclusively as a human rights issue, rather than one of criminal justice, could be considered to be progress in promoting human rights.[166] In February 1998, the High Commissioner, Mary Robinson, condemned the execution of Carla Fay Tucker by the State of Texas (United Nations, 1998d). In April 1998, she protested Rwanda's execution of twenty-two persons convicted for their role in the 1994 genocide. Indeed, she regularly issued statements condemning capital executions in various countries of the world (1999b).

---

164 UN Doc. E/CN.4/1997/60 (1996); UN Doc. E/CN.4/1996/614, paras. 507–517, paras. 540–557.

165 UN Doc. E/CN.4/1998/61, paras. 38, 81.

166 UN Doc. E/CN.4/Sub.2/1998/19, para. 66.

Success in the General Assembly, however, remains the big prize. The failures in 1994 and 1999 continue to haunt the abolitionist camp, and create doubt about the claim that an international consensus on the subject is being established. In December 2006, abolitionist countries in the General Assembly tried a somewhat innovative approach. Instead of a resolution, some eighty-five Member States delivered a 'statement' to the General Assembly within the context of the presentation of the report of the Third Committee.[167] The statement said:

> The right of everyone to life was universally affirmed in article 3 of the Universal Declaration of Human Rights and reaffirmed in other international instruments, such as article 6 of the International Covenant on Civil and Political Rights and articles 6 and 37 (a) of the Convention on the Rights of the Child. Over the past decade, the Commission on Human Rights adopted in all consecutive sessions a resolution on the question of the death penalty, expressing deep concern at its continuing use around the world and calling upon States that still maintain the death penalty to abolish it completely and, in the meantime, to establish a moratorium on executions. We firmly believe that the abolition of the death penalty contributes to the enhancement of human dignity and the progressive development of human rights. The death penalty provides no added value in terms of deterrence. Any miscarriage or failure of justice is irreversible when, in a cruel and inhumane way, the punishment deprives one of his or her right to life. The signatories of this statement are pleased to note that the trend towards the worldwide abolition of the death penalty continues, and they welcome the abolition of capital punishment in three States over the past year, together with positive developments towards its complete abolition in many other countries. However, despite these developments, there is still cause for great alarm. The signatories of this statement remain deeply concerned about the resort to the death penalty all over the world. The signatories of this statement commit themselves to working towards the abolition of the death penalty and, where the death penalty still exists, call for its use to be progressively restricted, insist that it be carried out according to minimum standards such as those set out in Economic and Social Council resolution 1984/50, and, in the meantime, call for the establishment of a moratorium on executions. The signatories call upon the General Assembly to be seized of this matter in the future.[168]

---

167 Albania, Andorra, Angola, Argentina, Armenia, Australia, Austria, Belgium, Bolivia, Bosnia and Herzegovina, Brazil, Bulgaria, Cambodia, Canada, Cape Verde, Chile, Colombia, Costa Rica, Côte d'Ivoire, Croatia, Cyprus, the Czech Republic, Denmark, the Dominican Republic, Ecuador, El Salvador, Estonia, Finland, France, Georgia, Germany, Greece, Guatemala, Guinea-Bissau, Haiti, Honduras, Hungary, Iceland, Ireland, Israel, Italy, Latvia, Liechtenstein, Lithuania, Luxembourg, Macedonia, Malta, Marshall Islands, Mauritius, Mexico, Micronesia, Moldova, Monaco, Montenegro, Nepal, the Netherlands, New Zealand, Nicaragua, Norway, Palau, Panama, Paraguay, the Philippines, Poland, Portugal, Romania, San Marino, São Tomé and Príncipe, Senegal, Serbia, Seychelles, Slovakia, Slovenia, Solomon Islands, Spain, Sweden, Switzerland, Timor-Leste, Turkey, Tuvalu, the United Kingdom, Ukraine, Uruguay, Vanuatu and Venezuela.

168 UN Doc. A/RES/61/PV.81, 33.

The statement was actually a prelude to a renewed effort within the General Assembly planned for the 2007 session.

In November 2007, there was a vigorous and quite unpleasant debate in the Third Committee when the European Union, with broad support from many regions of the world, tried yet again to secure the adoption of a draft resolution with the General Assembly.[169] The text reads as follows

Moratorium on the use of the death penalty

The General Assembly,

Guided by the purposes and principles contained in the Charter of the United Nations,

Recalling the Universal Declaration of Human Rights, the International Covenant on Civil and Political Rights and the Convention on the Rights of the Child,

Recalling also the resolutions on the question of the death penalty adopted over the past decade by the Commission on Human Rights in all consecutive sessions, the last being its resolution 2005/59,4 in which the Commission called upon States that still maintain the death penalty to abolish it completely and, in the meantime, to establish a moratorium on executions,

Recalling further the important results accomplished by the former Commission on Human Rights on the question of the death penalty, and envisaging that the Human Rights Council could continue to work on this issue,

Considering that the use of the death penalty undermines human dignity, and convinced that a moratorium on the use of the death penalty contributes to the enhancement and progressive development of human rights, that there is no conclusive evidence of the

169 *In favour*: Albania, Algeria, Andorra, Angola, Argentina, Armenia, Australia, Austria, Azerbaijan, Belgium, Benin, Bolivia, Bosnia and Herzegovina, Brazil, Bulgaria, Burkina Faso, Burundi, Cambodia, Canada, Cape Verde, Chile, Colombia, Costa Rica, Côte d'Ivoire, Croatia, Cyprus, Czech Republic, Denmark, Dominican Republic, Ecuador, El Salvador, Estonia, Finland, France, Gabon, Georgia, Germany, Greece, Guatemala, Haiti, Honduras, Hungry, Iceland, Ireland, Israel, Italy, Kazakhstan, Kyrgyzstan, Latvia, Liechtenstein, Lithuania, Luxembourg, Mali, Malta, Marshall Islands, Mauritius, Mexico, Micronesia (Federated States of), Moldova, Monaco, Montenegro, Mozambique, Namibia, Nepal, Netherlands, New Zealand, Nicaragua, Norway, Panama, Paraguay, Philippines, Poland, Portugal, Romania, Russian Federation, Rwanda, Samoa, San Marino, São Tomé and Príncipe, Serbia, Slovakia, Slovenia, South Africa, Spain, Sri Lanka, Sweden, Switzerland, Tajikistan, The former Yugoslav Republic of Macedonia, Timor-Leste, Turkey, Turkmenistan, Tuvalu, Ukraine, United Kingdom, Uruguay, Uzbekistan, Vanuatu, and Venesuela.

death penalty's deterrent value and that any miscarriage or failure of justice in the death penalty's implementation is irreversible and irreparable,

Welcoming the decision taken by an increasing number of States to apply a moratorium on executions, followed in many cases by the abolition of the death penalty,

1. Expresses its deep concern about the continued application of the death penalty;

2. Calls upon all States that still maintain the death penalty to:

(a) Respect international standards that provide safeguards guaranteeing the protection of the rights of those facing the death penalty, in particular the minimum standards, as set out in the annex to Economic and Social Council resolution 1984/50 of 25 May 1984;

(b) Provide the Secretary-General with information relating to the use of capital punishment and the observance of the safeguards guaranteeing the protection of the rights of those facing the death penalty;

(c) Progressively restrict the use of the death penalty and reduce the number of offences for which it may be imposed;

(d) Establish a moratorium on executions with a view to abolishing the death penalty;

3. Calls upon States which have abolished the death penalty not to reintroduce it;

4. Requests the Secretary-General to report to the General Assembly at its sixty-third session on the implementation of the present resolution;

5. Decides to continue consideration of the matter at its sixty-third session under the same agenda item.

As in the past, so-called 'wrecking amendments' were proposed in an attempt to derail the process. None of these was successful, however. When the vote on the resolution was taken in the Third Committee, the result was 99 in favour to 52 against, with 33 abstentions. Confirmation of the vote in the plenary General Assembly was little more than a formality. On 18 December 2007, the resolution was passed by a vote of 104 in favour to 54 against, with 29 abstentions.[170] Mexico,

170 *In favour*: Albania, Algeria, Andorra, Angola, Argentina, Armenia, Australia, Austria, Azerbaijan, Belgium, Benin, Bolivia, Bosnia and Herzegovina, Brazil, Bulgaria, Burkina Faso, Burundi, Cambodia, Canada, Cape Verde, Chile, Colombia, Congo, Costa Rica, Côte d'Ivoire, Croatia, Cyprus, Czech Republic, Denmark, Dominican Republic, Ecuador, El Salvador, Estonia, Finland, France, Gabon, Georgia, Germany, Greece, Guatemala, Haiti, Honduras, Hungary, Iceland, Ireland, Israel, Italy, Kazakhstan, Kiribati, Kyrgyzstan,

spoke on behalf of the 87 co-sponsors of the resolution, expressing the wish that this text would impel the Assembly to move forward in the struggle to improve human rights. The matter had been a source of concern in the international community, and the co-sponsors were pleased, after so many years, that the Assembly was adopting the resolution to establish a moratorium on the death penalty. Several delegations who opposed the resolution took the floor to register their discontent. Antigua and Barbuda spoke on behalf of the thirteenth Caribbean Community states who had voted against the draft as a bloc. Singapore said the vote demonstrated that the issue was not universally accepted and was, in fact, quite divisive. Nigeria, China, Syria and Malaysia made comments along similar lines. Egypt said it had voted against because the resolution was contrary to 'religious, practical and legal norms', and that the death penalty was only imposed 'according to the provisions of Islamic law'. Bangladesh conceded that the resolution was representative of the growing trend against the death penalty but said 'the time was not right for its total abolition'.

Early in the year, on 2 January 2007, United Nations Secretary-General Ban Ki Moon held his first press conference upon taking office. Saddam Hussein had been executed in a barbaric and undignified manner only a few days earlier. Perhaps predictably, the matter was at the top of the list of questions from the assembled press corps:

Latvia, Liechtenstein, Lithuania, Luxembourg, Madagascar, Mali, Malta, Marshall Islands, Mauritius, Mexico, Micronesia (Federated States of), Moldova, Monaco, Montenegro, Mozambique, Namibia, Nauru, Nepal, Netherlands, New Zealand, Nicaragua, Norway, Palau, Panama, Paraguay, Philippines, Poland, Portugal, Romania, Russian Federation, Rwanda, Samoa, San Marino, São Tomé and Príncipe, Serbia, Slovakia, Slovenia, South Africa, Spain, Sri Lanka, Sweden, Switzerland, Tajikistan, The former Yugoslav Republic of Macedonia, Timor-Leste, Turkey, Turkmenistan, Tuvalu, Ukraine, United Kingdom, Uruguay, Uzbekistan, Vanuatu, Venezuela; *Against*: Afghanistan, Antigua and Barbuda, Bahamas, Bahrain, Bangladesh, Barbados, Belize, Botswana, Brunei Darussalam, Chad, China, Comoros, Democratic People's Republic of Korea, Dominica, Egypt, Ethiopia, Grenada, Guyana, India, Indonesia, Iran, Iraq, Jamaica, Japan, Jordan, Kuwait, Libya, Malaysia, Maldives, Mauritania, Mongolia, Myanmar, Nigeria, Oman, Pakistan, Papua New Guinea, Qatar, Saint Kitts and Nevis, Saint Lucia, Saint Vincent and the Grenadines, Saudi Arabia, Singapore, Solomon Islands, Somalia, Sudan, Suriname, Syria, Thailand, Tonga, Trinidad and Tobago, Uganda, United States, Yemen, Zimbabwe; *Abstain*: Belarus, Bhutan, Cameroon, Central African Republic, Cuba, Democratic Republic of the Congo, Djibouti, Equatorial Guinea, Eritrea, Fiji, Gambia, Ghana, Guinea, Kenya, Lao People's Democratic Republic, Lebanon, Lesotho, Liberia, Malawi, Morocco, Niger, Republic of Korea, Sierra Leone, Swaziland, Togo, United Arab Emirates, United Republic of Tanzania, Viet Nam, Zambia; *Absent*: Guinea-Bissau, Peru, Senegal, Seychelles, Tunisia.

Q: Should Saddam Hussein have been executed, Mr. Secretary-General?

SG: Saddam Hussein was responsible for committing heinous crimes and unspeakable atrocities against the Iraqi people. We should never forget the victims of his crimes. The issue of capital punishment is for each and every Member State to decide. As a Secretary-General, at the same time, while I am firmly against impunity, I also hope that the members of the international community should pay due regard to all aspects of international humanitarian laws. During my entire tenure, I will try my best to help Member States, the international community, to strengthen the rule of law.

Q: Will his death help in bringing stability to Iraq in your opinion, with the death of Saddam Hussein in this way, or might it break a civil war there?

SG: The Iraqi people and Government have taken steps to address their past, and I hope that the international community should also understand the stakes and try to build the rule of law nationally and internationally.

…

Q: [inaudible on death penalty, moratorium]

SG: I said that capital punishment, the death penalty, is the issue for each and every Member State to decide. At the same time, I would hope that the international member states would pay due regard to all aspects of international humanitarian laws.

The answer was perhaps spontaneous, and seemed to reflect the personal views of the Secretary-General rather than those of the organisation. It was particularly disturbing that they seemed to echo the reaction of the President of the United States. But almost immediately, damage control was underway. At the 11 January 2007 news conference, the Secretary-General made it clear that life is precious and that he believed the death penalty should be eliminated. He called on the government of Iraq to suspend the execution of those who were already sentenced to die. The Secretary-General endorsed the position taken by the High Commissioner for Human Rights, which was one of unequivocal condemnation of the Hussein execution. The initial statement by the Secretary-General was disconcerting, but the subsequent rectification provided an unplanned confirmation of the unwavering position of the United Nations with respect to the abolition of capital punishment. On 18 December 2007, Ban Ki Moon enthusiastically welcomed the success of the resolution on capital punishment in the General Assembly.

Bibliography

Amnesty International (1989), *When the State Kills...* (New York: Amnesty International).

Ancel, M. (1962), *Capital Punishment*, UN Doc. ST/SOA/SD/9, Sales No. 62.IV.2 (New York: United Nations).

Clark, R.S. (1990), 'The Eighth United Nations Congress on the Prevention of Crime and the Treatment of Offenders, Havana, Cuba, August 27–September 7, 1990' (1990) 1 *Criminal Law Forum* 513.

Dennis, M.J. (2001), 'The Fifty-sixth Session of the UN Commission on Human Rights' (2001) 95 *AJIL* 213.

Hood, R. (1989), *The Death Penalty: A World-wide Perspective* (Oxford: Clarendon Press).

Lauren, P.G. (2003), *The Evolution of International Human Rights, Visions Seen*, 2nd Edition (Philadelphia: University of Pennsylvania Press).

Leone, U. (1987), 'UNSDRI's Activities Related to the Death Penalty Issue', 58 *Revue internationale de droit pénal* 325.

Morris, N (1967), *Capital Punishment: Developments, 1961–1965*, Sales No. E.67.IV.15.

Patten, C. (2000a), 'Excerpts from a Statement Delivered by the Rt. Hon. Christopher Patten,' EU Commissioner for External Relations to the European Parliament, 16 February 2000.

_______(2000b), 'Speech to European Parliament', 25 October 2000.

Rodley, N. (1987), *The Treatment of Prisoners Under International Law* (Oxford: Clarendon Press).

Schabas, W.A. (2000a), 'Islam and the Death Penalty', 9 *William & Mary Bill of Rights Journal* 223.

______(2000b) 'Life, Death and the Crime of Crimes: Supreme Penalties and the ICC Statute', 2 *Punishment & Society* 263.

Schabas, W.A. and Sax, H. (2006), 'Article 37, Prohibition of Torture, Prohibition of Death Penalty and Life Imprisonment and the Deprivation of Liberty', in Alen, A. et al. (eds) *A Commentary on the United Nations Convention on the Rights of the Child* (Leiden / Boston: Martinus Nijhoff Publishers).

Strafer, M. (1983), 'Volunteering for Execution: Competency, Voluntariness and the Propriety of Third Party Intervention', 74 *J. Criminal Law and Criminology* 860.

United Nations (1983), *Yearbook of the United Nations, 1980* (New York: United Nations).

______(1993), 'Extrajudicial, Summary or Arbitrary Executions, Report of the Special Rapporteur', UN Doc. E/CN.4/1993/46.

______(1994), 'Report by the Special Rapporteur, Mr. Bacre Waly Ndiaye, submitted pursuant to Commission on Human Rights resolution 1993/71', UN Doc. E/CN.4/1994/7.

______(1995), 'Report by the Special Rapporteur, Mr. Bacre Waly Ndiaye, submitted pursuant to Commission on Human Rights resolution 1994/82', UN Doc. E/CN.4/1995/61.

______(1997a), 'Report on the situation of human rights in the Islamic Republic of Iran, prepared by the Special Representative on the Commission on Human Rights, Mr. Maurice Copithorne, pursuant to Commission resolution 1996/84 and Economic and Social Council decision 1996/287', UN Doc. E/CN.4/1997/63.

______(1997b), 'Report of the Special Rapporteur, Mr. Bacre Waly Ndiaye, submitted pursuant to Commission on Human Rights resolution 1996/74', UN Doc. E/CN.4/1997/60/Add.1.

______(1998a), 'Report on the mission to Rwanda on the question of violence against women in situations of armed conflict', UN Doc. E/CN.4/1998/54/Add.1; UN Doc. E/CN.4/1998/54.

______(1998b), 'Interim report on the situation of human rights in the Islamic Republic of Iran, prepared by the Special Representative of the Commission on Human Rights in accordance with General Assembly Resolution 51/107 and Economic and Social Council Decision 1997/264', UN Doc. A/52/472, E/CN.4/1998/59.

_______(1998c), 'Report of the Special Rapporteur on extrajudicial, summary or arbitrary executions, Mr. Bacre Waly Ndiaye, submitted pursuant to Commission resolution 1997/61', Addendum, Mission to the United States of America, UN Doc. E/CN.4/1998/68/Add.3.

______(1998d), 'Statement by Mary Robinson, United Nations High Commissioner for Human Rights', UN Doc. HR/98/6, 4 February 1998.

______(1999a), 'The death penalty, particularly in relation to juvenile offenders', UN Doc. E/CN.4/Sub.2/RES/1999/4.

______(1999b), 'Daily Press Briefing of Office of Spokesman for Secretary-General', 16 June 1999.

______(2004), 'Extrajudicial, summary or arbitrary executions, Report of the Special Rapporteur, Asma Jahangir', UN Doc. E/CN.4/2004/7.

______(2005), 'Extrajudicial, summary or arbitrary executions, Report of the Special Rapporteur, Philip Alston', UN Doc. E/CN.4/2005/7.

______(2007a), 'Extrajudicial, summary or arbitrary executions, Report of the Special Rapporteur, Philip Alston', UN Doc. A/HRC/4/20.

______(2007b), UN Press Release, 'High Commissioner for Human Rights Hails Abolition of Capital Punishment in Rwanda', 27 July 2007.

______(2007c), 'Human Rights Council Opens Fourth Session', HRC/07/3, 12 March 2007.

Urofsky, M.L. (1984), 'A Right to Die: Termination of Appeal for Condemned Prisoners', 75 *J. Criminal Law and Criminology* 553.

White, W.S. (1991), *The Death Penalty in the Nineties* (Ann Arbor: University of Michigan Press).

Chapter 3
The Evolving Human Rights Discourse of the Council of Europe: Renouncing the Sovereign Right of the Death Penalty

Jon Yorke[1]

In the United Europe of the future the solemn abolition of the death penalty ought to be the first article of the European Code we all hope for.
Albert Camus, *Reflections on the Guillotine* (1957)

Introduction

The Enlightenment social contract theorists proposed differing political calculations for the formation of society and a governing sovereign. However, without exception, they identified that the resultant sovereign should possess the *right* to choose whether or not to use the death penalty as the ultimate penal sanction. Thomas Hobbes envisioned the possibility of the punishment when he stated, 'a subject may be put to death by the command of the sovereign' (Hobbes 1996, 141), John Locke reasoned that the political power of the sovereign encompassed 'a right of making laws with penalties of death' (Locke 1980, 8), Jean-Jacques Rousseau affirmed that 'putting the guilty to death' was a justifiable action of the sovereign (Rousseau 2004, 209), and Immanuel Kant went so far as to exclaim in his formulation of the *lex talionis* that '[a]ll murderers … must suffer the death penalty' (Kant 1970, 157). It has been generally accepted that the punishment became an 'essential aspect of sovereignty' of the early modern state (Evans 1996, 893), and such political philosophy then placed the sovereign state and the death penalty within a symbiotic relationship.

---

1 This chapter represents a larger work in progress on the Council of Europe and the abolition of the death penalty. A previous version was presented at the Surrey European Law Unit Seminar Series, School of Law, University of Surrey, on 7 November 2007. I would like to thank the participants for their very insightful comments and the dialogue which resulted. Thanks also to Roger Hood, Peter Fitzpatrick, Susan Breau, Christina Eckes, Opi Outhwaite and Regina Rauxloh, for reading this chapter and their very helpful comments. The usual *caveats* apply.

Jacques Derrida observed this juxtaposition through his writings on sovereignty post-1989 (see Derrida 1992; 2004), and he deconstructed such philosophical lineage during his seminar on the death penalty at Cardozo Law School in 2001. Engaging with this Enlightenment political philosophy he stated:

> It is impossible to separate political sovereignty from the power over life and death … In order to maintain an essential aspect of its sovereignty, the state must reserve the right to impose the death penalty, at least in exceptional cases (Huigens 2001, 23).

Derrida then positioned this devastating observation within a critique. He identified that the intrinsic relationship of sovereignty and the death penalty was a repugnant philosophical *truth* which required deconstruction. He *understood* the symbiotic relationship but he did not comfortably *accept* it. Derrida's main point of enquiry focused on the processes 'contesting or limiting the sovereignty of the sovereign' (Derrida 2004, 201), and he observed that the European 'public discourse against the death penalty' (*ibid*, 204) was not a specific *philosophical* exposition but was declared through *inter alia* considering a 'history of *cruelty*', the '"impure" phenomena of executions', and 'state sovereignty' *vis-á-vis* political pressure applied by the European supra-national structure (*ibid*, 199, 201, 202, 212).

Perhaps the most significant *public discourse* currently utilised in Europe is that provided by the Council of Europe through the different organs (the Committee of Ministers, the Parliamentary Assembly and the European Court of Human Rights), and the *Convention for the Protection of Human Rights and Fundamental Freedoms* 1950 (more commonly known as the 'European Convention on Human Rights', hereinafter, '*Convention*').[2] This *Convention* system of human rights now provides legal mechanisms for the restriction and removal of the death penalty within Member States. But this was not always the Council's policy. At the creation of the Council and the drafting of the *Convention*, the manifestation of the Member State's right to impose the death penalty would more accurately reflect the position of the Enlightenment social contract theorists mentioned above. Hence, the story which this chapter sets out to tell is how this Enlightenment philosophical heritage has now been penetrated, and suspended, as the Council and the Member States have produced and maintained a region which is now described as 'death penalty free' (Council of Europe 2007a, 8). The main players in this story are the Council (for a consideration of the anti-death penalty policies of the European Union, see Schabas 2002, 302–308; Girling 2005; Yorke 2006; 2007), sovereign Member States, non-governmental organisations and the individuals condemned to death.

---

2 213 UNTS 221 (1955). The *Convention for the Protection of Human Rights and Fundamental Freedoms* was signed in Rome on 4 November 1950 by Belgium, Denmark, France, German Federal Republic, Iceland, Ireland, Italy, Luxembourg, Netherlands, Norway, Turkey and the United Kingdom. It was later signed in Paris on 28 November 1950 by Greece and Sweden.

This chapter is divided into five sections. The first three sections analyse the arguments concerning the drafting processes of the *Convention, Protocol No. 6 to the Convention for the Protection of Human Rights and Fundamental Freedoms concerning the abolition of the death penalty*[3] and, *Protocol No. 13 to the Convention for the Protection of Human Rights and Fundamental Freedoms concerning the abolition of the death penalty in all circumstances*.[4] Within these different drafting debates, it is questioned whether an evolution has occurred which demonstrates that the right of the death penalty has been gradually suspended through sovereign choice, and to what extent the Council discourse has contributed to this change. The effect of terrorism on this penological choice is evaluated in the fourth section. It is argued that the *Convention* system of human rights has shifted its idiomatic focus from adopting what may be termed 'pure' human rights language specifically extracted from the text of the *Convention*, to an embracing of axioms of the political philosophy of 'liberal legitimacy', and 'legitimate government', to maintain that the execution of terrorists is itself a violation of human rights.

The chapter then concludes by arguing that the Council has adopted a further pedagogical tool to dismantle the possibility of the punishment: one which seeks to identify that the very imposition of the death penalty is against the 'conscience' of Europeans. The Council is seeking to formulate a moral authority which cognitively enhances the right to life. Friedrich Karl von Savigny stated that law resides in the 'very life of men' (Agamben 1998, ix) and that '[l]aw is nothing but life considered from a particular point of view' (Agamben 2005, 85) and the Council is stalwartly promoting the view that there is no place for the death penalty in the *life* of Europeans. Our perception on life and punishment is evolving, and Beccaria had reasoned in the eighteenth century that we should look to our 'hearts' to find the legitimacy for punishment (Beccaria 1983), and so the Council is attempting to banish the punishment from our hearts. It will be investigated whether the construction of this cognitive element has produced a departure from the traditional Enlightenment philosophy which rendered the acceptability of the death penalty at the social contract, and whether a new European social contract has been constructed which renders illegitimate any clause reserving the death penalty to the sovereign Member States.

But hearts and consciences can change, and Sigmund Freud reminded us that emotional shifts can occur especially when questions of life and death are confronted (see Freud 2005, 167–194, 219–232). Hence it is argued that the Council needs to ensure a continued renunciation of the punishment through the *Convention* human rights policies being repeatedly supported by municipal scholastic and political mechanisms, and the general public of Council Member States. As such, the discourse on the death penalty must be viewed as a 'never-

3 As amended by Protocol No. 11, Strasbourg, 28 April 1983. The headings of articles added and text amended according to the provisions of Protocol No. 11 (ETS No. 155) as from its entry into force on 1 November 1998.

4 Vilinus, 3 May 2002.

ending story' necessitating that the death penalty scholarship within the countries that have removed the punishment must not *die* just because the Council has declared that Europe is a 'death penalty-free area' (Council of Europe 2007a, 8). Although the death penalty is now completely removed from the statutes of English law, Michael Mansfield QC, in a public lecture at Warwick University in 2004, stated:

> there is a *great need* to ensure that we recognise that the job is, and always will be, education. There is a need to ensure that the ... public regularly understand the arguments so that the threat is diminished. The threat of the return of capital punishment is diminished ... If the public did understand properly what the debate was then one can be safe in the assurance that its return would be limited (Mansfield 2004; emphasis added).

This chapter is an attempt to engage with the 'great need' of continued education in the Council and its Member States. We begin by investigating, perhaps, the root issue (Foucault 1981) of how Member State sovereignty was utilised to preserve the right of the death penalty during the drafting of the *Convention* text.

The Drafting of the European Convention on Human Rights

European nation states have historically pronounced in resilient rhetoric the right to impose the death penalty (Guizot 1848; Foucault 1976; Spierenburg 1984; Evans 1997). This phenomenon of political power was so potent that it even exerted itself within the drafting debates of the *Convention* in 1949–50. The unalloyed presence of the state right of the death penalty was paradoxically juxtaposed against the very deontology of the formulated text. How did this happen when the *Convention* itself purported to elevate the human rights of Europeans?

The drafting process of the *Convention* was specifically guided by the *Statute of the Council of Europe* 1949,[5] article 1, which called for *inter alia*, a recognition of the, 'ideals and principles which are [the Member State's] common heritage'. The identification of such 'common heritage' is of fundamental importance and the Group of Officials of the Secretariat outlined the essential aspects of such historicity as being 'the cumulative influence of Greek philosophy, Roman law, the Western Christian Church, the humanism of the Renaissance and the French Revolution' (Group of Officials of the Secretariat 1970, 8). One reading of this philosophical and historical genealogy could point to moral and ethical developments culminating with the humanist arguments for recognition of individual deontology. However, the historical records also recount the acceptance of the death penalty in Greek philosophy by Aristotle (Aristotle 1981, 227) and Plato (Plato 1987, 355–360), the sanguine use of the death penalty in the Roman Draconian Code (Plutarch 1952,

5 *Statute of the Council of Europe*, ETS. No.1, 5.5.1949.

70), Christianity brought the devastating inquisitions (Megivern 1997, 97–122), the Renaissance witnessed the evolution of Kant's argument that the death penalty was a categorical imperative for the satisfaction of the *lex talionis* (Kant 1970, 154–159) and the French Revolution advanced execution technologies through Dr. Ignace Guillotin's invention of the decapitating machine (Soubiran 1964).

A further reading may be offered which reveals that this European heritage also heralded the arguments *against* the death penalty. Thucydides first documented a debate on the death penalty which occurred in Athens in 427 BCE, and the result was that the Mytilenian revolt was not punished with death by the Athenians (Thucydides 1972, 212–222). Marcus Tullius Cicero in his infamous oratory argued in Roman courts against the death penalty (Cicero 1990), and in early Christianity the Waldensian sect were opposed to the Catholic imposition of the punishment (Megivern 1997, 99–103). The Italian humanist Cesarea Beccaria was perhaps the father of the modern anti-death penalty movement in Europe (Beccaria 1983), and Voltaire exported the Italian's humanism to France (Voltaire 1994). Before he turned to a virile use of the guillotine once in power, Maximilien Robespierre vehemently renounced the punishment (Matrat 1975, 106–107), and Jeremy Bentham adopted his utilitarian theory to specifically attack the efficacy of the French use of the guillotine (Bentham 1831). Both the application of the death penalty and arguments against its imposition, are laced within this genealogy of European history, all the way to the 1949–50 drafting of the *Convention*. Thus the identification of a 'common heritage' asked for by *Statute* article 1 becomes problematical. However, if the manifestation of the sovereign power to implement the death penalty is distilled, we are left with a common heritage of a sanguine penal history (Spierenburg 1984).

The other *Statute* article which had significant influence upon the drafting process was article 3, as it mandated *inter alia* the acceptance of the 'principles of the rule of law'. To understand the interpretation of this article by the drafters we must recount the symbolism of the executions of war criminals following the Nuremburg Tribunal and other trials across Europe. The executions of captured Nazis and their supporters in Europe was considered to be compatible with the defence against 'tyranny', as Sir David Maxwell-Fyfe stated during the drafting debates that 'by this Convention we give a warning, a challenge and a first counter-stroke to the intending tyrant' (*Travaux Préparatoires* 1976, 1, 120). In 1946, the Supreme Court of Norway ruled in *Public Prosecutor v. Kling*,[6] that even though the death penalty was not applicable for ordinary crimes in Norway, international law allowed for the death penalty in times of war. This ruling is consistent with the Norwegian testimony to the Great Britain Select Committee on Capital Punishment in 1930, and points to a legitimacy of executing war criminals post-World War Two (SCCP 1930). Furthermore, following the war, the National Coalition for the Abolition of the Death Penalty, based in London, recorded that Norway, Denmark, Holland and Belgium all reserved the death penalty for 'the

6 (1946) 13 Ann. Dig. 262 (Supreme Court, Norway), cited in Schabas 2002, 1.

worst crimes of collaboration with the enemy' (National Council for the Abolition of the Death Penalty 1945–46, 4).

The promotion of the rule of law, as recognised by *Statute* article 3, enabled the death penalty to be an acceptable punishment within the *Convention*. At this time the death penalty for war crimes was part of the majority of municipal state law, and no state is recorded to have argued in the drafting debates that such punishment was against the formulation of *Convention* human rights. The critical question here is to ask why the nine countries[7] who signed the original *Convention* and which had removed the death penalty for ordinary crimes, were *silent* on the issue? It is argued that during this period of European history this silence was the result of the continued political sentiment that the death penalty was a product of the exclusive jurisdiction of the state. Human rights did not penetrate this political control of domestic criminal law, and the punishment was simply not seen as a *per se* violation of *Convention* human rights (Simpson 2004, 876).

The *Convention* drafting debates were published in an edited collection of the *travaux préparatoires*, and they record few direct references to any debates on the death penalty. Torkel Opsahl stated, '[i]f there was any discussion of what was intended [concerning the death penalty] the published *travaux préparatoires* reveal little of it' (Opsahl 1993, 208; see also Ramcharan 1985, 57–61) and J.E.S. Fawcett remarked concerning the absence of debate on article 2(1) that, 'there is almost no reported discussion in the drafts' (Fawcett 1987, 34). However, the published *travaux préparatoires* do reveal that there were numerous participants who commented on the death penalty. These included M. Maccas, the Greek representative at the first session of the drafting debates, who identified the execution of Socrates, the Ancient Greek philosopher (*Travaux Préparatoires* 1976 1, 108). Also at the first session the question of what was meant by 'security of person' was not debated or whether an execution violated this 'security' (*Travaux Préparatoires* 1976 1, 160). In the same debate the Turkish representative, M. Düsünsel, questioned the validity of 'so-called popular courts condemning to death and executing deputies', and stated that such courts were a 'travesty of justice' (*Travaux Préparatoires* 1976 2, 30). But these comments were not picked up as essential questions of the right of the death penalty and whether this punishment would be (in)compatible with human rights. Furthermore, there are no recorded reasons *why* the United Kingdom proposal to the drafting committee, which stated:

> 1. No one shall be deprived of his life intentionally.

---

7 The countries represented in the drafting debates and which had removed the death penalty for ordinary crimes were Belgium who removed the death penalty in 1949 (but subsequently reintroduced it in 1975 as a discretionary penalty for kidnapping and in 1976 for aircraft hijacking), Denmark (1933), West Germany (1949), Iceland (1928), Italy (1947), Luxembourg (1950), the Netherlands (1870), Norway (1905), and Sweden (1921).

> 2. There shall be no exception to this rule save where death results in those States where capital punishment is lawful, from the execution of such a penalty in accordance with the sentence of a court (*Travaux Préparatoires* 1976, 3, 158)

ultimately evolved into article 2(1) being worded as:

> Everyone's right to life shall be protected by law. No one shall be deprived of his life intentionally save in the execution of a sentence of a court following his conviction of a crime for which this penalty is provided by law.

Opsahl observed that the 'United Kingdom proposal was not opposed and there are no signs that restrictions nor limitations on its use were intended or even discussed' (Opsahl 1993, 217). All we have is the tabled proposal and then the amended proposal, which is recognisably euphemistic. The United Kingdom proposal adopted the phrases 'where death results', and 'where capital punishment is lawful', and such idiomatic usage clearly, and aptly, describes the consequences of the punishment of death. However, article 2(1) changed the description to 'deprivation of his life' and 'for which this penalty is provided by law'. Both the specific references to actual 'death' and the name of the punishment, 'capital punishment' were erased.

Albert Camus referred to the journalistic articles and death penalty scholarship during this period in Europe and stated that '[p]eople write of capital punishment as if they are whispering ... since everyone strives to refer to it only through euphemisms' (Camus 1957, 176). Sigmund Freud helps us to understand a psychoanalytical view of 'death' in the pre-war period when he states, '[w]e have shown the unmistakable tendency to "shelve" death, to eliminate it from life. We tried to hush it up' (Freud 1968, 15). Although not specifically related to the *Convention* text, both Camus and Freud perhaps provide interpretive insights into the drafting process which removed (shelved) the words 'death' and 'capital punishment' from article 2(1). Whether the drafters intended the wording to be euphemistic or otherwise, the consequence of the final wording of the article minimises the description of the bodily *violation* upon the capital criminal. To paraphrase Upendra Baxi, the *human* violation pronounced by the death sentence and execution was not considered to be a *human rights* violation (Baxi 2006, 9).

From my reading of the drafting debates I argue that although the Member States of the Council wanted to ensure that the choice of whether or not to impose the death penalty remained a sovereign 'right', the euphemistic change from the United Kingdom proposal to the final wording of article 2(1) reveals an inherent political uncertainty about the punishment. James Megivern identified that following World War Two the 'old argument used to justify the theoretical legitimacy of the state's right to execute ... would never sound the same after Hitler' (Megivern 1997, 282). The governments were becoming increasingly uncomfortable with the power they had following mass death in World War Two. This political uncertainty following war would work against the death penalty as indeed by 1981, Western Europe witnessed the removal of the punishment for ordinary crimes. In Western Member States this political unease with the punishment resulted in the governments making their *own* choices to 'shelve' the punishment.[8] Significantly this cognitive change was made through different societal and political sentimentalities (Rorty, 1993; Garland 1990; 2001), and such political shift was determined without a centralised, codified, *Convention* human rights discourse (Zimring 2002, 28–33). We now explore this penological phenomenon below.

The Removal of the Death Penalty in Western Europe

Following the adoption of the *Convention* the nine signatory states which had removed the death penalty were joined by Austria who abandoned the punishment for ordinary crimes in 1950, then between 1950 and 1981, the United Kingdom (suspended in 1965, and confirmed in 1969), Portugal (1976[9]), Spain (1978) and finally France (1981[10]). By 1981 Western Europe had collectively refused to impose the death penalty for ordinary crimes. This was nothing short of a penological revolution which had occurred without any *official* Council statement against the punishment. It is difficult to pinpoint a general theory to suggest why the death penalty was renounced. William Schabas has argued, '[t]here appears to be no formula as each country finds its own path [to abolition]' (Schabas 2004, 444), and Roger Hood has similarly stated that 'there has been no one pattern' (Hood 2002, 25). Hood pointed to various methods being reflected in that some countries removed the death penalty in one political act when new regimes came into power, and other countries went through a process of restriction, moratoria and final removal (Hood 2002, 24).

The *Convention* system of human rights had not directly provided a paradigm for this change in penal policy. In many ways, a cognitive shift occurred concerning the role and responsibility of the state with regards to its protection of the right to life of inhabitants. Following World War Two the retentionist Western European governments began to offer anti-death penalty proponents a more sympathetic ear. This wave of change swept over European shores and for the first time in its history, every Western European government had accepted that the death penalty

---

8 This governmental choice is to be seen as the political and legislative process for debate within municipal parliaments, which brings about the removal of the punishment from statute and constitutional law for ordinary crimes. As noted above, Belgium had reintroduced the death penalty in the 1970s but the courts refused to impose the sentence and it was not applied. In the UK, the process for removal of the punishment from statute law was initiated through a free vote in Parliament, and I am grateful to Roger Hood for pointing this out to me.

9 Portugal had removed the death penalty for military crimes in 1976, but it had abolished the penalty for ordinary crimes in 1867.

10 France removed the punishment for all crimes in 1981.

was not an efficient penological tool. The Oxford jurist, H.L.A. Hart, had affirmed the central issue for debate of the punishment as being:

> [i]n any public discussion of this subject the question which is likely to be the central one is 'What is the character and weight of the evidence that the death penalty is required for the protection of society? What is the evidence that it has a uniquely deterrent force compared with the alternative of imprisonment?' (Hart 1968, 71).

Hart stated that the deterrent effect and general utility of the punishment was the 'root of the matter' the 'fundamental question in considering whether the death penalty should be abolished or retained' (*ibid*). Jeremy Bentham had clearly demonstrated that there was no special deterrent quality inherent within the punishment in 1831 (Bentham 1831), but only after World War Two were such arguments becoming a more serious political realisation (Koestler 1956). The governments were, to borrow from Michel Foucault, deciding 'not to punish less, but to punish better' (Foucault 1977, 82). This *punishing better* was evident as the flaws of the utilitarian position were acknowledged. The findings of the Select Committee on Capital Punishment in 1930 took root, and the Royal Commission on Capital Punishment 1949–1953, reviewed comparative examples from Europe and elsewhere, and both reports identified that the punishment could not be demonstrated to provide a greater deterrent effect than a prison sentence (SCCP 1930, lxvii; RCCP 1953). Following his evidence before the Royal Commission, Lord Templewood stated:

> [t]he conclusion seems to be inescapable that, whatever may be argued to the contrary, the existence of the death penalty makes little or no difference to the security of life. This is a conclusion that needs to be repeated over and over again (Templewood 1951, 85).

This recognition of the failure of the utilitarian value was juxtaposed with the arguments that innocent people may be executed. Such a repugnant possibility became a troubling issue for the Select Committee on Capital Punishment, and they gave thorough attention to the debates and concluded that 'the evidence before the Committee was unable completely to dispel these disquieting and awful considerations' (SCCP 1930, xlix). In his evidence to the Select Committee, Sir Herbert Samuel stated, 'I do not think that we can ever say that no innocent man has been executed for murder in the past, nor can we have an absolute assurance that no innocent man will be convicted and executed in the future' (*ibid*). Also the Lafayette statement in the French Assembly was quoted by the Select Committee, as the French jurist had stated, 'I shall ask for the abolition of the punishment of death until I have the infallibility of human judgment demonstrated to me' (*ibid*, 222) and Lord Shaw of Dunfermline similarly articulated, '[e]very human judgment is mingled with human error, and in the issues of life and death no judge should be charged with an irreparable doom' (*ibid*, xlix). Furthermore, after the war there was a shift away from the death penalty being used as a tool of retributive punishment. Lord Templewood had stated to the Royal Commission on Capital Punishment that, 'the reforming element has come to predominate' (RCCP 1953, 17) and although Sir John Anderson did not argue for the removal of the death penalty his testimony clearly demonstrates a renunciation of retribution when he argued, '[t]here is no longer in our regard of the criminal law any recognition of such primitive conceptions as ... retribution' (*ibid*).

Hart stated that the Royal Commission report, 'introduced altogether new standards of clarity and relevance into discussions [of the death penalty]' (Hart 1968, 58) and Franklin Zimring confirmed that the 'Royal Commission's report... was the launching pad for rethinking capital punishment throughout the developed world' (Zimring 2004, 20). Certainly the abolitionists, Arthur Koestler and Albert Camus, in the 1940s and 1950s, used both the 1930 and 1949–53 reports in their arguments against the punishment (Koestler 1956, 60; Camus 1957, 192, 195). Hence, the cogent anti-death penalty position can be seen to *not* be specifically influenced by the *Convention*, but was determined by a political calculation based upon the best penal mechanisms of municipal government. In 1961, Arthur Koestler and C.H. Rolph, formulated 'A Creed for Abolitionists', and it did not specifically mention human rights or the *Convention*, but based the anti-death penalty arguments on the failure of utilitarianism, the irremediable nature of the punishment, and the incompatibility of retribution with civilised society (Koestler and Rolph 1961, 142–3). At the dawn of its removal from French statutes in 1981, Michel Foucault questioned:

> Do we want the debate on the death penalty to be anything other than a discussion on the best punitive techniques? Do we want it to be the occasion for and beginning of a new political reflection? Then it must take up the problem of the right to kill at its root, as the state exercises that right in its various forms (Foucault 1981 in Faubion 2002, 460–461).

Foucault identified that the main form of enquiry into the death penalty at this time in France should take the form of a 'new political reflection', which observed the 'right to kill at its root'. Foucault's main theoretical focus concerned the technologies of sovereign power and how such power is manifested, and hence he would not have had in mind a human rights critique. Before the complete removal of the death penalty for ordinary crimes in Western Europe, the leading scholarship reveals that the predominant argument ultimately revolved around punishment techniques and utility (Hart 1968, 71).

However, leaving the discussion there would not reveal the complete picture and we would not be able to fully grasp how the *Convention* came to be influential. What should be observed is that although the specific mandates of the *Convention* were not referred to during this period, humanitarian notions were relied upon to argue against the cruelty of executions (see Hart 1968, 64), and in France, Camus, Robert Badinter, and others, had argued about the inhumane nature of the guillotine

(Camus 1957; Foucault 1976). Hence, what may be determined is that although the *Convention* is not specifically prominent in guiding the arguments against the death penalty, what had occurred was the humanist sentiments incorporated within the *Convention* did indirectly contribute to the demise of the punishment. An interweaving of discourses then paved the way for the formulation of a Council policy on the death penalty. Below we now investigate how the death penalty has been encompassed as a specific human rights issue by the Council.

The Evolution of the Human Rights Discourse and the Interpretation of Protocol No. 6

By 1981, the Council discourse on the death penalty can be seen as an initiation of *catch-up* with Western European state renunciation of the punishment. The Council began what may be termed an 'experiment' to determine whether Member State renunciation could be transformed into a human rights discourse. During the opening session of the *Convention* drafting debates, the *rapporteur*, Henri-Pierre Teitgen had identified that:

> [w]e should need years of mutual understanding, study, and collective experiments, even to attempt after many years, with any hope of success, to formulate a complete and general definition of all the freedoms and all the rights which Europe should confer on Europeans (*Travaux Préparatoires* 1976 1, 44).

During this time, as has been argued above, the Council had not been able to establish that the death penalty violated the 'general definition' of the 'rights which Europe should confer on Europeans' and the evaluation of the punishment remained an exclusive state issue. This was confirmed in 1957 as the application of the death penalty in Cyprus by British Colonial authorities, was held by the European Commission of Human Rights not to be a violation of the *Convention*.[11] Marc Ancel, for the European Committee on Crime Problems, authored the first official Council report on the death penalty in 1962. He set out the methodological mandate for the report as being to investigate the death penalty, 'principally from the angle of substantive law and current practice in Council countries' (Council of Europe 1962, 9). As such, Ancel stated that the 'study deliberately leaves aside the philosophical, moral and theological aspects of the question' (*ibid*, 38). But some within the Parliamentary Assembly were arguing that the scope of the investigations

11 *Application by the Government of the Kingdom of Greece, lodged against the Government of the United Kingdom of Great Britain and Northern Ireland*, No. 176/56, *Application of the European Convention of Human Rights and Fundamental Freedoms to the Island of Cyprus, Report of the European Commission of Human Rights*, Doc. No. A 42.048 (Article 31 of the Convention) (Strasbourg, 26 September, 1958).

into the death penalty needed to be widened as Hans Christian Krüger observed that the Council's initial work 'did not yield results' (Krüger 1999, 65).

Change in the approaches to the discourse was forthcoming. In 1973, Astrid Bergegren, a Swedish parliamentarian, proposed a Motion in the Parliamentary Assembly, and argued that 'capital punishment must now be seen to be inhuman and degrading within the meaning of Article 3 of the European Convention of Human Rights' (Council of Europe 1973), and in a 1976 report for the Parliamentary Assembly, Committee of Legal Affairs, Bertil Lidgard, stated, '[t]he abolition of the death penalty is one of those problems that involves the very principles of moral, philosophical, legal and criminological, political and other sciences' (Council of Europe 1976, 1). Although Lidgard attempted to extend the scope of the investigations, at this time the Parliamentary Assembly could not unify its position to bring the death penalty within the realm of human rights. However, the widening of the scope of enquiry would eventually lead to the Parliamentary Assembly adopting its strongest human rights platform through a Report, a Resolution, and a Recommendation in 1980. These Parliamentary Assembly provisions maintained that the death penalty was now a human rights issue and that *Convention* article 2(1) should be amended to repudiate the possibility of the imposition of the punishment (Council of Europe, Report 1980; Resolution 727 (1980); Recommendation 819 (1980)). Resolution 727 stated:

> The Assembly,
>
> 1. Considering that capital punishment is inhuman
>
> 2. Appeals to the parliaments of those member states of the Council of Europe which have retained capital punishment for crimes committed in times of peace, to abolish it from their penal systems

These early steps in the search for the parameters of human rights saw the Parliamentary Assembly declare the death penalty as a *per se* violation of *Convention* article 3, which prohibits *inter alia* inhuman punishment. Point 1 stated that 'capital punishment is inhuman' and as a consequence of this new position, Point 2 called for abolition in peacetime. Point 3 then concluded with the Parliamentary Assembly recommending 'that the Committee of Ministers amend article 2 of the European Convention on Human Rights to bring it into line with Assembly Resolution 727(1980)'. However, it is not clear what the amended wording should have been. One reading would be that because of Point 1, the complete second sentence of article 2(1) should be removed because it is a purported violation of article 3. Another reading can be put forward to suggest that Point 2 necessitates the amendment to reflect that the death penalty can only be applied in times of war. It was this later reading that would be reflected during the drafting of what became *Protocol No. 6* in 1983. *Protocol No. 6* article 1 calls for the abolition of the death penalty, and article 2 states:

> A state may make provision in its law for the death penalty in respect of acts committed in time of war or of immanent threat of war; such penalty shall be applied only in the instances laid down in the law and in accordance with its provisions...

Under *Protocol No. 6* the death penalty is restricted to wartime offences or the immanent threat of war. However, the Committee of Ministers had not legislated to provide for the amendment of article 2(1), and Renate Wohlwend, *rapporteur* for the Committee on Legal Affairs and Human Rights, stated that *Protocol No. 6* had three essential weaknesses. Firstly it did not abolish the death penalty in times of war or imminent threat of war, secondly that it provided no formal obstacle to a reinstating of the death penalty, and finally that it did not amend article 2(1) of the *Convention* (Council of Europe 2002a). This clearly problematised the Parliamentary Assembly's arguments that the death penalty is a *per se* violation of *Convention* article 3. But from 1973 up until the present time, the Parliamentary Assembly has repeatedly argued that the death penalty *is* a violation of article 3 (for example see, Council of Europe 1994; 2001; 2003; 2005), and Wohlwend confirmed that by 2006:

> Over the past twelve years, the Parliamentary Assembly has adopted no fewer than five resolutions and four recommendations on the abolition of the death penalty, ceaselessly reaffirming its absolute opposition to capital punishment, which it regards as an act of torture and an inhuman and degrading punishment, and undeniably the most serious of all human rights violations (Council of Europe 2006a, 1).

The frustration inherent within this quote reveals an interpretive friction between the Parliamentary Assembly and the Committee of Ministers. As Council legislator, the Committee of Ministers is frequently more reserved in its approach to the formulation of Council Conventions and Protocols. The Committee of Ministers comprises the Ministers of Justice of the Member States, and so the restrictive legislation is perhaps indicative of the shadow of the sovereign state hovering over the different drafting processes in order to reserve to itself the right of making definitions of human rights (Baxi 2006) and this is explored in more detail below. Danny Nicol has noted that the Parliamentary Assembly is 'enthusiastic' in the drafting of human rights legislation but the Committee of Ministers is more 'cautious', and this can be seen in the above examples on the death penalty (Nicol 2005, 154). The reason for these different interpretive approaches can be located in the inability of the organs to unify its approach to the sovereignty question: *how far can human rights go to penetrate the sovereign right of the death penalty*? The Parliamentary Assembly was attempting to advance radical human rights boundaries, while the Committee of Minister's caution lay in the fact that it wanted to ensure the role of the Member State in the determination of the renunciation of the punishment.

Furthermore, the resulting jurisprudence of the European Court of Human Rights (Court) is more in line with the restricted approach of the Committee of

Ministers, than the radical advances of the Parliamentary Assembly. The Court (and previously the European Commission of Human Rights) had established that until article 2(1) is amended, article 3 cannot provide a *per se* prohibition on the death penalty. In *Kirkwood v. the United Kingdom,*[12] the European Commission of Human Rights first considered this possibility and held:

> [t]he Commission notes that one may see a certain disharmony between Articles 2 and 3 of the Convention. Whereas Article 3 prohibits all forms of inhuman and degrading treatment and punishment without qualification of any kind, the right to life is not protected in an absolute manner. Article 2(1) expressly envisages the possibility of imposing the death penalty.[13]

This decision in 1985 is contrary to the Parliamentary Assembly's current position, and it does reflect the conflict in the Council organs. In the 1989 Court decision in *Soering v. the United Kingdom*, Amnesty International submitted an *amicus curiae* brief and building on their 1977 Stockholm Declaration, argued that the evolving standards of *Convention* interpretation meant that the death penalty should now be considered as a breach of article 3.[14] The Court rejected the possibility of such evolutive interpretation which would have in effect made article 2(1) inoperative (see Mowbray 2005, 66–68). The Court considered the coming into force of *Protocol No. 6* and Member State signature and ratification and stated:

> [t]he Convention is to be read as a whole and article 3 should therefore be construed in harmony with the provisions of article 2. On this basis article 3 evidently cannot have been intended by the drafters of the Convention to include a general prohibition of the death penalty since that would nullify the clear wording of article 2(1). Subsequent practice in *national penal policy*, in the form of a generalised abolition of capital punishment, could be taken as establishing the agreement of the Contracting States to abrogate the exception provided for under article 2(1) and hence to remove a textual limit on the scope for evolutive interpretation of article 3. However, Protocol No. 6, as a subsequent written agreement, shows that the *intention of the Contracting Parties* as recently as 1983 was to adopt the normal method of amendment of the text in order to introduce a new obligation to abolish capital punishment in time of peace and, what is more, to do so by an optional instrument *allowing each State to choose the moment when to undertake such an agreement.* In these conditions, notwithstanding the special character of the Convention, article 3 cannot be interpreted as generally prohibiting the death penalty (emphasis added).[15]

---

12 *Kirkwood v. the United Kingdom* (Application No. 10308/83) (1985) 37 DR 158, p. 184.

13 *ibid*, p. 190.

14 *Soering v. the United Kingdom* (Application No. 14038/88) Series A, No. 161 (1989) para 8.

15 *ibid*, para 102–4.

This decision confirmed that article 3 should be read in harmony with article 2(1),[16] and in the event of a conflict, the 'right' of the Member States to choose whether or not to apply the death penalty will have prominence as no 'general prohibition of the death penalty' was established. In 1989, article 3 was considered by the Court as confined to scrutinising the extent of the 'right' of the Member States to impose the death penalty, but not to attack the actual 'right' itself. As such the Court observed that the central determining feature in the restriction of the punishment occurred through the individual choices made by the Member States through signature and ratification of *Protocol No. 6* as an expression of 'national penal policy'. What had occurred by 1989 was that although there was a conflict present within the different organs of the Council, the human rights scrutiny of the death penalty was initiated and evolving. With the coming into force of *Protocol No. 13* in 2002, which mandates for the abolition of the death penalty in all circumstances, this friction concerning the harmony of articles 2(1) and 3 would inevitably be revisited.

The Drafting and Interpretation of Protocol No. 13

According to the Parliamentary Assembly, the next logical legislative project was to formulate a protocol for the complete removal of the death penalty in Council Member States. Such a protocol would remove the wartime exception provided by *Protocol No. 6*. However, the legislative friction between the Parliamentary Assembly and the Committee of Ministers was again evident. The Rapporteur Group on Human Rights submitted the Draft Protocol (Council of Europe 2001b) and the Committee of Ministers considered the draft and explanatory report and presented it to the Parliamentary Assembly for opinion (Council of Europe 2001c). Article 2(1) was not specifically amended by the Draft Protocol text, and this was considered a failing of the legislation by the Parliamentary Assembly, as 'ultimately it is in the Assembly's interest to delete the second sentence of Article 2' (Council of Europe 2002). The Rapporteur Group on Human Rights considered the Parliamentary Assembly's Opinion and stated:

> With regards to the Assembly's Opinion the Group, whilst welcoming its strong political support for such a protocol, came to the conclusion that it was not advisable to accede to the Recommendation...In the Group's view such an amendment would present only limited interest given that the purported legal effect in respect of Article 2, ECHR will in practice also be achieved through an additional protocol. Furthermore, the amendment could, in the opinion of the [Rapporteur Group on Human Rights], give rise to some legal questions, not least with regard to territorial declarations and reservations,

16 Following the reasoning in *Klass and others v. Germany*, judgment of 6 September 1978, Series A No. 28, p. 31, para 68.

> extending beyond the scope of the consideration of the protocol itself, which could delay unduly the adoption of this important text (Council of Europe 2002b).

The Rapporteur Group on Human Rights were advancing complex, although not completely justifiable, legal arguments which thwarted the efforts of the Parliamentary Assembly. It argued that *Protocol No. 13* would alter article 2(1) by implication, and that the 'purported legal effect' would be achieved 'in practice'. Such an interpretation does not provide a coherent legal position. *Protocol No. 13*, article 5 outlined the relationship of the Protocol with the *Convention*, and it stated that the, '... Protocol shall be regarded as additional articles to the Convention', and not that it amends the *Convention* in practice. But the final 'Commentary on the provisions of the Protocol', on article 5, was an attempt to clarify the situation:

> As an additional Protocol, it does not, as far as the Parties to the Protocol are concerned, supersede Article 2 of the Convention, since the first sentence of paragraph 1 and the whole of paragraph 2 of that article still remain valid ... It is clear that the second sentence of paragraph 1 is no longer applicable in respect of the States Parties to this Protocol.[17]

Although the Commentary proposes that 'the second sentence of paragraph 1 is no longer applicable', it nevertheless is still part of the *Convention* itself. The Rapporteur Group on Human Rights allowed this to remain for two specific reasons concerning possible Member States' arguments on such an amendment. Firstly, it presumed that the amendment of article 2(1) would only be of 'limited interest', to the signatory states, and secondly, that the proposal of such amendment may 'give rise to some legal questions, not least with regard to territorial declarations and reservations'. However, territorial considerations have been a central factor of the sovereignty of modern European states since their legal mandate within the Treaty of Westphalia in 1648. So the importance of the recognition of state issues should not have been underestimated. As a result the stern warning by Renate Wohlwend is to be understood in this context. In her opinion the door had been left ajar to the Member States by *Protocol No. 13*, as she argued, '[a]re we then going to draw up another (the third!) Protocol on the same subject – the abolition of the death penalty – in order to at long last amend Article 2 of the Convention itself?' (Council of Europe 2002b).

By 2003, all Member States except Russia had signed and ratified *Protocol No. 6*, and *Protocol No. 13* had come open for signature and ratification. The states began to sign and ratify this later protocol, and this shift in collective penal policy

17 *Protocol No. 13 to the Convention for the protection of human rights and fundamental freedoms, concerning the abolition of the death penalty in all circumstances*, Vilnius, 3 May, 2002, Commentary on the provisions of the Protocol, Article 5: Relationship to the Convention.

was considered by the European Court of Human Rights in *Öcalan v. Turkey*.[18] The Chamber of the Court firstly outlined the general interpretive principles of article 3 consistent with the *Soering* decision, and it held that articles 2(1) and 3 should be read in harmony. Although the Chamber was adhering to internal state jurisdiction, it noted that since 1950 the municipal penal policy had evolved, as through the ratifications of *Protocol No. 6* and *Protocol No. 13*, Member States had independently chosen not to impose the death penalty and restrict it, and remove it, from their most current statutes. The Chamber further noted that article 3 can be interpreted as prohibiting the death penalty in peacetime, and it appears to be the case with the presence of *Protocol No. 6*, when there is no imminent threat of war, article 2(1) cannot now apply. William Schabas has argued that 'the European Court clearly rules that the death penalty in peacetime is contrary to article 3', and thus 'it is not sheltered by article 2(1)' (Schabas 2004, 428). The Partially Dissenting Opinion of Judge Türmen supports this argument when he stated, 'Article 2 still permits [the] death penalty in wartime. The logical conclusion would then be that the death penalty constitutes a breach of Article 3 in peacetime but not in wartime (because it is permitted in Article 2)'.[19]

The refusal of the Chamber to hold that article 3 now provides an absolute ban on the death penalty was challenged by the applicant on appeal to the Grand Chamber of the European Court of Human Rights in 2005. The applicant submitted arguments that a penological evolution had taken place since the drafting of the *Convention* in 1950, and that the change in Member State policy meant that article 3 should now be interpreted as renouncing the death penalty.[20] However, the Grand Chamber agreed with the Chamber's *ratio* that article 3 cannot be interpreted as providing a *per se* ban. This is a holding which has not changed since *Kirkwood* in 1985. The Grand Chamber also agreed with the conclusions of the Chamber on the harmonisation of articles 2(1) and 3 following the opening for signature of *Protocol No. 13*,[21] and it followed the *Soering* 'traditional method of amendment' analysis when it held:

> The Court notes that by opening for signature Protocol No. 13 concerning the abolition of the death penalty in all circumstances the *Contracting States have chosen the traditional method of amendment of the text of the Convention in pursuit of their policy of abolition.* At the date of this judgment, three member States have not signed this Protocol and sixteen have yet to ratify it. However, this final step toward complete abolition of the death penalty – that is to say both in times of peace and in times of war – can be seen as confirmation of the abolitionist trend in the *practice of the Contracting*

18 *Öcalan v. Turkey* [C] Application No. 46221/99, 12 March 2003.

19 *ibid* p. 71.

20 *Öcalan v. Turkey*, [GC] Application No. 46221/99, 12 May 2005, paras 157–158.

21 *Öcalan v. Turkey*, [C] paras 189–196.

> *States*. It does not necessarily run counter to the view that Article 2 has been amended in so far as it permits the death penalty in times of peace[22] (emphasis added).

The *Öcalan* Grand Chamber, following the adoption of *Protocol No. 13*, refused to apply an evolutionary interpretation. It was not prepared to reinterpret article 3, but allowed the Member States to guide this penological issue through 'their policy of abolition', and it did not want to pre-empt any possible unanimous Member State position.

By June 2007, the Parliamentary Assembly noted that the Russian Federation still had not ratified *Protocol No. 6* (Council of Europe 2007b; see also 1999; 2002; 2005). *Protocol No. 13* has still not been signed by Azerbaijan and the Russian Federation, and the protocol had not been ratified by Armenia, France,[23] Latvia, Poland, and Spain (Council of Europe 2007b). Latvia abolished the death penalty only for ordinary crimes and retained the death penalty for crimes with aggravating circumstances committed in wartime (Council of Europe 2006). Furthermore, only in October 2007 did Italy completely remove the death penalty from the Italian Constitution, article 27, paragraph 4, which had previously stated that the death penalty can be applied in 'cases provided for by military laws in case of war'. This article was removed with the eventual ratification of *Protocol No. 13* at the Council of Europe and European Commission conference 'Europe Against the Death Penalty' in Lisbon, 9 October 2007 (Council of Europe 2007d).

The possible reinstating of the death penalty in Central and Eastern Europe has been continually debated. Poland considered reintroduction in 2004–5 (Gliszczyńska *et al* 2006, 23–25), when the Law and Justice Party made the adoption of the death penalty one of the main points of its election platform. Agata Fijalkowski stated that both Polish society and the political elites support the application of the death penalty as a 'notion of a strong state' (Fijalkowski 2006, 162). Such support for the death penalty was revealed as on 22 October 2004, the lower house of the Polish Parliament rejected the proposal to reintroduce the punishment by a vote of 194 in favour and 198 against, with 14 abstentions (Council of Europe 2006). Renate Wohlwend exclaimed, '[t]he result hardly gives cause for rejoicing; there is, quite the contrary, every reason to be disturbed, even scandalised, by such a result. After all, 194 MPs were willing to vote for the restoration of the death penalty in Poland!' (*ibid*).

There are some separatist territories within Europe, which are not officially recognised internationally and are not subject to international treaties. Chechnya, Abkhazia, and South Ossetia, have retained the death penalty as an appropriate punishment in both peacetime and wartime (Fawn 2001, 85). These break-away states are still heavily influenced by Russian and Georgian legislation, with South Ossetia making Russian law applicable within its territory in 1992, and Abkhazia, initiating a moratorium on executions although death sentences are still applied

22 *Öcalan v. Turkey*, [GC] para 164.

23 France ratified Protocol No. 13 on 10 October 2007.

(Council of Europe 2006a). Furthermore, the separatist territory Dnestr Moldovian Republic, retained the death penalty following its split from Moldova, and the Parliamentary Assembly adopted a resolution calling for the commutation of all death sentences in all the separatist states (Council of Europe 2006b). Belarus is the only mainland European country which currently imposes executions and is also the only European state that is not a member of the Council of Europe. The statistics on the death penalty and executions in Belarus are a state secret, but what is known is that Belarus carried out four executions in 2004, two executions in 2005 and the actual figures are thought to be higher (Council of Europe 2006a). In a 'provisional edition' of Resolution 1560 (2007), the Parliamentary Assembly noted that executions were still being carried out in Belarus (Council of Europe 2007b).

What the legislation of *Protocols No. 6* and *No. 13* and the Court's use of them in the interpretation of article 2(1) and 3 demonstrates, is that the human rights discourse and the Member State choice to abandon the death penalty is being formulated side-by-side. In some circumstances the States are choosing themselves to abandon the death penalty, and in others, the human rights principles are guiding the states. Although there are still anomalous situations with some countries not ratifying *Protocols No. 6* and *No. 13*, and break-away territories carrying out executions, the human rights discourse is becoming hegemonic and the Council will not give up until all Member States have *de jure* abolished the punishment. A severe test of the strength of the discourse has recently been supplied by the social and political ruptures caused by terrorist violence and we now turn to consider this issue below.

The Council's Response to Terrorism

Terrorism poses one of the main threats to peace in Europe and the Council is concerned with the possibility of the return of death penalty for terrorist offences (Council of Europe 2002c). In June 2007, Fátima Aburto Baselga, stated in a Parliamentary Assembly Opinion:

> I am afraid that there is a real risk that in our times, in the context of the fight against terrorism, our societies loose sight of their principles and values and take steps backwards, driven by fear ... The fact that society is not prepared to relinquish the death penalty is often invoked as an argument against its abolishment, and it is true that in this matter there is often a gap between the electorate on the one hand, and parliaments and governments on the other (Council of Europe 2007c).

Baselga's fears are legitimate and they are based upon the consequences of terrorist violence on the cognition and sentimentality of European society: as 'fear' can make Europe 'take steps backwards'. Under the heading, 'Some major concerns', she warned the 'risk that in the context created by the fight against terrorism' the recourse to the death penalty is considered 'more acceptable' (*ibid*). The Parliamentary Assembly was particularly unnerved by a French National Assembly debate on 8 April 2004 for the reintroduction of the death penalty for terrorist offences (Council of Europe 2004a). This was a serious challenge to the current removal of the death penalty by a leading Council member which is supposed to be a *poster*-country against the punishment. In arguing against the French National Assembly 'proposition de loi', members of the Parliamentary Assembly issued a Written Declaration which stated that the devastating consequences of France bringing the death penalty back would be, '[o]nce one exception is admitted, the same hollow arguments can be rephrased with increased confidence in calling for further exceptions' (Council of Europe 2004a). The possibility of a domino-effect for the reintroduction of the death penalty was clearly a concern, and the symbolism of a country such as France bringing the punishment back would have severely damaged the credibility of the human rights discourse.

Perhaps in recent times, the terrorist case which could have undermined the Council position, was the Russian trial of Nur-Pashi Kulayev for his part in the 2004 Beslan school siege in North Ossetia, in which 330 people died. This case should be seen as a test case because the Russian Deputy Prosecutor-General Nikolay Shepel called for the death penalty, but Judge Tamerlan Aguzarov stated 'Kulayev deserves the death penalty but is sentenced to life imprisonment because a moratorium is in place' (BBC News 2006). As Russia has not ratified *Protocol No. 6*, it cannot be claimed that the Council edicts directly influenced the case. However, it is surely evident that the membership of the Council and the various mechanisms of the *Convention* system of human rights inherently influenced the Russian court's refusal to apply the death penalty. As such, the Council position against the use of the punishment for terrorist crimes is currently holding strong within Member States.

A similar test case against the use of the death penalty for terrorism occurred in the United States. Zacarias Moussaoui was charged in Virginia for his role in the 11 September 2001 terrorist attacks on New York and Washington D.C., and the United States sought the death penalty. But on 4 May 2006, the jury gave a life sentence adopting a similar approach to that of Russia in Kulyev's case. These two verdicts in terrorist cases may be described as representative of an *emerging* legal standard which is grounded within a new liberal critique on how the state treats individuals, even those which threaten the life and security of the state. In fact, the Moussaoui jury displayed that it was especially attuned to not only its role as decider of fact, but also in making decisions as representatives of a world community. Gerard Baker, writing for *The Times*, stated:

> It is this ability of the jurors to weigh the evidence in a sober way and to set aside the claims of rightful vengeance that is most impressive and most uplifting about the verdict. It was especially impressive that the jury decided a month ago that the defendant Moussaoui was *eligible* for the death penalty, but then subsequently decided that he

> should not actually receive it, a pair of decisions that reflects an almost *philosophical sensitivity* (Baker 2006, emphasis added).

The sovereign has the 'right' to choose the death penalty, but it also has the 'right' not to apply the penalty in an effort to demonstrate its preservation of the right to life. Virtually the whole of the Platonic discipline of political philosophy would agree that the imposition of the death penalty was a manifestation of 'rightful vengeance', but, as Baker correctly states, what is 'uplifting' is that the jury possessed a 'philosophical sensitivity', which is more akin to a promotion of a sentimentality against the punishment (Rorty 1993). The Kulyev and Moussaoui trials point the way forward in arguing that the death penalty is not a legitimate punishment in terrorism cases. The decisions are educative decisions on how political liberalism is evolving in its promotion of the right to life. Robert Badinter in his usual educative erudition stated:

> In reality, no one is denying the threat posed by terrorism, but not only does the war against terrorism not require the death penalty, it must actually ensure that it does not resort to it. In the face of terrorism, abolition gives democracy an ethical dimension, essential in such a war. The terrorist kills innocent victims in the name of his ideology; democracy defends freedom and recognises all lives as sacred, even that of the terrorist. The conflict is one of values in which, eventually, democracy always triumphs and even more so when it upholds, loud and clear, the principles on which it is founded. Faced with crime and cruelty, a democracy's justice system rejects vengeance and death. It punishes but it does not kill; it prevents the terrorist from harming others but respects his life; by refusing to give him death, democracy guarantees the humanity the terrorist denies through his crimes. Democracy comes out as the moral victor of the test inflicted on it by terrorism. That will not be the least of its victories in the eyes of generations to come (Badinter 2006).

The foundations of the promotion of life and livelihood by an enhanced evaluation of liberal democracy, are being affirmed in the face of terrorist violence (see also Glover 1977, 241). It is a returning to the (on the whole, forgotten) sentiments of M. François Guizot, the Nineteenth Century European historian, who observed, '[p]unishments may destroy men, but they can neither change the interests nor sentiments of the people' (Guizot 1848, 327). Guizot was advancing the argument that the death penalty is a futile instrument for preventing threatening attacks and as a consequence the punishment:

> may kill one or several individuals, and severely chastise one or several conspiracies; but if it can do no more than this, it will find the same perils and the same enemies always before it. If it is able to do more, let it dispense with killing, for it has no more need of it: less terrible remedies will suffice (*ibid*).

Arguments for better ways to punish terrorists must encompass alternative penological options as 'less terrible remedies will suffice'. Hugo Bedau has researched the death penalty in the United States for over 40 years. He has come to the conclusion on what he thinks is the 'best argument against the death penalty', which is what he terms the 'Minimal Invasion principle' (Bedau 2004). The Minimal Invasion principle can perhaps be described as searching for a Guizotian 'less terrible remedy'. Bedau argues that if governments are built upon democracy they must 'use the least restrictive means sufficient' to achieve penological aims (Bedau 2004, 32). Bedau recognises that this argument is outside of human rights considerations as it, 'does not rely on such familiar values as the right to life', and also that the argument does not rest on traditional criminological considerations except 'the debate over deterrence' (*ibid*). The Minimal Invasion principle is built upon three propositions which firstly recognise that punishment is an adopted state practice. Secondly, that the death penalty is recognised as the most invasive punishment, and thirdly, that 'the death penalty must be judged not to play a necessary role in securing public safety either by way of general deterrence or specific incapacitation' (Bedau 2004, 33). Bedau argues that when the death penalty is confronted in the United States, these three propositions are true and so the death penalty should not be imposed.

Advancing a New Standard of Legitimate Government

Hans Göran Franck, who was the author of a 1994 Parliamentary Assembly Report on the Abolition of Capital Punishment, stated '[t]he Assembly considers that the death penalty has no legitimate place in the penal systems of modern civilised societies' (Council of Europe 1994, 3). The Parliamentary Assembly was proposing the argument that the 'modern civilised societies' comprising the Council considered that the death penalty was not 'legitimate' and hence an unjustifiable punishment. What had changed was that article 3 was now analysed through a new European political liberalism by stating that the death penalty is not 'legitimate': hence attaching political liberalism to affirm the human rights prohibition of 'inhuman and degrading punishment'. This rhetoric has been repeated by the *rapporteur*, Renate Wohlwend when she affirmed the 1994 position in a 2001 Resolution which stated:

> [t]he Assembly considers that the death penalty has no legitimate place in the penal systems of modern civilised societies, and that its application constitutes torture and inhuman and degrading punishment within the meaning of Article 3 of the European Convention on Human Rights (Council of Europe 2001).

There appears to be no turning back from the Parliamentary Assembly's exclaiming of this position that the death penalty is illegitimate because it is inhuman, and this argument has been repeated like a mantra within successive Reports and Resolutions (see Council of Europe 2001; 2002; 2003; 2006; 2007). In 2003, Resolution 1349 stated:

> [t]he Assembly once more reaffirms its complete opposition to capital punishment, which has no legitimate place in the penal systems of modern civilised societies. The Assembly considers that its application constitutes torture and inhuman and degrading punishment, and is thus a severe violation of universally recognised human rights (Council of Europe 2003).

The Parliamentary Assembly is seeking to develop a new human rights norm against the death penalty. Costas Douzinas has argued that 'human rights have the ability to create new worlds, by pushing and expanding the boundaries of society, identity and law' (Douzinas 2000, 343). The Parliamentary Assembly is expanding the boundaries of the Council's human rights discourse, and has taken the reach of the arguments and policies away from a literal extraction of the *Convention* text.

The initiation of the political philosophical arguments of legitimacy, demands that the Member States justify their application of the punishment both via the established human rights principles, but also through the language of political legitimacy: there must be a political justification for executions. Hitherto, such arguments have been lacking. The Member States have not displayed any principled, and justifiable, reasons why the initiation of the death penalty would not violate human rights. In the language of European liberalism, it has not been explained how the punishment now can be seen to be a legitimate practice of government in civilised societies. As such the reliance on this political philosophy is helping to enhance and create a human rights bulwark.

But the Parliamentary Assembly has not rested there. The organisation has taken the discourse beyond political philosophy to encompassing psychoanalytical formulations. We now turn to consider this cognitive element below.

A European 'Conscience' to Guide the Pedagogy Against the Death Penalty

The discourse against the death penalty has revealed another idiomatic shift which attempts to rupture the traditional political philosophy on the social contract that aligned the sovereign with the right of the death penalty. The Enlightenment theorists thought that during the social contract, the preservation of life would only occur through transferring the right to life to the sovereign. Such a social construct was made on the basis of a psychoanalytical view necessary for the preservation of the life of the citizens. However, the Parliamentary Assembly is constructing the argument that the death penalty is against the 'conscience' of Europe. Renate Wohlwend has argued that in promoting the abolition of the death penalty the Parliamentary Assembly has 'successfully played its role as the Council of Europe's conscience', and Fátima Aburto Baselga has affirmed that the 'Assembly, who represents the conscience of Europe … reiterate[s] its strong and unequivocal call against the death penalty' (Council of Europe 2007c). Freud is useful here when he identified that '[c]onscience is the inner perception of the repudiation of a wishful impulse within us' (Freud 2005, 70). History has clearly demonstrated to us Europeans that there is an inherent impulse *within* to resort to the death penalty at the threshold of violent circumstances, and as such it should be remembered that this development of a European 'conscience' which renounces the impulse is just in its neonatal stage: after 5 millennia, we have only had *de facto* abolition for around 10 years. As such the Parliamentary Assembly understood the need to reach and understand the 'inner perception' of penology. It is attempting to establish itself as a moral authority which has identified the emotional, or perhaps, psychoanalytical 'moment', which now renounces the punishment from the core of sovereignty and law. Savigny stated that 'Law is nothing but life' and with each Member State ratification of *Protocols No. 6* and *No. 13*, the Member States are agreeing and assimilating. They are joining the Parliamentary Assembly in renouncing the psychological urge to impose the punishment. Thomas Hobbes had argued concerning the right to life that:

> [n]evertheless we are not to understand, that by such liberty, the sovereign power of life, and death, is either abolished or limited ... And therefore it may, and doth happen in commonwealths, that a subject may be put to death by the command of the sovereign power (Hobbes, 1996, 141).

But by 'such liberty' which is now formulated under the *Convention* system of human rights, this sovereign power of life and death is indeed both limited and abolished. This evolved regional and individual Member State conscience against the punishment has changed the Enlightenment social contract as referred to at the beginning of this chapter. Life is now *outside*, and not *inside*, the new contractual terms: in 1949–50 the original *Convention* ensured that the right to take life remained within the realm of the sovereign, but the new contract supplied by *Protocols No. 6* and *No. 13*, takes life outside of the contract and protects it. Michel Foucault had asked that when the social contract was theorised:

> Can life actually become one of the rights of the sovereign? Isn't life the foundation of the sovereign's right, and can the sovereign actually demand that his subjects grant him the right to exercise the power of life and death over them, or in other words, simply the power to kill them? Mustn't life remain outside the contract to the extent that it was the first, initial, and foundational reason for the contract itself? (Foucault 2004, 241)

The Council has intricately engaged with the removal of the possibility of the death penalty as a clause of the new European social contract. Gradually, the Member States have affirmed this principle and determined through the *bios*, as life in the political realm, has ensured that *zoe*, the existence of life, cannot be now judicially taken away by sanguine, tyrannical, sovereigns.

Conclusion: The 'Never-Ending Story'

The arguments against the death penalty are required to be part of a human rights 'never-ending story'. This is because any identified European conscience may change when confronted with difficult questions of life and death, and possible public opinion which calls for the death penalty may manifest a serious political challenge. Freud reminded us concerning issues of life and death that emotions can be ambivalent (Freud 2005, 23–78). This is why the anti-death penalty story is required to be repeated to each generation within each Council Member State: even within those who have abolished the punishment. The key to maintaining the European moral sentimentality against the punishment is to ensure that the scholarship on the punishment does not disappear when the punishment disappears. This is because when horrific crimes take place, the calls for the death penalty reappear.

Anti-death penalty scholarship must be sympathetic to victim's families needs (Hodgkinson 2004), but also must be able to specifically, culturally, deal with the issues surrounding the crimes so that the state will not revert back and pander to the powerful *talionic* cry. In 1969, Louis Blom-Cooper opened his edited collection, *The Hanging Question*, by stating, '[p]robably more words have been uttered – in public and in private – over the issue of capital punishment than over any other single issue of public or social policy ... Yet the debate rages on' (Blom-Cooper 1969, 1). The debate is still raging on, and this is because of the transcendent nature of the punishment: the shadow of the monster is always on the horizon. The interview of a capital lawyer in the United States by the death penalty scholar, Austin Sarat, is poignant when the lawyer stated, '[i]t doesn't matter if you live from now until eternity, there will always be more to do' (Sarat 1996, 353), and in a seminal article on this very point, Peter Fitzpatrick confirms that this is the only option for anti-death penalty scholarship because 'there can be no end to all this, neither an ending nor some end in view' (Fitzpatrick 1999, 132).

Niccolò Machiavelli offered his advice to the Magnificent Lorenzo, Son of Piero De' Medici, upon the Medici's return to power in Florence in 1513, and concerning the Prince's application of the death penalty, he stated, 'reasons for taking life are not easily found, and are more readily exhausted' (Machiavelli 1997, 65). Machiavelli was uncomfortable with the administration of the punishment and warned against its application, and Michel Foucault similarly argued, 'the authority that exercises the right to punish should always be uneasy about that strange power and never feel too sure about itself' (Foucault 1981, 461). The battle ground is that when a Council Member State does claim that its security is threatened to argue that, firstly, why such threat is not a challenge to the very *life of the state*; we don't *need* the death penalty. Secondly, to argue why the imposition of executions would have future detrimental effects; for example, producing a brutalising effect on society and making martyrs of those executed. Thirdly, that as a consequence of the first two arguments, the death penalty is not necessary and thus an illegitimate practice of modern government for the preservation of the life and livelihood of the state. Furthermore, the argument can be placed within a deeper phenomenological horizon of political philosophy, in that if the questions by the government *are actually being put forward* then there will *never* be room for the death penalty. The existence of the possibility of the *question* renders the death penalty illegitimate. From the question should emanate the Derridarian response that, 'I can only say I prefer life' (Crosara 2000) and as we are alive, *we prefer to begin with the promotion of life.* The death penalty is antithetical to this aim of humanism and human rights.

In many ways, the removal of the death penalty in Council Member States has resulted in Council discussions, scholarship and legislation, evolving at a tremendous rate, but such evolution has also meant the Member States being (somewhat) left behind. Concerning the European region Roger Hood and William Schabas, have produced the leading scholarship, and the regional publications by the Council, are invaluable. But these regional approaches must be enhanced with a burgeoning municipal perspective. The Council publications in 1999 and 2004 (Council of Europe 1999b; 2004b) are a very good starting point, but there needs to be a greater municipal and regional structure for reporting on issues of the death penalty from pluralistic disciplines such as; political theory, criminology, philosophy, religion, feminism, economics, culture, anthropology, history, and literature. However, the Amnesty International, Hands Off Cain, and the Organisation for Security and Co-operation in Europe, campaigns within Member States, and the recently created World Coalition for the Abolition of the Death Penalty, are proving invaluable for the bridging of the Council's supra-national approaches with the ground roots municipal issues.

Only from a multifaceted approach will the monster remain in abeyance. We finish with the words of Hans Göran Franck:

> The death penalty must be abolished because it is inhuman and thus incompatible with our system of values ... Capital punishment must come to be regarded in the same way as any other cruel, inhuman or degrading treatment and punishment for the world to become a better place where mankind can live in peace and prosperity; this means the death penalty has to be abolished for all offences, be they peace-time or war-time offences, as soon as possible – worldwide (Council of Europe 1994).

Bibliography

Agamben, G. (1998), *Homo Sacer: Sovereign Power and Bare Life* (Stanford: Stanford University Press).

_________(2005), *State of Exception* (Chicago: The University of Chicago Press).

Aristotle (1981), *The Politics* (trans: T.A. Sinclair) (London: Penguin).

Badinter, R. (2006), 'The OSCE and the Death Penalty', in *The Death Penalty in the OSCE Area* (Warsaw: OSCE Office for Democratic Institutions and Human Rights).

Baker, G. (2006), 'No Lethal Injection, No Single Blow of A Sword: American Justice Triumphed', *The Times*, 5 May.

Baxi, U. (2006), *The Future of Human Rights*, 2nd Ed (New Delhi: Oxford University Press).

Beccaria, C. (1983), *An Essay on Crimes and Punishment* [1775] (Chicago: Branden Press).

Bedau, H.A. (2004), 'An Abolitionist's Survey of the Death Penalty in America Today', in Bedau, H. and Cassell, P. (ed), *Debating the Death Penalty: Should America Have Capital Punishment?* (New York: Oxford University Press).

Bentham, J. (1831), *To His Fellow Citizens of France on Death Punishment* (London: Robert Heward).

Blom-Cooper, L. (1969), *The Hanging Question* (London: Gollancz).

Camus, A. (1957), 'Reflections on the Guillotine,' in *Resistance, Rebellion, and Death* (New York: Vintage Books, 1998).

Cicero (1990), *Murder Trials* (trans: Michael Grant) (London: Penguin).

Council of Europe (1962), *The Death Penalty in European Countries* (Strasbourg: Council of Europe).

________(1973), Consultative Assembly, Doc. 3297; Consultative Assembly, Debates, 18 May 1973.

________(1976), *Collected Edition of the "Travaux Préparatoires" of the European Convention on Human Rights*, vols. I–V (The Hague: Martinus Nijhoff).

________(1980), Parliamentary Assembly Document, Report of the Legal Affairs Committee, Document. 4509 (2nd and 3rd sittings), 22 April 1980.

________Resolution 727 (1980), *on the abolition of capital punishment*, text adopted by the Parliamentary Assembly, 22 April 1980 (3rd sitting).

________Recommendation 891 (1980), *Parliamentary Assembly debate* on 22 April 1980 (2nd and 3rd Sittings).

________(1994), *Report on the Abolition of Capital Punishment*, Doc. 7154, 15 September 1994.

________(1999a), Resolution 1187 (1999) *on Europe – a death penalty-free continent.*

________(1999b), *The Death Penalty: Abolition in Europe* (Strasbourg: Council of Europe Press).

________(2001a), Resolution 1253 (2001).

________(2001b), *Draft Protocol No. 13 to the Convention for the Protection of Human Rights and Fundamental Freedoms, concerning the abolition of the death penalty in all circumstances*, Ministers' Deputies Meeting (773rd meeting) 21 November.

________(2001c), *European Convention on Human Rights – Draft Protocol No. 13 on abolition of the death penalty in all circumstances*, Parliamentary Assembly, Doc. 9291, 14 December.

________(2002a), *Report: Draft Protocol to the European Convention on Human Rights concerning the abolition of the death penalty in all circumstances*, Parliamentary Assembly, Doc. 9316, 15 January.

________(2002b), *Reference Documents: 4.5 European Convention on Human Rights, Draft Protocol No. 13 on the abolition of the death penalty in all circumstances*, Ministers' Deputies Meeting (784th Meeting), 21 February.

________(2002c), *Guidelines on Human Rights and the Fight Against Terrorism*, adopted on 11 July 2002 at the 804th meeting of the Ministers' Deputies.

________(2003), Resolution 1349 (2003).

________(2004a), *Recent Initiative in France to Reintroduce the Death Penalty for the Perpetrators of Terrorist Acts*, Doc. 10211, 17 June.

________(2004b), *Death Penalty: Beyond Abolition* (Strasbourg: Council of Europe Press).

________(2006a), *Position of the Parliamentary Assembly as Regards the Council of Europe Member and Observer States which have not Abolished the Death Penalty*, Doc. 10911, 21 April.

________(2006b), Recommendation 1760 (2006), *Position of the Parliamentary Assembly as Regards the Council of Europe Member and Observer States which have not Abolished the Death Penalty*, 28 June.

________(2007a), *Death is Not Justice: The Council of Europe and the Death Penalty* (Strasbourg: Council of Europe Publishing).

________(2007b), *Resolution 1560 (2007) Promotion by Council of Europe Member States of an International Moratorium on the Death Penalty*, 26 June.

________(2007c), *Promotion by Council of Europe Member States of an International Moratorium on the Death Penalty*, Parliamentary Assembly, Doc. 11321, 25 June.

________(2007d,) Conference: Europe Against the Death Penalty, Lisbon, 9 October 2007.

Crosara, S. (2000), 'I'm Against the Death Penalty', University of Trieste, 9 November, <http://www.triestecontemporanea.it/pag20-e.htm>.

Derrida, J. (1992), 'Force of Law: The "Mystical Foundation of Authority"', in Cornell, D., Rosenfled, M., and Carlson, D.G. (eds) *Deconstruction and the Possibility of Justice* (New York: Routledge).

________(2004), 'Capital Punishment: Another "Temptation of Theodicy"', in Benhabib, S. and Fraser, N. (eds) *Pragmatism, Critique, Judgment: Essays for Richard J. Bernstein* (Cambridge: The MIT Press).

Douzinas, C. (2000), *The End of Human Rights: Critical Legal Thought at the Turn of the Century* (Oxford: Hart Publishing).

Evans, R.J. (1996), *Rituals of Retribution: Capital Punishment in Germany*, 1600–1987 (London: Penguin).

Fawcett, J.E.S. (1987), *The Application of the European Convention on Human Rights* (Oxford: Clarendon Press).

Fawn, R. (2001), 'Death Penalty as Democratization: Is the Council of Europe Hanging Itself?' 8:2 (Summer) Democratization, pp. 69–96.

Fijalkowski, A. (2005), 'Capital Punishment in Poland: An Aspect of the "Cultural Life" of Death Penalty Discourse', in Sarat, A. and Boulanger, C. (ed) *The Cultural Lives of Capital Punishment: Comparative Perspectives* (Stanford: Stanford University Press).

Fitzpatrick, P. (1999), '"Always More to Do": Capital Punishment and the (De)Composition of Law', in Sarat, A. (ed) *The Killing State: Capital Punishment in Law, Politics, and Culture* (New York: Oxford University Press).

Foucault, M. (1976), *Discipline and Punish: The Birth of the Prison* (London: Penguin).

________(1981), 'Against Replacement Penalties', in Faubion, J. D. (2002) *Michel Foucault: Power: Essential Works of Foucault 1954–1984* (London: Penguin).

________(2004), *Society Must Be Defended: Lectures at the Collège de France, 1975–76* (London: Penguin).

Freud, S. (2005), *On Murder, Mourning and Melancholia* (London: Penguin).

________(1968) 'Thoughts for the Times of War and Death,' in Pickham, J. (ed) *Sigmund Freud:Civilisation, War and Death* (London: Hogarth Press).

Garland, D. (1990), *Punishment and Modern Society: A Study in Social Theory* (Oxford: Clarendon Press).

________(2001), *The Culture of Control: Crime and Social Order in Contemporary Society* (Chicago: University of Chicago Press).

Girling, E. (2005), 'European Identity and the Mission Against the Death Penalty in the United States', in Sarat, A., and Boulanger, C. (ed) *The Cultural Lives of Capital Punishment* (Stanford: Stanford University Press).

Gliszczyńska, A., Sękowska, K., and Wieruszewski, R. (2006), 'The Abolition of the Death Penalty in Poland' in OSCE, *The Death Penalty in the OSCE Area, 2006* (Warsaw: OSCE).

Glover, J. (1977), *Causing Death and Saving Lives* (London: Penguin).

Group of Officials of the Secretariat (1970), *Manual of the Council of Europe: Structure, Functions and Achievements* (London: Stevens and Sons Ltd).

Guizot, M.F. (1848), *A Treatise on Death Punishments*, in, *ibid*, *General History of Civilisation in Europe: From the Fall of the Roman Empire Till the French Revolution* (Edinburgh: William and Robert Chambers Press).

Hart, H.L.A. (1968), 'Murder and the Principles of Punishment: England and the United States', in *Punishment and Responsibility: Essays in the Philosophy of Law* (Oxford: Clarendon Press).

Hobbes, T. (1996), *Leviathan* (Oxford: Oxford University Press).

Hodgkinson, P. (2004), 'Capital punishment – The Families of the Homicide Victim and the Condemned', in Council of Europe, *Death Penalty: Beyond Abolition* (Strasbourg: Council of Europe Press).
Hood, R. (2002), *The Death Penalty: Worldwide Perspectives*, 3rd ed (Oxford: Oxford University Press).
Huigens, K. (2001), 'Derrida on the Death Penalty', Cardozo Life, Winter 2001.
Kant, I. (1970), *The Metaphysics of Morals*, in Reiss, H.S. (ed), *Kant: Political Writings* (Cambridge: Cambridge University Press).
Koestler, A. (1956), *Reflections on Hanging* (London: Gollancz).
_________ and Rolph, C.H. (1961), *Hanged by the Neck* (London: Penguin).
Krüger, H.C. (1999), 'Protocol No. 6 to the European Convention on Human Rights', in Council of Europe, *The Death Penalty: Abolition in Europe* (Strasbourg: Council of Europe).
Locke, J. (1980), *Second Treatise of Government* (Indianapolis: Hackett Publishing).
Machiavelli, N. (1997), *The Prince* (trans: C.E. Detmold) (Ware: Wordsworth Editions Limited).
Mansfield, M. (2004), 'Is the Death Penalty About to Execute Itself?' Keynote Speech, School of Law, University of Warwick, 28th February.
Matrat, J. (1975), *Robespierre: Or the Tyranny of the Majority* (trans: Alan Kendall) (London: Angus and Robertson).
Megivern, J.J. (1997), *The Death Penalty: An Historical and Theological Survey* (New York: Paulist Press).
Mowbray, A. (2005), 'The Creativity of the European Court of Human Rights', 5 *EHRLR*, 57.
National Council for the Abolition of the Death Penalty (1945–46), Annual Report, in Tuttle, E.O. *The Crusade against Capital Punishment in Great Britain* (London: Stevens and Sons, 1961).
Nicol, D. (2005), 'Original intent and the European Convention on Human Rights', *Public Law* 152.
Opsahl, T. (1993), *The Right to Life*, in Macdonald, R. St. J. (*et al*, ed) *The European System for the Protection of Human Rights* (Dordrecht: Nijhoff, 1993).
Plato (1987), *The Republic* (trans: Desmond Lee) (London: Penguin).
Plutarch (1952), *The Lives of the Noble Grecians and Romans* (Chicago: Encyclopaedia Britannica).
Ramcharan, B.G. (ed) (1985), *The Right to Life in International Law* (Dordrecht: Martinus Nijhoff).
Report of the Select Committee on Capital Punishment (1930) (London: HMSO).
Rorty, R. (1993), 'Human Rights, Rationality, and Sentimentality', in Shute, S. and Hurley, S. (ed) *On Human Rights: The Oxford Amnesty Lectures 1993* (New York: Basic Books).
Rousseau, J.J. (2004), *The Social Contract and Discourses* (London: Everyman Publishers).

Royal Commission on Capital Punishment (1953) (1949 R. St. J. 1953) (London: HMSO).
Sarat, A. (1996), 'Narrative Strategy and Death Penalty Advocacy', *Harvard Civil Rights-Civil Liberties Law Review* 31.
Schabas, W. (2002), *The Abolition of the Death Penalty in International Law*, 3rd ed (Cambridge: Cambridge University Press).
_________(2004), 'International Law, Politics, Diplomacy and the Abolition of the Death Penalty', 13 *Wm. & Mary Bill Rts. J.* 417.
Simpson, A.W.B. (2004), *Human Rights and the End of Empire: Britain and the Genesis of the European Convention* (Oxford: Oxford University Press).
Soubiran, A. (1964), *The Good Dr. Guillotin and his Strange Device* (Souvenir Press Ltd).
Spierenburg, P. (1984), *The Spectacle of Suffering: Executions and the Evolution of Repression* (Cambridge: Cambridge University Press).
Templewood, V. (1951), *The Shadow of the Gallows: The Case Against Capital Punishment* (London: Gollancz).
Thucydides (1972), *History of the Peloponnesian War* (trans: Rex Warner) (London: Penguin).
Voltaire (1994), 'Commentary on the book "On crimes and punishments", by a provincial lawyer', in Williams, D. (ed), *Voltaire: Political Writings* (Cambridge: Cambridge University Press).
Yorke, J. (2006), 'Part One: The Evolving European Union Strategy Against the Death Penalty: From Internal Renunciation to a Global Ideology', 16 *Amicus Journal* 25.
________(2007), 'Part Two: The Evolving European Union Strategy Against the Death Penalty: From Internal Renunciation to a Global Ideology', 17 *Amicus Journal* 26.
Zimring, F. (2003), *The Contradictions of American Capital Punishment* (New York: Oxford University Press).

Chapter 4

Taking the Death Penalty Debate Further: The African Commission on Human and Peoples' Rights

Lilian Chenwi

Introduction

Africa remains one of the death penalty regions in the world, as most African states still retain the punishment in their statutes. Fourteen African states have abolished the death penalty in law and practice.[1] Of these, seven have ratified the *Second Optional Protocol to the International Covenant on Civil and Political Rights* (ICCPR) that aims at the abolition of the death penalty.[2] No *de facto* abolitionist African state has signed or ratified this Protocol. This raises questions about the commitment of some African states to human rights standards and in some cases, their *de facto* abolitionist status. Africa also remains the only region with a human rights treaty that has not yet adopted a protocol on the abolition of the death penalty. The European and Inter-American human rights systems already have protocols on the subject.

In addition, the *African Charter on Human and Peoples' Rights* (African Charter) is silent on the death penalty.[3] The right to life provision of the *African*

---

1 Cape Verde (1981), Mozambique (1990), Namibia (1990), São Tomé and Príncipe (1990), Angola (1992), Guinea Bissau (1993), Seychelles (1993), Mauritius (1995), Djibouti (1995), South Africa (1997), Côte d'Ivoire (2000), Senegal (2004), Liberia (2005) and Rwanda (2007).

2 The Second Optional Protocol was adopted by the United Nations General Assembly on 15 December 1989 and entered into force on 11 July 1991 (G.A. Res. 44/128, UN Doc. A/44/49(1989)). It has been ratified by Mozambique (21 July 1993), Namibia (28 November 1994), Seychelles (15 December 1994), Cape Verde (19 May 2000), South Africa (28 August 2002), Djibouti (5 February 2003) and Liberia (16 September 2005). São Tomé and Príncipe (6 September 2000), and Guinea-Bissau (12 September 2000) are signatories. The ICCPR was adopted by the General Assembly on 16 December 1966 and entered into force in 23 March 1976 (Res. 2200A, UN Doc. A/6316 (1966)).

3 The African Charter was adopted on 27 June 1981 and entered into force on 21 October 1986 (OAU Doc. CAB/LEG/67/3 rev.5 (1982) 21 I.L.M 58). The African Charter has been ratified by all 53 African states except Morocco. For the status of ratification of the African Charter, see Heyns 2004, 106.

Charter reads as follows: 'Human beings are inviolable. Every human being shall be entitled to respect for his life and the integrity of his person. *No one may be arbitrarily deprived of this right*'.[4] The language of article 4 with its reference to arbitrary deprivation of life is similar to that of article 6(1) of the ICCPR, indicating a prohibition of the arbitrary use of the death penalty. Although there is little interpretative material to assist in construing article 4, article 60 of the *African Charter* invites recourse to international law on human and peoples' rights. The analysis of the death penalty in international and national human rights instruments, which point towards abolition, may therefore be very useful for the purposes of interpreting article 4 of the *African Charter*. Since the object of human rights treaties is to protect the basic rights of individual human beings, in interpreting these treaties, objective criteria of interpretation that look to the text itself are more appropriate than subjective criteria that seek to ascertain only the intent of the parties.[5] Hence, I have argued elsewhere that if one applies an objective as opposed to a subjective analysis of article 4 of the *African Charter*, it points towards abolition as a goal (Chenwi 2007, 65–68).

Though the *African Charter* makes no mention of the death penalty, some African human rights instruments at least make reference to it. These are the *African Charter on the Rights and Welfare of the Child* (African Children's Charter)[6] and the *Protocol to the African Charter on Human and Peoples' Rights on the Rights of Women in Africa* (African Women's Protocol),[7] which place restrictions regarding the imposition of the death penalty on persons below 18 years of age and expectant mothers or mothers of infants and young children.

Despite these restrictions and the fact that most African states are parties to major international human rights instruments, some of which aim at limiting the imposition of the death penalty (see Heyns 2004, 48, 106), the standards in these instruments have had only a limited impact on most African states partly because of the general perception of international law in African states as a threat to sovereignty. Governments guard their sovereignty closely (Heyns and Viljoen 2002, 31). They view such standards as a threat to their sovereignty and are thus hesitant to implement them. The impact of international human rights standards at the domestic level has also been limited by the fact that some of the treaties have

4 Art. 4 of the African Charter (emphasis added).

5 See Inter-American Court of Human Rights, Advisory Opinion OC-3/83 of 8 September 1983, Restrictions to the death penalty (arts. 4(2) and 4(4) American Convention on Human Rights), series A, no. 3, para 50.

6 Adopted in July 1990 and entered into force on 19 November 1999 (OAU Doc. CAB/LEG/24.9/49 (1990). See arts. 5(3) & 30(e).

7 Adopted by the 2nd ordinary session of the Assembly of the African Union (AU) in Maputo, 11 July 2003, art. 4(2)(j).

not been incorporated into domestic law, in addition to the widespread ignorance of the standards among lawyers and civil society.[8]

Notwithstanding, there has been a growing trend towards the abolition of the death penalty at the international level as well as in Africa, which I have engaged with elsewhere (Chenwi 2007, 201–206). There have been specific developments in Africa that point towards abolition. These include the increased willingness of courts to deal with the death penalty in a constitutional context; progress in commutation of death sentences; the enforcement of a (*de facto*) moratorium in some states; and the carrying out of studies in different states on the death penalty and whether it is desirable. In addition, a crucial development has been the fact that the African Commission on Human and Peoples' Rights (African Commission) is encouraging debate on the question of the abolition of the death penalty in Africa. The African Commission was persuaded to initiate this debate by the international human rights developments and trends towards abolition of the death penalty and by the initiatives already taking place in several African countries such as Zambia, Kenya, Malawi, Uganda and Nigeria (African Commission 2004a). This development is crucial because, as is explored below, the African Commission is yet to take a clear stance on the death penalty. It could therefore pave the way for the African Commission to adopt a clear and firm position on the subject.

This chapter reviews the African Commission's initiatives including its decisions thus far relating to the death penalty. The chapter begins with a discussion of the position of the African Commission as regards the death penalty as well as initiatives towards abolition such as the 1999 resolution and the Working Group on the Death Penalty. The jurisprudence of the African Commission is then discussed. The chapter concludes with proposals towards the abolition of the death penalty in Africa.

The African Commission and its Position on the Death Penalty

The African Commission was set up as a monitoring mechanism under the *African Charter*. It was established in 1987, one year after the entry into force of the *African Charter*. The African Commission consists of eleven experts, serving in their personal capacity.[9] It is mandated to promote and protect the rights in the *African Charter* as well as interpret all its provisions.[10] The African Commission therefore has a broad interpretative function, similar to that of an advisory opinion jurisdiction (Murray 2000, 25). The functions of the African Commission also

---

8 For factors limiting the impact of UN human rights treaties on the domestic level, see Heyns and Viljoen, The Impact of the United Human Rights Treaties on the Domestic Level (2002) (Kuwer Law International) pp. 31–32.

9 Art. 31 of the African Charter.

10 Art. 30 and 45 of the African Charter.

extend to performing any other tasks which may be entrusted to it by the Assembly of Heads of State and Government.[11]

Though the African Commission is encouraging debate on the question of the death penalty, it is yet to take a clear and firm position on the issue.[12] This could partly be attributed to the fact that it has not yet been presented with a direct challenge to the death penalty.

The death penalty appeared for the first time on the African Commission's agenda during its 36th ordinary session in November-December 2004, almost two decades after its establishment.[13] However, expressing their personal opinions, some commissioners had stated their opposition to the death penalty or that they favour abolition. For example, the late Commissioner Beye, at the African Commission's 12th session in October 1992, openly and explicitly identified himself as an abolitionist by stating that he was personally opposed to the death penalty. Also, at the time he was commissioner, Umozurike indicated though not explicitly, his interest in the abolition of the death penalty (Viljoen 2004, 400). Similarly, former Commissioner Chirwa, during her time as commissioner, made it clear that she favoured abolition of the death penalty in Africa and regarded the death penalty as a human rights issue. In fact, she initiated the debate and urged the African Commission to take a firm stance on the subject. This was met with some resistance from Egypt, Sudan and Nigeria. Egypt for instance, argued that the abolition of the death penalty is against *Shari'a* law and that there is no international consensus on it. Nonetheless, it has been a welcomed proposal resulting in the establishment of the Working Group on the Death Penalty.

African Commission Initiatives

The 1999 Resolution

The African Commission had not paid much attention to the death penalty or addressed the issue of the death penalty in any of its resolutions prior to 1999. However, the situation changed in November 1999 when the African Commission passed the 'Resolution Urging the State to Envisage a Moratorium on the Death Penalty'.[14] The resolution was adopted because non-governmental organisations had expressed concern about recent death sentences carried out in Africa. Following this and in view of the international developments towards abolition

11 Art. 45 of the African Charter.

12 For a discussion of the African Commission's stance on the death penalty, see Chenwi, 2005b.

13 Though the death penalty had not yet been included in the African Commission's agenda, in 1999, it adopted a resolution on the death penalty, discussed below.

14 Adopted in Kigali on 15 November 1999, ACHPR / Res.42(XXVI)99 (see African Commission 2000).

of the death penalty, Ben Salem, who was then Special Rapporteur on Summary, Arbitrary and Extrajudicial Executions proposed that the African Commission should make a statement on the subject and call for a moratorium. Although Sudan and Rwanda (the latter now an abolitionist country) opposed the resolution, the Special Rapporteur on the request of the African Commission went ahead to prepare a draft text. The resolution was subsequently adopted. This initiative is a major and encouraging step towards the abolition of the death penalty in Africa.

The African Commission noted in the preamble that article 4 of the *African Charter* affirms 'the right of everyone to life' and article 5(3) of the *African Children's Charter* provides that 'the death penalty shall not be pronounced for crimes committed by children'. The preamble further makes reference to the following: the resolutions of the United Nations Commission on Human Rights and the Sub-Commission on the Promotion and Protection of Human Rights that call for the establishment of a moratorium on the death penalty with a view to abolishing it; the Second Optional Protocol to the ICCPR and the fact that three African states had ratified it (at the time); and the exclusion of the death penalty for grave international crimes under the statutes of the International Criminal Tribunal for Former Yugoslavia and the International Criminal Tribunal for Rwanda. The African Commission further noted the number of African states that had *de facto* or *de jure* abolished the death penalty at the time, which stood at 19. The African Commission then expressed concern, still in the preamble, that the death penalty is being imposed in African states under conditions that do not comply with fair trial rights guaranteed in the *African Charter*.

Accordingly, the African Commission in the resolution urges state parties to the *African Charter* that still maintain the death penalty to comply fully with their obligations under the *African Charter* and to ensure that persons accused of capital offences are afforded 'all' the guarantees of the *African Charter*. The resolution further calls upon states to limit the imposition of the death penalty only to the most serious crimes, to consider establishing a moratorium on executions, and to reflect on the possibility of abolishing the death penalty.

The African Commission's concern, as can be deduced from the resolution, was mainly on the implementation of the death penalty without respect for due process safeguards. Urging states to reflect on the possibility of abolishing the death penalty is evidence of the fact that the African Commission has been thinking about the issue. Furthermore, this is supported by the subsequent inclusion of the death penalty in the African Commission's agenda and the establishment of the Working Group on the Death Penalty.

The Working Group on the Death Penalty

The establishment of a Working Group on the Death Penalty has been another key focus of the African Commission towards initiating discourse on the question of the death penalty in Africa. At its 38th ordinary session in December 2005, the African Commission adopted a 'Resolution on the Composition and the Operationalisation of the Working Group on the Death Penalty' (African Commission 2005, 21). In the preamble to the resolution, the African Commission recalls the 1999 resolution and as in that resolution, acknowledges the trends in international law towards the abolition of the death penalty. In particular, it makes reference to the Second Optional Protocol to the ICCPR, the statute of the International Criminal Court, United Nations Commission on Human Rights resolution 2005/59 on the question of the death penalty as well as the debates and initiatives undertaken by civil society and other stakeholders on the issue. The African Commission further noted that 14 African states have already abolished the death penalty and 13 others are exercising a moratorium on its application. It then calls upon states that have abolished the death penalty *de jure* to encourage retentionist states of the necessity of abolishing the death penalty.

The Working Group is mandated to: elaborate further a concept paper on the death penalty in Africa; develop a strategic plan(s), including a practical and legal framework on the abolition of the death penalty; collect information and continue to monitor the situation of the application of the death penalty in African states; develop a funding proposal with the view to raising funds to meet the cost of the Working Group; and submit a progress report at each ordinary session of the Commission. In fulfilling this mandate, the Working Group is required to collaborate with other partners, including international, national, governmental and non-governmental institutions.

The Working Group is composed of two members of the African Commission (African Commission 2005, 8)[15] and five experts chosen from the different legal systems and the different regions in Africa. Its first meeting was held on 20 November 2005, in Banjul, The Gambia, thanks to financial assistance from *Fédération Internationale des Droits de l'Homme* (FIDH), an international non-governmental organisation (African Commission 2005, 45). The group discussed a draft position paper on the death penalty and agreed on the need to involve the public in debating the issue. At the time of its first meeting, the five experts had not yet been appointed. During the 39th ordinary session of the African Commission in May 2006, the Working Group submitted a report stating that it had not been able to meet again owing to the fact that the appointment of the five experts was yet to be concluded and also due to financial reasons (African Commission 2006, 37). However, the five experts were appointed at the 40th ordinary session in November 2006.[16] But resource constraints are still hampering the proper functioning of the

15 These are Commissioner Yasser El Hassan (Chair) and Commissioner Bahame Tom Nyanduga (see African Commission 2005, 8). In 2007, a new Chair was appointed – Commissioner Kayitesi Zainabo Sylvie (see Resolution on the Renewal of the Mandate and Appointment of the Chairperson of the Working Group on the Death Penalty, adopted at the 42nd ordinary session of the African Commission held in Brazzaville, Republic of Congo, from 15 to 28 November 2007; African Commission 2007; African Commission 2008, 3).

16 They are: Alya Cherif Chammari (Tunisia), Alice Mogwe (Botswana), Mactar Diallo (Senegal), Philip Francis Iya (Uganda), Carlson E Anyangwe (Cameroon), and

group, as the group has not been able to meet since the experts were appointed in May 2008. In the Resolution on the Composition and Operationalisation of the Working Group, the African Commission requested that the African Union provide adequate resources, assistance and support in ensuring its implementation. It appears that the assistance and support has not yet been forthcoming, as it depends largely on political will.

Notwithstanding, the work on improving the draft document on the death penalty in Africa is on course. At its recent meeting held from 4 to 5 May 2008, in Manzini, Swaziland, the Working Group drew up a detailed plan for the elaboration of the form and content of the draft document on the death penalty in Africa (African Commission 2008, 47–48). In this regard, for instance, the Working Group has decided that the first draft of the elaborated document would be produced by the World Coalition against the Death Penalty, an observer at its meeting (Final Communiqué of the meeting of the Working Group held in May 2008). The Working Group has further reported that it will continue to monitor the abolition and moratorium trends in Africa (African Commission 2008, 13). The Working Group also intends to pursue its efforts in collecting contributions and ideas from partners, the public and from as many sources as possible (African Commission 2006, 37). It is unquestionable that the Working Group would provide a forum for enlightening people on how the death penalty has been administered in the past as well as how alternatives to capital punishment can and do work, and whether the death penalty is desirable in the present.

African Commission Decisions

Although the African Commission is yet to take a firm stance on the death penalty, it has been faced with the issue in a number of cases before it. It has found a violation of fair trial rights and the right to life in cases in which the question of the death penalty was raised not only in the context of fair trial rights but also in the context of the right to life. With regard to whether the death penalty is cruel, inhuman and degrading, the African Commission has failed to find a violation where the challenge related to whether the failure to give reasonable notice of the date and time of execution and the fact that the death sentence in the case in question was a disproportionate penalty amounted to cruel, inhuman and degrading punishment and treatment.

The African Commission has had more impact where the challenge to the death penalty was raised in the context of the deprivation of fair trial rights than in the context of the right to life. As seen below, the African Commission has in fact laid down procedural benchmarks in capital cases. For instance, summary executions and deprivation of due process rights during the trial process would constitute a violation of not just the right to a fair trial but also the right to life and the duty of

Mohamed S. El- Awa (Egypt).

states to guarantee the independence of the courts. Also, the mere appearance of partiality alone will suffice to find a violation of the right to be tried by an impartial court or tribunal. The subsequent paragraphs provide an overview of the African Commission's jurisprudence.

Procedural Benchmarks in Capital Cases

Various human rights bodies have emphasised the imperative nature of fair trial rights. The Inter-American Commission on Human Rights and the Inter-American Court of Human Rights have indicated that the respect for fair trial rights is a necessary prerequisite to ensure the adequate protection of the rights of individuals (Davidson 1997, 296).[17] The European Court of Human Rights has also emphasised the importance of respecting fair trial rights.[18]

With reference to the death penalty, the United Nations General Assembly in various resolutions has pointed out the importance of respecting fair trial standards in capital cases by all countries.[19] The United Nations Special Rapporteur on extrajudicial, summary or arbitrary executions has also reiterated that proceedings leading to the imposition of capital punishment must conform to the highest standards of independence, competence, objectivity and impartiality of judges and juries, in accordance with the relevant fair trial standards in legal instruments (United Nations 1996, 81). In addition, the United Nations Economic and Social Council has encouraged United Nations member states in which the death penalty has not yet been abolished to ensure that defendants facing a possible death sentence are given all guarantees to ensure a fair trial.[20]

In like manner, the African Commission has on numerous occasions emphasised the imperative nature of fair trial rights and the need to strengthen the provisions of the *African Charter* relating to these rights.[21] And as seen above, in the 1999 resolution, the African Commission was concerned that the death penalty is imposed after trials in which due process guarantees are not respected and called upon states to ensure that persons accused of capital offences are afforded all the guarantees of the *African Charter*.

---

17 See, Inter-American Court of Human Rights, Advisory Opinion OC-9/87 of 6 October 1987, 'Judicial Guarantees in States of Emergency', para 29.

18 *Delcort v Belgium* (1970) 1 EHRR 355, para 25.

19 See, Res. 2393 (XXIII) of 26 November 1968 and Res. 35/172 of 15 December 1980.

20 Res. 1996/15 of 23 July 1996.

21 See 'Resolution on the Right to Recourse and Fair Trial', 11th session in Tunis, Tunisia, 2-9 March 1992 (reprinted in Heyns 2004, 526); 'Resolution on the Right to a Fair Trial and Legal Assistance in Africa', 26th session in Kigali, Rwanda, 1–15 November 1999 (reprinted in Heyns 2004, 584); 'Principles and Guidelines on the Right to a Fair Trial and Legal Aid in Africa', adopted at its 33rd ordinary session in May 2003 (see African Commission 2004b).

Article 7 of the *African Charter* guarantees every individual the right of appeal to competent national organs;[22] the right to be presumed innocent until proved guilty by a competent court or tribunal;[23] the right to defence, including the right to be defended by counsel of one's choice;[24] and the right to be tried within a reasonable time by an impartial court or tribunal.[25] The African Commission has found a violation of these rights in a number of cases in which the issue of the death penalty was raised.[26] The cases illustrate that a violation of fair trial rights may result in other violations, such as an execution becoming arbitrary or violations of article 26 of the *African Charter*, which places on state parties a duty to guarantee the independence of the courts.

The African Commission has found a capital trial before a traditional court consisting of chiefs with no legal training and in which the defendants are not defended by counsel to constitute a violation of the right to defence. This was in a case in which the Southern Regional Traditional Courts in Malawi had sentenced Orton and Vera Chirwa to death for treason after a trial that did not meet fair trial standards.[27] It was alleged that the Chirwas were denied legal representation during the trial.[28] Though the traditional Appeals Court upheld their sentences, it however criticised many aspects of the conduct of the trial. Before the African Commission decided the case, and after international protest, the sentences were commuted to life imprisonment.[29] The African Commission held that the trial of the Chirwas without being defended by legal counsel amounted to a violation of article 7(1)(c) of the *African Charter*.

Furthermore, it is a requirement of the right to defence, including the right to be defended by counsel of one's choice guaranteed under article 7(1)(c) that counsel representing an accused should not be intimidated or harassed during a trial. In a case against Nigeria, it was alleged that counsel for the accused as well as the accused themselves, were constantly harassed and intimidated during the trial, resulting in the withdrawal of the defence counsel.[30] The case concerned seven

22 Art. 7(1)(a) of the African Charter.

23 Art. 7(1)(b) of the African Charter.

24 Art. 7(1)(c) of the African Charter.

25 Art. 7(1)(d) of the African Charter. Art. 6 of the African Charter on the right to liberty and security of the person is also relevant with regard to the pre-trial phase in ensuring a fair trial.

26 These cases have also been discussed, in relation to fair trial rights, in Chenwi 2006.

27 *Amnesty International (on behalf of Orton and Vera Chirwa) v Malawi*, Communications 68/92 and 78/92, 8th Annual Activity Report: 1994–1995 (African Commission).

28 Para 2.

29 Para 3.

30 *Constitutional Rights Project (in respect of Lekwot and Others) v Nigeria*, Communication 87/93, 8th Annual Activity Report: 1994–1995 (African Commission); (2000) AHRLR 183 (ACHPR 1995).

men from Nigeria who had been sentenced to death under the Civil Disturbances (Special Tribunal) Act of 1987. The Act makes no provision for judicial appeal against the decisions of the special tribunals and prohibits the courts from reviewing any aspects of the operation of the special tribunal. Despite the lack of defence, following their withdrawal, the tribunal proceeded with the trial and condemned the accused to death for culpable homicide, unlawful assembly and breach of peace.[31]

It was argued before the African Commission that the prohibition on judicial review of the tribunals and lack of judicial appeals for judgments of the tribunals was in breach of article 7(1)(a) of the *African Charter*, guaranteeing the right to an appeal to competent national organs against acts violating fundamental rights. It was also argued that the harassment of the defence counsel and the subsequent lack of counsel violated the right to be defended by counsel of one's choice under article 7(1)(c). Further still, it was argued that the composition of the tribunals, comprising members of the armed forces and police as well as judges, violates article 7(1)(d) on the right to be tried by an impartial tribunal.[32]

The African Commission observed that a decision, sentence, judgment or order of the tribunals may certainly constitute an act violating fundamental rights as described in article 7(1)(a).[33] The fundamental rights in this case were the rights to life and liberty. The African Commission then held that 'to foreclose any avenue of appeal to "competent national organs" in criminal cases bearing such penalties clearly violates article 7(1)(a) of the African Charter'.[34] The African Commission further saw the right to defence, including the right to be defended by counsel of one's choice guaranteed under article 7(1)(c) as requiring that the counsel representing the accused should not be intimidated or harassed during the trial. Intimidation and harassment of counsel to the extent that they withdraw would amount to a violation of this right. If after such withdrawal the accused is not given the opportunity to procure the services of another counsel, the right to be represented by counsel of one's choice is violated.[35] With regard to the composition of the tribunal, the African Commission observed that the tribunal is composed of persons belonging largely to the executive branch (one judge and four members of the armed forces), the same branch that passed the Act. Its composition alone, irrespective of the character of the individual members, the African Commission held, 'creates the appearance, if not actual lack, of impartiality' in violation of article 7(1)(d) of the *African Charter*. After finding a violation of article 7(1)(a) (c) and (d), the African Commission recommended that the complainants be freed.

With regard to the right to appeal, the severity of a sentence is pertinent in establishing whether denial of this right constitutes a violation. This was the African

31 Para 2.

32 Paras 3–4.

33 Para 12.

34 Para 13.

35 *ibid.*

Commission's view in another case against Nigeria where the complainants had been sentenced to death under the Robbery and Firearms (Special Provision) Decree of 1984, which created special tribunals composed of one serving or retired judge, one member of the armed forces and one member of the police force.[36] The Decree does not provide for any appeal of sentences but merely subjects them to confirmation or disallowance by the governor of the state. It was argued that the prohibition on judicial review and lack of judicial appeals for judgments of these tribunals violates the right to appeal to competent national organs against acts violating fundamental rights under article 7(1)(a) of the *African Charter*.[37] It was further argued that the composition of the tribunals violates the right to be tried by an impartial tribunal guaranteed by article 7(1)(d).[38]

The African Commission found a violation of article 7(1)(a) in this case on the grounds that special tribunals created in 1984 in Nigeria foreclosed any avenue of appeal to competent national organs in criminal cases bearing severe penalties.[39] It further found a violation of article 7(1)(d) on account of the fact that an appearance of partiality had been created by the composition of the special tribunals.[40] The character of the individual members of the tribunal was immaterial in deciding whether the right to be tried by an impartial court or tribunal had been violated.

Similarly, in a case against Sierra Leone, the African Commission held that the denial of the right of appeal to competent national organs in such a serious offence (alleged roles in the *coup d'ètat* that overthrew the elected government) falls short of the requirement of the respect for fair trial standards expected of courts.[41] It was alleged in the case that the trials of 24 soldiers were flawed and in violation of Sierra Leone's obligation under the *African Charter*. The court martial that tried and convicted the soldiers allowed no right to appeal against the conviction or sentence to a higher tribunal.[42] It was argued that this is in violation of fair trial rights and that the public execution of the soldiers after they were denied the right to appeal constitutes an arbitrary deprivation of life.[43] The African Commission concluded that the execution of the soldiers without the right to appeal amounted to a violation of article 7(1)(a) of the *African Charter*. It further observed that 'this is more serious given the fact that the said violation is irreversible'.[44]

---

36 *Constitutional Rights Project (in respect of Akamu and Others) v Nigeria*, Communication 60/91, 8th Annual Activity Report: 1994–1995 (African Commission); (2000) AHRLR 180 (ACHPR 1995).

37 Para 3.

38 Para 4.

39 Para 13.

40 Para 12.

41 *Forum of Conscience v Sierra Leone*, Communication 223/98, 14th Annual Activity Report: 2000–2001 (African Commission); (2000) AHRLR 293 (ACHPR 2000).

42 Para 4.

43 Para 5.

44 Para 17.

In one of the high profile cases before it, the African Commission also found special tribunals in Nigeria with an appearance of partiality to be in violation of the right to be tried by an impartial tribunal and consequently found Nigeria in breach of its duty to guarantee the independence of judicial bodies.[45] The case concerned the detention and trial of Ken Saro-Wiwa (a writer and Ogoni activist) and subsequent human rights violations suffered by him and his co-defendants. His trial and that of his co-defendants took place before a tribunal established under the Civil Disturbances (Special Tribunal) Act of 1987.[46] He and some of his co-defendants were later sentenced to death, despite alleged irregularities in the conduct of the trial itself such as harassment of defence counsel, presence of military officer at confidential meetings between defendants and counsel, bribery of witnesses, and bias on the part of the tribunal members.[47] The initial communications to the African Commission were submitted before the trial began. And following their sentencing, an urgent supplement to the communication was submitted to the African Commission on 2 November 1995 requesting it to adopt provisional measures to prevent the executions. The secretariat of the African Commission then faxed a *note verbale* to the government of Nigeria invoking interim measures under Rule 111 of its Rules of Procedure of 1995. There is no provision in the *African Charter* providing for the adoption of interim measures, which explains why the African Commission relies on the provision in its Rules of Procedure. The African Commission requested that, as the case was already before it, the executions should be delayed until it had discussed the case with the Nigerian authorities.[48] However, the government ignored the African Commission's request and Ken Saro-Wiwa was executed together with the others in secret on 10 November 1995.[49]

With regard to the conduct of the trial, the African Commission recalled its view in previous cases that special tribunals established under the Civil Disturbances Act violate article 7(1)(d) of the *African Charter* since their composition is at the discretion of the executive branch, hence compromising their impartiality. The African Commission added that 'this violation of the impartiality of tribunals occurs in principle, regardless of the qualifications of the individuals chosen for a particular tribunal'.[50] It therefore found that Ken Saro-Wiwa and his co-defendants were denied the right to a fair trial in violation of article 7(1)(d),[51] and a violation of article 7(1)(a) of the *African Charter*, as the accused persons had no possibility

45 *International Pen and Others (on behalf of Saro-Wiwa) v Nigeria*, Communications 137/94, 139/94, 154/96 and 161/97, 12th Annual Activity Report: 1998–1999 (African Commission); (2000) AHRLR 212 (ACHPR 1998).

46 Para 5.

47 Paras 6–7.

48 Para 8.

49 Paras 9–10.

50 Para 86.

51 Para 90.

of appeal to competent national organs.[52] The Civil Disturbances Act ousts all possibility of appeal to ordinary courts. Consequently, and considering that article 26 of the *African Charter* places an obligation on state parties to guarantee the independence of the courts, the African Commission found a violation of article 26 on the basis that the special tribunals are not independent.

Furthermore, the African Commission found a violation of the right to be presumed innocent under article 7(1)(b) because the government openly pronounced the accused guilty prior to and during the trial at various press conferences and before the United Nations.[53] The right to defence, including the right to be defended by counsel of one's choice guaranteed under article 7(1)(c) of the *African Charter* was also found to have been breached. This was on the basis of the fact that the defence counsel was harassed to the extent that they withdrew, and after the withdrawal of their chosen counsel, the team subsequently assigned by the tribunal also complained of harassment. After this, the accused refused to have a new defence team, and the court proceedings were closed without the accused having legal representation. Moreover, it was alleged that the government withheld evidence from the defence, which the former did not respond to.[54]

The African Commission was also faced with the issue of the composition of special courts in a series of four cases against Sudan.[55] These cases concerned the imposition of the death penalty after unfair trials and the carrying out of executions after summary and arbitrary trials. It was alleged that the government executed members and suspected supporters of the Sudan People Liberation Army (SPLA) without trial.[56] Executions were also alleged to have been carried out by militia groups with close connections to the government.[57] It was further alleged that 28 army officers were executed after a trial in which they had no legal representation,[58] and the trials were carried out by special courts in which lawyers were not allowed to address the court.[59]

The African Commission observed that giving a tribunal the power to veto the choice of counsel of defendants is an unacceptable infringement of the right to freely choose one's counsel under article 7(1)(c), which is essential to the assurance of a fair trial.[60] It then reiterated the duty of state parties to the *African Charter* to guarantee the independence of courts under article 26 and the link between this

52 Para 93.

53 Para 96.

54 Para 97–101.

55 *Amnesty International and Others v Sudan*, Communications 48/90, 50/91, 52/91, 89/93, 13th Annual Activity Report: 1999–2000 (African Commission); (2000) AHRLR 297 (ACHPR 1999).

56 Paras 6–7.

57 Paras 8.

58 Paras 13.

59 Paras 15.

60 Para 66.

article and article 7 on fair trial rights. The government of Sudan had not met this duty. The African Commission also found a violation of article 7(1)(d) on the following basis: Firstly, the composition of special courts in Sudan created the impression, or indicated the reality, of a lack of impartiality.[61] The courts consisted of three military officers or other persons of integrity and competence appointed by the President, his deputies and senior military officers. The African Commission added that by providing for courts whose impartiality is not guaranteed, the government violated article 26 of the *African Charter*.[62] Secondly, on the basis that the government dismissed judges opposed to the formation of these courts. The African Commission stated that the dismissal of the judges deprived the courts of the personnel qualified to ensure that they operate impartially, thus denying individuals the right to have their case heard by such bodies.[63]

However, in another high profile case against Botswana the African Commission did not find a violation of fair trials rights.[64] This was the case of Mariette Bosch who was convicted of murder by the High Court of Botswana on 13 December 1999 and sentenced to death.[65] Following an unsuccessful appeal to the Court of Appeal of Botswana in 2001, a petition was submitted to the African Commission on her behalf alleging violations of her rights in the *African Charter*. Upon receipt of the petition, the chairman of the African Commission wrote to the President of Botswana on 27 March 2001 appealing for a stay of execution pending consideration of the communication.[66] There was no response to the appeal and the authorities in Botswana went ahead with her execution by hanging on 31 March 2001.[67]

A number of issues were raised in the case relating to fair trial rights, the right to life and the prohibition of cruel, inhuman and degrading punishment and treatment. The issue that related to fair trial rights was whether the misdirection of the trial judge with regard to the burden of proof was so fatal as to deny the right to a fair trial in the circumstances of the case, amounting to a violation of the right to be presumed innocent until proved guilty by a competent court or tribunal. According to the trial judge, the burden of proof was on Bosch to prove on a balance of probabilities that someone else was responsible for the murder she was accused of committing. This resulted in a reversal of the presumption of innocence. Despite recognising this reversal, the Court of Appeal of Botswana upheld Bosch's conviction on the grounds that the reversal did not result in a

61 Para 68.

62 *ibid.*

63 Para 69.

64 *Interights et al (on behalf of Bosch) v Botswana*, Communication 240/2001, 17th Annual Activity Report: 2003–2004 (African Commission); (2003) AHRLR 55 (ACHPR 2003).

65 Para 2.

66 Paras 7–10.

67 Para 11.

miscarriage of justice. The African Commission was of the view that there is no general rule or international norm to the effect that any misdirection by itself vitiates a verdict of guilt, and that a breach of article 7(1) would arise only if the conviction had resulted from such misdirection.[68] Drawing inspiration from, amongst others, the case law of the European Court on Human Rights and based on the fact that Bosch's conviction for murder did not result from the misdirection but from the evidence presented, the African Commission concluded that there had not been a violation.[69] It held that there could be a basis for finding a violation of article 7(1) as well as article 4 of the *African Charter*, if it is shown that the High Court and Court of Appeal of Botswana's evaluation of the facts were manifestly arbitrary or amounted to a denial of justice.[70] But this was not the case.

A reversal of the presumption of innocence in my view is a fundamental violation of article 7(1)(b) of the *African Charter*. Generally, in any system of criminal justice, the presumption of innocence is fundamental to the protection of human rights (United Nations 1984, 7). It is essential to ensure a fair trial.

Execution after Unfair Trial as an Arbitrary Deprivation of Life

The right to life is a prerequisite for the enjoyment of other human rights. It is therefore the most fundamental of all human rights. The African Commission has considered the right to life in a number of individual cases before it. But the provision is yet to be interpreted in the context of the death penalty *per se*, independent of fair trial rights. The decisions show that the death penalty is not a *prima facie* violation of the right to life, as article 4 of the *African Charter* is violated only if due process in the imposition of the death sentence is not respected. The African Commission has emphasised the importance of the right to life stating that it is 'the fulcrum of all other rights. It is the fountain through which other rights flow, and any violation of this right without due process amounts to arbitrary deprivation of life'.[71]

Consequently, the African Commission has found the execution of the 24 soldiers after a trial that was in breach of due process of law to constitute an arbitrary deprivation of life. As mentioned above, it was argued in the case that the public execution of the soldiers after they were denied the right to appeal amounted to an arbitrary deprivation of life.[72] The African Commission held that since the trial of the soldiers breached due process of law, particularly the right to appeal as guaranteed under article 7(1)(a) of the *African Charter*, the subsequent execution amounted to an arbitrary deprivation of their rights to life.[73]

68 Paras 24 & 26.

69 Paras 27 & 28.

70 Para 29.

71 *Forum of Conscience v Sierra Leone*, para 20.

72 Para 5.

73 Para 19.

In the series of four cases against Sudan discussed above, the African Commission also found the execution of prisoners after summary and arbitrary trials to constitute an arbitrary deprivation of life.[74] The African Commission observed that even if all the executions after summary or arbitrary trials were not the work of forces of the government, the government has a duty to protect all people residing under its jurisdiction.[75] It accordingly found a violation of the right to life on the basis that the trials were unfair.[76]

The African Commission concluded in the Ken Saro-Wiwa case that since the trial which ordered the executions itself violated fair trial rights, any subsequent implementation of sentences rendered the deprivation of life arbitrary, in violation of article 4 of the *African Charter*.[77] The violation was compounded by the fact that the executions were carried out despite the African Commission's request for a stay of execution and while the case was pending. In this regard it noted that Rule 111 of its Rules of Procedure is an important rule that aims at preventing irreparable damage being caused to a complainant before the African Commission, and an execution in the face of the invocation of this rule defeats that purpose.[78] In the past, executions had been stayed in Nigeria on the request of the African Commission but this was not the situation in this case.[79] The African Commission saw this negative response to its request as 'a blot on the legal system of Nigeria which will not be easy to erase' and expressed its disappointment in the following words:

> To have carried out the execution in the face of pleas to the contrary by the Commission and world opinion is something which we pray will never happen again. That it is a violation of the Charter is an understatement.[80]

In addition, the African Commission also found a violation of article 1 of the *African Charter* because the government ignored the pleas of the African Commission and others, hence ignoring its obligations to institute provisional measures.[81]

The African Commission's hope that executions will never be carried out again in the face of pleas to the contrary definitely 'hit deaf ears' in Botswana, as just two

74 *Amnesty International and Others v Sudan*, paras 47–52.

75 Paras 50.

76 Paras 52.

77 *International Pen and Others (on behalf of Saro-Wiwa) v Nigeria*, para 103.

78 Para 114.

79 The first decision on interim measures was taken in 1993 in a communication against Togo. By the end of 2002, the Commission had used interim measures on six occasions (see Killander 2006, 106).

80 Para 115.

81 Article 1 states: 'The Member States of the Organization of African Unity parties to the present Charter shall recognize the rights, duties and freedoms enshrined in this Chapter [human and peoples' rights] and shall undertake to adopt legislative or other measures to give effect to them'.

years after its decision in the Ken Saro-Wiwa case, a request for a stay of execution to the government of Botswana proved futile.[82] However, unlike in the case of Ken Saro-Wiwa, the African Commission avoided dealing with the question of whether the execution of Mariette Bosch following this request amounted to a violation.

Two of the issues in the Mariette Bosch case related to alleged violations of article 4 of the *African Charter*. The first issue was whether the President, in exercising his clemency, arbitrarily deprived Bosch of her right to life. The Commission was of the view that the clemency process did not fall under article 4 of the *African Charter*. It observed that the process that can be challenged as arbitrary is that which includes the holding of a trial so that an accused is given an opportunity to defend his or her cause, and that the intervention of the President does not affect the non-arbitrariness of the process.[83] The African Commission noted that the clemency process, unlike the trial process, is discretionary in most jurisdictions and based on a written report of the case from the trial judge together with other information the President may require.[84] It stated further that the President does not sit as a court to hear submissions on clemency and the attendance of the applicant and her lawyers at the hearing was therefore impractical and will result in undermining the office and dignity of the President.[85] It added that, in appropriate circumstances, the right to be heard may be confined to the submission of written presentations.[86] This case was one of such circumstances.

One can deduce from the African Commission's decision that if the issue related to Bosch not being afforded adequate time to assemble the relevant information, and to prepare and put forward her representations with regard to the clemency process, then the finding of a violation would have been possible. As seen in earlier decisions, it has found a violation where due process of law was not respected during the trial process.

The second issue before the African Commission was whether the execution of Bosch pending the consideration of her communication amounted to an arbitrary deprivation of life, in violation of article 4, and subsequently article 1 of the *African Charter*, which requires states to adopt legislative and other measures (including interim measures) to give effect to the rights in the Charter. The African Commission avoided dealing with this issue, stating that it was not in possession of any proof that the President of Botswana did receive the written letter in which it requested a stay of execution.[87] Actually, the government did argue in its oral submission that the fax was never received by the President.[88] Once the letter had

82 Communication 240/2001, 17th Annual Activity Report: 2003–2004 (African Commission); (2003) AHRLR 55 (ACHPR 2003).

83 *Interights et al (on behalf of Bosch) v Botswana*, para 43.

84 Para 44.

85 Para 46.

86 Para 47.

87 Para 50.

88 *ibid.*

been faxed, it was for the government of Botswana to ensure that the appropriate channels are in place to ensure that the President receives the letter. The approach adopted by the African Commission in this regard could open a door for future abuse, since states can claim that they did not receive a request for provisional measures, even in cases where they did, as an excuse not to comply with the African Commission's request. Consequently, it did not find a violation of article 1 of the *African Charter* as it did in the case of Ken Saro-Wiwa.

Sadly, the African Commission did not find the retention of the death penalty *per se* to constitute a violation of the right to life, despite the fact that it acknowledged the evolution of international law and the trend towards abolition,[89] and the fact that the death penalty has increasingly been found to constitute a violation of the right to life. In fact, the South African Constitutional Court has found the imposition of the death penalty to be 'inherently' arbitrary.[90] This implies that there is no guarantee that all due process rights can be respected in the course of its imposition. Article 4 of the *African Charter* would allow for the death penalty only if substantive and procedural safeguards and the restrictions on its imposition are respected. But if this cannot be guaranteed, then the death penalty cannot be saved by article 4 since its imposition without respect for fair trial rights will constitute an arbitrary deprivation of life.

The African Commission's approach has so far been consistent. Where fair trial rights are not respected, the imposition of the death penalty will amount to an arbitrary deprivation of life. This approach is in harmony with that of other human rights bodies at the United Nations and regional levels. Its approach is similar to that of the UN Human Rights Committee. The Human Rights Committee is of the view that the imposition of the death penalty following an unfair trial is a breach not only of procedural standards but also of the right to life (Schabas 2002, 112–113). In *Burrel v Jamaica* for instance, the Human Rights Committee found a violation of the right to have adequate time and facilities for the preparation of one's defence and to communicate with counsel of one's choosing (article 14(3)(b) of the ICCPR). It consequently found a violation of the right to life under article 6 of the ICCPR because the death penalty was imposed after a trial in which the provisions of the ICCPR were not respected.[91] *Burrel* was not informed that his legal aid counsel was not going to argue any grounds in support of his appeal and he was not given an opportunity to consider any remaining options open to him.[92] The African Committee therefore considered this to be in violation of the right to have adequate time and facilities for the preparation of one's defence and to communicate with counsel of one's own choosing.[93] As *Burrel* had been executed

89 Para 52.

90 *S v Makwanyane* (1995) 3 SA 391 (CC) para 153.

91 *Burrel v Jamaica*, Communication 546/1993, UN Doc. CCPR/C/57/D/546/1993, 1 August 1996, para 9.4.

92 Para 9.3.

93 Art. 14(3)(b) of the ICCPR.

before the Committee could decide on the matter, the remedy in the case entailed the payment of compensation to the family.[94] The African Commission is yet to issue a remedy of compensation in capital cases, as it did not do so in the case of Ken Saro-Wiwa, who had already been executed before it decided the case and in which it found a violation. In the Ken Saro-Wiwa case, the African Commission requested the government to annul the decrees that lead to the imposition of the death penalty without respect for due process rights.

The Inter-American Commission on Human Rights (Inter-American Commission) and Inter-American Court of Human Rights (Inter-American Court) also have similar views as regards the relationship between fair trial rights and the right to life. The Inter-American Commission has found the imposition of the death penalty without respect for due process rights to be in violation of the right to life. In the case of *Andrews* for instance, who had been sentenced to death and executed despite a precautionary measures request, it had to deal with, amongst others, the right to an impartial hearing guaranteed under article XXVI of the *American Declaration of the Rights and Duties of Man*.[95] The Inter-American Commission observed that inherent in the right to life provision (article I) of the *American Declaration* is a requirement that before the death penalty can be imposed and before a death sentence can be executed, the accused must be given all the guarantees established by pre-existing laws, including guarantees both at the national and international levels.[96] It held that:

> the evidence indicates that Andrews did not receive an impartial hearing because there was a reasonable appearance of 'racial bias' by some members of the jury, and the omission of the trial court to *voir dire* the jury tainted his trial and resulted in him being convicted, sentenced to death and executed.[97]

Accordingly, the United States was found to have violated article XXVI of the *American Declaration*.[98] The Inter-American Commission further reiterated that in capital punishment cases, state parties have an obligation to observe rigorously all the guarantees for an impartial trial. The African Commission, as seen above, has also reiterated the importance of respecting fair trial standards in cases bearing such severe penalties (like the death sentence). Consequently, as has been the case with the African Commission, the Inter-American Commission went ahead and found a violation of the right to life because *Andrews* was tried by a partial and

94 Para 11.

95 O.A.S. Res. XXX, adopted by the Ninth International Conference of American States (1948), *reprinted in* Basic Documents Pertaining to Human Rights in the Inter-American System, OEA/Ser.L.V/II.82 doc.6 rev.1 at 17 (1992).

96 *Andrews v United States* Case 11.139, Report No 57/96, 6 December 1996, OEA/Ser.L/V/II.98 Doc. 6 Rev. 13 April 1998 (Inter-American Commission) para 177.

97 Para 165.

98 Para 172.

incompetent court that did not provide him with equal treatment at law.[99] Like the Human Rights Committee, the Inter-American Commission recommended that the United States provide adequate compensation to Andrews' next of kin, which the United States refused to comply with.[100]

The Inter-American Court has considered the imposition of capital punishment without respect for due process to constitute an arbitrary deprivation of life. The Court has stated that the failure to respect the right to consular information, recognised in article 36(1)(b) of the *Vienna Convention on Consular Relations*,[101] is prejudicial to the guarantees of due process and that the imposition such punishment violates the right not to be deprived of life 'arbitrarily', as stipulated in the relevant provisions of human rights treaties.[102]

Cruel, Inhuman and Degrading Punishment and Treatment

The death penalty has not been challenged before the African Commission on the grounds of cruel, inhuman and degrading punishment and treatment, with the exception of the case of *Mariette Bosch*. Two of the issues in this case related to whether the death penalty was cruel, inhuman and degrading.

The first was whether the death sentence in the case was a disproportionate penalty, hence a violation of article 5 of the *African Charter*. Article 5 provides that 'every individual shall have the right to respect of the dignity inherent in a human being and to the recognition of his legal status. All forms of ... cruel, inhuman or degrading punishment and treatment shall be prohibited'. The African Commission was of the view that the question of the imposition of the death penalty being disproportionate to the gravity of the crime in this case is based on a mistaken assumption of what amounts to extenuating circumstances.[103] While the African Commission recognised that the death penalty should be imposed after full consideration of not only the circumstances of the individual offence but also the circumstances of the individual offender, it however erroneously added that 'there is no rule of international law which prescribes the circumstances under which the death penalty may be imposed'.[104] On the contrary, article 6 of the ICCPR and other United Nations standards such as the *Safeguards Guaranteeing Protection of the*

---

99 Paras 175–177 & 184.

100 Para 188 & 190.

101 Adopted on 24 April 1963 and entered into force on 19 March 1967.

102 Inter-American Court of Human Rights Advisory Opinion OC-16/99 of 1 October 1999, 'The Right to Information on Consular Assistance in the Framework of the Guarantees of the Due Process of Law' (paras 137 & 141), endorsed by the United Nations General Assembly in December 1999 in the preamble of the Resolution on Protection of Migrants (UN Doc. A/RES/54/166).

103 Para 31.

104 Para 31.

Rights of Those Facing the Death Penalty[105] for instance, prescribe circumstances under which the death penalty may be imposed.

The African Commission went further to hold that extenuating circumstances must relate to the criminal conduct in question and the state of mind of the accused at the time of the commission of the offence.[106] It added that in deciding on the proportionality of a sentence one would have to fully weigh the seriousness of the offence against the sentence.[107] The African Commission did not find any extenuating circumstances because, as evident from the Court of Appeal records, the murder involved considerable effort and careful planning on the part of Bosch.[108] Hence, it found no basis for finding a violation of article 5 of the *African Charter* since it was also not established that the courts in this case failed to consider the full circumstances before imposing the death penalty.[109]

The second issue was whether the failure to give reasonable notice of the date and time of execution amounted to cruel, inhuman and degrading punishment and treatment in breach of article 5 of the *African Charter*. The African Commission was of the view that it would be fundamentally unfair to the respondent state if it deals with the substance of this issue because the issue had not been communicated to the state.[110] It added that because the issue only surfaced shortly before the hearing, the Commissioners had not had an opportunity to consider it. At this stage it gave priority to procedure at the expense of substance, as the communication of the issue to the state is a matter of procedure. As an independent body, one would expect the African Commission to give its opinion on substantive issues. It should have set further minimum standards that states have to respect in imposing the death penalty, besides the requirement of respect of due process (Hye-Young and Ramaroson 2006, 116). The African Commission failed to do so in this case. However, if it had considered this issue, it would certainly have found a violation of article 5 of the *African Charter*, as can be deduced from the following observation it made:

> A justice system must have a human face in matters of execution of death sentences by affording a condemned person an opportunity to arrange his affairs, to be visited by members of his intimate family before he dies, and to receive spiritual advice and comfort to enable him to compose himself as best as he can, to face his ultimate ordeal.[111]

---

105 Economic and Social Council Resolution 1984/50 of 25 May 1984, endorsed by the United Nations General Assembly in Resolution 39/118, adopted without a vote on 14 December 1984.

106 Paras 31–32.

107 Para 36.

108 Para 36.

109 Paras 31 & 37.

110 Para 40.

111 *ibid.*

However, in this case, Bosch was executed without having been given reasonable notice of the date and time of execution or without informing her family.

Proposals Towards Abolition

The adoption of the 1999 resolution, placing the death penalty on the African Commission's agenda and establishing the Working Group on the Death Penalty are major and very encouraging steps towards the abolition of the death penalty in Africa. However, there is need for the African Commission to go beyond these initiatives. In addition to encouraging states to consider putting in place a moratorium on the punishment as a means to achieving abolition, the African Commission should also request that states include in their periodic reports,[112] the measures they have taken towards realising abolition in their respective countries. For a debate on the question of the death penalty in Africa to have more force, the African Commission has to take a clear and firm stance on the subject. There are various means in which the African Commission can take the debate on the death penalty in Africa further, two of which are stated below.

Resolution on Article 4 of the African Charter

The African Commission could adopt a resolution in which it explicitly interprets article 4 of the African Charter in the context of the death penalty, thus going further than the 1999 resolution. As stated in article 60 of the *African Charter*, such an interpretation has to be done in the light of international law on human and peoples' rights, other instruments adopted by the United Nations and by African countries in the field of human and peoples' rights. According to article 45(3) of the *African Charter*, the African Commission can interpret all the provisions of the Charter at the request of a state party, an institution of the Organisation of African Unity (OAU) – now African Union – or an African organisation recognised by the OAU. Abolitionist state parties (including *de facto* abolitionist states), institutions of the African Union and African organisations are therefore encouraged to request an interpretation of article 4 of the *African Charter* in the light of international law developments and worldwide abolition trends.

112 Art. 62 of the *African Charter* requires states 'to submit every two years … a report on the legislative or other measures taken with a view to giving effect to the rights and freedoms recognised and guaranteed by the present Charter'.

Protocol to the African Charter on Abolition

The African Commission could also further the debate through initiating the adoption of a protocol to the *African Charter* on the abolition of the death penalty in Africa. In fact, as stated earlier, the African continent remains the only region that is yet to adopt a protocol on the abolition of the death penalty as the Inter-American and European human rights systems already have abolitionist protocols. The legal basis for the adoption of such a protocol is found in article 66 of the *African Charter*, which states that 'special protocols or agreements may, if necessary, supplement the provisions of the present Charter'. As article 4 of the *African Charter* makes no mention of the death penalty and considering that one of the principles of the African Union is the respect for the sanctity of life,[113] this initiative is vital to achieving the goal of abolition in Africa. This initiative should certainly not prevent the African Commission from encouraging African states to ratify the Second Optional Protocol to the ICCPR. However, since the protocol would most likely take into consideration the unique problems of the continent, it stands a better chance of effectively supplementing the provisions of the *African Charter* than the Second Optional Protocol. An African instrument would gain more legitimacy because African states believe that international human rights instruments do not always address the unique problems of the continent (Nsibirwa 2001, 40). The above explains in part why not all the abolitionist and *de facto* abolitionist African states have ratified the Second Optional Protocol. In addition, a protocol on the abolition of the death penalty in Africa has an important place in the framework of human rights protection in Africa. It would be essential in enhancing human rights protection in Africa and in clarifying the situation of the death penalty in Africa.[114]

Conclusion

The African Commission has certainly taken the death penalty debate in Africa further. It has adopted a resolution urging states to consider establishing a moratorium on executions and reflected on the possibility of abolishing the punishment. It has now initiated a regional debate on its abolition and has established a working group to, *inter alia*, develop strategic plans, including a practical and legal framework on the abolition of the death penalty. The African Commission's decisions on fair trial rights have been progressive and are clearly procedural benchmarks in capital cases. Its jurisprudence on the right to life is insightful, and some have viewed its decision in the Mariette Bosch case as a step backwards (Hye-Young

113 See art. 4(o) of the Constitutive Act of the African Union, adopted on 11 July 2000 and entered into force on 26 May 2001(CAB/LEG/23.15).

114 I have suggested elsewhere how this process can be done and provided guidelines as regards its content (see Chenwi 2007, 211–212; and Chenwi 2005b, 101–103).

and Ramaroson 2006, 114). However, it is an excellent inroad for international law to help future African Commission decisions relating to the death penalty since, in line with article 60 of the *African Charter*, the African Commission did acknowledge the evolution of international law and the trend towards abolition. It also noted its previous acknowledgment of this trend when it adopted the 1999 resolution and encouraged states, albeit in weak language, 'to take all measures to refrain from exercising the death penalty'.[115] This decision in fact underscores the need to strengthen the jurisprudence of the African Commission as well as that of the African Court on Human and Peoples' Rights by persistently drawing their attention to the jurisprudence of similar bodies and developments in other human rights systems on the abolition of the death penalty.

References

African Commission (1988), 'First Activity Report: November 1987–April 1988' (African Commission on Human and Peoples' Rights).

_________(2000), 13th Annual Activity Report (1999–2000) Annex IV (African Commission).

_________(2004a), 'The Question of the Death Penalty in Africa', DOC/OS/(XXXVI)/387o, November 2004.

_________(2004b), Final Communiqué of the 33rd Ordinary Session and 17th Annual Activity Report: 2003–2004 (African Commission).

_________(2005), 19th Annual Activity Report: July–December 2005 (African Commission).

_________(2006), 20th Activity Report: January–June 2006 (African Commission).

_________(2007) Final Communiqué of the 22nd Ordinary Session (African Commission).

_________(2008) 23rd and 24th Activity Report: May 2007–May 2008 (African Commission).

Chenwi, L. (2005a), 'The African Commission and the death penalty' 11 *Amicus Journal* 13–15.

_________(2005b), 'Initiating Constructive Debate: A Critical Reflection on the Death Penalty in Africa', 38:3 *Comparative and International Law Journal of Southern* Africa 474–491.

_________(2005c), 'Breaking New Ground: the Need for a Protocol to the African Charter on the Abolition of the Death Penalty in Africa', 5:1 *African Human Rights Law Journal* 89–104.

_________(2006), 'Fair Trial Rights and their Relation to the Death Penalty in Africa', 55 *International and Comparative Law Quarterly* 609–634.

115 Para 52.

________(2007), *Towards the Abolition of the Death Penalty in Africa: A Human Rights Perspective* (Pretoria: Pretoria University Law Press).

Davidson, S. (1997), *The Inter-American Human Rights System* (Aldershot: Dartmouth).

Hands Off Cain (2004), *The Death Penalty Worldwide: 2004 Report* (Rome: Quaderni Radicali).

Heyns, C. (ed.) (2004), *Human Rights in Africa* (Leiden: Martinus Nijhoff Publishers).

Heyns, C. and Viljoen, F. (2002), *The Impact of the United Nations Human Rights Treaties on the Domestic Level* (The Hague: Kluwer Law International).

Hye-Young, L. and Ramaroson, M. (2006), 'Like a Candle in the Wind: Commentary on Communications Decided by the African Commission of Human and Peoples' Rights in 2003', 10:2 *Law, Democracy and Development* 101–121.

Killander, M. (2006), 'Communications before the African Commission on Human and Peoples' Rights', 10:1 *Law, Democracy and Development* 101–117.

Murray, R. (2000), *The African Commission on Human and Peoples' Rights and International Law* (Oxford-Portland Oregan: Hart Publishing).

Nowak, M. (2000), 'Is the Death Penalty an Inhuman Punishment?' in Orlin, T. et al. (eds.) *The Jurisprudence of Human Rights Law: A Comparative Interpretative Approach* (Turku: Institute of Human Rights, Åbo Akademi University).

Nsibirwa, M. (2001), 'A Brief Analysis of the Draft Protocol to the African Charter on Human and Peoples' Rights on the Rights of Women', 1:1 *African Human Rights Law Journal* 40–52.

Schabas, W. (2002), *The Abolition of the Death Penalty in International Law* (Cambridge: Cambridge University Press).

United Nations (2004), United Nations Human Rights Committee General Comment 13, 'Equality before the Courts and the Right to a Fair and Public Hearing by an Independent Court Established by Law (article 14 of the ICCPR)', 13 April 1984.

________ (1996), Report by the Special Rapporteur on extrajudicial, summary or arbitrary executions, UN Doc. E/CN.4/1997/60, 24 December 1996.

Van Zyl Smit, D. (2004), 'The Death Penalty in Africa', 4:1 *African Human Rights Law Journal* 1–16.

Viljoen, F. (2004), 'Introduction to the African Commission and the Regional Human Rights System' in Heyns, C. (ed.) *Human Rights in Africa* (Leiden: Martinus Nijhoff Publishers).

Chapter 5
Challenging the Death Penalty in the Caribbean: Litigation at the Privy Council

Quincy Whitaker

Introduction

The Judicial Committee of the Privy Council is the Supreme Court to the Commonwealth countries that choose to retain its jurisdiction.[1] Although it is comprised of Law Lords, the Privy Council's function is distinct from that performed by the same judges when they sit as the United Kingdom's most senior judges in the Judicial Committee of the House of Lords. Unlike the United Kingdom, the countries that retain the jurisdiction of the Privy Council have written constitutions with entrenched fundamental rights for the protection of their citizens.

It is the task of the Privy Council, as the Supreme Constitutional Court, to interpret the constitution and to ensure that citizens receive its full protection, and to ensure that all actions of the executive are taken in accordance with it and the rule of law. In this chapter I intend to examine the extent to which the Privy Council can be considered to have properly functioned as a Constitutional Court in the context of death penalty litigation in the Commonwealth Caribbean. As such, I will examine the Privy Council's ability to redefine its function beyond that shaped by the weight of its imperial origins and focus on its willingness and capability to operate as a modern supreme appellate body. It is only if it succeeds in discharging this function that the Privy Council can claim to be a legitimate court rather than a mere anachronistic vestige of Empire.

Furthermore, the Caribbean Court of Justice is now functioning and provides Caribbean countries with an alternative supreme appellate jurisdiction if they choose[2] and its existence brings the issues of the Privy Council's continued legitimacy to the fore.

---

1 Principally Caribbean countries: Antigua & Barbuda, Bahamas, Barbados, Belize, Repub. Dominica, Grenada, Jamaica, St Christopher & Nevis, St Lucia, St Vincent & the Grenadines, Repub. Trinidad & Tobago and Kirabati, Tuvalu, and the Cook Islands.

2 The Caribbean Court of Justice was inaugurated 16 April 2005 in Port of Spain, Trinidad. It has original jurisdiction for all Caricom states and an appellate jurisdiction for those states that choose to accept it, which currently includes only Barbados and Guyana.

The Death Penalty in its Historical Context

An appreciation of the political and historical function which capital punishment, and in particular, hanging (the only method of execution practised in the Caribbean) was administered following adoption into colonial society, is essential to an examination of the extent to which the Privy Council have succeeded in protecting the liberal values it is constitutionally required to uphold (see Hay *et al* 1975; Gatrell 1994). Such an appreciation ought, I would suggest, to cause one to critically scrutinise claims that judicial interference with the capacity of Caribbean governments to carry out the death penalty is nothing more than an exercise in neo-colonialism.

Capital punishment has been a constant feature of English history until abolition this century (Hodgkinson 2004, 164–170; Hood 2002, 25–26).[3] Throughout this history the crimes for which it was applied demonstrates the political nature of its imposition. The protection of the rights of the ruling elite, property rights and later the emerging capitalist economy characterise crimes for which the death penalty was imposed. The penalty itself was reserved for poor men, while decapitations were a luxury reserved for the nobility, although the extent of the concession depended on the skill of the swordsman (Whitman 2003).[4] While the labour needs of increased industrialisation and the Empire lead to a more moderate use of capital punishment during the seventeenth century, the execution of common criminals was an extravagant waste of resources which could more usefully be employed as slave labour in mines, galleys, civil engineering projects and plantations until the discovery of more efficient African slaves made this no longer necessary (Morris 1999). And there was a ferocious upsurge in its usage in the eighteenth century brought about by the introduction of the infamous Waltham Black Act of 1723,[5] the so called "Bloody Code" which added over fifty capital offences to the statute book (see Thompson 1975).

With other new statutes, there were over 200 capital offences (Koestler 1956, 13) on the statute books at the time of the Bloody Code primarily directed not only at protection of the political order at a time when it was perceived to be under threat, but also on a wider level through the protection of property as the cornerstone of capitalism. At a time when some other societies were defining and enshrining the rights of their citizens through the use of constitutional law, Britain used capital punishment to underscore its fundamental values which required

---

3 The Murder (Abolition of the Death Penalty) Act 1965 Ch.71 abolished the death penalty for a trial period of five years which was then confirmed in 1969.

4 Anne Boleyn was allowed to choose her method of execution and requested that a skilled swordsman be brought from France. See exhibits at the Clink Museum, Clink St, London.

5 The Criminal Law Act, 9 George I C.22.

political dissent to be punished with death[6] and valued the property rights of some above the right to life of others. The criminal law in eighteenth and nineteenth century Britain undoubtedly played a central role in ensuring that the power enjoyed by the Ruling classes was not unduly diminished by the claims of the masses and capital punishment was an essential tool in its performance of this function. By 1872 even *The Times* acknowledged that under the Bloody Code, 'It was not justice that was administered, it was a war that was waged between classes of the community' (The Times, 1872).

British Colonial Rule in the Caribbean

Just as capital punishment performed a particular political role in domestic British society, so too did it function in British colonies. From the days of slavery the political order of colonial rule was enforced by rigorous application of the criminal law and extensive use of the death penalty for those who attempted to assert their freedom. The law is not a neutral construct and all law reflects the values of a society at any given time. An Act passed in Barbados in 1688 for instance made thefts by slaves of articles valuing a shilling a capital offence providing protection for the twin pillars of capitalism and slavery that were so vital to British interests while conversely in 1723 it was confirmed by the Assembly of Antigua that nowhere in the Caribbean was a free man who killed a slave triable for his life (Williams 1970, 186).

Revolts by slaves were suppressed by the execution of rebel leaders and the body was displayed to deter others. For example, in 1639 a slave who led a rebellion in St Kitts was shot and then his body quartered and the limbs hung in the most frequently visited places (Williams 1970, 194). Following the Jamaican Slave Rebellion of 1865, the Jamaica Royal Commission was set up to enquire into the excessive punishments that had been inflicted. The Commission found that the death penalty had been inflicted on 354 convicted criminals, which was considered to be an excessive amount, and that the floggings were barbarous and the burning of houses wanton and cruel (Jamaica Royal Commission 1866). In self defence the Governor argued it was 'necessary to strike terror into the Negro population' and 'Negroes cannot be treated like the peasantry of Europe' (Williams 1970, 401).

Even as pressure to abolish slavery began to be voiced in Britain,[7] the legislatures of the colonies were clear that their purpose was to protect the commercial fruits of the Empire and difficulties over abolition and other issues led the British government to remove internal self rule by the expedient of abolishing elections through the 'surrender' of the islands' constitutions in the 1860s and they

6 The last people executed by the axe in Britain were the Cato Street conspirators in 1820.

7 The Abolition Society in England was formed in 1787.

were to be replaced with Crown colony government. Legislatures were replaced by a single chamber consisting of representatives nominated by the Queen in all islands except Barbados and the Bahamas (Hart 1998, 80–84). Whatever else British rule in the colonies was therefore, it was not government which had democracy as its legitimising underpinning. This historical fact is ignored by the Privy Council when it approaches statutory construction (of colonial laws) with supreme deference to legislative intent. The death penalty and the law surrounding its use cannot, I would suggest, be separated from the function and purposes of the legal system in the colonies.

The death penalty is one of the lasting legacies of British colonial rule. Certainly, some of the more barbaric aspects of the British criminal justice system were reserved for the colonies after they were abolished in Britain. Flogging for instance had declined dramatically in use in Britain since 1912 and was formally abolished in 1948, no doubt reflecting emerging twentieth century concerns about the appropriateness of such a punishment. In contrast, no such concern was apparent in relation to Britain's colonies where it continued to be used on the native population with imprisonment being reserved for whites (Roberts-Wray 1966). Flogging remained on the statute books at independence since which time it has been protected from constitutional challenge by the drafters of the Constitution (see below). It remains a punishment regularly imposed to this day in Trinidad and Jamaica at least, the two countries most anxious to carry out the death penalty. The reason why flogging could be considered unacceptable in British society and yet appropriate for the colonies is a reflection of an ideology which was necessary to the continuing operation of imperial rule, specifically a denial of the essential humanity of the native population and attendant deprivation of their fundamental rights.

Seen in this context there is an irony to the claims of those who react to the attempts by the Privy Council to address the issue of the death penalty from a basis of constitutionalism with allegations of neo-imperialism, claims, incidentally, which were not voiced in relation to the jurisdiction over commercial disputes and business transactions. Institutionally-imposed violence cloaked in the sanctity of judicial authority can perhaps be seen as one of the real vestiges of the Empire.

General Challenges to the Death Penalty

On finally shedding the yoke of imperial rule, 'Westminster' style Constitutions were enacted in most of the Commonwealth Caribbean. All of which contained entrenched protection for the fundamental freedoms that had so conspicuously been undefended by the British.[8] Thus from the perspective of a constitutional

8 Based on the European Convention of Human Rights, though Trinidad & Tobago passed a second Constitution in 1976 on becoming a Republic where the relevant Chapter was based on the Canadian Bill of Rights 1962.

lawyer, the political choice of the newly-sovereign people would elevate these rights to a height which informs all statutory construction and by which the lawfulness of government action is to be tested.

However, in the Caribbean, the practical exercise of such rights is severely limited by the inclusion in the majority of the Constitutions of those islands which retain the jurisdiction of the Privy Council and carry out the death penalty[9] of 'savings clauses' for pre-existing law (Fitzgerald 2001). These clauses have the effect of preventing any constitutional claim that fundamental freedoms are infringed by any law that was in existence prior to independence, thus preserving the status quo for constitutional protection of such freedoms as that which existed under colonial law for the life of the constitution.

Whether these provisions exist through misguided British benevolence or whether the independent political powers considered that they might also benefit from some of the values that existed under colonisation is a matter of debate and perspective. However, one might surmise that the political purpose served by colonial laws does not necessarily have uppermost the welfare of those colonised (Williams 1970, 408). The fact is, because of the insertion of the savings clauses, the constitutionality of various colonial legal practices is immune from challenge for the very reason that such practices existed, namely they were considered appropriate under colonial rule. Attempts to encourage the adoption of practices both penal and procedural into the criminal justice system that are more in keeping with values recognised internationally, albeit through the colonial anachronism of the Privy Council, are vigorously resisted by respondent states in the name of independence.

The Caribbean

The reasons why the Caribbean stands out against the current global trend towards abolition (Hood 2002; Schabas 2002) are the subject of much debate. Many of the islands have the death penalty but have not carried it out for many years. The Bahamas and St Kitts both carried out executions in 1998 although there have been periods of political moratoria. Trinidad & Tobago resumed hanging after a five year hiatus when it executed nine people in June of 1999 and Jamaica is endeavouring to carry out the death penalty after a ten year moratorium.

The motives of those in power who favour a return to the death penalty appear to be principally political. Undoubtedly Trinidad and Jamaica have a spiralling crime problem and a horrendous murder rate. It is arguable that the resumption of hanging represents a cheap and easy political action (or distraction) for a government otherwise short of crime prevention strategies and it can be carried out in the name of democracy because 'that's what the people want' (People's

9 Jamaica, Trinidad & Tobago, The Bahamas, Belize, St Lucia, St Vincent & the Grenadines, St Christopher & Nevis, Antigua & Barbuda. The death penalty was abolished in the dependent territories by SI No. 988 in 1991 and in Bermuda in 1998.

National Movement 1998). It is true that the death penalty is extremely popular in those jurisdictions (one calypso song from Trinidad contained the memorable lines 'Break their necks /it's the law /Don't let the foreign lawyers interfere /Hang the lawyers on Monday and the killers on Tuesday!') and there is much public anger that convicted killers claim the protection of the fundamental rights under the Constitution when their victims had not been accorded such rights.

However, Eric Williams, the esteemed Trinidadian Statesman and historian, writing in 1970 suggested that the Caribbean has remained not only economically but culturally, institutionally and psychologically, dependent on systems and ideas prominent under colonial rule. Political and social institutions reflect the forms existing in the countries from which they were derived and still to the most part 'reflect the concepts and vocabulary of nineteenth century Europe'. Of particular relevance to the current subject under discussion, Williams commented that 'Legal systems ... reflect past practices which are now hastily being abandoned in the metropolitan countries in which they originated' (Williams 1970, 502). Williams argued that it is only by the Caribbean defining and asserting an autonomous cultural identity that it can progress beyond this state of dependence.

Aside from the remarks above about the origins of the culture of the death penalty (see Sarat and Boulanger 2005), the argument justifying the death penalty under the mantra of the 'people's will' requires some dissecting. On closer scrutiny the argument turns out to be less one of raising issues of cultural relativism, namely 'we do not consider hanging to be cruel and inhuman treatment in our culture', but rather one of the appropriateness of convicted murderers being protected from inhuman and degrading treatment at all, namely 'they have forfeited their "human" rights by behaving like animals and thus the more inhuman the treatment the better'. Despite Caribbean judgments being peppered with references to 'public confidence' there has been little judicial examination of the legitimacy of the role of public opinion from a constitutional perspective. The public will is in direct conflict with the constitution because therein citizens are guaranteed the 'dignity of the human person and the equal and inalienable rights with which all members of the human family are endowed by their Creator',[10] Constitutional judges, and indeed politicians, need to correctly apply the Constitution as enshrining the protection of all including the social outcasts and the despised.

Challenges to Hanging and the Mandatory Nature of the Death Penalty

In *Jones v AG of Bahamas*[11] the challenge to the mandatory nature of the death sentence was based on the fact that the statute authorising the punishment merely states that whoever committed murder 'shall be liable to suffer death'[12] thus it was

10 Preamble to the Constitution of Trinidad & Tobago 1976.
11 [1995] 1 WLR 891.
12 s. 312 of the Bahamas Penal Code 1927.

argued that the death penalty was discretionary. The Board acknowledged that the use of the word 'liable' was ambiguous but approached the issue as simply one of statutory construction. They held that had the drafters of the Penal Code intended to embark on such a radical change of the law they would surely have done so in clear and express terms and seen in the context of other provisions in the Penal Code it was clear that 'liable' meant 'shall'.

Undoubtedly the Board is correct in assuming that British colonial rulers in the 1920s had no such enlightened intention as introducing a discretionary sentence when mandatory death sentences for murder were the rule in the mother country. Mandatory sentences are particularly appropriate within the political context that I have tried to outline above. The prerogative of mercy was routinely exercised, in Britain at least, to mitigate the rigours of the mandatory sentence; but this transforms the right to life to a discretionary benefaction wholly within the gift of the executive and stripped of any right-like qualities (Gatrell 1994).

It would, however, surely have been open to the Privy Council to have embarked on an interpretative exercise that was more in keeping with their role as a constitutional court. But the approach of the Privy Council in this case provides a prime example of its failures as a constitutional court. The Board in fact undertook their task as if they were the House of Lords, where ultimate deference to Parliamentary sovereignty underlies the legitimacy of their judicial authority. The exercise is conducted using English rules of constitutionalism without the central underpinning of democratically-imposed legislation or the moderating effect of fifty years worth of post-colonial changing attitudes to penal policy.[13]

In this respect, at least, those that describe the operation of the Privy Council as an exercise in neo-colonialism are right. An English constitutional approach constructing colonial legislation in its original meaning rather than acceptance of the political choice of the entrenched protection of fundamental freedoms through a written constitution is to deny the rights of individuals. The challenge to hanging as the method of execution on the basis that nowhere was it stipulated that such a method should be used was dismissed using a similar approach. The common law of England, by which hanging was the lawful method of execution, was made part of the law of the Bahamas by the Declaratory Act of 1799 and thus preserved at the time of the constitution, and it was during this period that the common law required a mandatory death sentence for pick-pocketing goods to the value of 12 pence.[14]

Over the last few years the issue of the constitutionality of the mandatory death penalty has reoccurred in a series of cases which provide a paradigm example of the competing approaches between what effectively have become two factions within the Law Lords. In the case of *R v Reyes*[15] it was argued that the mandatory

13 Except in relation to women where notions of equality, perhaps, have stripped them of their immunity from hanging.

14 Abolished 1808.

15 [2002] 2 AC 259.

nature of the death penalty in Belize amounted to inhuman and degrading treatment because it prevented the individual circumstances of the offender and the offence from being considered in determining what the appropriate punishment was. Belize's temporally limited savings clause had expired and thus the Board could approach the issue directly. The Privy Council's acceptance of the appellant's arguments was foreshadowed by the decision of the Eastern Caribbean Supreme Court in the linked cases of *R v Spence and R v Hughes*[16] that had already held that the mandatory death penalty was unconstitutional in St Vincent & the Grenadines and St Lucia. The decision was also applied to Nevis and St Kitts in the case of *R v Fox*,[17] As there were no savings clauses operative in the relevant constitutions these decisions were relatively uncontroversial. The cases that followed from Trinidad and Barbados, both with savings clauses, however provide an ultimately tragic example of the tensions within the Privy Council itself as to how it should perform its function.

In *R v Roodal*[18] the majority of the Privy Council accepted the appellant's imaginative argument that a correct constitutional approach necessitated using the Trinidadian Interpretation Act whereby any fixed penalty could be construed as a maximum to render the death penalty discretionary. The majority held that it was not necessary for Parliament to have intended to abolish the mandatory nature of the death penalty when passing the Interpretation Act provided the words could permit of such an interpretation. The 1962 Trinidadian Constitution contained a clause requiring all existing laws to be applied with such modifications as were necessary to bring them into conformity with the new Constitution. In 1976 a further Constitution was brought into force when Trinidad became a Republic which provided that any law that was inconsistent with the new Constitution was void to the extent of the inconsistency. As the mandatory death sentence was incompatible with the prohibition on inhuman and degrading treatment it was necessary to modify it to make it compatible with the constitution, namely by making it a discretionary sentence through the use of the Interpretation Act. The decision of the majority demonstrates the exemplary approach to purposive constitutional construction characteristic of the judgments of Lord Steyn and Lord Bingham in this area. However the later decisions of *R v Boyce*[19] from Barbados and *R v Matthew*[20] which overruled *Roodal* led the Privy Council back from this high watermark of their functioning as a legitimate Constitutional Court, where the majority of Law Lords (both cases had an unprecedented 9 judge

16 Upheld by the Privy Council and reported at [2002] UKPC 12.

17 [2002] 2 A.C. 284 (PC).

18 [2005] 1 A.C. 378.

19 [2005] 1 AC 400; Barbados subsequently left the jurisdiction of the Privy Council. Mr Boyce's sentence was commuted by the Court of Appeal of Barbados, a decision upheld by the Caribbean Court of Justice on Nov. 8 2006 (CCJ Appeal No CV 2 of 2005) in one of its first judgments concerning the death penalty.

20 [2005] 1 AC 433.

Board) demonstrate a reversion to 'the austerity of tabulated reasoning' that Lord Wilberforce had cautioned against.[21] Lord Hoffman led this flawed approach as he has done in so many of the cases in this area, rejecting the application of a similar argument to that which succeeded in Trinidad and Barbados as 'arbitrary to the point of absurdity'[22] despite acceptance that the mandatory penalty was incompatible with the prohibition on inhuman and degrading treatment.

By a majority of five to four the Privy Council dismissed the appeal and this majority again triumphed in *R v Matthew*, overruling *Roodal*, and removed the most substantial inroad that had hitherto been made to the application of the death penalty in the Caribbean, despite universal acceptance that the mandatory penalty breached the prohibition on inhuman treatment.

Delays in Execution and the Death Row Phenomenon

The jurisprudence arising from arguments concerning delay in carrying out the death sentence was the first area where the emergence of an approach compatible with a modern constitutional court could be identified.

The argument that delay in carrying out the sentence of death could amount to cruel and unusual treatment had been accepted in Indian and Zimbabwean jurisprudence prior to its acceptance by the Privy Council in the landmark case *Pratt & Morgan v AG Jamaica.*[23] While greater evidential material was available in *Pratt* than when the argument had been rejected by the Board previously, the decision may be as much a reflection of the changing composition of the Privy Council, but also evidence of a greater enthusiasm for undertaking its task as a constitutional court.

Delay was first relied upon before the Privy Council in the case of *de Freitas v Benny*[24] (the case of Michael X). It was argued that despite the savings clause the execution of the appellant nonetheless contravened the prohibition of cruel and unusual treatment or punishment in the Trinidadian constitution. The appellant argued for a distinction between the passing of the sentence (a judicial act and thus immune from challenge) and carrying out of sentence (which was an executive administrative act and not immune). In their Lordships' view however this distinction did not 'bear examination'[25] and the case was dismissed without the respondent government being called upon, stating that 'their Lordships [found] some difficulty in [even] formulating the ... argument based on delay' and 'this contention only needed to be stated to be rejected'.[26]

21 *Minister of Home Affairs v Fisher [*1980] AC 319, 329.
22 *ibid*, p. 447.
23 [1994] 2 AC 1.
24 [1976] AC 239.
25 *ibid*, 245.
26 *ibid*, 246.

A challenge based on delay also failed in the case of *Abbott v AG Trinidad & Tobago*[27] where a different constitutional route was tried by arguing that a delayed execution would not be in accordance with 'due process of law' as required by the constitution. Not surprisingly the argument based on eight months delay failed. However, some useful dicta were produced which would be successfully relied upon in future cases, such as the view that 'due process of law does not end with the pronouncement of sentence in a criminal matter'[28] and:

> their Lordships accept it is possible to imagine a case in which the time allowed by the authorities to elapse between the pronouncement of a death sentence and notification to the condemned man that it was to be carried out was so prolonged as to arouse in him the reasonable belief that his death sentence must have been commuted to life imprisonment … [but] such a case would involve delay measured in years not months[29]

Such change in emphasis of Privy Council jurisprudence was advanced in *Noel Riley & Others v AG of Jamaica*[30] by the far sighted minority opinions of Lords Scarman and Brightman, and the legal evolution continued through the seven member court[31] in *Pratt & Morgan.* The appellants in *Pratt* had been held on death row for some fourteen years and it was argued that to execute them after such a period would expose them to inhuman and degrading punishment contrary to section 17(1) of the Jamaican Constitution. The major obstacle, as with the Trinidadian cases, was the savings clause in section 17(2). This section provides that 'Nothing … shall be held to be inconsistent with ... this section to the extent that the law in question authorises the infliction of any description of a punishment which was lawful immediately before the appointed day' and which had been interpreted in the earlier judgement of *Riley* as conclusively preventing such a challenge. The majority in *Riley* construed section 17(2) as focussing on the description of the act of punishment and proceeded on the assumption that the legality of a long delayed execution could never have been questioned before independence. The Board in *Pratt* preferred the narrow interpretation of section 17(2) which had been advocated by the minority in *Riley,* limiting the scope of the subsection to authorising the passing of a judicial sentence lawful in Jamaica before independence. They held the subsection was not concerned with the act of the executive in carrying out the punishment. Thus while it prevented any challenge to the imposition of the death sentence, it presented no barrier to examining the lawfulness of the decision of the executive to read the death warrant and carry out the execution. This far-sighted approach (though also argued seven

27 (1979) 1WLR 1342.
28 *ibid,* 1347.
29 *ibid,* 1348.
30 (1983) AC 719.
31 A seven member court was convened because the Privy Council was being asked to overrule one of its previous decisions.

years previously) to constitutional construction is in keeping with the modern two tier approach to defining rights and restrictions.

Their Lordships then considered the question as to whether such delay would amount to inhuman and degrading treatment. Lord Griffiths reviewed two competing strands of jurisprudence. First, the approach of the courts in America, and indeed of the Privy Council prior to *Pratt*,[32] that it cannot be inhuman or degrading to allow a defendant every opportunity to prolong his life by resorting to appellate procedures. In the words of Lord Diplock 'where there's life there's hope'.[33] Secondly, the approach in Zimbabwe and India had focused on the effect on the condemned man rather than the cause of the delay and had followed the minority judgment in *Riley* (in a pleasant demonstration of Commonwealth jurisprudential cross-fertilisation) 'it is no answer to say that a man will struggle to stay alive. In truth it is this ineradicable human desire which makes prolongation inhuman and degrading'.[34] The words of Gubbay CJ in the leading Zimbabwean case[35] were adopted:

> It seems to me highly artificial and unrealistic to discount the mental agony and torment experienced on death row on the basis that by not making the maximum use of the judicial process the condemned man would have shortened not lengthened his suffering.

This 'effect on the individual' approach has the advantage of logic and humanity as it recognises the essentially inhuman and degrading nature of the death row phenomenon, a quality that does not alter because it occurs by virtue of resorting to a legitimate appellate process. These two competing views were brought into sharp relief in the extradition case of *Soering v United Kingdom*[36] when the European Court of Human Rights held that the United Kingdom would violate Mr Soering's right under the *European Convention on Human Rights* not to be subjected to inhuman or degrading punishment or treatment if he was extradited to Virginia on a capital charge in view of the long period of delay experienced by condemned men prior to execution in that State (average 8 years). Following these decisions, the Privy Council departed from its previous case law and held that the delay experienced by Mr Pratt and Mr Morgan, even though it occurred as a result of resorting to the appellate process, amounted to inhuman and degrading treatment and thus it would be unconstitutional to execute them now. Their sentences were commuted to life imprisonment.

32 See generally, *Abbot v AG Trinidad & Tobago, supra.*

33 *Ibid.*

34 Minority judgment, 753.

35 *Catholic Commissioners for Peace and Justice v. Attorney General* (1993) 1 ZLR 242 (S).

36 (1989) 11 EHRR 439.

Their Lordships then proceeded to lay down a timetable whereby the domestic appeal process should be completed within two years and appeals to the United Nations Human Rights Committee within eighteen months thereafter. These considerations led them to the view that a presumption of inhuman or degrading punishment would arise in any case where execution is to take place more than five years after sentence. This decision had an extraordinary impact across the Commonwealth Caribbean and led to automatic commutation of sentence for several hundred men languishing on death row.

Inevitably there was a level of arbitrariness about the five year period. Several cases following *Pratt* questioned whether it was necessary to refine the jurisprudence away from the executing state's view of 5 years as a rigid cut-off point, and indeed to correct the Privy Council's own understanding of the rationale behind their decision.

In *Bradshaw v AG of Barbados*[37] the Privy Council held that *Pratt* applied to Barbados, rejecting the government's argument that the addition of 'the administration of treatment' to the savings clause distinguished the constitutional position of Barbados from Jamaica. Their Lordships rejected the contention that keeping a condemned man in prison prior to execution amounted to 'the administration of treatment' and even if it were, over-long detention would not have been lawful prior to independence for the reasons set out in *Pratt*. Further they rejected a suggestion from the Government that the five year period should be extended because appeals to international human rights bodies were taking two years or that these periods be excluded from the reckoning altogether. While there is some force in the argument that procedures of international bodies are beyond the control of the state, the notion of fault is at odds with the focus of the impact upon the individual.

Their Lordships stated that they wished to discourage the minute examination of weeks and months when delay has occurred in an attempt to apportion blame to one party or another. The approach as set out in *Pratt* was to take the total period of time which has elapsed and then to ask whether 'the delay is due entirely to the fault of accused such as an escape from custody or frivolous and time wasting resort to legal procedures which amount to an abuse of process'.[38]

There is no denying that this jurisprudence was deeply unpopular with those Caribbean governments anxious to hang their convicted capital murderers. Frustration turned to judicial murder in a low point in Trinidad & Tobago's judicial history when collusion between the judiciary and the state led to the hanging of Glen Ashby while his constitutional appeal was being argued in front of the Court of Appeal. A stay of execution had arrived by fax from the Privy Council minutes after Mr Ashby had been hanged.

Trinidad & Tobago also took a strict view of the five year limit and sought to execute Lincoln Guerra and Brian Wallen when they had been on death row

37 (1995) 1 WLR 936.

38 *ibid*, 943 quoting *Pratt*, 33.

for four years and ten months. In both cases the state's desire to implement an execution was frustrated, in Brian Wallen's case by his dying in prison of a heart attack two days after the Court of Appeal dismissed his constitutional motion. In Guerra's case the Privy Council commuted his sentence following a successful constitutional challenge on the grounds, *inter alia*, of delay. Even though the five year period had not been exceeded, the men's domestic appeal against conviction had taken four and a half years to be disposed of, principally because it had taken over four years to provide the appellant's lawyers with the notes of evidence from the trial. The Court of Appeal in Trinidad had held that the *Pratt* period of five years was too short for Trinidad and further openly based their reasoning on the constitutionally flawed basis of public opinion.

Apart from their wholly selective approach to which laws ought to be enforced at the behest of the public, the Court of Appeal's reasoning showed an attempt to resurrect notions of fault. They argued that courts in Trinidad & Tobago had an increased workload as a result of the crime wave and the condemned prisoner had to recognise that his appeal is not the only one and a balance must be maintained. Furthermore, as the five year period had not been exceeded there could be no arguable case on delay. Their Lordships disagreed, as they held *Pratt* was equally applicable to Trinidad & Tobago and the reasoning of the case shows the 'limited extent to which regard can be had in the present case to problems facing the judicial system. It follows that such problems cannot be used to excuse delay'.[39] Their Lordships explained that the five year period was merely advice to the executive to enable them to deal expeditiously with the large number of men who had spent many years on death row. Falling just short of the five year period therefore was not an end of the matter. It was held that the four years and ten months which it had taken to complete the domestic appeal process was so excessive when compared to the target period of two years, that it could not be said that the appellate process was being carried out with 'all due expedition' as required by *Pratt*.

Moratoria

The Privy Council's confusion concerning the rationale underlying their jurisprudence relating to the death row phenomenon was evident in the case of *Reckley (No 1)* from the Bahamas.[40] Mr Reckley had been sentenced to death in 1990 and his domestic appeals were completed within eighteen months. However, a suspension of executions had been ordered pending the outcome of the challenge to the mandatory nature of the death penalty in *Jones*. These proceedings were commenced in 1989 and not determined at the Privy Council until 1995, when the government sought to resume executions and a warrant of execution was read to Mr Reckley in May 1995, some four and a half years after his conviction. The Privy Council approached Mr Reckley's position simplistically, holding that as the

39 *Guerra v Baptiste* [1996] 1 AC 397, 414.
40 [1995] 2 AC 491.

delay was due to a moratorium rather than any fault on behalf of the Bahamian State there could be no question of the *Pratt* principle applying. His appeal was rejected. The Privy Council did not question why the *Jones* proceedings had taken the extraordinary time of almost six years to complete and the responsibility that the Bahamas had for that delay, which directly impacted upon Mr Reckley's own delay. More substantially, the Board failed to explain why the death row phenomenon was any less an inhuman and degrading experience because it arose as a result of a moratorium rather than delay in the appellate process. This represents a failure to approach the issue from a constitutional basis.

A more sophisticated approach was demonstrated in another case from the Bahamas, that of *Henfield & Farrington v Minister of Public Safety*.[41] Mr Henfield had been on death row for six years eight months when he applied for a declaration under the *Pratt* principle that his sentence should be commuted. This was granted by the judge at first instance. Virtually the entire period had been covered by the *Jones* moratorium and the Court of Appeal allowed the state's appeal against the first instance decision on this basis. At the Privy Council it was argued that the Bahamas were responsible for the delay by failing to take steps to process the *Jones* litigation expeditiously. This argument was accepted, without the Board taking the more radical approach that it is the impact on the individual by virtue of the death row phenomenon, *irrespective of the cause*, which makes execution unconstitutional.

The second argument that was advanced concerned Mr Farrington who had been on death row for three years and four months when the execution warrant was read to him. On his behalf it was argued that the applicable period in the Bahamas was not the five years in *Pratt* but three and a half years in view of the fact that the Bahamas, unlike Jamaica (at the time[42]), had not ratified the Optional Protocol permitting complaints from individuals under the ICCPR.[43] Thus citizens of the Bahamas had no right of access to the UNHRC (nor indeed had the Bahamas ratified the *American Convention on Human Rights*, although this was not argued and see *Fisher (No. 1)* below). Therefore the eighteen months that the Board had allowed for petitions to the UNHRC in *Pratt* ought to be deducted in relation to the Bahamas. While their Lordships stated that it was 'too simplistic' to simply deduct an eighteen month period, 'taking all relevant considerations into account' they held that a delay of three and a half years where there was no access to international human rights bodies was an inordinate period of delay amounting to inhuman and degrading treatment and hence was unconstitutional. As Mr Farrington was two months short of this period, their Lordships applied the *Guerra* principle and his sentence was commuted. Unfortunately Mr Reckley did not have the benefit of this jurisprudence and had been executed eight months previously, but on the

41 [1997] AC 413.

42 Jamaica denounced the Optional Protocol permitting individual petitions under the ICCPR to the UNHRC in 1997.

43 (1976) 999 UNTS 171.

authority of *Henfield*, or even simply *Guerra* his four and a half years on death row would have led to commutation.

Prison Conditions

The issue of prison conditions is a useful prism through which to view the Privy Council's more recent approach to its constitutional task as it raises the pertinent issue of relativism within human rights. The first substantive opportunity to demonstrate its approach on this issue arose in the case of *Darrin Thomas & Hanif Hilaire v AG of Trinidad.*[44]

No one had been hung in Trinidad since the disgraceful case of Glen Ashby referred to above, and Darrin Thomas was the first unlucky beneficiary of the then Attorney General, Ramesh Maharaj's stated policy of resuming hangings as an antidote to Trinidad's spiralling crime problem. The warrant was read to Hanif Hilaire shortly afterwards. The argument mounted on behalf of Thomas and Hilaire was that following *Guerra*, where there was delay falling short of five years an examination of the individual circumstances was required. Clearly the conditions in which a person had been kept are a relevant circumstance as they are highly material to the quality of the punishment the condemned man is exposed to. It is conceptually artificial to separate the conditions of detention from the period for which such conditions have been endured. This was the approach adopted by Mr Justice Jamadar, the judge at first instance in Mr Thomas's case. In a detailed and careful ruling the judge set out his findings of fact on the principle area of dispute between the parties, namely the amount of exercise that Mr Thomas received.[45] Despite the contrary assertion of the Commissioner of Prisons, Mr Thomas stated in an affidavit that he was allowed out for an hour every two weeks. On occasion three or four weeks passed without any exercise and on one occasion three months had passed without exercise (it was said by one inmate that the only time they received the correct amount of exercise was when the prison officers were on a Work to Rule protest!)[46]

Mr Thomas was assisted by the official record of exercise which recorded him as having received twelve periods of exercise over five months. Further it was agreed that inmates were handcuffed throughout their exercise. Mr Justice Jamadar preferred Mr Thomas's evidence to that of the Commissioner and further accepted that his cell was stuffy and without natural light or adequate ventilation. It was likely to be claustrophobic and oppressive. These conditions breached the Prison Rules and the judge pointed out that the Prison Rules had remained virtually unchanged since 1838, quoting Davis J in an earlier first instance decision in Trinidad, that of *Re Andy Thomas and Kirkland Paul*:

44 [2000] 2 A.C. 1.

45 Unrep. HCA No. Cv1373 of 1998, 58 *et seq.*

46 Said to the author at Port of Spain Prison, Trinidad, June 1988.

> What strikes me here again, is that cells in death row were not intended to house a condemned prisoner for a prolonged period of time. They were intended, it appears to me, to be in effect, holding bays where the condemned man was kept for a limited period of time on his way to the gallows. Our post independence system has rendered the law governing this system anachronistic and the cells which served the system equally so.[47]

Jamadar J adopted this reasoning, relying particularly on the discussion in *Pratt* concluding that the death penalty was carried out in terms of weeks or months and certainly not years as now was invariably the case. The Court of Appeal disagreed with the judge, and while holding that the conditions 'were completely unacceptable in a civilised society', nonetheless took the view they did not amount to cruel and unusual treatment, with no attempt to explain the distinction. The majority of the Privy Council followed a similar route stating that:

> prison conditions in third world countries often fall lamentably short of the minimum which would be acceptable in more affluent countries. It would not serve the cause of human rights to set such demanding standards that breaches were commonplace. Whether or not the conditions in which the appellants were kept amounted to cruel and unusual treatment is a value judgement which is necessary to take account of local conditions both inside and outside prison[48]

It is unclear why the Privy Council shied away from requiring standards which 'civilised society' finds acceptable, but in addition the judgment ignores the fact that the local finder of fact took the view that the conditions *do* amount to cruel and unusual treatment. This conclusion was overturned by the Court of Appeal (all trained in Britain) without holding that the judge (trained in the West Indies) had erred in reaching the factual basis for his conclusion. No examination was made of the resources available or whether the issue was in fact a resource question, but, without evidence, the Board assumed that it was.

It was not even asserted by the government that they did not have the resources to remedy the breaches of the prison rules which had led to Jamadar J's finding of fact. Indeed he specifically stated that no explanation had been offered. In fact the matters relied upon, such as the handcuffing of prisoners during exercise periods, have minimal resource implications. However, many Trinidadians are of the view that their country is a relatively prosperous oil-rich country where people by and large are not found sleeping on the streets and the decision not to house condemned men in the new prison, or indeed not to provide them with their minimum exercise period and handcuffing them when they do exercise, would appear to be less a resource issue than an attitude issue ('they do not deserve it'). The excusing of appalling conditions on the basis they emanate from a 'third world' country is also

47 Unrep. HCA No. 6346 and 6347 of 1985, 19th July 1987, 28.

48 *ibid*, 17.

an attitude which may bear the hallmarks of the first world imperialism that the Board was trying to avoid. As the advocate who addressed the Court of Appeal in Trinidad on behalf of Thomas and Hilaire said 'if we consider ourselves a third world country then we are a Third World country',[49] and proceeded to quote the novel but apt source of Bob Marley, in suggesting 'we should emancipate ourselves from mental slavery, none but ourselves shall free our mind'.[50]

Constitutional and human rights standards exist as minima which regulate the lawfulness of state conduct irrespective of which country they operate in. Whatever their view of what best serves *the cause of human rights*, the Privy Council were engaged in an exercise in constitutional interpretation. The Constitution of Trinidad does not stipulate that the fundamental freedoms are to be observed 'resources permitting', it lays down an absolute prohibition which the reasoning of the Board is at odds with. Mr Justice Jamadar had a clear understanding of the role he was required to perform as a constitutional judge, quoting the esteemed Trinidadian judge Telford Georges in the case of *Thornhill*: 'The Court has been appointed the sentinel of the rights of the subject under the constitution and should be ever vigilant to offer protection whenever there has been an infringement', Jamadar J added 'No court can dare shirk that responsibility, to do so would be to betray the Nation and the people that it serves'.[51]

The majority of the Privy Council failed to discuss the relevance of relativism within a constitutional context, surely a central concept to any exercise in constitutional interpretation and of particular resonance for the Privy Council. Lord Steyn, in his minority opinion, alone addressed this issue when he stated:

> Contrary to the view of the Court of Appeal, there is no tenable argument based on cultural relativism. There was a fundamental breach of irreducible minimum standards of treatment of prisoners recognised among civilised nations. And I count Trinidad & Tobago among those nations.

One could ask whether it is the view of the Court of Appeal of Trinidad or that of Lord Steyn which displays an attitude that could most aptly be described as neo-colonialist?

The Prerogative of Mercy

The colonial legacy of the mandatory death sentence for murder raises the importance of the role of the administrative committee in advising on the exercise of the prerogative of mercy. In the colonial Caribbean, the prerogative of mercy was exercised by the governor of the colony on behalf of the Queen and the

49 Trinidadian lawyer Gregory Delzin addressing the CA, July 27 1998.

50 Lyrics from *Redemption Song*, on the album *Uprising* by Bob Marley.

51 (1974) 27 WLR 281, 288.

power was a purely personal executive decision, although he usually reached his decision after he had consulted with the relevant advisory committee. Because of the mandatory nature of the death sentence, the real sentencing exercise took place at this stage. It can be seen from some remaining records that traditional sentencing factors were taken into account in deciding whether the sentence should be commuted. In one case the defendant's sentence was commuted where there was doubt about the safety of the conviction and he had failed to lodge his appeal within the requisite time.[52]

The precise constitutional status of such committees (usually called Advisory Committees' on the Power of Pardon, although in Jamaica this function is exercised by the Jamaican Privy Council) varies from island to island with the relevant Minister being obliged to follow their advice in some jurisdictions but only to consider their advice in others.

It was first argued in 1976 in the case of *de Freitas v Benny*[53] that the principles of natural justice ought to be applied to the activities of the Advisory Committee in Trinidad & Tobago. These principles required that the condemned man should have disclosed to him the material that was placed before the Committee so that he could have an opportunity to comment on it and to deal with any inaccuracies or prejudicial material. While it was accepted that prior to independence the exercise of the prerogative of mercy could not have been questioned, the prerogative, it was argued, had been wholly superseded by the statutory provisions of the constitution. The protection of due process of law guaranteed to all Trinidadian citizens under section 1 of the constitution extended to administrative process as well as the legislative process. Thus the Advisory Committee was required to carry out its function in accordance with the rules of natural justice, particularly in respect of disclosure and representation. This argument was made at a time when the judicial review jurisdiction had not developed in England to anything like the wide-ranging jurisdiction that it is today. Lord Diplock held that except insofar as it has been altered by the constitution the legal nature of the exercise of the prerogative of mercy remained the same as it was in England at common law.[54] At common law the prerogative had always been a matter which lay solely in the discretion of the sovereign, exercised by the Home Secretary through constitutional convention. But the condemned man had no legal right to have his case considered by the Home Secretary because 'mercy is not the subject of legal rights. It begins where legal rights end'.[55] This Shakespearian-sounding approach ignores the central

52 Minutes of the Jamaican Privy Council 19 June 1951 (sentence of Roy Thompson commuted on grounds of his youth), 13 February 1947 (sentence of Mervin Westey commuted on grounds of his mental condition), 25 February 1950 (sentence of Adolphus Delpratt commuted as appeal not lodged in time). PRO – CO 140/359.

53 [1976] AC 239.

54 *ibid*, 247.

55 *Ibid.*

feature that by virtue of the constitution the condemned man does have a right to have the matter considered by the Advisory Committee.[56]

The act of the Home Secretary was, according to Lord Diplock, the exemplar of a purely discretionary rather than a quasi-judicial act and as there had been no practice of disclosing the material before the Committee prior to independence there was no requirement to do so thereafter.[57] This case provides a good example of how what constitutes lawful practice is fossilised at the point of independence to restrict the development of Caribbean jurisprudence to that which was appropriate under colonial rule. Lord Diplock's interpretation of the 'savings clause' proceeded on the basis that the fundamental freedoms referred to in the constitution were already secured for Trinidadian citizens by the law in force at its commencement (i.e. independence). The constitution framers were merely concerned, on Lord Diplock's analysis, to ensure that the fundamental freedoms previously protected by the British Empire continued to be protected once the colonial subjects were released from the benign paternalism of British rule.

The premise that the well-being of its subjects was at the forefront of objectives of imperial British rule has already been discussed, and the view of colonial law as the high watermark of citizen protection from acts of the state ignores the contradictory basis of colonialism. One sees in Lord Diplock's reasoning a strand that continues to occur in British jurisprudence, namely the naïve equation between the common law and human rights. Lord Diplock's attitude to constitutional interpretation as essentially no different from any other exercise in statutory interpretation demonstrates the limitations of the Privy Council as a constitutional court at the time. The decision in *de Freitas & Benny* pre-dates Lord Wilberforce's classic dictum on constitutional interpretation by three years but Lord Diplock's view that the colonial law remained fundamentally unchanged, unless specifically so by the constitution, is in conflict with the approach advocated by his fellow Law Lord.

While Lord Diplock may be forgiven for not foreseeing Lord Wilberforce's more sophisticated approach to constitutional interpretation, the same cannot be said of the next time the issue of the prerogative of mercy was considered by the Privy Council in 1996 in the case of the hapless Mr Reckley.[58] It was argued on Mr Reckley's behalf that *de Freitas v Benny* was no longer good law as the prerogative of mercy was now considered justiciable. The Divisional Court in the English case of *R v Secretary of State ex parte Bentley*[59] had held, albeit rather circuitously, that decisions taken under the prerogative could be reviewed where the subject matter was amenable to judicial process, provided the challenge did not require the court to review questions of policy. The court ordered that the Home Secretary

---

56 The Constitution of Trinidad, s. 70.

57 [1976] A.C. 239 at, 248.

58 Already discussed in the context of delay, *Reckley (No. 1)*. This issue was dealt with in *Reckley (No. 2) v Minister of Immigration,* [1996] 1 AC 527.

59 [1994] QB 349.

consider afresh whether it would be just to exercise the prerogative in such a way as to acknowledge the generally accepted view that Derek Bentley should have been reprieved. *de Freitas v Benny* was distinguished on the basis it was decided before the *Council of Civil Service Unions v Minister for the Civil Service* (the GCHQ case)[60] (and therefore presumably wrong) and that it did not concern an error of law as Bentley's case had. It is however hard to see how an error of law can be identified if the basic principles of natural justice are not applied; without disclosure of the material before the Committee it is not possible to say whether they have taken into account irrelevant material and without the provision of reasons one cannot suggest that an error of law concerning the offence itself or the Committee's understanding of its own powers has occurred.

Mr Reckley's counsel also relied on a decision of the Lord Chief Justice of Belize in the case of *Lauriano v AG Belize*,[61] which held that *ex parte Bentley* demonstrated the prerogative was now reviewable, although the Lord Chief Justice was subsequently forced to overrule himself in the light of *Reckley (No 2)* as an indication of the way indigenous constitutional development was hindered by the Privy Council's reasoning. Furthermore, he argued that as English law had recognised that fairness in the case of life prisoners required disclosure of the material placed before the Parole Board, so that the prisoner could make effective representations thereon, because it was a matter affecting his liberty.[62] The argument must apply with even greater force where it concerned the deprivation of life.

Under the Bahamian Constitution, as with that of Trinidad, the Minister is required to refer a capital case to the Advisory Committee but he is not bound by their advice.[63] Their Lordships considered it of note that this section of the Bahamian Constitution had been enacted before capital punishment was abolished in Britain and at a time when the position regarding the exercise of the prerogative by the Home Secretary had been accurately described by Lord Diplock in *de Freitas*. Without any reference to Lord Wilberforce's approach in *Fisher*, the Board held that 'it appeared to be the statutory intention … to replicate that discretion [in articles 90 to 92 of the Bahamian constitution]', citing the analysis in *de Freitas* with approval. Their Lordships particularly relied on the fact that the Minister was not bound by the advice of the Advisory Committee which 'provides a strong indication of an intention to preserve the status of the minister's discretion as a purely personal discretion'[64] and suggested (with little basis) that:

> It may be inferred that the reason why provision was made in the Constitution for an advisory committee was to provide a constitutional safeguard in circumstances where

60 [1985] AC 374.

61 Unrep. 20 September 1985, Supreme Court of Belize.

62 *R v Secretary of State for the Home Department ex parte Doody* [1994] 1 AC 531.

63 Section 92(1) of the Bahamian Constitution.

64 *ex parte Doody*, 539.

> the minister's discretionary power was of such a nature that it was not subject to judicial review. [65]

Thus a constitution which guarantees to its citizens the 'protection of law',[66] apparently provides a further constitutional safeguard of an advisory committee which, however, is not susceptible to the protection of the law in one of its most basic ways, namely the application of the rules of natural justice and scrutiny by the courts.

Their Lordships dismissed *ex parte Bentley* as a case which was not 'directly concerned with the possibility of judicial review of the exercise of the prerogative of mercy in a death sentence case',[67] although the only distinction would appear to be that the sentence had already been carried out on Mr Bentley. Somewhat surprisingly their Lordships concluded that that decision did not 'have any bearing on the present case' and in any event concerned an 'exceptional situation'.

Consequently, their Lordships rejected the argument that the condemned man had any right to make representations or could have any right to see the material disclosed to him. Twenty years and much international constitutional jurisprudence later the approach of the Privy Council on this issue remained governed by the spirit of Lord Diplock, whatever the developments elsewhere.

However in the case of *Neville Lewis* referred to above in the context of prison conditions the Privy Council took the opportunity to re-visit the decision in *Reckley (No. 2)* which had been subject to much academic criticism and was at odds with developments that have occurred elsewhere in the common law world (see Blom-Cooper 1997; Gelber 1997). In Guyana for instance, which is no longer within the jurisdiction of the Privy Council, there had been judicial acceptance that the principles of natural justice apply to the operation of the Advisory Committee when considering clemency. In *Abdool Yassin & Noel Thomas v The Attorney General of Guyana*,[68] a challenge to the decision not to exercise clemency was mounted on the basis that the Attorney General, who presided over the Advisory Committee's deliberations, had represented both appellants at various stages of their criminal murder trials while still in private practice. Relying on Indian jurisprudence, the GCHQ case, *ex parte Bentley* and the New Zealand case of *Burt v Governor General of New Zealand*,[69] the Supreme Court of Guyana held that the operation of the Advisory Committee was susceptible to judicial review in appropriate circumstances. Further, that the presence of the Attorney General had violated the rules of natural justice as expressed in Lord Hewart C.J's oft-quoted maxim that 'It is not merely of some importance but of fundamental importance that justice should not only be done, but should manifestly and undoubtedly be

65 *ibid*, 540.

66 Article 15(a) of the Bahamian Constitution.

67 *ex parte Doody*, 541.

68 Unrep. Criminal Appeal No. 40 of 1996, 30 August 1996.

69 (1993) 4 LRC 1.

seen to be done'.[70] The Supreme Court went on to hold that this 'grave irregularity' with its 'attendant attributes of unfairness and injustice' violated the appellant's constitutional 'right to life' protection and rendered unenforceable the President's decision that the sentences of death should be carried out.

In the case of *Neville Lewis* despite there being no material jurisprudential developments since *Reckley (No 2),* the Privy Council (with Lord Hoffman in a lone dissent, unable to accept that his previous decision in *Reckley* should be overturned) held that natural justice and procedural fairness required that the condemned men had a right to see all the material that was placed before the Jamaican Privy Council and had a right to make representations upon it. They further held that the Jamaican Privy Council was required to consider such representations and to consider reports from an international human rights body and when they do not accept the body's recommendations they should explain why. The process is susceptible to challenge in the courts if it has been applied unfairly, all such litigation being required to take place within the 5 year period. The contrast between this decision and that of *Reckley (No 2)* demonstrates the two opposing approaches to constitutionalism within the Privy Council, and the difference the composition of the Board can make to a man's fate.

Conclusion

At a time when the future of the Privy Council's jurisdiction is being vigorously debated in the Caribbean, particular scrutiny is required of the extent to which they have successfully performed their function as a supreme constitutional court. I have tried to show that the approach of the Privy Council has in some cases failed to discharge this function principally because of the legal culture of parliamentary sovereignty within which they operate as British judges. In these cases the Privy Council has been reluctant to embrace a culture of constitutionalism which sees the protection of entrenched freedoms at the forefront of any legal analysis, with a secondary role being accorded to the intention of the legislature. This failure has led to a non-interventionist approach in some of the worst aspects of the colonial legacy of penal practice and procedure.

The Privy Council are rightly concerned about the legitimacy of their anachronistic status. But by applying English rules of constitutional construction they do truly lay themselves open to the allegations of neo-imperialism that they are so keen to avoid. Such an approach denies the Caribbean peoples the fruit of independence – namely the right to have the actions of those who run their islands on their behalf determined in line with their political choice of entrenched constitutional values, rather than at the whim of the British. In fact, the Privy Council has a legal and arguably a moral duty to re-affirm and protect the transition

70 *R v Sussex Justices ex parte McCarthy* [1924] 1 KB 256.

in the political order which independence from colonial rule was intended to bring about through its constitutional framework.

The increasing use of dissenting judgments seen in the Privy Council in this area demonstrates the different results that differing approaches have produced and the authority of the court is undermined when a person is to be executed on the basis of the lottery of a bare majority of judges.

One of the more persuasive arguments concerning the retention of the Privy Council's jurisdiction concerns the benefits of a unified Commonwealth jurisprudence and reformers suggest this role could be undertaken more satisfactorily if more judges from the relevant jurisdictions sat on the Board, indeed if it were to go 'on circuit' to such jurisdictions. However, the Privy Council's approach has often lagged far behind some of the more impressive Commonwealth constitutional jurisprudence from countries such as India and South Africa that have abolished its jurisdiction.

If the Privy Council is to have any role in the second millennium it should be as a modern constitutional court for a range of jurisdictions united by a shared acceptance of the values of the entrenched fundamental freedoms. To continue to operate as the House of Lords by another name deprives the Caribbean populations of a properly functioning constitutional appellate body and adds further weight to the heavy burden already carried by Britain as a result of its history of colonial domination.

Bibliography

Blom-Cooper, L. (1997), 'Justice and Mercy in the Caribbean', *Criminal Law Review* 116.

Fitzgerald, E. (2001), *Savings Clauses and the Colonial Death Penalty Regime,* Commonwealth Caribbean Human Rights Seminar, 12–14 September 2000 (Paris: Penal Reform International).

Gatrell, V.A.C. (1994), *The Hanging Tree: Execution and the English People 1770–1868* (New York: Oxford University).

Gelber, C. (1997), 'Reckley (No 2) and the Prerogative of Mercy: Act of Grace or Constitutional Safeguard?', *Modern Law Review*, July 1997, 572.

Hart, R. (1998), *From Occupation to Independence* (London: Pluto Press).

Hay, G. *et al.* (1975), *Albion's Fatal Tree, Crime and Society in Eighteenth Century England* (London: Penguin).

Hodgkinson, P. (2004), 'Alternatives to the Death Penalty: The United Kingdom Experience', pp. 164–170, in Council of Europe, *Death Penalty: Beyond Abolition* (Strasbourg: Council of Europe Publishing).

Hood, R. (2002), *The Death Penalty: A Worldwide Perspective*, 3rd ed (Oxford: Oxford University Press).

Jamaica Royal Commission (1866), *Report of the Jamaica Royal Commission 1866* (London: G.E Eyre and W.M. Spottiswoode).

Koestler, A. (1956), *Reflections on Hanging* (London: Victor Gollancz).
Morris, T. (1999), *'What's all this about Punishment?'*, The Howard League Magazine, Vol 17, pp.6–7, February.
People's National Movement (1998), *Statement on the execution of the death penalty extracted from the address of the Political Leader of the People's National Movement to the Special Convention*, 19 July 1998.
Roberts-Wray, K. (1966), *Commonwealth and Colonial Law* (London: Stevens & Stevens).
Sarat, A. and Boulanger, C. (ed) (2005), *The Cultural Lives of Capital Punishment: Comparative Perspectives* (Stanford: Stanford University Press).
Schabas, W.A. (2002), *The Abolition of the Death penalty in International Law*, 3rd ed (Cambridge: Cambridge University Press).
The Times, 25 July 1872.
Thompson, E.P. (1975), *Whigs and Hunters* (London: Penguin Books).
Whitman, J.Q. (2003), *Harsh Justice and the Widening Divide between America and Europe* (New York: Oxford University Press).
Williams, E. (1970), *From Castro to Columbus: The History of the Caribbean* (Harper and Row).

PART II
PERSPECTIVES AND QUESTIONS FOR RETENTIONIST COUNTRIES

Chapter 6

Constraining America's Death Penalty: The Eighth Amendment and Excessive Punishment

Julian Killingley

For most of America's recorded history the death penalty has been widely accepted as part of the nation's criminal justice regime. Since a majority of the States and the federal government have been unwilling to abandon capital punishment voluntarily, abolitionists have had to look to the text of the United States Constitution or to the several constitutions of the retentionist States to develop constitutional arguments for prohibiting the practice. This chapter looks at the role that might be played by the United States Constitution in advancing this aim.

Much of the United States Constitution and its Amendments (together hereafter called 'the Constitution') is written in very general terms. The generality of its language is both a strength and a weakness and has led to competing schools of constitutional interpretation. At different times in the nation's history this has allowed the Supreme Court of the United States (the Court) the flexibility to interpret its text expansively or restrictively. However, even the most liberal and activist Court faces a seemingly insuperable problem if it were minded to find a constitutional imperative for abolition. The text of the Constitution seemingly recognises the propriety of the practice and even the most myopic member would be challenged to evade its plain language.

If a constitutional objection to the penalty exists then its source will have to be found in the text of the Constitution's Bill of Rights or its Fourteenth Amendment.[1] In modern times challenges have been made under four different clauses[2] of the Constitution but no advocate has yet persuaded a majority – or even a near majority – of the Court that its text demands an outright ban on the practice. As the Court's capital punishment jurisprudence has developed over the last 35 years, capital penalty litigators have come to realise that the best prospect for systemic reform

1 The Bill of Rights comprises the first ten Amendments to the United States Constitution that were together adopted by the United States in 1791. The Fourteenth Amendment was adopted in 1868 in the aftermath of the Civil War.

2 These are the Due Process Clauses of the Fifth and Fourteenth Amendments, the Cruel and Unusual Punishments Clause of the Eighth Amendment and the Equal Protection Clause of the Fourteenth Amendment.

is near *de facto* abolition rather than outright *de jure* proscription. Experience has shown that this is most likely to be achieved by strict confinement of the penalty through imaginative application of the Eighth Amendment. I look at why this should be so and how this might be brought about.

The Historical Background

The fourteen States[3] that presently prohibit capital punishment do so for a variety of reasons. Michigan has a constitutional prohibition on the practice[4] while the Court of Appeals of New York has ruled[5] that New York's 1995 death penalty statute is facially unconstitutional because a jury deadlock instruction violates the State constitution's Due Process clause. Michigan's constitutional prohibition can only be negated by constitutional amendment while New York's *de facto* prohibition could be overcome readily by legislative amendment.

The remaining thirty-six States and the federal government conceive their constitutions as imposing no prohibition on the infliction of death as a criminal sanction. This is because these constitutions, unlike Michigan's, contain no explicit prohibitions of the practice and their courts have interpreted other constitutional protections as not impliedly proscribing executions or as being manageable in such a way as to permit them to take place if their protections are properly observed.

The safeguards afforded citizens by the Bill of Rights, as part of the 1791 Constitution, originally applied only to protection from the actions of the federal government. Any attempt to argue that it prohibited the infliction of the death penalty would founder inevitably upon textual problems. The text of the Fifth Amendment recognises that a person may be sentenced to death. The Grand Jury Clause of that Amendment explicitly recognises the availability of the death penalty in that, '[n]o person shall be held to answer for a capital, or otherwise infamous crime, unless on a presentment or indictment of a Grand Jury'. The Due Process clause of the same Amendment reads, '[n]o person shall [...] be deprived of life, liberty or property, without due process of law', the implication being that a person may be deprived of their life if afforded due process of law.

The Eighth Amendment states: 'Excessive bail shall not be required, nor excessive fines imposed, nor cruel and unusual punishments inflicted'. When these words are read in conjunction with the Fifth Amendment it is clear that the Framers did not view capital punishment as a cruel and unusual punishment *per se*. Indeed, almost one of the first acts of those who drafted the Bill of Rights was

3 These comprise: Alaska, Hawaii, Iowa, Maine, Massachusetts, Michigan, Minnesota, New Jersey, New York, North Dakota, Rhode Island, Vermont, West Virginia, and Wisconsin. The practice is also prohibited within the District of Columbia.

4 See M.C.L.A. Const. Art. 4, § 46: "No law shall be enacted providing for the penalty of death".

5 See *People v. LaValle* 3 N.Y.3d 88 (2004), 817 N.E.2d 341 (N.Y., 2004).

to enact a law in the first United States Congress[6] creating offences punishable by death and by whipping.

The U.S. Supreme Court has long recognised that the Framers of the Constitution did not write in a vacuum. The Court has stated that the phrase 'cruel and unusual punishments' is derived from the English Bill of Rights of 1689.[7] The Court has a rule of construction that when common law terminology is used then the ordinary common law meanings of those terms are incorporated into American domestic law.[8] Yet as Justice Brennan pointed out in his dissent in *McGautha v. California*, when the Framers drafted the Bill of Rights this was only a few years after the Reverend William Paley had written (Paley 1785) his *Principles of Moral and Political Philosophy* justifying 'England's 'Bloody Code' of more than 250 capital crimes'.[9]

The Fourteenth Amendment, adopted in 1868, extended most of the protections of the Bill of Rights and made them enforceable against the several States. This was achieved by operation of Section 1 of the Due Process Clause which provided, 'nor shall any State deprive any person of life, liberty, or property without due process of law'. Just as the Fifth Amendment's Due Process Clause permitted the federal government to deprive citizens of life after giving them due process, so did the Fourteenth Amendment allow States to do the same. However, the Court's expansionary interpretation of the protection of liberty interests under the Fourteenth Amendment's Due Process Clause, its Privileges and Immunities Clause[10] or its Equal Protection Clause[11] – or some combination of all three – has also extended, *inter alia*, the citizen's protection from State infliction of cruel and unusual punishments.[12]

---

6 1 Stat. 117 (1st Cong., 2d Sess. 1790), act of 30 April 1790.

7 For example, see *Harmelin v. Michigan* 501 U.S. 957 (1991) per Scalia J. at, 966, 'In fact, the entire text of the Eighth Amendment is taken almost verbatim from the English Declaration of Rights, which provided "[t]hat excessive Baile ought not to be required nor excessive Fines imposed nor cruell and unusuall Punishments inflicted"'.

8 See *United States v. Smith* 18 U.S. (5 Wheat.) 153 (1820) per Story J at, 160, 'When the act of 1790 declares, that any person who shall commit the crime of robbery, or murder, on the high seas, shall be deemed a pirate, the crime is not less clearly ascertained than it would be by using the definitions of these terms as they are found in our treatises of the common law. In fact, by such a reference, the definitions are necessarily included, as much as if they stood in the text of the act'.

9 *McGautha v. California* 402 U.S. 183 (1971) at, 281.

10 'No State shall make or enforce any law which shall abridge the privileges or immunities of citizens of the United States'.

11 'Nor shall any State [...] deny to any person within its jurisdiction the equal protection of the laws'.

12 As early as 1892 three Justices would have applied the Eighth Amendment directly to the States. See Justice Harlan dissenting in *O'Neil v. Vermont* 144 U.S. 323 (1892), 370–371, 'Among those rights is immunity from cruel and unusual punishments secured by the eighth amendment against federal action, and by the fourteenth amendment

Capital punishment was so firmly entrenched as part of the cultural and legal landscape that there were few challenges to it in the nineteenth century as being a 'cruel and unusual' punishment. Such challenges as there were confined themselves to the propriety of a State's manner of executing a death sentence. The first was an unsuccessful challenge to a sentence that a condemned man be executed by firing squad in Utah[13] and the other an equally unsuccessful challenge to New York's adoption of electrocution as its means of execution.[14] Two other cases challenged unsuccessfully the right of a State to detain a prisoner in solitary confinement while awaiting his execution on the ground that it was a cruel and unusual addition to the sentence of death itself.[15]

During the first half of the twentieth Century there was little Supreme Court litigation to help clarify the Eighth Amendment's meaning. In the early decision *Weems v. United States*[16] the Court found a fine of 4,000 pesetas plus 15 years of cadena temporal imprisonment[17] imposed for a minor fraud in the Philippines to be a cruel and unusual punishment proscribed by the Eighth Amendment. The central issue for the Court was whether it was fundamental to the law that punishment for crime should be graduated and proportioned to the offence. It reviewed the prior history of the Eighth Amendment and observed that it received little debate in the Congress prior to its adoption to help clarify its reach but that one member objected to it as being 'too indefinite'[18] and another thought it 'unnecessary' as 'it is sometimes necessary to hang a man' and mused whether the nation was to be prevented in future from imposing such punishments.[19]

The Court seemed to recognise clearly that the present meaning of the Constitution did not necessarily lie in its history:

> Legislation, both statutory and constitutional, is enacted, it is true, from an experience of evils but its general language should not, therefore, be necessarily confined to the

---

against denial or abridgment by the states. A judgment, therefore, of a state court, even if rendered pursuant to a statute, inflicting, or allowing the infliction of a cruel and unusual punishment , is inconsistent with the supreme law of the land'. Here the Court's majority decided that although the question was raised it was not a federal question as it arose under the Vermont constitution.

13 *Wilkerson v. Utah* 99 U.S. 130 (1878).

14 *In re Kemmler* 136 U.S. 436 (1890).

15 *McElvaine v. Brush* 142 U.S. 155 (1891) and *Trezza v. Brush* 142 U.S. 160 (1891).

16 217 U.S. 349 (1910) on writ of error to the Supreme Court of the Philippine Islands, then an American colonial territory.

17 The cadena temporal was a sentence of imprisonment to be served in chains and subject to performance of hard labour; the person so sentenced lost many basic civil rights such as parental and marital authority, the right to dispose of his property, the right to vote or hold public office and was also subjected to lifetime surveillance and supervision.

18 *Weems*, 369.

19 *ibid*, 369.

> form that evil had theretofore taken. Time works changes, brings into existence new conditions and purposes. Therefore a principle, to be vital, must be capable of wider application than the mischief which gave it birth.[20]

Justice McKenna also reviewed scholarly commentaries and State interpretations of their own constitutional prohibitions on the inflictions of cruel and unusual punishments before concluding:

> But general discussion we need not farther pursue. We may rely on the conditions which existed when the Constitution was adopted. As we have seen, it was the thought of Story, indeed, it must come to a less trained reflection than his, that government by the people, instituted by the Constitution, would not imitate the conduct of arbitrary monarchs. The abuse of power might, indeed, be apprehended, but not that it would be manifested in provisions or practices which would shock the sensibilities of men.[21]

The opinion in *Weems* seemed to suggest that the Eighth Amendment is not merely an admonition to legislatures but that its prohibitions adapt to societal changes and impose some requirement of proportionality in sentences.

The next significant case picked up on those themes and elaborated them in a majority opinion that has become one of the cornerstones of modern American death penalty jurisprudence and the present guide to how the Court approaches interpretation of the Eighth Amendment's Cruel and Unusual Punishments Clause. In *Trop v. Dulles*[22] the petitioner had been a private in the U.S. Army serving in French Morocco in 1944. While under detention in barracks at Casablanca for a disciplinary offence, he escaped. The following day he and a companion were discovered walking along the road to Rabat in the general direction of Casablanca. An Army truck stopped and the petitioner willingly boarded it. No words were spoken and in Rabat he was turned over to military police. A general court martial later convicted Trop of desertion and sentenced him to three years at hard labour, forfeiture of all pay and allowances and a dishonourable discharge. In 1952 Trop applied for a passport only to find it denied to him on the ground that under the provisions of Section 401(g) of the Nationality Act of 1940, as amended, he had lost his citizenship by reason of his conviction and dishonourable discharge for wartime desertion. He commenced an action in federal district court for a declaration that he was a citizen. The government was granted summary judgment against him and his appeal ultimately came to the U.S. Supreme Court.

The Court had to consider the constitutionality of a statute that effectively made the military the arbiters of whom among those convicted of desertion should be made stateless. This arose because it was the act of being given a dishonourable discharge that had the legal effect of expatriating the convicted serviceman. As

20 *ibid*, 373.

21 *ibid*, 375.

22 356 U.S. 86 (1958).

the Court pointed out,[23] although the crime was one of the most serious known to military law, convictions for it were not uncommon. U.S. Army estimates suggested that during World War II some 7,000 convicted soldiers and airmen had been made stateless as a consequence of receiving dishonourable discharges following conviction for desertion.

The case divided the Court 5-4 with Chief Justice Warren writing the opinion for the Court.[24] The government sought to defend its actions by claiming, *inter alia*, that the divestiture of citizenship provision was a regulation of nationality or a regulatory provision authorised by the war power and so not a punishment. The majority readily dismissed these claims and concluded that the provision was penal in nature and thus leaving it only to be decided 'whether the Constitution permits the Congress to take away citizenship as a punishment for crime'.[25] Chief Justice Warren noted that since wartime desertion was punishable by death there could be no argument whether divestiture of citizenship was excessive in relation to the gravity of the crime. Rather the question was whether the penalty subjected the individual to a fate forbidden by the principle of civilised treatment guaranteed by the Eighth Amendment.[26] The Chief Justice thought it plain that the existence of the death penalty was not a licence for the Government to devise any punishment short of death within the limit of its imagination.

While noting that the exact scope of the phrase 'cruel and unusual' had not been defined by the Court, the Court looked back to its opinion in *Weems* and remarked that it had not hesitated there 'to declare that the penalty was cruel in its excessiveness and unusual in its character'.[27] Citing the *Weems* Court's willingness to give the meaning of the Eighth Amendment a dynamic interpretation, Chief Justice Warren declared:

> The Court recognized in that case that the words of the Amendment are not precise, and that their scope is not static. The Amendment must draw its meaning from the evolving standards of decency that mark the progress of a maturing society.[28]

Despite being part of a plurality opinion in a deeply divided Court, the Chief Justice's words have come to have great significance in death penalty cases and have been used time and time again to try to persuade the Court that some hitherto accepted practice has become offensive to 'the evolving standards of decency that mark the progress of a maturing society'. This case was what is called a 'sleeper' – there is little evidence that its future significance was appreciated fully at the time

23 *ibid*, 90–91.

24 The majority opinion was joined by Black, Douglas and Whittaker JJ and with Brennan J concurring in the result.

25 *ibid*, 99.

26 *ibid*.

27 *ibid*, 100.

28 *ibid*, 100–101.

it was handed down. Contemporary law review articles dealing with it are mainly notes and comments by members of the student editorial boards. The majority saw its importance as a nationality case rather than as a significant addition to Eighth Amendment jurisprudence that it was to become later (see Anon 1958a, 1959a and 1959b). However, at least one student editorial board (Anon 1958b: 168–70) did pick up on its significance for Eighth Amendment interpretation and its future application to capital cases.

One of the great debates of American constitutional law is how to approach the text of the Constitution. One school, whose members are sometimes called 'textualists', 'originalists' or 'strict constructionists' according to the strength of their views, would treat its text with reverence and, whenever possible, give its words narrow interpretations or the same meaning they would have had for those who originally drafted them. One of its leading proponents is current U.S. Supreme Court Justice Antonin Scalia who has expressed his views pungently on the subject both on and off the Bench – see Scalia 1989a, 1989b, 1997 and 2006 and (more humorously) Scalia 1990. Justice Scalia has described himself (Scalia 1989) as a 'faint-hearted orginalist' and would not allow the original intention of the Framers expressed in the Eighth Amendment to require him to uphold a law imposing brutal punishment. As he stated, 'I cannot imagine myself, any more than any other federal judge, upholding a statute that imposes the punishment of flogging' (Scalia 1989: 864). Other members of the U.S. Supreme Court presently favouring this interpretative approach include Chief Justice John Roberts and Associate Justices Clarence Thomas and Samuel Alito.

Another school of thought would approach the Constitution as a dynamic text speaking to us in the language of our own times and capable of the flexibility necessary to meet changing needs and mores. Adherents of this view of the Constitution as a living document rather than as a static text are sometimes called 'pragmatists' or, more pejoratively, 'judicial activists'. This approach is more a vision of what the Constitution should be than a canon of interpretation. It is associated with liberal judges (itself often a pejorative term in America) and reflects the approach taken by Chief Justice Warren in *Trop*. Members of the U.S. Supreme Court leaning to a greater or lesser extent towards this view include Associate Justices John Paul Stevens, David Souter, Ruther Bader Ginsburg and Stephen Breyer.

The conservative view is well expressed by Justice Scalia (Scalia 1997: 23):

> Textualism should not be confused with so-called strict constructionism, a degraded form of textualism that brings the whole philosophy into disrepute. I am not a strict constructionist, and no one ought to be – though better that, I suppose, than a nontextualist. A text should not be construed strictly, and it should not be construed leniently; it should be construed reasonably, to contain all that it fairly contains.

Notwithstanding the textualists' views, no member of the present U.S. Supreme Court has challenged *Trop*'s command that the Eighth Amendment's Cruel and

Unusual Punishments Clause must be interpreted to reflect 'the evolving standards of decency that mark the progress of a maturing society'. As we shall see, the present dispute is where the Court is to look for evidence that society's standards of decency have evolved in any particular direction.

The NAACP/LDF Moratorium Strategy

The National Association for the Advancement of Colored People (NAACP) was formed in 1909. Its charter describes its aims as being:

> To promote equality of rights and to eradicate caste or race prejudice among the citizens of the United States; to advance the interest of colored citizens; to secure for them impartial suffrage; and to increase their opportunities for securing justice in the courts, education for the children, employment according to their ability and complete equality before law.[29]

Many of its early years were taken with fighting lynchings and Jim Crow laws.[30] However, in 1940 Thurgood Marshall founded the NAACP's Legal Defense and Educational Fund (LDF) to handle litigation that might advance the NAACP's aims. Marshall and his team embarked upon a plan to bring about change and overturn the 'separate but equal' doctrine endorsed in *Plessy v. Ferguson*.[31] Mark Tushnet has described (Tushnet 1987) how the NAACP had worked towards this from as early as 1925 and how Thurgood Marshall's team devised a strategy of structural litigation to desegregate education.

Owen Fiss (2003) has explained the nature of structural litigation. He describes a hypothetical complacent legal system that assumes the function of legal adjudications is to resolve abnormal events that disrupt an otherwise satisfactory world. The function of adjudication is to restore the *status quo*. He compares the structural litigant's view of the adjudicative process thus:

> Structural litigation, on the other hand, denies that assumption and reflects doubt as to whether the status quo is, in fact, just. It is premised upon skepticism about the existing distribution of privilege and power in American society. (Fiss 2003: 53)

Structural litigation requires a concerted effort and long-term strategy – in this case extending over decades – to bring about changes in society through constitutional adjudication. Part of that strategy requires the careful selection of plaintiffs whose cases' fact patterns frame the problem appropriately and maximise the prospects of success. The NAACP and the LDF's strategy to overturn *Plessy v. Ferguson*

29 NAACP Charter (1911).

30 Laws, named after a character in minstrel shows in America, that required segregation of the races in public facilities and often criminalised mixed race marriages.

31 163 U.S. 537 (1896).

came to fruition in the landmark case of *Brown v. Board of Education of Topeka*[32] (now called *Brown I*) when the U.S. Supreme Court ruled:

> We conclude that in the field of public education the doctrine of 'separate but equal' has no place. Separate educational facilities are inherently unequal. Therefore, we hold that the plaintiffs and others similarly situated for whom the actions have been brought are, by reason of the segregation complained of, deprived of the equal protection of the laws guaranteed by the Fourteenth Amendment.[33]

Emboldened by it success in *Brown I*, the NAACP, the LDF and the American Civil Liberties Union (ACLU) embarked upon a blizzard of litigation to dismantle institutionalised racism through an energised civil rights movement.

The NAACP and the LDF had long been concerned about the over-representation of minorities among those sentenced to death. Michael Meltsner has described (Meltsner 1973a and 1973b) how the LDF embarked upon a course of structural litigation to block executions in the United States. This course was beset with ethical and practical difficulties. In its desegregation structural litigation, the NAACP and the LDF had the benefit of acting for the plaintiffs. They could select 'attractive' plaintiffs and cherry pick the most egregious examples of discrimination to litigate. Cases could be developed at leisure and the commencement of proceedings timed to suit their convenience.

The LDF's original strategy in its capital litigation had been to litigate what became known as the 'Southern rape cases'. In these, race-neutral laws that provided for death as a possible penalty for rape were in practice applied so that the death penalty was only imposed upon black men who raped white women. In 1950 the LDF's lawyers raised a claim unsuccessfully that this was a constitutional violation.[34] There they had claimed:

> [It is] the policy, practice and custom of the Commonwealth of Virginia, to inflict the death penalty upon negroes, because of their race and color, convicted of rape upon white women, while failing and refusing to inflict the death penalty upon white or any other persons convicted of rape of negro women.[35]

Nearly a decade later it had considered (see Haines 1996: 27) raising a similar challenge in a case[36] where a black defendant was convicted of breaking and entering a house with intent to rape and had been sentenced to death.

Epstein and Kobylka (1992: 50–51) relate how the NAACP collected data on rape cases in twelve Southern states that were heard between 1945 and 1965.

32 347 U.S. 483 (1954).
33 *ibid*, 495.
34 *Hampton v. Commonwealth*, 58 S.E.2d 288 (Va. 1950).
35 *ibid*, 298.
36 *Hamilton v. State* 116 So.2d 906 (Ala. 1960).

Analysis showed that 110 of the 119 defendants sentenced to death during that period were black. After performing multiple regression analysis of the data variables, the study found '[i]n less than one time in a thousand could these associations have occurred by the operation of chance factors alone'. In the mid-1960s this evidence persuaded Jack Greenberg, the LDF's Director Counsel, to attack systematically the discriminatory application of the death penalty for rape.

However, Greenberg (who had been among the plaintiff's counsel in *Brown*) and the LDF faced a problem. As he has explained (Greenberg 1982: 912–3), their professional duty as counsel for the defendants obliged them to raise every defence open to their clients. Their briefs[37] did not just concentrate upon the discriminatory application of the penalty but also raised other significant issues such as arbitrariness and juror scruples in capital trials as well as more general due process issues such as right to counsel, unlawful search and seizure, coerced confessions and jury selection. The result was that it was difficult to frame the issues as they had in *Brown* so that courts could not evade the discriminatory application issue.

It soon became clear to the LDF's attorneys that a sharply focussed attack would not succeed and that they would have to attempt to block all executions and not just those of rapists. As Meltsner (1973a: 1112) explained:

> One factor prompting the decision was the unpleasant lesson taught by the reaction of the courts to attempts to prove racial discrimination in the death sentencing of Southern black rapists: notwithstanding that the evidence was as convincing as men with finite resources could produce, judges resisted an argument that on the basis of statistics asked them to brand hundreds of juries as prejudiced.

However, another ethical dilemma for the lawyers was that once they saw these collateral constitutional attacks were overturning death sentences they could not withhold them from other prisoners. Meltsner quotes Professor Anthony Amsterdam as saying:

37 The expression 'brief' requires some explanation for those unfamiliar with American procedure. A brief is a formal document setting out the legal argument in support of an application or motion of some kind. This chapter's references to briefs are to briefs in proceedings before the US Supreme Court. Most appeals arrive at the US Supreme Court by way of petition for a writ of certiorari. Very rarely a matter arrives there by way of application for original writ of habeas corpus – see *In re Stanford* 537 U.S. 968 (2002). The petitioner files a 'petitioner's brief' along with the petition setting out reasons why the writ should be granted. If the writ of certiorari is granted then the petitioner files a further 'brief on the merits' setting out *in extenso* the constitutional arguments for reversing the lower court. The respondent files a reply brief seeking to refute the petitioner's arguments. Only after briefs from both sides have been filed does the Court hear oral argument. Oral argument in the US Supreme Court is usually limited to one hour when the Justices question counsel on their argument – each side's real case is made in the briefs rather than in oral argument.

> We could no more let men die that we had the power to save [...] than we could have passed by a dying accident victim sprawled bloody and writhing on the road without stopping to render such aid as we could. (Meltsner 1973a: 1113):

The ambition and audacity of this strategy was breath-taking. If it was to work, the LDF had to take on hundreds of capital cases from across the nation. Fortunately for the LDF, the Ford Foundation made a million dollar grant to enable it to set up an office to bring test cases to improve the legal system's treatment of poor offenders. By pooling talent and expertise the LDF was able to develop a set of precedents that could be deployed by even the least experienced attorney to obtain stays of execution for their clients. These precedents – wittily named 'Last Aid Kits' – rapidly gained notoriety and were distributed to hundreds of lawyers.[38]

The implementation of the moratorium strategy coincided with a nationwide trend of declining executions and soon had its desired effect. National statistics show that executions had dwindled from 42 in 1961 to just two in 1967 and none between 1968 and 1972.[39] The LDF's desired logjam had occurred – the numbers of prisoners on death row had increased from 219 in 1961 to 620 in 1972.[40] The accumulating appeals from across the country put pressure on the U.S. Supreme Court to grant certiorari to review the question of whether the imposition of the death penalty constituted *per se* a cruel and unusual punishment proscribed by the Eighth Amendment.

From Furman to Gregg

In June 1971 the Court granted a writ of certiorari to the Supreme Court of Georgia in the case of William Henry Furman.[41] On the same day it also granted certiorari to the Supreme Court of California in the case of Earnest James Aikens.[42] Many counsel in the briefs on the merits were common to both cases – in particular the names of Jack Greenberg and Jack Himmelstein of the LDF, Michael Meltsner from Columbia University Law School, and Anthony Amsterdam from Stanford University Law School appear on both briefs.[43] Oral argument in both cases took place on 17 January 1972 with Anthony Amsterdam appearing for both Aikens and Furman.

---

38 For a more detailed description of these mass-produced pleadings and their use see Vila and Morris 1997, 130–32.

39 See Zimring and Hawkins 1989:34–35.

40 *ibid*, 35.

41 403 U.S. 952 (1971).

42 403 U.S. 952 (1971) – the grant was limited to the question: 'Does the imposition and carrying out of the death penalty in this case constitute cruel and unusual punishment in violation of the Eighth and Fourteenth Amendments?'

43 See *Aikens v. California*, Petitioner's brief, 1971 WL 134168 and *Furman v. Georgia*, Petitioner's brief, 1971 WL 134167.

Before the Court could render its verdict in *Aikens v. California*, the Supreme Court of California declared capital punishment to be unconstitutional under California's State constitution.[44] The Court, on the petitioner's application, dismissed Aikens' writ in a *per curiam* opinion on the ground that it was now moot.[45] In *Furman v. Georgia* the petitioner's brief on the merits adopted the same arguments (*inter alia*) that had been advanced in the brief on the merits in *Aikens*.[46] Amsterdam summarised their argument in *Aikens* in these words:[47]

> The penalty of death for first-degree murder is a cruel and unusual punishment because it affronts the basic standards of decency of contemporary society. Those standards are manifested by a number of objective indicators which this Court can properly notice, but principally by the extreme rarity of actual infliction of the death penalty in the United States and the world today. Worldwide and national abandonment of the use of capital punishment during this century has accelerated dramatically, and has now become nearly total.
>
> In historical context, this development marks an overwhelming repudiation of the death penalty as an atavistic barbarism. The penalty remains on the statute books only to be-and because it is-rarely and unusually inflicted. So inflicted, it is not a part of the regular machinery of the state for the control of crime and punishment of criminals. It is an extreme and mindless act of savagery, practiced upon an outcast few. This is exactly the evil against which the Eighth Amendment stands.

The issue before the Court was deeply divisive for a number of reasons. The power to set limits for behaviour and prescribe punishments for those who transgress those limits is a fundamental characteristic of the police powers that are the peculiar prerogative of the States in the federal system. Also significant was the long standing acceptance of capital punishment and the trial processes of the several States associated with its imposition. A successful attack on the institution and its implementation would be seen as a diminution of 'States' Rights'[48] and a corresponding increase in the power of the federal government.

---

44 *People v. Anderson* 493 P.2d 880 (Cal. 1972).

45 406 U.S. 813 (1972).

46 See 1971 WL 134167, 11: 'The Brief for Petitioner in *Aikens v. California* fully develops the reasons why we believe that the death penalty is a cruel and unusual punishment for the crime of murder, as that penalty is administered in the United States today. At the heart of the argument is the principle that the Eighth Amendment condemns a penalty which is so oppressive that it can command public acceptance only by sporadic, exceedingly rare and arbitrary imposition' (footnote reference omitted).

47 1971 WL 134168, 6.

48 'States' Rights' is convenient shorthand that is often used by conservative judges and scholars to remind others that the Constitution divides sovereignty between the federal government and the States. As Justice Thomas put it in *Federal Maritime Commission v. South Carolina State Ports Authority* 535 U.S. 743, 751 (2002): 'Dual sovereignty is a defining feature of our Nation's constitutional blueprint. [...] States, upon ratification of

At the end of its 1971–2 Term, the Court announced its decision in *Furman v. Georgia*[49] on 29 June 1972. At first appearance it looked like a victory for the abolitionists and the end of capital punishment in the United States. The Court reversed the lower courts' death sentences in the petitioners' cases and in 120 others. The shock was such that many believed the Court had outlawed capital punishment as a cruel and unusual punishment *per se*.[50] Unfortunately, as the LDF and others came to realise all too soon, *Furman* had none of the authority of the *Brown I* decision. Where the Court was unanimous in *Brown I* and all Justices joined Chief Justice Warren's opinion for the Court without filing separate concurrences, *Furman* was a weak decision. The Court was fractured 5-4 and there was no opinion for the Court other than an anodyne *per curiam* opinion. After reciting the petitioners' convictions and death sentences the opinion continued:

> The Court holds that the imposition and carrying out of the death penalty in these cases constitute cruel and unusual punishment in violation of the Eighth and Fourteenth Amendments. The judgment in each case is therefore reversed insofar as it leaves undisturbed the death sentence imposed, and the cases are remanded for further proceedings.[51]

In his concurrence Justice Douglas found the petitioners' cases 'pregnant with discrimination and discrimination is an ingredient not compatible with the idea of equal protection of the laws that is implicit in the ban on 'cruel and unusual' punishments'.[52]

Justice Brennan took a stronger line and would have abolished capital punishment as cruel and unusual *per se.* He saw the imposition of the death penalty 'as fatally offensive to human dignity. The punishment of death is therefore "cruel and unusual", and the States may no longer inflict it as a punishment for crimes'.[53]

Justice Stewart found that death sentences were both cruel in kind and unusual in the sense that they were infrequently imposed. In a famous phrase he characterised their imposition as being 'cruel and unusual in the same way that being struck by lightning is cruel and unusual'.[54] He went on to conclude 'that the Eighth and Fourteenth Amendments cannot tolerate the infliction of a sentence of

---

the Constitution, did not consent to become mere appendages of the Federal Government. Rather, they entered the Union with their sovereignty intact' (internal quotations omitted).

49 408 U.S. 238 (1972).

50 See Zimring and Hawkins (1989, 37–8).

51 *Furman*, 239–40.

52 *ibid*, at 257.

53 *ibid*, 305.

54 *ibid*, 309.

death under legal systems that permit this unique penalty to be so wantonly and so freakishly imposed'.[55]

Justice White took a narrower view. His concern was capital statutes where the legislature did not itself mandate the penalty in any particular kind of case but left it to judges or juries to decide when the penalty would be utilised and where judges and juries had ordered the death penalty with such infrequency that the odds were very much against imposition and execution of the penalty with respect to any convicted murderer or rapist. He felt that 'the death penalty is exacted with great infrequency even for the most atrocious crimes and that there is no meaningful basis for distinguishing the few cases in which it is imposed from the many cases in which it is not'.[56]

Finally, Justice Marshall reviewed the history of capital punishment in England and America and the justifications for its imposition. 'What purpose has it served?' he asked. 'The evidence is that it has served none'.[57] Like Justice Brennan, he concluded that its imposition violated the Eighth Amendment and that by banning it '[w]e achieve a major milestone in the long road up from barbarism and join the approximately 70 other jurisdictions in the world which celebrate their regard for civilization and humanity by shunning capital punishment'.[58]

The effect of the decision in *Furman* was electric and electrifying – but the LDF soon discovered that the fruits of its success had a bitter taste. The LDF moratorium strategy of building a logjam of cases and then winning a victory in the Court was intended to show America that it could do without executions. However, the States saw it in a very different way. They perceived *Furman* as an assault on their traditional police powers and a repudiation of the values of federalism. As Zimring and Hawkins put it, '[s]ome of the initial reaction to this seeming judicial abolition of the death penalty bordered on the hysterical' (1989: 38). Congress even considered promoting a constitutional amendment to permit imposition of the death penalty.[59]

The death penalty States rapidly consulted their attorneys generals and soon learned the true effect of *Furman*. The majority sentiment on the Court showed that the death penalty had not been proscribed – it was merely its procedural requirements that had been scrutinised. If the States could put their houses in order then capital punishment could be restored. Zimring and Hawkins (1989: 39–40) describe how opinion polls had shown that national support for the death penalty had steadily declined by twenty-five percent between 1953 and 1966. Opposition stayed high until 1972 when a dramatic increase in support for the penalty was recorded. While little more than forty-five percent of the nation was in favour in 1970, this increased to sixty percent in 1973.

55 *ibid*, 310.

56 *ibid*, 313.

57 *ibid*, 369.

58 *ibid*, 371 (internal quotations omitted).

59 See Meltsner 1973b, 291.

The States whose death penalty statutes had been struck down rapidly passed new capital statutes and as convictions and appeals under their new laws began to accumulate these were fast-tracked for hearing in the Court. In a series of cases all argued on the same day,[60] a 7-2 majority of the Court approved new capital statutes in three jurisdictions[61] and a 5-4 majority struck down statutes in two others.[62] The leading case where arguments were most fully articulated is *Gregg v. Georgia.* The opinion for the Court announced by Justice Stewart put paid to the LDF and NAACP's hopes in its opening pages:

> The Court on a number of occasions has both assumed and asserted the constitutionality of capital punishment. [...] But until *Furman v. Georgia* [...] the Court never confronted squarely the fundamental claim that the punishment of death always, regardless of the enormity of the offense or the procedure followed in imposing the sentence, is cruel and unusual punishment in violation of the Constitution. Although this issue was presented and addressed in *Furman*, it was not resolved by the Court. [...] We now hold that the punishment of death does not invariably violate the Constitution.[63]

It went on to consider Georgia's amendments to its capital sentencing scheme and concluded:

> The basic concern of *Furman* centered on those defendants who were being condemned to death capriciously and arbitrarily. [...] The new Georgia sentencing procedures, by contrast, focus the jury's attention on the particularized nature of the crime and the particularized characteristics of the individual defendant. While the jury is permitted to consider any aggravating or mitigating circumstances, it must find and identify at least one statutory aggravating factor before it may impose a penalty of death. In this way the jury's discretion is channeled. No longer can a jury wantonly and freakishly impose the death sentence; it is always circumscribed by the legislative guidelines. In addition, the review function of the Supreme Court of Georgia affords additional assurance that the concerns that prompted our decision in *Furman* are not present to any significant degree in the Georgia procedure applied here.[64]

The two dissenters were Justices Brennan and Marshall, both of whom had held in their concurrences in *Furman* that the death penalty was invariably a cruel and unusual punishment proscribed by the Eighth Amendment. Brennan noted that the Court felt unable to agree with the proposition that the State's deliberate infliction of death was uniquely degrading to human dignity yet three members

---

60 *Gregg v. Georgia* 428 U.S. 153 (1976), *Proffitt v. Florida* 428 U.S. 242 (1976), *Jurek v. Texas* 428 U.S. 262 (1976), *Woodson v. North Carolina* 428 U.S. 280 (1976) and *Roberts v. Louisiana* 428 U.S. 325 (1976).

61 Georgia, Florida and Texas.

62 North Carolina and Louisiana.

63 *Gregg v. Georgia* at 168–9.

64 *ibid*, 206–7.

of the majority felt that the mandatory infliction of death was a cruel and unusual punishment.[65] Justice Marshall reiterated his argument in *Furman* that infliction of the death penalty was, at heart, a 'total denial of the wrongdoer's dignity and worth' and accordingly the death penalty was 'an excessive penalty forbidden by the Eighth and Fourteenth Amendments'.[66]

In two other cases the Court struck down statutes requiring the mandatory imposition of the death penalty. In *Woodson v. North Carolina* the State had enacted a statute stipulating death as the penalty on conviction for first degree murder, which included any wilful, deliberate and premeditated killing and any murder committed in perpetrating or attempting to perpetrate a felony.[67] The opinion for the Court began by reiterating the Court's rejection of the proposition that the death penalty is under any circumstances a cruel and unusual punishment.[68] The Court, quoting *Trop v. Dulles*,[69] noted that the Eighth Amendment stood to assure that the State's power to punish was 'exercised within the limits of civilized standards'. It concluded that the Eighth Amendment required 'consideration of the character and record of the individual offender and the circumstances of the particular offense as a constitutionally indispensable part of the process of inflicting the penalty of death'.[70]

In the other mandatory penalty scheme, the Court considered Louisiana's capital penalty statute which reserved its mandatory death sentences for a wider range of offences than did North Carolina. Under its new scheme, the death penalty was mandatory for those found guilty of first degree murder,[71] aggravated rape,[72] aggravated kidnapping,[73] or treason.[74] The Louisiana capital homicide offence caught a much narrower range of offenders than did its North Carolina counterpart. The statute defined first degree murder as homicide where the offender had a specific intent to kill or to inflict great bodily harm and was engaged in the perpetration or attempted perpetration of aggravated kidnapping, aggravated rape, or armed robbery. It also specified other particular circumstances relating to the victim or other circumstances where a homicide would constitute first degree murder, e.g. where there were multiple victims, or where the homicide was a contract killing.

A further difference between the North Carolina and Louisiana capital homicide statutes was that Louisiana utilised a unique system of responsive verdicts under

65 *ibid*, 230.
66 *ibid*, 240–41.
67 See NC Gen Stat § 14–17 (Cum Supp 1975).
68 *Woodson, supra*, at 285.
69 *ibid*, 288 quoting *Trop*, 356 U.S. 86, 100.
70 *ibid*, 304.
71 La Rev Stat Ann § 14:30 (1974).
72 *ibid*, § 14:42.
73 *ibid*, § 14:44.
74 *ibid*, § 14:113.

which the jury in every first-degree murder case had to be instructed on the crimes of first-degree murder, second-degree murder, and manslaughter and had to be provided with the potential verdicts of guilty, guilty of second-degree murder, guilty of manslaughter, and not guilty.

The Court was not convinced that this cured the constitutional infirmities of the statute. The opinion for the Court observed:

> The futility of attempting to solve the problems of mandatory death penalty statutes by narrowing the scope of the capital offense stems from our society's rejection of the belief that every offense in a like legal category calls for an identical punishment without regard to the past life and habits of a particular offender. As the dissenting Justices in *Furman* noted, the 19th century movement away from mandatory death sentences was rooted in the recognition that individual culpability is not always measured by the category of crime committed.[75]

The Court saw another problem in Louisiana's scheme that involved its responsive verdicts. As the Court saw it, this procedure:

> not only lacks standards to guide the jury in selecting among first-degree murderers, but it plainly invites the jurors to disregard their oaths and choose a verdict for a lesser offense whenever they feel the death penalty is inappropriate. There is an element of capriciousness in making the jurors' power to avoid the death penalty dependent on their willingness to accept this invitation to disregard the trial judge's instructions.[76]

The Court accordingly struck down Louisiana's capital penalty statutes as violating the Eighth and Fourteenth Amendments' prohibition of cruel and unusual punishments.

The decisions in these five cases announced on 2 July 1976 ushered in what has become known as the modern era of the death penalty in America.[77] If Anthony Amsterdam and the LDF had taken stock of the situation on the following day, some things could have been said with certainty about the sweep of the Eighth Amendment's words in 1976. Their meaning was dynamic and reflected the evolving standards of a maturing society (*Trop v. Dulles*). They controlled the mode of execution and proscribed gratuitous infliction of unnecessary suffering (*Wilkerson v. Utah*, *In re Kemmler* and *Weems v. United States*). The infliction of punishments seemingly had to be proportionate to the gravity of the offence

75 *Roberts*, supra, at 333 (internal quotations omitted).

76 *ibid*, 335. Invitations for jury nullification of repugnant statutes were also to prove problematic in a later case – see *Penry v. Johnson* 532 U.S. 782, 796–804 (2001).

77 Although most commentators consider *Gregg* in 1976 to be the dawn of the modern era of the death penalty (e.g., King 2007, 198), others consider that *Furman* in 1972 was its dawn (e.g. Hindson et al 2006, 551), while yet others would sit on the fence and say that it spans the period from *Furman* to *Gregg* (e.g., Kirchmeier 2006, 403 (footnote 4)).

committed (*Weems v. United States*) yet, while it could not be imposed as a mandatory punishment for any offence (*Woodson v. North Carolina* and *Roberts v. Louisiana*), neither was it a cruel and unusual punishment in all circumstances (*Gregg v. Georgia*). Sentencing schemes infected with standardless procedures that might lead to capricious death sentencing by juries would also be considered to be inflictions of cruel and unusual punishment (*Furman v. Georgia*).

There was still unfinished business in clarifying the existing rulings. It was unclear as to what was needed to satisfy the requirement for proportionality in sentencing seemingly set out in *Weems*. The issue of which crimes might appropriately attract a death sentence had still to be directly addressed by the Court. Most importantly of all, the Court had managed to evade discussion of the effect of the racism that the NAACP and LDF believed infected capital sentencing. Indeed, the sentencing disparities originally identified in the Southern rape cases that had first excited the attention of the NAACP remained unresolved. These were battles yet to be fought but the abolitionists must have felt regret that they had been able to persuade only two members of the Court that capital punishment could not be administered in a fair and principled way.

The Modern Era of the Death Penalty

The very next year one of these issues came before the Court in *Coker v. Georgia*.[78] The Court was called to rule upon the constitutionality of one of Georgia's capital statutes[79] that provided a maximum penalty of death for the offence of rape. Coker was convicted of raping an adult woman and his sentencing was carried out in accordance with the protocol approved in *Gregg*.[80] The question presented for decision on the grant of certiorari was '[w]hether the imposition and carrying out of the sentence of death for the crime of rape under the law of Georgia violates the Eighth or Fourteenth Amendment to the Constitution of the United States?' In a companion case, *Eberheart v. Georgia*,[81] the Court considered also whether the death penalty could be imposed for a non-fatal kidnapping.

In their brief on the merits in *Coker*,[82] the petitioner's attorneys did not have an opportunity to explore the racial disparities in capital rape sentencing that so concerned the NAACP because both Coker and his victim were white.[83] They

78 433 U.S. 584 (1977).

79 Ga. Code Ann. § 26-2001 (1972).

80 A general procedure for sentencing in capital crimes was laid down in Ga. Code s 26-3102 (Supp. 1976) as Georgia's response to the Court's decision in *Furman*.

81 433 U.S. 917 (1977) – here the Court granted certiorari and, without other briefing or oral argument, summarily overturned Eberheart's death sentence citing *Coker* as authority for doing so.

82 See 1976 WL 181481.

83 See Kennedy 1997, 324.

framed their argument upon proportionality grounds founded firmly on the Court's decisions in *Weems* and *Trop*. They summarised their argument in these words:

> The Eighth Amendment forbids punishments which are grossly excessive and disproportioned to the offense. While the rape of an adult woman is a serious crime, it almost nowhere except in Georgia [is] warranting the punishment of death. [...] By a unanimous concurrence of the relevant objective indicators of contemporary societal values, capital punishment for rape is excessive. It therefore violates the Eighth Amendment.[84]

The Court, by a 7-2 majority, found that the sentence of death for rape was grossly disproportionate. In his opinion for the Court, Justice White pointed out that the Eighth Amendment not only prohibited punishments that were barbaric but also those that were excessive in relation to the crime committed.[85]

The requirements for sentencing proportionality enunciated in *Weems* and *Coker* were revisited in 1982 in *Enmund v. Florida*.[86] In this case Enmund was sentenced to death for felony murder where he was not the actual killer – he had aided and abetted others in the commission of a robbery in the course of which two people had been killed. Florida's law made Enmund a principal in the first degree despite the fact that he had been sitting in the getaway car outside while the murders took place. By a majority of 5-4 the Court overturned Enmund's sentence. Justice Brennan, writing for the Court, found that punishment in this case was excessive:

> For purposes of imposing the death penalty, Enmund's criminal culpability must be limited to his participation in the robbery, and his punishment must be tailored to his personal responsibility and moral guilt. Putting Enmund to death to avenge two killings that he did not commit and had no intention of committing or causing does not measurably contribute to the retributive end of ensuring that the criminal gets his just deserts.[87]

Unfortunately, hopes that the Court would require a more onerous proportionality review in capital cases have been dashed by its later 5-4 decision in a non-capital case, *Harmelin v. Michigan*.[88] Harmelin was sentenced to mandatory life imprisonment without possibility of parole for possession of 650g of cocaine. He claimed that Michigan's statute did not allow for individualised sentencing and was therefore a cruel and unusual punishment. Justice Scalia, announcing the opinion for the Court, upheld the Michigan statute noting that, '[s]evere,

84 1976 WL 181481, 28–29.
85 *Coker*, 591–2.
86 458 U.S. 782 (1982).
87 *ibid*, 801.
88 501 U.S. 957 (1991).

mandatory penalties may be cruel, but they are not unusual in the constitutional sense, having been employed in various forms throughout our Nation's history'.[89] In an earlier section of his opinion, joined by Chief Justice Rehnquist, he concluded that the Eighth Amendment contained no proportionality guarantee.[90] A plurality of the Court, citing *Coker* and *Enmund*, noted that in capital cases there was a test for gross disproportionality. The Cruel and Unusual Punishments Clause encompassed a narrow proportionality principle but the plurality observed, '[t]hough our decisions recognise a proportionality principle, its precise contours are unclear'.[91]

The NAACP and others continued their pursuit of a ruling on racial disparities in the criminal justice system. A modest advance was made in 1986 when the Court decided in *Batson v. Kentucky*[92] that the racially motivated exercise of peremptory challenges during jury selection offended the Equal Protection Clause of the Fourteenth Amendment. However, in a major challenge described (Goldfarb 2007, 551) as 'a searing case that reveals ugly realities about American law and American society', the LDF sought to force the Court in *McCleskey v. Kemp*[93] to face up to the fact that there was systemic racial discrimination in the way the death penalty was applied. If that could be demonstrated then it reasoned that the Court would have to deal with the constitutional consequences of that discrimination which it believed would be necessarily fatal to the administration of the death penalty in Georgia.

The LDF used a meticulous data gathering and statistical analysis exercise on homicide disposals in the state of Georgia over an extended period of time. The study, known as the 'Baldus study' (fully described in Baldus et al 1990), revealed startling sentencing discrepancies strongly correlated to the race of both victim and perpetrator. In their merits brief McCleskey's attorneys summarised their argument in these uncompromising terms:

> The principal questions before the Court on certiorari involve intermediate issues of evidence and proof. Fundamental constitutional values are nonetheless at the heart of this appeal. Our primary submission is that the lower courts, by their treatment of petitioner's evidence, have effectively placed claims of racial discrimination in the death penalty – no matter how thoroughly proven – beyond effective judicial review. [...]Reduced to its essence, petitioner's submission to the Court is a simple one. Evidence of racial discrimination that would amply suffice if the stakes were a job promotion, or the selection of a jury, should not be disregarded when the stakes are life and death. Methods of proof and fact-finding accepted as necessary in every other area of law should not be jettisoned in this one.[94]

89 *ibid*, 994–5.
90 *ibid*, 965.
91 *ibid*, 998 (per Kennedy J).
92 476 U.S. 79 (1986).
93 481 U.S. 279 (1987).
94 1986 WL 727359, 23–32.

Goldfarb points out (Goldfarb 2007: 555–6) that McCleskey only had to establish a discriminatory pattern of law enforcement to show that his punishment violated the Eighth Amendment's Cruel and Unusual Punishments Clause. The Baldus study did just this and, in his opinion for the Court, Justice Powell did not challenge the correctness of the study.[95] Nevertheless the Court denied relief on the ground that maintaining jury discretion was of higher importance than eliminating racial discrimination. Similarly, McCleskey's claim that purposeful discrimination in his sentencing denied him the Fourteenth Amendment's promise of the equal protection of the laws was readily evaded by requiring a higher standard of proof of purposeful discrimination in his case than the Court had required in *Batson v. Kentucky*.

There is little doubt that the strength of evidence in *McCleskey v. Kemp* troubled the Court. It was divided 5-4 on the issues and Justice Powell later regretted his decision.[96] The real reason for this pragmatic decision was the floodgates argument that Justice Powell articulated in the closing section of his opinion for the Court:

> Thus, if we accepted McCleskey's claim that racial bias has impermissibly tainted the capital sentencing decision, we could soon be faced with similar claims as to other types of penalty. Moreover, the claim that his sentence rests on the irrelevant factor of race easily could be extended to apply to claims based on unexplained discrepancies that correlate to membership in other minority groups, and even to gender.[97]

McCleskey seemed to put paid to the LDF's hope of using racial factors in sentencing to strike down or limit the death penalty as cruel and unusual punishment and also any broad attack on it based on equal protection grounds. The excesses proscribed by the Eighth Amendment's Cruel and Unusual Punishments Clause could be seen to fall broadly into categories of excesses in modes of execution, arbitrary impositions or disproportionate punishments. Some progress had been made in narrowing the circumstances in which death could be inflicted constitutionally but death rows continued to expand. It was around this time that abolitionists began to turn their attention to scrutinising characteristics of offenders that might disqualify them from capital sentences rather than the more traditional approach of disqualifying particular modes of execution or particular offences.

---

95 *McCleskey*, 291 n.7, the Court would 'assume the [Baldus] study is valid statistically'.

96 After his retirement from the Court, Powell told Jeffries, his biographer and former law clerk, that the one vote he participated in on the Supreme Court bench that he would change was that in *McCleskey* – see Jeffries 1994, 451–52.

97 *McCleskey*, 315–17. A full discussion of the significance of this important case is beyond the scope of this chapter but it is discussed extensively in law review articles. The interested reader is referred to Amsterdam and Bruner's (2000, 194–216) succinct discussion of the rhetoric employed by Justice Powell to justify the Court's conclusions without appearing to be too partisan.

In a series of cases beginning with *Ford v. Wainwright*[98] in 1986 the Court began to identify certain classes of offenders who were declared categorically exempt from execution. Such offenders all shared the common characteristics of having reduced understanding – either of their condition or of the consequences of their actions – and thus the retributive and exemplary value of executing them was thereby reduced. To execute persons in such a condition might then be considered to be excessive punishment for the offence proscribed by the Cruel and Unusual Punishments Clause. Since such persons had been executed in the past it would be necessary in every case to establish that contemporary standards had evolved so as to prohibit the practice.

In *Ford* the Court was called upon to consider whether Florida could execute a man who was competent to stand trial but who had become insane during the period of his incarceration awaiting execution. By a 7-2 majority the Court, applying common law principles and *Trop v. Dulles,* concluded that the insane were categorically exempted from execution[99] and that the State was obligated to put in place robust adversarial procedures for ensuring that the constitutional prohibition was not evaded.[100]

Two years later the Court considered whether another class of defendant was categorically exempted from execution. In *Thompson v. Oklahoma*[101] the Court concluded by a 5-3 majority that the execution of a defendant convicted as a 15-year-old juvenile would constitute a cruel and unusual punishment. In his opinion for the Court Justice Stevens discussed at length where evidence of the 'evolving standards of decency that mark the progress of a maturing society' referred to in *Trop* might be found. Justice Stevens looked primarily to the actions of legislatures and juries. As he explained:

> Our capital punishment jurisprudence has consistently recognized that contemporary standards, as reflected by the actions of legislatures and juries, provide an important measure of whether the death penalty is "cruel and unusual". Part of the rationale for this index of constitutional value lies in the very language of the construed clause: whether an action is "unusual" depends, in common usage, upon the frequency of its occurrence or the magnitude of its acceptance.[102]

Justice Stevens concluded his opinion by observing:

> Although the judgments of legislatures, juries, and prosecutors weigh heavily in the balance, it is for us ultimately to judge whether the Eighth Amendment permits

98 477 U.S. 399 (1986).
99 *ibid*, 410.
100 *ibid*, 416–18.
101 487 U.S. 815 (1988).
102 *ibid*, 822 n. 7.

> imposition of the death penalty on one such as petitioner who committed a heinous murder when he was only 15 years old.[103]

The following year the Court had to consider whether the same exemption applied to those who were 16-year-olds or 17-year-olds at the date of the commission of their offences. In *Stanford v. Kentucky*[104] it concluded that the imposition of the death penalty on 16- and 17-year-old offenders did not breach the Eighth Amendment's prohibitions. In his opinion for the Court, Justice Scalia dwelt at some length on where evidence of evolving standards was to be found. He reiterated that first and foremost the Court must look for objective indicia of changing sentiment – and that this was to be found most reliably in the actions of legislatures and juries. He expressly rejected the petitioners' invitation to look to wider evidence:

> Having failed to establish a consensus against capital punishment for 16- and 17-year-old offenders through state and federal statutes and the behavior of prosecutors and juries, petitioners seek to demonstrate it through other indicia, including public opinion polls, the views of interest groups, and the positions adopted by various professional associations. We decline the invitation to rest constitutional law upon such uncertain foundations. A revised national consensus so broad, so clear, and so enduring as to justify a permanent prohibition upon all units of democratic government must appear in the operative acts (laws and the application of laws) that the people have approved.[105]

In the same year the Court considered another possible category of exempt offender – those suffering from learning difficulties. In *Penry v. Lynaugh*[106] Justice O'Connor writing for a 5-4 majority of the Court declined to find that persons suffering from learning difficulties (or 'mental retardation' as it was then called in America) should be categorically exempted from execution. In reaching this conclusion the Court found neither evidence of evolving standards nor did it find disproportionality of punishment on account of Penry's degree of reduced personal responsibility. Justice O'Connor remarked, '[t]he clearest and most reliable objective evidence of contemporary values is the legislation enacted by the country's legislatures. We have also looked to data concerning the actions of sentencing juries'.[107]

In *Atkins v. Virginia*[108] in 2002, the Court revisited its earlier decision and, by a 6-3 majority, concluded that standards had evolved since its 1989 decision in

---

103 *ibid*, 833 (internal quotations omitted).

104 492 U.S. 361 (1989). *Stanford* involved a 17-year-old offender. The case was consolidated for hearing and judgment with *Wilkins v. Missouri* involving a 16-year-old offender.

105 *ibid*, 377.

106 492 U.S. 302 (1989).

107 *ibid*, 331.

108 536 U.S. 304 (2002).

Penry. Writing for the Court, Justice Stevens acknowledged that the behaviour of legislatures was the clearest and most reliable indicator of evolving standards.[109] Nevertheless, he declared that the Court had to bring its own judgement to bear on the acceptability of the death penalty under the Eighth Amendment, 'Thus, in cases involving a consensus, our own judgment is "brought to bear" by asking whether there is reason to disagree with the judgment reached by the citizenry and its legislators'.[110]

However, what proved to be the most controversial part of Justice Stevens' opinion was contained in a footnote where he noted that the legislative consensus reflected 'a much broader social and professional consensus'.[111] He instanced the views of professional associations and religious leaders, but most controversially, the disapproval of the 'world community' and 'polling data'.

These comments drew furious dissents from Chief Justice Rehnquist and Justice Scalia. The Chief Justice wrote separately to call attention to what he saw as the defects in the Court's decision to place weight on foreign laws, the views of professional and religious organisations, and opinion polls in reaching its conclusion. He considered that the Court should take account of only State legislative actions and jury determinations and these 'ought to be the sole indicators by which courts ascertain the contemporary American conceptions of decency for purposes of the Eighth Amendment'.[112] Abandoning the usual conventions of judicial politeness, he ended by saying:

> There are strong reasons for limiting our inquiry into what constitutes an evolving standard of decency under the Eighth Amendment to the laws passed by legislatures and the practices of sentencing juries in America. Here, the Court goes beyond these well-established objective indicators of contemporary values. It finds further support to its conclusion that a national consensus has developed against imposing the death penalty on all mentally retarded defendants in international opinion, the views of professional and religious organizations, and opinion polls not demonstrated to be reliable. Believing this view to be seriously mistaken, I dissent.[113]

Justice Scalia was even more scathing. He accused the majority of basing its opinion 'upon nothing but the personal views of its Members',[114] of relying upon 'embarrassingly feeble evidence of consensus',[115] and of 'thrashing about

109 *ibid*, 312.
110 *ibid*, 313 (citation omitted).
111 *ibid*, 316 n. 21.
112 *ibid*, 324.
113 *ibid*, 328 (internal quotations omitted).
114 *ibid*, 338.
115 *ibid*, 344.

for evidence of consensus'[116] before concluding in a spectacularly contemptuous dismissal of the majority view:

> But the Prize for the Court's Most Feeble Effort to fabricate "national consensus" must go to its appeal (deservedly relegated to a footnote) to the views of assorted professional and religious organizations, members of the so-called "world community", and respondents to opinion polls. I agree with the Chief Justice, that the views of professional and religious organizations and the results of opinion polls are irrelevant. Equally irrelevant are the practices of the "world community", whose notions of justice are (thankfully) not always those of our people.

In the same year the Court had a chance to revisit its earlier decision in *Stanford v. Kentucky* allowing the execution of 16- and 17-year-olds but the requisite majority to grant habeas corpus could not be found.[117] However, in 2003 when the Supreme Court of Missouri granted relief to such a defendant,[118] ignoring precedent and second guessing what the U.S. Supreme Court would do if it had to again confront the constitutionality of juvenile executions, the Court was compelled to reconsider the issue.

In a 5–4 majority decision Justice Kennedy, writing for the Court, found that standards had evolved so as to proscribe juvenile executions. He defiantly referred to international law and opinion. While noting that such law and opinion was 'instructive' rather than 'controlling', he continued:

> It is proper that we acknowledge the overwhelming weight of international opinion against the juvenile death penalty, resting in large part on the understanding that the instability and emotional imbalance of young people may often be a factor in the crime. [...] The opinion of the world community, while not controlling our outcome, does provide respected and significant confirmation for our own conclusions.

In her dissent Justice O'Connor, who had joined the majority in *Atkins*, agreed with much of the majority opinion. She saw the Eighth Amendment's Cruel and Unusual Punishments Clause as proscribing a punishment 'if it makes no measurable contribution to acceptable penal goals' or is 'grossly out of proportion to the severity of the crime'.[119] She took issue with the Court's failure to reprove, or even to acknowledge, the Supreme Court of Missouri's unabashed refusal to follow *Stanford.* However, she raised the issue of the majority's view that the international consensus provided confirmatory evidence of evolving standards in these terms:

---

116 *ibid*, 346.

117 See *In re Stanford* 537 U.S. 968 (2002). Grants of habeas corpus require five votes in the US Supreme Court but certiorari is granted on four votes.

118 *State ex rel Simmons v. Roper*, 112 S.W.3d 397 (Mo., 2003).

119 *Roper v. Simmons* 543 U.S. 551 (2005) at 589 (internal quotations omitted).

> [T]he evidence of an international consensus does not alter my determination that the Eighth Amendment does not, at this time, forbid capital punishment of 17-year-old murderers in all cases.
>
> Nevertheless, I disagree with Justice Scalia's contention [...] that foreign and international law have no place in our Eighth Amendment jurisprudence. Over the course of nearly half a century, the Court has consistently referred to foreign and international law as relevant to its assessment of evolving standards of decency.[120]

Justice Scalia was forceful in his condemnation of the majority opinion. After roundly attacking the majority's evidence of evolving standards and the exercise of its own judgment, he moved on to the object of his special scorn – the Court's references to international law and foreign legal opinion. He advised that 'the basic premise of the Court's argument – that American law should conform to the laws of the rest of the world – ought to be rejected out of hand'.[121]

He had clearly noted the *amicus curiae* brief interventions by the English Bar in a number of capital cases and that the fact that its submission in *Roper v. Simmons* had been cited with approval in the opinion for the Court in this case.[122] But Justice Scalia and his fellow dissenters would consign modern British legal thought on these constitutional issues to mere historical interpretation:

> The Court's special reliance on the laws of the United Kingdom is perhaps the most indefensible part of its opinion. It is of course true that we share a common history with the United Kingdom, and that we often consult English sources when asked to discern the meaning of a constitutional text written against the backdrop of 18th-century English law and legal thought.[...] It is beyond comprehension why we should look, for that purpose, to a country that has developed, in the centuries since the Revolutionary War – and with increasing speed since the United Kingdom's recent submission to the jurisprudence of European courts dominated by continental jurists – a legal, political, and social culture quite different from our own.

Finally, the most recent cases concerning the interpretation of the Cruel and Unusual Punishments Clause of the Eighth Amendment have brought the continuing debate full circle. In *Baze v. Rees*[123] the issue before the Court was the traditional one of whether a particular mode of execution constitutes cruel and unusual punishment. In this case the challenge was to the constitutionality of a lethal injection protocol widely adopted by the death penalty States.

Counsel for the petitioner and the numerous supporting *amici curiae* briefs argued for a position that it was not enough for States to eschew barbaric methods

120 *ibid*, 604.
121 *ibid*, 624.
122 *ibid*, 576.
123 U.S., 128 S.Ct. 1520 (2008).

of execution but rather that it was incumbent upon them to choose optimal methods to ensure the least possibility of a painful death. Baze argued that the State violates the Eighth Amendment when its execution procedures create a significant and unnecessary risk of inflicting severe pain that could be prevented by the adoption of reasonable safeguards.[124] In a 7-2 majority decision the Court rejected that argument. In his opinion for the Court Chief Justice Roberts began by reaffirming that capital punishment was constitutional under *Gregg* and that '[s]ome risk of pain is inherent in any method of execution – no matter how humane – if only from the prospect of error in following the required procedure'.[125] After noting that the petitioner conceded that Kentucky's protocol was humane and constitutional if performed properly,[126] he declared that an execution method must present a 'substantial' or 'objectively intolerable' risk of serious harm if it was to constitute a cruel and unusual punishment.[127] On the facts of the case, he concluded that the petitioners had not discharged their burden of showing that the risk of pain from maladministration of the protocol and the State's failure to adopt an untried alternative amounted to cruel and unusual punishment.[128]

In *Kennedy v. Louisiana*[129] the court will revisit the vexed question of the 'precise contours' of the allegedly narrow proportionality principle in capital cases mentioned by the plurality in *Harmelin v. Michigan*.[130] Kennedy was sentenced to death for raping his eight-year-old stepdaughter. One of the questions presented for decision is whether the Cruel and Unusual Punishments Clause permits a State to punish the crime of rape of a child with the death penalty. The case attracted a larger than usual number of *amicus curiae* briefs for both sides, including a British brief on behalf of The Law Society, the Bar Human Rights Committee, four former Law Lords and close to 100 leading counsel.

During oral argument[131] Kennedy's counsel advanced arguments that there was a national consensus against imposing death as a punishment for rape and secondly that Louisiana's child rape statute did not sufficiently narrow the category of which rapists of children were eligible for the death penalty. Questioning by members of the Court suggested that it was most interested in what *Coker v. Georgia* stood for and how Louisiana's statute might be narrowed. Louisiana tried to hoist conventional abolitionist strategists with their own petard – it argued that there was a trend among States to introduce capital statutes for aggravated rapes. Questioning of Louisiana focussed on the slippery slope of where this might

124 Petitioner's brief on the merits, 2007 WL 3307732, 28.

125 *Baze v. Rees*, 1529.

126 *ibid*, 1530.

127 *ibid*, 1531.

128 *ibid*, 1532-1538.

129 Docket No. 07-343.

130 See, *supra*, 30.

131 See <http://www.supremecourtus.gov/oral_arguments/argument_transcripts/07-343.pdf>.

lead to if capital punishment was not confined to cases involving the death of a victim. However, much of the questioning focussed on whether Louisiana had narrowed sufficiently jury discretion in such cases. The outcome is difficult to read but is likely to turn upon Justice Anthony Kennedy. He holds the balance of power in the present Court in capital cases and it was he who first raised in *Harmelin* the question of the precise contours of the proportionality requirement in capital cases.

The Future Contours of the Cruel and Unusual Punishments Clause

In his opinion concurring in the outcome in *Baze v. Rees*, Justice Stevens predicted that, far from settling the issue of the constitutionality of three-drug-protocol lethal injection executions, the decision would generate more litigation. He advised, 'In my view, therefore, States wishing to decrease the risk that future litigation will delay executions or invalidate their protocols would do well to reconsider their continued use of pancuronium bromide'.[132] During the period between the Court's grant of certiorari in *Baze* and its decision, there was a *de facto* moratorium on executions in the United States. The Court's decision was announced on 16 April 2008 and within days the first State had applied for the stays of execution to be lifted.[133]

Again, if the Court were to uphold Louisiana's child rape capital statute in *Kennedy v. Louisiana* or find that there was no capital proportionality of the kind suggested by Justice Kennedy in *Harmelin* but only a requirement for *Furman/Gregg* narrowing of the class of persons eligible for the penalty, this would open the way for the States to test the waters as to what other crimes might legitimately attract a capital sentence. In particular there are a number of existing federal statutes that potentially attract capital sentences and whose constitutionality has yet to be tested.

It is almost certain that abolitionists will continue to press vigorously for certain categories of inmate to be declared categorically exempt from execution. The two categories of offender whose cases have excited the greatest national and international attention are those who have endured excessively long periods of detention pending their execution (the so-called 'death row phenomenon' defendants) and offenders suffering from serious mental illness.

The death row phenomenon is of particular interest to British jurists because of the role that the European and British courts have played in declaring those subjected to it as suffering inhuman treatment. In *Soering v. United Kingdom*[134] the European Court of Human Rights declared that Britain's proposed extradition of Mr Soering to Virginia to stand trial for murder would subject him to risk

132 *Baze v. Rees*, 1546.

133 Florida applied to vacate the Court's stay of execution in *Schwab v. Florida* on 18 April 2008.

134 161 European Court of Human Rights (ser. A) (1989).

of a death sentence and therefore of exposure to the death row phenomenon.[135] This would amount to subjecting him to 'inhuman or degrading treatment or punishment' contrary to article 3 of the European Convention of Human Rights. The court defined the 'death row phenomenon' as 'consisting of a combination of circumstances to which the applicant would be exposed if, after having been extradited to Virginia to face a capital murder charge, he were sentenced to death'. The principal ingredients of these circumstances were the anguish of a prisoner's contemplation of his own death and the extraordinarily long periods of detention before final execution of sentence.

After *Soering* the British Judicial Committee of the Privy Council, sitting as the court of last appeal for Jamaica, applied the death row phenomenon argument to Jamaica in *Pratt & Morgan v. Attorney General for Jamaica*[136] and set aside the appellants' death sentences as violations of the Jamaican constitution. In the United States the Court has never decided whether it would be a cruel and unusual punishment to subject a prisoner to the death row phenomenon and then seek to execute him. In *Lackey v. Texas*[137] the Court denied certiorari on just this issue but, in an explanatory memorandum,[138] Justice Stevens pointed out that denial of certiorari did not constitute a ruling on the merits and that Lackey's claims raised important undecided issues. So far numerous American courts have rejected (sometimes summarily) death row phenomenon arguments but only two courts are recorded as having taken action on death row phenomenon grounds.[139] Appellate courts usually take a robust view that delay is inherent in the full exercise of a prisoner's Fifth and Fourteenth Amendment due process rights. However, a colourable case can be made out that to serve what amounts in most cases to a typical 'life sentence' before execution is excessive punishment, especially when coupled with the conditions of close confinement endured by death row prisoners and their general anguish of mind over their uncertain fate.

Another potential source of Eighth Amendment violation claims are those cases where a defendant suffers from serious mental illness short of *Ford* insanity.

---

135 *ibid*, 28–30, paras. 93–99.

136 [1993] 2 A.C. 1.

137 514 U.S. 1045 (1996).

138 *ibid.*

139 In *State v. Koskovich* 776 A.2d 144, 161 (N.J., 2001) the New Jersey Supreme Court noted that the trial court, when imposing the death sentence, provided that if defendant's death sentence was not implemented by May 7, 2004 (i.e. within 5 years of imposition), his sentence would be automatically modified to a life sentence with a thirty-year period of parole ineligibility, but that it had summarily amended the judgment to remove that modification. In *Jones v. State* 740 So. 2d 520, 525 (Fla., 1999) the Florida Supreme Court vacated a death sentence on grounds of egregious delay by the State – in this case the defendant had experienced 23 years on death row and 18 of those years were accounted for by successful appeals. The court found and emphasised that '*he has experienced that delay because of the State's own faulty procedures and not because of frivolous appeals on his own part*'.

Just such a case vexed Florida's courts for years where the defendant suffered from severe delusions that made it difficult to discover the true extent of his understanding.[140] The Florida Supreme Court eventually resolved the problem by ruling that as long as there was substantial, competent evidence supporting a finding that the defendant knew why the State was proposing to execute him and that he understood that he would die as a result of the execution, that satisfied *Ford*. The court acknowledged that:

> … this case is troubling because there is evidence that Provenzano has mental health problems of some degree. The circuit court acknowledged these problems in its findings of fact and concluded that Provenzano suffers from mental illness, but because he also exaggerates symptoms and utilizes deception, it is difficult to determine Provenzano's exact mental status.[141]

Who can say which other groups of offenders may be singled out for exemption? The mere fact that claims are raised on their behalf and litigated fully can raise public awareness and eventually bring about changes in national sentiment. Other groups whose members are infrequently executed yet who may be able to raise plausible claims for exemption from execution include women, the elderly and the severely disabled. However, the principal problem facing any attempt to persuade the Court to exempt such persons now is that their conditions are not ones that reduce their understanding of or culpability for the offences they committed.

Female executions always arouse greater than ordinary interest and protest for a variety of reasons.[142] These executions certainly satisfy the Eighth Amendment's requirement that the punishment be unusual but it cannot be said to be 'cruel' in the constitutional sense. A sentimental exemption for women would throw an equal protection question over male executions.

Similarly, executions of the old and the infirm are unusual and provoke public distaste. When California executed Clarence Ray Allen in 2006 there was widespread disgust. At the date of his execution Allen was aged 76 and confined to a wheelchair. He had to be helped onto the execution table by four guards. Allen was legally blind and had previously had a heart attack a few months earlier. Anticipating a possible repetition, he had asked prison officials not to revive him if he suffered a heart attack in the execution chamber. Without any apparent irony, a prison spokesman said, '[a]t no point are we not going to value the sanctity of life. We would resuscitate him'.[143]

---

140 See *Provenzano v. State* 760 So.2d 137 (Fla., 2000).

141 *ibid*, 140.

142 See, the numerous press reports surrounding the execution of Karla Faye Tucker in Texas in February 1998. Tucker was the first woman to be executed in Texas since the Civil War and the first in the U.S. in more than a decade.

143 The Associated Press, 10 February 2006.

References

Amar, A. R. (1991), 'The Bill of Rights as a Constitution', 100 *Yale Law Journal* 1131.

Amsterdam, A. G. and Bruner, J. (2000), *Minding the Law*, Harvard University Press, Cambridge, MA.

Anon (1958a), 'Recent Case: Expatriation for Voting in Foreign Political Election Held Necessary and Proper to Congress' Foreign Affairs Power', 107 *University of Pennsylvania Law Review* 118.

Anon (1958b), 'Business of the Court', 72 *Harvard Law Review* 98.

Anon (1959a), 'Comment–Expatriation: Flexible or Strict Statutory Construction?', 11 *Stanford Law Review* 352.

Anon (1959b), 'Notes and Comments: Expatriating the Dual National', 68 *Yale Law Journal* 1167.

Baldus, C. D. et al (1990), *Equal Justice and the Death Penalty*, Northeastern University Press, Boston, MA.

Carter, S. L. (1992), 'Originalism and the Bill of Rights', 15 *Harvard Journal of Law and Public Policy* 141.

Epstein, L. and Kobylka, J. F. (1992), *The Supreme Court and Legal Change*, University of North Carolina Press, Chapel Hill, NC.

Fiss, O. M. (2003), *The Law as it Could Be*, New York University Press, New York, NY.

Goldfarb, P. (2007), 'Pedagogy of the Suppressed: A Class on Race and Death Penalty', 31 *New York University Review of Law and Social Change* 547.

Greenberg, J. (1982), 'Capital Punishment as a System', 91 *Yale Law Journal* 908.

Haines, H. H. (1996), *Against Capital Punishment: The Anti-Death Penalty Movement in America 1972–94*, Oxford University Press, New York, NY.

Hindson, S. et al (2006), 'Race, Gender, Region and Death Sentencing in Colorado', *1980–1999, University of Colorado Law Review* 549.

Jeffries, J. C. (1994), *Justice Lewis F. Powell Jr.: A Biography*, Charles Scribner's Sons, New York, NY.

Kennedy, R. (1997), *Race, Crime, and the Law, Pantheon Books*, New York, NY.

King, R. (2007), 'No Due Process: How the Death Penalty Violates the Constitutional Rights of the Family Members of Death Row Prisoners', 16 *Boston University Public Interest Law Journal* 195.

Kirchmeier, J. L. (2006), 'Dead Innocent: The Death Penalty Abolitionist Search for a Wrongful Execution', 42 *Tulsa Law Review* 403.

Lain, C. B. (2007), 'Furman Fundamentals', 82 *Washington Law Review* 1.

Meltsner, M. (1973a), 'Litigating Against the Death Penalty: The Strategy Behind Furman', 82 *Yale Law Journal* 1111.

Meltsner, M. (1973b), *Cruel and Unusual – The Supreme Court and Capital Punishment*, Random House, New York, NY.

Paley, W. (1785), *Principles of Moral and Political Philosophy*, London.

Scalia, A. (1989a), 'The Rule of Law as a Law of Rules', 56 *University of Chicago Law Review* 1175.

_________(1989b), 'Originalism: The Lesser Evil', 57 *University of Cincinnati Law Review* 849.

_________(1990), 'Assorted Canards of Contemporary Legal Analysis', 40 *Case Western Reserve Law Review* 581.

_________(1997), *A Matter of Interpretation: Federal Courts and the Law* (ed. Gutmann, A.), Princeton University Press, Princeton, NJ.

_________(2006), 'Review of Steven D. Smith's Law's Quandary', 55 *Catholic University Law Review* 687.

Tushnet, M. (1987), *The NAACP's Legal Strategy Against Segregated Education, 1925–1950*, University of North Carolina Press, Chapel Hill, NC.

Vila, B. and Morris, C. (1997), *Capital Punishment in the United States*, Greenwood Press, Westport, CT.

Zimring, F. E. and Hawkins, G. (1989), *Capital Punishment and the American Agenda*, Cambridge University Press, New York, NY.

Chapter 7

Walking the Eighth Amendment Tightrope: 'Time Served' in the United States Supreme Court

Jane Marriott

Introduction

Of the 50 American states, 37 make provision for the death penalty.[1] Thirteen states, along with the District of Columbia, have abolished the practice. In terms of the number of executions, in the modern era[2] capital punishment has claimed the lives of 1,057 prisoners but, from a high of 98 executions in 1999, its use has declined markedly, with 2006 seeing 'only' 53 death sentences carried out (NAACP 2007, 7). Progress over the last 30 years has largely been due to the expansion of the constitutional parameters of the Eighth Amendment at the hands of the United States Supreme Court.[3] The reduction in numbers of inmates put to death, albeit culled from a large death row population of almost three and a half thousand (NAACP 2007, 1), is driven by a progressively narrowing range of circumstances in which the death penalty may be applied – so that capital punishment may not now be sought for certain offences[4] or applied to certain types of offender[5] – and a series of maturing procedural safeguards aimed at the fair and equitable administration of capital punishment.[6] In that same 30-year period,

1 As at 13 December 2007. The death penalty is also sanctioned at federal level by the US Government and the US military. The figure of 37 includes New York, whose death penalty was declared unconstitutional in 2004 but which retains one inmate on Death Row.

2 Subsequent to the decision in *Gregg v. Georgia* 428 US 153 (1976).

3 The Eighth Amendment states that '[e]xcessive bail shall not be required, nor excessive fines imposed, nor cruel and unusual punishments inflicted'.

4 See *Coker v. Georgia* 433 US 584 (1977), *Enmund v. Florida* 458 US 782 (1982).

5 See *Thompson v. Oklahoma* 487 US 815 (1988), *Atkins v. Virginia* 536 US 304 (2002), *Roper v. Simmons* 543 US 551 (2005).

6 See *Furman v. Georgia* 408 US 238 (1972), *Godfrey v. Georgia* 446 US 420 (1980), *Lockett v. Ohio* 438 US 586 (1978), *Turner v. Murray* 476 US 28 (1986), *Burger v.*

the average time spent on death row prior to execution has risen from 4 years and 3 months to 12 years and 3 months, with many death row inmates serving considerably in excess of that (Snell 2006, 17).

The notion that an inordinate delay between sentencing and being put to death might bar an inmate's eventual execution on Eighth Amendment grounds has been given judicial expression on several occasions in the Supreme Court but significant challenges must be faced if it is to be established as a means of further limiting the application of the death penalty, not least that such a principle would most easily find its roots either extra-jurisdictionally or by reference to penal practices no longer considered acceptable. Whilst time served has intrinsic appeal as a means of further constraining America's death penalty, here it will be argued that its development should neither feature prominently in the short-term in American death penalty jurisprudence nor lead imminently to the 'back door' (Hatchard 1993, 188) abolition of the death penalty in the United States, due largely to the Constitution's due process imperatives, a distinct lack of coherence in both domestic and international approaches to the matter and a range of unintended practical consequences that might ensue from its adoption.

Time Served as a Potential Eighth Amendment Prohibition: *Lackey* Claims

The idea that time on death row might place constitutional fetters on a state's ability to execute its capital criminals first arose in *Lackey v. Texas*.[7] Lackey claimed that executing a prisoner who had already spent 17 years on death row, measured against an average lapse of 11 years and 2 months (Snell 2006, 11) between sentencing and execution, would constitute cruel and unusual punishment under the terms of the Eighth Amendment. The Supreme Court declined to hear the appeal but, in a memorandum issued in conjunction with his own denial of certiorari, Justice Stevens expressed the view that the 'importance and novelty'[8] of the question were sufficient to warrant review. In arriving at this conclusion he relied heavily on domestic constitutional history and the social purposes of capital punishment, but also dipped a toe into foreign jurisdictional waters.

In the domestic setting, *Gregg v. Georgia* had, for the moment at least, incontrovertibly established the legitimacy of capital punishment: if carefully employed, it was permissible because it was so considered by the Framers of the Constitution,[9] had not yet been rejected 'by the elected representatives of the

Kemp 483 US 776 (1987).

7 514 U.S. 1045 (1995).

8 *ibid*, 1045.

9 428 U.S. 153, 177 (1976).

people'[10] was accepted by juries,[11] and was warranted by 'two principal social purposes', namely 'retribution and deterrence'.[12] It was, however, arguable that neither of *Gregg's* social purposes retained force for prisoners who had spent many years on death row. Firstly, lengthy delays in the carrying out of a sentence would not have been contemplated or deemed acceptable by the Constitution's Framers.[13] Secondly, capital punishment's attendant social purposes would be more than satisfied by the retributive nature of the 'severe punishment already inflicted'.[14] The 'minimal' additional deterrent effect of actual execution would easily be eclipsed by 'the deterrent value of incarceration during that period of uncertainty', which was 'comparable to the consequences of the ultimate step itself'.[15] The same point had been made in *Furman v. Georgia*, which had effected a temporary suspension of the death penalty on the basis of defective procedures between 1972 and 1976. There Justice White had stated that when capital punishment:

> ceases realistically to further these purposes ... its imposition would then be the pointless and needless extinction of life with only marginal contributions to any discernible social or public purposes. A penalty with such negligible returns to the State would be patently excessive and cruel and unusual punishment violative of the Eighth Amendment.[16]

Extra-jurisdictionally, and significantly in Justice Stevens' view, 'English jurists'[17] were already moving towards a constitutional bar on the execution of long-term death row inmates. Basing its reasoning on the terms of the Bill of Rights of 1689 (from which the Eighth Amendment derives) the majority of the Judicial Committee of the Privy Council (Privy Council) had, in *Riley v. Attorney General for Jamaica*,[18] rejected the idea that execution after long delay violated s.17(1)[19] of the Jamaican Constitution. Lords Scarman and Brightman, however, were in no doubt that 'execution after inordinate delay would have infringed the prohibition against cruel and unusual punishments'[20] contained in the Bill of Rights, and further maintained that it was:

> no exaggeration ... to say that the jurisprudence of the civilized world, much of which is derived from common law principles and the prohibition against cruel and unusual

10 *ibid*, 181.

11 *ibid.*

12 *ibid*, 183.

13 *supra*, n7, 1045.

14 *ibid.*

15 *ibid*, 1046.

16 408 U.S. 238, 312 (1972).

17 *supra*, n7, 1046.

18 [1983] 1 AC 719.

19 'No person shall be subjected to torture or to inhuman or degrading punishment or treatment'.

20 *supra*, n18, 734.

> punishments in the English Bill of Rights, has recognized and acknowledged that prolonged delay in executing a sentence of death can make the punishment when it comes inhuman degrading.[21]

The dissent laid the groundwork for the Privy Council's subsequent reversal of *Riley* in *Pratt and Morgan v. Attorney General for Jamaica*[22] which identified 'an instinctive revulsion against the prospect of hanging a man after he has been held under sentence of death for many years',[23] as a ground for commuting sentences of death to life imprisonment. Pratt and Morgan had been on death row for 14 years. The Privy Council noted that a further 23 prisoners had been awaiting their fate for more than 10 years, and 82 for more than five, the point at which their Lordships concluded there would be 'strong grounds for believing that the delay is such as to constitute inhuman or degrading punishment or other treatment' to the extent that commutation should occur in the interests of achieving 'substantial justice'.[24]

Lackey did not see the Supreme Court debating the merits of time served as a bar to execution. It merely indicated that, in the view of Justice Stevens, the claim might have some constitutional mileage. The remainder of the Supreme Court bench, in simply denying Lackey certiorari without discussion or debate, was effectively silent on the issue and, for the most part, remains so. The years since *Lackey* have seen Justice Stevens' efforts to engage the Supreme Court in deliberating the constitutional and practical implications of a time served doctrine largely dismissed or ignored – only Justice Breyer has firmly grasped the baton.

In *Gomez v. Fierro*[25] Justices Stevens and Breyer, joined in dissent, argued that the Court's decision to remand for further proceedings in light of an amendment to a California statute, concerning the state's method of execution, exhibited 'callous indifference'[26] to the fact that the petitioners had each spent almost twenty years on death row suffering 'under a Sword of Damocles'.[27] Such delay, they argued, 'frustrates the public interest in deterrence and eviscerates the only rational justification for that type of punishment'.[28] *Elledge v. Florida*[29] followed and saw Justice Breyer dissent forcefully from the Supreme Court's denial of certiorari, claiming that execution after 23 years on death row would 'cease to serve the legitimate penological purposes that otherwise provide a necessary constitutional justification for the death penalty'.[30] Then, proceeding to attack the Court again

21 *ibid.*
22 [1993] 4 All ER 769.
23 *ibid*, 783.
24 *ibid.*
25 519 U.S. 918 (1996).
26 *ibid*, 919.
27 *ibid.*
28 *ibid*, 918.
29 525 U.S. 944 (1998).
30 *ibid*, 945.

for its reluctance to address the issue, he argued firstly that, by any yardstick of domestic law, 23 years under sentence of death when set against an average at that time of 10 years and 10 months (Snell 2006, 11) was, in Eighth Amendment parlance, 'unusual'[31] and, secondly, that neither 'current practice' nor 'practice in this country ... at the time our Constitution was written'[32] could justify it. Moreover, execution at this stage would be cruel within the meaning of the Eighth since the petitioner had 'faced the threat of death for nearly a generation'.[33] It was also readily apparent that the Supreme Court was swimming against the international tide. In addition to the Privy Council's decision in *Riley,*[34] the European Court of Human Rights (ECtHR) had, in *Soering v. U.K.*,[35] held that the extradition of a capital defendant to the United States would violate Article 3 of the European Convention on Human Rights (ECHR)[36] due to the 'real risk' of the extraditee 'being subjected to torture or to inhuman or degrading treatment or punishment in the requesting country'.[37] *Soering* is generally considered to constitute the first explicit judicial recognition of the 'death row phenomenon' which refers to the psychological effects of death row confinement (Hudson 2000; Connolly 1997; Strafer 1983).[38] Whilst the ECtHR found that the death penalty *per se* was consistent with democratic ideals, and with Article 3, it expressed concern that 'the condemned prisoner has to endure for many years the conditions on death row and the anguish and mounting tension of living in the ever-present shadow of death'.[39] 'Many years', in this instance, amounted to between 6 and 8, the average time to elapse between sentencing and execution in Virginia, Soering's destination state. As a result, the Court suggested that, in determining whether a potential extraditee would be surrendered for extradition, a number of factors should be taken into account, 'such as the nature and context of the treatment or punishment, the manner and method of its execution, its duration, its physical or mental effects'.[40] In Justice Breyer's view, at the very least *Soering* created a 'practical anomaly'[41] in American law enforcement which the Court's consideration of the time served issue might resolve. These themes were further developed in *Knight v. Florida*[42] the following year.

31 *ibid*, 944.

32 *ibid*, 945.

33 *ibid.*

34 *supra*, n18.

35 (1989) 11 EHRR 439.

36 'No one shall be subjected to torture or to inhuman or degrading treatment or punishment'.

37 *supra*, n.35, para 100.

38 See *People* v. *Anderson* 6 Cal 3d 628 (1972), *Furman* v. *Georgia* 408 U.S. 238 (1972), *Solesbee* v. *Balkcom,* 339 U.S. 9 (1950).

39 *supra*, n.35, para 106.

40 *ibid*, para 100.

41 *supra*, n.29, 946.

42 528 U.S. 990 (1999).

Knight petitioned for review of his death sentence for inordinate delay some 24 years after the sentence was first passed. The average elapse of time between sentencing and execution was, by this stage, 11 years and 11 months (Snell 2006, 11). Justice Breyer revisited the inverse relationship between time served and the purposes of capital punishment and, again, found no justification in 'constitutional tradition'[43] for proceeding to execution where an inmate had spent many years on death row. In *Knight*, however, the extra-jurisdictional references ranged across the world, taking in the Caribbean,[44] Canada,[45] India[46] and Zimbabwe,[47] along with the supranational bodies, the ECtHR[48] and United Nations Human Rights Committee.[49]

For current purposes it is probably sufficient to point out that, in their totality, the extra-jurisdictional precedent cited in *Knight* does not demonstrate a coherent or consistent approach to the time served issue. Indeed, Justice Breyer concedes that 'not all foreign authority reaches the same conclusion'.[50] The Supreme Court of Zimbabwe had adopted *Soering*, stating that:

> [h]aving regard to the impressive judicial and academic consensus concerning the death row phenomenon, the prolonged delays and harsh conditions of incarceration, I am convinced that a sufficient degree of seriousness has been attained as to entitle the applicant to invoke on behalf of the condemned prisoners the protection against inhuman treatment afforded them by ... the Constitution[51]

Likewise, the Indian Supreme Court considered it:

> well established that a prisoner cannot be tortured or subjected to unfair or inhuman treatment. It is a logical extension of the self same principle that the death sentence, even if justifiably imposed, cannot be executed if supervening events make its execution harsh, unjust or unfair. A prisoner who has experienced living death for years on end is entitled to invoke the jurisdiction of this Court for examining the question whether, after all the agony and torment he has been subjected to, it is just and fair to allow the sentence of death to be executed.[52]

---

43 *ibid*, 996.

44 *supra*, n22.

45 *Kindler v. Minister of Justice* [1990] 2 SCR 779.

46 *Sher Singh v. State of Punjab* AIR 1983 SCR 465.

47 *Catholic Commission for Justice and Peace in Zimbabwe v. Attorney-General* [1993] 1 Zimb LR 239.

48 *supra*, n35.

49 Communication Nos 210/1986 and 225/1987 *Pratt v. Morgan v Jamaica* UN GAOR Hum Rts Comm 44th Session, Supp No 40 at 230 UN Dec A/44/40 (1989).

50 *supra*, n.42, 996.

51 *supra*, n.47, 313–4.

52 *supra*, n.46, 593.

Not all took the same view, however. Prior to the ECtHR's decision in *Soering*, the European Commission of Human Rights had held, by six votes to one, that the risk of *Soering*'s exposure to death row phenomenon, were he to be extradited to Virginia, was not grave enough to amount to inhuman or degrading treatment or punishment (Lillich 1996). The Canadian Supreme Court found itself unable to bar extradition to the United States on grounds of delay or the psychological effects of death row confinement – though it was later to do so[53] – and declared *Soering* limited to its own facts.[54] The United Nations Human Rights Committee had not subscribed either, stating that '[i]n principle prolonged judicial proceeding do not *per se* constitute cruel, inhuman or degrading treatment even if they can be a source of mental strain for prisoners'.[55] It may be surmised, therefore, that Justice Breyer was deploying them in an attempt to show that courts and supra-national bodies outside America had time served in the spotlight. In this way, *Knight* should be viewed, not as prescription, but as a plea to the Supreme Court to tackle a growing problem, albeit one that threatened to undercut the claim that lengthy detention on death row could be deemed, in Eighth Amendment terms, unusual since a long delay was becoming increasingly commonplace as Justice Breyer pointed out:

> the constitutional issue, even if limited to delays of close to 20 years or more, has considerable practical importance. Available statistics indicate that as of two years ago, December 1997, 24 prisoners sentenced to death had been on death row for more than 20 years. At that time 125 prisoners on death row had been sentenced in or before 1980 and therefore may now fall within the relevant category.[56]

Knight also saw a more explicit articulation of the death row phenomenon, the hallmarks of which had been referred to only obliquely in *Elledge* and *Lackey*. Justice Breyer noted that the Supreme Court had, in other cases, made reference to the 'frightful toll'[57] exacted by lengthy incarceration on death row and 'the onset of insanity'[58] pending execution, whilst state courts had cited the 'dehumanizing effects'[59] of lengthy imprisonment in advance of a sentence of death being carried out. Death row phenomenon was addressed again in *Foster v. Florida*[60] which, along with *Knight* in terms of its appeal to the Court on the range of factors applicable to long-term confinement on death row, must represent the high water mark of Justices Stevens and Breyers' attempts to force consideration of

53 *US v. Burns* [2001] 1 SCR 283.
54 *supra*, n.45.
55 *supra*, n.49.
56 *supra*, n.42, 999.
57 *supra*, n16, 288–9.
58 *Solesbee v. Balkcom* 339 U.S. 9, 14 (1950).
59 *People v. Anderson* 6 Cal 3d 628, 629 (1972).
60 537 U.S. 990 (2002).

time served. Justice Breyer cast the petitioner's 27 years awaiting execution as 'extraordinarily long confinement under sentence of death' which extended 'from late youth to later middle age'[61] and which 'by any standard' was 'unusual'.[62] The length of Foster's incarceration had inevitably caused the sharpening of death row's 'anxieties and uncertainties' and brought 'an immense mental anxiety amounting to a great increase in the offender's punishment'.[63] Moreover, the Supreme Court had long since recognised the deleterious psychological effects of prolonged confinement prior to execution: 'when a prisoner sentenced by a court to death is confined in the penitentiary awaiting the execution of the sentence, one of the most horrible feelings to which he can be subjected during that time is the uncertainty during the whole of it'.[64] If executed now, Breyer argued, Foster would have been 'punished both by death and also by more than a generation spent in death row's twilight'.[65] Despite this, and a reiteration of the fact that 'courts of other nations' had found that 'delays of 15 years or less can render capital punishment degrading, shocking, or cruel',[66] enough to violate 'principles of fundamental justice',[67] the Court was as unmoved as ever. Justice Thomas decried the 'musings' of Justice Breyer in promoting 'this meritless claim'.[68] Had the petitioner wished to end the uncertainties of life on death row, argued Justice Thomas, he could have done so 'by submitting to what the people of Florida deemed him to deserve'.[69] 'Moreover', he added, 'this judgment would not have been made had petitioner not slit Julian Lanier's throat, dragged him into bushes, and then, when petitioner realized that he could hear Lanier breathing, cut his spine'.[70]

For four years after *Foster*, time served was not, again, brought to the attention of the Supreme Court. It has, however, recently risen up the judicial agenda once more, seemingly as a result of successes in abolishing the executions of juveniles and the mentally retarded on the basis of evolving standards of decency and international norms. In its latest appearances, the issue has surfaced indirectly in *Ayers v. Belmontes*[71] and directly in *Smith v. Arizona.*[72] The former presented

61 *ibid*, 993.
62 *ibid*, 992.
63 *ibid*, 993.
64 *Re Medley* 134 U.S. 160, 172 (1890).
65 *supra*, n60, 993.
66 *ibid*, 992.
67 *ibid*, 993.
68 *ibid*, 990.
69 *ibid*, 991.
70 *ibid.*
71 127 S.Ct. 469 (2006). Page numbers refer to slip opinion, docket number 05-493.
72 552 US ___ (2007). Page numbers refer to slip opinion, docket number 07-5847. Another recent, related manifestation of Justice Breyer's tilting at the time served windmill arose in *Allen v Ornoski* 546 US ___ (2006) (Docket 05-8369). Here he dissented from the Supreme Court's denial of certiorari with regard to Clarence Allen, a 76 year-old murderer

a narrow question for the Supreme Court, namely whether, under a provision of California's Penal Code known as Factor K, the jury in the sentencing phase of Fernando Belmontes' trial had been properly directed on mitigation prior to imposing a sentence of death for the first-degree murder of nineteen year old Steacy McConnell some 25 years earlier. In *Lockett v. Ohio*[73] the Court decreed that a death penalty statute which unduly restricted the presentation of mitigating evidence was incompatible with the Eighth Amendment's prohibition of cruel and unusual punishment, but here California's jury instruction was found not to prevent the consideration of such evidence where a defendant sought life imprisonment rather than execution. Belmontes' death sentence was, thus, reinstated. The decision did not spring any particular surprises since Factor K had previously been tested for constitutional soundness by the Supreme Court and passed fit.[74] What was notable about *Ayers* was the dissent of Justice Stevens, which, as well as indicating its disagreement with the substance of the majority's decision on the basis that Factor K caused the jury 'significant residual confusion',[75] suggested that the quarter of a century Belmontes had spent awaiting execution was punishment enough, with little to be gained by proceeding to put him to death.[76]

Unlike *Ayers*, inordinate delay formed the basis of the petition in *Smith v. Arizona.* Smith was one of the longest-serving death row prisoners in the United States, having first been sentenced to death in 1977. He had appealed successfully and been permitted to present new evidence at a further sentencing hearing in 1979, at which he again received the death penalty. His death sentence was overturned once more in 1999 but reinstated in 2004. In the instant case, the explicit contention was that 'evolving standards of decency'[77] in the United States would render unconstitutional his execution after the length of time he had served on death row – some 30 years, as opposed to the average of 12 years 3 months (Snell 2006, 11). The significance of the fact that Smith's claim was based on 'evolving standards of decency' will be addressed shortly but, in terms of the outcome here, the Court disagreed and denied certiorari over Justice Breyer's dissent. Breyer highlighted the 'serious constitutional question'[78] that arose and stated that Smith could 'reasonably claim'[79] that his execution at this stage would

---

incarcerated on death row for 23 years. Justice Breyer's short dissent argued that Allen's circumstances raised a 'significant question' as to whether his execution would constitute cruel and unusual punishment but time served was but one factor briefly mentioned, along with the seemingly more weighty matters of Allen's blindness, diabetes and the fact that he was wheelchair-bound.

73 438 U.S. 586 (1978).

74 *Boyde v. California* 494 US 370 (1990) and *Brown v. Payton* 544 US 133 (2005).

75 *supra*, n. 71, 2 (Breyer's dissent).

76 *ibid.*

77 *Trop v. Dulles* 356 US 86, 101 (1958).

78 *supra*, n. 71, 1 (Breyer's dissent).

79 *ibid.*

be unusual, certainly in view of the fact that the delay seemed to be attributable to the state's 'constitutionally defective' sentencing proceedings.[80]

A number of themes emerge from the cases outlined above. Justices Stevens and Breyer have addressed the purposes of punishment, the nature of death row confinement, the length of death row confinement, the demands of modern standards of decency and attitudes prevailing beyond America's jurisdictional borders. Through *Lackey*, *Foster*, *Knight*, *Elledge*, *Gomez*, *Ayers* and *Smith*, therefore, time served has been pitched as a matter of both domestic law and of international or, perhaps more correctly, 'foreign' norms. It is readily apparent that consideration of the issues on both, or either, of these bases would entail the Supreme Court entering a tangled jurisprudential thicket of substantial proportions. In adjudicating on the Eighth, the Court is clearly a site of tension, between the members of its own bench, between itself and Congress, and itself and the states, between the norms generated by its own jurisprudence and those generated by the international community and between past and present constitutional adjudication. As a result, petitioners frequently find themselves occupying and operating in the uncomfortable space between America's democratically legitimised fidelity to the death penalty in principle and the Supreme Court's commitment to an evolving Constitution in practice. *Lackey* petitioners are no different in this regard. In what follows, the themes identified above are examined more closely in a bid to test their strength as foundations for time served as a species of cruel and unusual punishment under the Eighth Amendment. We will begin by addressing the significance of 'evolving standards' and their relationship with the norms of the international community.

The Significance of 'Evolving Standards' and Foreign Norms in Eighth Amendment Jurisprudence

To all intents and purposes, the United States appears obstinately defiant in the face of international condemnation of its retention of the right to execute its criminals. Seen in the context of the legislative branch's persistent failure to ratify international provisions directed at abolition, and passing of legislation expanding its remit over capital punishment (Aarons 1998), it may seem that such provisions have little to contribute to the demise of the American death penalty. Amman notes that, in general, there is 'no seamless history of isolationist decision making' and a 'receptivity to consulting external norms' but concedes that all the Supreme Court Justices have a tendency to blow hot and cold with regard to favouring the use of foreign norms (Amman 2004, 603). Whilst the Supreme Court has long since

80 *ibid.*

decreed that duly ratified treaties[81] and customary international law[82] may assume the status of federal law, that domestic statutes should always be interpreted in conformity with treaty obligations,[83] and has, on many occasions, concluded that the jurisprudence of the world community may be relevant to American adjudication (Calabresi and Zimdahl 2005; Amman 2004; Koh 2002; Martin 2001; Schabas 1998), its approach to foreign norms in death penalty jurisprudence has often been lukewarm at best, and frequently approaches outright hostility.[84] Nevertheless, largely at the instigation of the more liberal justices, such norms are beginning to impact on the Supreme Court's death penalty jurisprudence and, whilst neither their reception nor adoption is a given, international standards have begun to bite. As a result, the argument that 'the American ostrich is finally starting to take its head out of the sand' (Koh 2002, 48) might have some mileage but the most recent Eighth Amendment battles, fought over the execution of the mentally retarded and juveniles, are instructive in identifying the problems that must be overcome if full and legitimate use is to be made of extra-jurisdictional norms.

In determining whether a punishment is cruel and unusual under the Eighth Amendment, the Supreme Court employs a test which is triggered once the Court has satisfied itself that the punishment is not prima facie cruel and unusual, being outlawed at the time the Eighth Amendment was adopted. The test refers to *Trop v. Dulles* requirement that a punishment comports with the 'evolving standards of decency that mark the progress of a maturing society',[85] which involves the Court in an assessment of 'public attitudes concerning a particular sentence – history and precedent history and precedent, legislative attitudes, and the response of

81 *Foster v. Nielson* 27 US (2 Pet) 253, 314 (1829) 'Our Constitution declares a treaty to be the law of the land ... to be regarded ... as equivalent to an act of the legislature'. This outcome is a result of Article VI of the Constitution (the Supremacy Clause) which states 'This Constitution, and the Laws of the United States which shall be made in Pursuance thereof; and all Treaties made, or which shall be made, under the Authority of the United States, shall be the supreme Law of the Land; and the Judges in every State shall be bound thereby, any Thing in the Constitution or Laws of any state to the Contrary notwithstanding'.

82 *The Paquete Habana* 175 US 677, 700 (1900) 'International law is part of our law, ... and where there is no treaty and no controlling executive or legislative act or judicial decision, resort must be had to the customs and usages of civilized nations ... for trustworthy evidence of what the law really is'.

83 *Murray v. Supreme Courthooner Charming Betsy* 6 US (2 Cranch) 64, 118 (1804) 'an act of Congress ought never to be construed to violate the law of nations if any other possible construction remains', though a distinction has emerged between self-executing and non-self executing treaties.

84 See, for example, Justice Scalia in *Lawrence v. Texas* arguing that recourse to foreign norms was 'meaningless', 'dangerous' and reflected the imposition of 'foreign moods, fads, or fashions on Americans' 123 S.Ct. 2472, 2495 (2003).

85 *supra*, n. 77, 100–101.

juries reflected in their sentencing decisions'[86] for particular crimes. The death penalty will survive the Court's scrutiny if it is deemed compatible with those standards, which are to be determined by objective factors 'to the maximum possible extent'.[87] Although optimum weight is given to domestic legislative enactments as the 'clearest and most reliable objective evidence of contemporary values',[88] by no means does the *Trop* test explicitly exclude consideration of the values of the wider world. Indeed, it embraces fully the idea that the Supreme Court should factor prevailing international opinion into its judgments. *Trop* involved a punishment of statelessness for an army deserter and makes clear reference to the outlook of the 'international community of democracies', the fact that 'civilized nations of the world are in virtual unanimity' on the matter and that such punishment was 'universally decried by civilized people'.[89] *Trop* has been used to positive effect in a number of instances. The Court has, for example, made reference to 'the climate of international opinion concerning the acceptability of a particular punishment'[90] in barring execution for the rape of an adult woman and cited 'international opinion'[91] when considering whether a death sentence was an appropriate punishment for a person who arguably lacked *mens rea*. More recently *Trop's* 'evolving standards' test has been employed to import international opinion into consideration of the execution of the mentally retarded and juveniles. What emerges is evidence of a deep division on the Supreme Court bench.

In *Atkins v. Virginia*,[92] and despite relatively youthful precedent to the contrary,[93] the Supreme Court invalidated a Virginia statute that permitted the execution of the mentally retarded. Atkins, a serial violent offender with sixteen convictions, was sentenced to death for robbery and murder in 1997 but contended that his low IQ, of 59, amounted to mental retardation to the extent that he lacked the abilities in reasoning, judgment and self-control characteristic of the morally culpable criminal. On the bases of what it construed as a national consensus against executing the mentally retarded and the overwhelming disapproval of 'the world community',[94] the Supreme Court permitted Atkins, and others like him,[95] to escape execution. The majority's references to world opinion appeared in a footnote that, despite claiming that it was, among several factors, 'by no means

86 *Coker v. Georgia* 433 U.S. 584, 596 (1977).

87 *ibid*, 592.

88 *Penry v. Lynaugh* 492 U.S. 302, 331 (1989).

89 *supra*, n77, 592.

90 *ibid.*

91 *Emmund v. Florida* 458 U.S. 782, 788 (1982).

92 536 U.S. 304 (2002).

93 *supra*, n88.

94 *supra*, n. 92, 317, fn21.

95 Loveland notes that the Court seemingly deliberately omitted to provide guidance 'as to how exactly one should gauge whether a given person was indeed retarded' and predicts that this will 'no doubt provoke much litigation' (2003, 59). The same might also be said of those claiming to be suffering from death row phenomenon.

dispositive',[96] enraged the minority. In separately authored opinions, Chief Justice Rehnquist and Justice Scalia lambasted the majority for adverting to foreign disapproval, with the former 'fail[ing] to see ... how the views of other countries regarding the punishment of their citizens provide any support for the Court's ultimate determination'[97] and the latter awarding 'the Prize for the Court's Most Feeble Effort to fabricate national consensus' to its appeal to, *inter alia*, the views of members of the so-called 'world community' whose practices were 'irrelevant'[98] to American constitutional adjudication. *Atkins* provided a foretaste of what was to come in the undoing of the juvenile death penalty and, once again, supplied evidence of fundamental disagreement between the members of the Supreme Court on the use of foreign norms.

Prior to 2006, the Supreme Court had ruled twice on the constitutionality of the juvenile death penalty and twice declined to do so. In 1988, in *Thompson v. Oklahoma*,[99] it held that the Eighth Amendment barred the execution of those aged 15 and under at the time their crimes were committed. One year later, in *Stanford v. Kentucky*[100] the Court affirmed that the Constitution permitted the execution of 16- and 17-year old offenders. Since 1989, therefore, the line had been drawn at 16. Where the Court declined to revisit the constitutionality of the juvenile death penalty, in both instances the ruling was accompanied by a dissent arguing that the matter was ripe for reconsideration. The *Patterson v. Texas* minority urged the Court to revisit the issue 'at the earliest opportunity'[101] and, more forcefully, in *Re Kevin Nigel Stanford* declared that 'we should put an end to this shameful practice'.[102] The chance to do so came in *Roper v. Simmons*,[103] where the Court finally ruled that the Eighth Amendment barred the execution of offenders aged 18 and under at the time their crime was committed.

In *Stanford v. Kentucky*, the Court made the express claim that extra-jurisdictional approaches to sentencing were redundant in the exercise of gauging domestic conceptions of 'evolving standards of decency' for determining whether particular punishments would pass constitutional muster.[104] Though *Trop* had, for forty years, permitted the identification of evolving standards from both internal and external sources, Amann sees *Stanford* as an attempt by the Supreme Court's conservatives to usher in 'the revival of an interpretive tradition' (Amman 2004, 603), namely one that cleaved closely to the Framers' of the Constitution's original intent and whose focus was intensely domestic. The attempt clearly failed. In *Roper*

96 *supra*, n. 92, 317.
97 *ibid*, 324–5.
98 *ibid*, 347–8.
99 487 U.S. 815.
100 492 U.S. 361 (1989).
101 536 U.S. 984, 985 (2002).
102 537 U.S. 968, 972 (2002).
103 543 U.S. 551 (2005).
104 *supra*, n. 100, 380.

international norms played a much more significant part than they had in *Atkins*, with the majority noting that America was 'alone in a world that has turned its face against the juvenile death penalty' and, whilst not controlling the outcome in the instant case, it was only 'proper'[105] that the overwhelming weight of international opinion should be explicitly acknowledged. No argument was made that foreign law was determinative of the issue, but the majority declared itself content to refer to international jurisprudence to inform its judgment. Among the dissentients, only Justice O'Connor, in her separately authored opinion, agreed that this was the correct approach:

> This nation's evolving understanding of human dignity certainly is neither wholly isolated from, nor inherently at odds with, the values prevailing in other countries. On the contrary, we should not be surprised to find congruence between domestic and international values, especially where the international community has reached clear agreement – expressed in international law or in the domestic laws of individual countries – that a particular form of punishment is inconsistent with fundamental human rights.[106]

This perhaps implies that the Supreme Court had, to all intents and purposes, come to recognise the importance of employing selected international standards as a means of assessing specifically domestic practices and issues but that was argued by the remainder of the *Roper* minority to be an illegitimate tool of American constitutional adjudication.

Constitutional Legitimacy and Foreign Norms

On any reading, mere reference to extra-jurisdictional standards cannot amount to the jettisoning of constitutional norms developed over several hundred years yet, in a classic exposition of American exceptionalism, a trenchant minority grouping, led by Justice Scalia, reserved its most vitriolic condemnation of the majority for its reliance on the international community's attitude to juvenile executions. Being most troubled by the cherry-picking of alien methodologies and solutions simply because they masked, and were tailored to, the liberals' supposed ulterior moral purpose of dismantling the death penalty, the dissentients claimed that this was not reasoned decision-making but 'sophistry',[107] indicating the supremacy of internationally prescribed norms and foreign law that was 'powerful enough to supplant the judgment of the American people'[108] where a misguided Court desired that it should. Amman would appear to agree, noting that the 'dearth of

105 *supra*, n. 103, 577.
106 *ibid*, 605.
107 *ibid*, 627.
108 *ibid*.

methodological guideposts opens courts to the criticism that foreign practice does not really aid deliberation but merely cloaks otherwise unsupported policy decisions in a guise of constitutional legitimacy' (Amman 2004, 604–5).

According to this minority, in its selective and partial attitude to juveniles in *Roper*, the Court had contrived 'to look over the heads of the crowd and pick out its friends',[109] that error being compounded by its recourse to international legal standards adopted by countries 'of whatever tyrannical political makeup and with however subservient or incompetent a court system'.[110] For the minority, whilst the Court's recourse to international standards was unacceptable, its 'special reliance' on the laws of the United Kingdom (UK) was 'indefensible' and 'beyond comprehension' given the marked legal, political and social differences between America and the UK that had emerged from the latter's 'submission to the jurisprudence of European courts dominated by continental jurists'.[111] Nevertheless, in Scalia's view, reference to UK jurisprudence was legitimate and necessary, but only to support an originalist reading of the American Constitution, discerning its meaning through the medium of the English Bill of Rights of 1689 and against the 'backdrop'[112] of eighteenth century English law and legal thought. It should be noted, however, that this approach would render *Trop's* evolving standards test futile and cause the substance of the Eighth Amendment to be frozen in the seventeen-hundreds.[113] The Court has, in any case, repeatedly rejected this method of constitutional interpretation ('wrongly' in Scalia's opinion[114]) but, according to the minority, even without falling back on the doctrine of original intent, *Roper* made a 'mockery' of any expectation that life-tenured Supreme Court Justices, in possession of the power to invalidate statutes in determining the meaning of the Constitution, would be 'bound down by strict rules and precedents which serve to define and point out their duty'[115] rather than proceeding on the basis of moral impulses and a desire to conform to the rest of the world.

To seasoned observers of the Supreme Court, the robust quality of the minority opinion demonstrates a customary impatience with the majority's liberal tendencies and with the abolitionist movement. It should not be taken lightly, however, since the Supreme Court's deeply divided approach to the use of international standards in Eighth Amendment jurisprudence, threatens to raise particular difficulties for the development of a time served doctrine in that time served is not so possessed of the straightforward 'yes-no' quality that is readily apparent in relation to the execution of the mentally retarded and juveniles.

---

109 *ibid*, 617.

110 *ibid*, 623.

111 *ibid*, 626–7.

112 *ibid*, 626.

113 As the majority indicated, a strictly originalist reading of the Eighth would, today, permit the execution of seven-year-olds, see, *ibid*, 589.

114 *ibid*, 626.

115 *ibid*, 608.

Time Served and Foreign Norms

Irrespective of whether it is a constitutionally legitimate practice to refer to international norms, it is patently obvious that there existed a coherent and consistent attitude towards those two classes of death row inmates: foreign jurisdictions either executed juveniles and the mentally retarded, or they did not, and the jurisdictions and supra-national bodies that were deemed acceptable as reference points, carefully chosen by the Supreme Court's majority, either did not or had made it clear that the practice was disapproved of. Although the decisions in *Atkins* and *Roper*, in their internationally grounded approaches to evolving standards, may be said to have provided a Trojan horse for time served, as indicated by its use as a basis for the claim in *Smith*, the case of inordinate delay prior to execution may present problems since there are distinct discrepancies in the approaches of the foreign jurisdictions selected for comparative purposes. The discrepancies arise on three levels. Firstly, there is a lack of uniformity with regard the use of the death penalty *per se*. Secondly, the jurisdictions' precedents on the issue of whether it is simply inordinate delay that raises barriers to execution or whether something else – 'time served plus' – is required, suggest that the Supreme Court would need to formally subscribe to the existence of the death row phenomenon which it has, so far, refused to do. Thirdly, the length of delay that provides the tipping point at which commutation should occur is contestable both as a rule of thumb and as a reflection of the availability and integrity of particular jurisdictions' procedural safeguards.

Turning first to the death penalty itself, in *Knight*, one reading of Justice Breyer's jurisdictional jamboree might be that here was an attempt to play the hawks at their own game by not focussing comparative attention solely on abolitionist states in the international sphere. Justice Breyer explicitly included jurisdictions that 'accept or assume the lawfulness of the death penalty'[116] perhaps in an attempt to forestall the inevitable accusation that reference to countries where abolition had already occurred manipulated the apparent international consensus. On closer inspection, however, it is clear that death-qualified jurisdictions also make for unacceptable comparators where they fail to surmount the minority's hurdles regarding the need for their political systems to be democratic and their court systems to be neither servile nor incompetent. As a result, Justice Breyer finds himself in some difficulty with regard to the deployment of foreign norms since none of his comparators would seem to make the grade: broadly speaking, single- and pan-European jurisdictions are deemed unacceptably continental in their approach, whilst those drawn from the wider international community, even though they may be death-qualified and of common law heritage, may not count grounds of institutional quality or will be deemed irrelevant because their norms, expressed in international instruments, represent a consensus to which America has not formally subscribed.

116 *supra*, n. 42, 995.

As has been indicated above, the only satisfactory comparison for Justice Scalia is with post-revolutionary England but Justices Stevens and Breyer are seemingly wise to this tactical device and its deployment as a shield for the continuance of capital punishment. Their claim that neither the Framers nor their English contemporaries would have contemplated lengthy delays between sentencing and execution appears to be designed to divest the originalist argument of any force in resisting consideration of the time served issue. In some respects, it also grants greater persuasive authority to the Caribbean decisions of *Pratt* and *Riley* since the reasoning there was firmly grounded in the English Bill of Rights. That said, the dangers of this approach are all too clear since any appeal to originalism has the potential either to undo current Eighth Amendment jurisprudence or cause it to stagnate. On the former point, the Justices themselves recognise the hazards. Justice Brennan urged caution, stating that:

> during Colonial times, pillorying, branding, and cropping and nailing of the ears were practiced in this country. Thus if we were to turn blindly to history for answers to troubling constitutional questions, we would have to conclude that these practices would withstand challenge under the cruel and unusual clause of the Eighth Amendment (Brennan 1986, 327).

And on the latter point, Greenberg and Litman note that '[t]he combination of originalism's basic force and its apparent vulnerability in the face of constitutionally suspect traditional practices results in an odd stalemate: each side of the originalism debate seems to acknowledge the theoretical power of originalism while rejecting, or shying away from, its supposed implications' (Greenberg and Litman 1998, 571) Despite the appeal to originalism as a means of providing a foreign (namely, English) precedent-based justification for the Supreme Court's consideration of the time served issue, as a matter of domestic law it might prove a defective and, ultimately, unusable conduit because it ousts the norms of 'the international community of democracies' and 'evolving standards' from the Court's purview, which could be more damaging in the long-run. Moreover, it is apparent that Caribbean precedent may no longer provide a stable foundation for time served.

In *Pratt*, in reaching its conclusion that prolonged detention on death row was incompatible with the Jamaican Constitution, the Privy Council had canvassed and relied largely upon the same international opinion as Justices Stevens and Breyer in *Knight*. The effects have been dramatic. According to Helfer, in Caribbean jurisdictions, *Pratt* 'radically altered perceptions of the Privy Council among government officials, local judges, and some legal elites, who condemned its 'revolutionary' break from past jurisprudence, its usurpation of Caribbean legislative powers, and the 'great dislocation' it engendered in 'the system of the administration justice'. The Court's stature also 'declined among the Caribbean public' (Helfer 2002, 1872). These issues aside, the practical impact of the decision was to cause the 'near de facto abolition' (Helfer 2002, 1874) of the death penalty due to the 'unduly optimistic' (Helfer 2002, 1874) timetable it set for both national and supra-national review and the exploitation of that timetable by capital defendants, no doubt encouraged by the Privy Council's further statement that '[i]f the appellate procedure enables the prisoner to prolong the appellate hearings over a period of years, the fault is to be attributed to the appellate system that permits such delay and not to the prisoner who takes advantage of it'.[117] It may, of course, be considered a positive outcome, that abolition was, to all intents and purposes, achieved but subsequent events must surely give cause for concern since *Pratt* was partially responsible for propelling the Caribbean towards the severing of its ties with the Privy Council, the creation of the Caribbean Court of Justice as its final court of appeal and instances of withdrawals from human rights treaties.[118] As Helfer notes, by invoking the need for maintaining public order and security and upholding the domestic rule of law, Caribbean governments were enabled 'not only able to amass popular support ... but also to shore up regional backing for capital punishment and resistance to external pressures' (Helfer 2002, 1899). As a result, it becomes apparent that the strategy of invoking international norms can be counterproductive where it causes resistance or intransigence and further retreat from the international community's development of overriding human rights standards. These are both dangers to which Supreme Court is exposed by the drive for a time served doctrine based on foreign norms.

The second difficulty relates to whether a time served doctrine emerges with sufficient coherence internationally to enable it to be employed as a legitimate reference point. It must be said that, of the jurisdictions referred to in *Lackey* claims to date, there is no discernible temporal standard by which such claims have succeeded or failed. The Zimbabwe Supreme Court has prohibited the executions of prisoners with six years and three years on death row.[119] The Privy Council has taken a position whereby executions occurring after a five-year delay are unlawful.[120] The Indian Supreme Court has ruled that eight years between sentencing and execution violates the Indian Constitution and has overruled another of its judgments that a two-year delay is sufficient for commutation to occur.[121] No absolute or unqualified rule can be deduced from these cases since each court has emphasised that other factors must be taken into account in gauging whether a death sentence should be vacated. This is because inordinate delay

117 *supra*, n. 22, paragraph 33B–D.

118 Jamaica withdrew from the First Optional Protocol of International Covenant on Civil and Political Rights in October 1997, removing the right of individual petition to the UN Human Rights Committee.

Trinidad and Tobago withdrew then re-acceded with a reservation as to the competence of the Human Rights Committee on death penalty matters. Trinidad has also withdrawn from the American Convention on Human Rights.

119 *supra*, n. 47.

120 *supra*, n. 22.

121 *supra*, n. 46.

between sentencing and execution would appear, by itself, insufficient to trigger commutation.

Those factors which have been articulated by these courts are of two types, both of which add a qualitative dimension to the purely quantitative measurement of time served. The first consideration beyond pure time is the nature of death row confinement itself (including incidences of death row phenomenon) and the second, post-sentencing procedures available to death row inmates in different jurisdictions. Aarons refers to the 'procedural morass surrounding the inordinate delay claim' (Aarons 1998, 1) and the 'crazy quilt'[122] of post-conviction procedures and death row confinement in the United States alone would make legitimate domestic comparison difficult. The difficulties are, of course, exacerbated when international norms are added into the mix. Lillich, for example, whilst supporting the internationalisation of human rights law, conceded that normative consistency might be an issue, and cited the United Nations' concern that '[a]s standards proliferate and new treaty bodies are created the risks of inconsistency will grow. Confusion and diminished credibility could result' (Lillich 1996, 701). Such is the variation in procedural and penal forms, and individual prisoners' responses to them, it is contended here that the argument for the development of a time served doctrine in the United States simply cannot be advanced by reference to international procedural norms, since the rough comparability of comparative standards generally required by even the most liberal of Supreme Court Justices for legitimate comparison is absent.

With regard to death row confinement as a constituent element of 'time served plus', a similar conclusion might be reached, namely that foreign precedent is unlikely to hold sway. Lillich maintained that, in relation to the death row phenomenon, 'a cross-fertilization process is well underway' (Lillich 1996, 702). But it is argued here that three significant problems arise. Firstly, and probably fatally, the Supreme Court has consistently dismissed the idea of a formal condition classified as the 'death row phenomenon' and the idea that, if there were, it might have any substantive constitutional impact. In *Knight*, Justice Thomas's response to Justice Breyer was to state that 'were there any such support in our own jurisprudence [for invalidating death sentences based on the death row phenomenon], it would be unnecessary for proponents of the claim to rely on the European Court of Human Rights, the Supreme Court of Zimbabwe, the Supreme Court of India, or the Privy Council'.[123] Secondly, there is little normative consistency with regard to its exact substance, the weight that it carries and the weighing of its constituent elements *inter se*. Death row phenomenon's psychological terminology comprises 'stress', 'anxiety' and 'tension'. If that is sufficient to render the death row inmate insane in all likelihood he would be caught by *Ford v Wainwright*'s prohibition on executing the insane.[124] If insufficient, the inmate might then be medicated in accordance

122 *Kansas v Marsh* 548 U.S. (2006), Justice Scalia dissenting.

123 *supra*, n. 42, 990.

124 477 U.S. 399 (1986).

with the Supreme Court's confirmation of Arkansas's ability to administer drugs to Charles Singleton, a mentally ill death row inmate, to render him competent for execution.[125] Should the psychological impact of death row confinement be dealt with in either of these ways that would tend to suggest that the time served issue reverts to a matter of pure time, discussed in more detail below. Thirdly, there is a concern over the 'thin end of the wedge' in that the death row phenomenon may be difficult to confine. Yin makes the point that in the United States, onerous physical and mental conditions might cause 20,000 non-capital inmates to fall into the embrace of the death row phenomenon since they serve their sentences in identical conditions to capital inmates (Yin 2005, 1). He argues that *Soering*'s identification of harsh conditions on death row, namely a small cell, little recreation, limited access to common areas and facilities such as a library or infirmary and routine handcuffing and shackling, are replicated for lifers in America's 36 Supermax facilities (Yin 2005, 20–22). Moreover, where a sentence is handed down of life with the possibility of parole (LWP), Yin sees a sufficiently clear analogy with living under a sentence of death to suggest that the death row phenomenon simply could not be confined to inmates under threat of execution:

> [t]o the extent that the death row inmate may suffer special stress from being repeatedly exposed to death warrants that are vacated and re-obtained for later dates, a similar phenomenon occurs with LWP inmates: they may get repeated parole hearings, only to be denied parole each time ... Of course, the exact cause of the uncertainty looks different; potential execution in one instance, compared to potential release in the other ... But this is dependent on how one characterizes the baseline by which one measures the anguish. Arguably, uncertainty about release from prison is more anguishing to the prisoner, since it is the difference between dying in prison and being freed. Uncertainty about execution, on the other hand, lies in wondering if one will die in prison of natural causes or violence at the hands of other inmates, or on a gurney due to a lethal injection (Yin 2005, 15–17).

Yin takes the view that excessive delay is miscast as a 'negative' (Yin 2005, 13), that the death row phenomenon requires a counterintuitive assumption to be made that conditions on death row are 'worse than dying immediately' (Yin 2005, 1) and that, ultimately, the suffering of inmates is 'so individualized as to be beyond the ability of the courts' (Yin 2005, 19) either to generalise a phenomenon or keep it from escaping the death row compound.

That is not to say, however, that what is left in place is a system under which the duration and nature of the time a person spends on death row should remain free of constitutional scrutiny since there may be some scope for the issues to be addressed on the basis of domestic law alone, and it is on this that attention will now be focussed.

---

125 319 F3d 1018 (8th Cir 2003) and *Singleton v. Norris* 124 S.Ct. 74 (2003).

Lackey Claims as a Matter of Pure Time

In *Lackey* Justice Stevens concluded his dissent with an invitation to the lowers courts to 'serve as laboratories'[126] in testing the issue 'with its legal complexity and ... potential for far-reaching consequences'.[127] At Justice Stevens' bidding, therefore, the legitimacy of the *Lackey* claim has been addressed by the lower courts but in no instance has the claim succeeded. In *Knight*, concurring in denial of certiorari, Justice Thomas considered that, given the lower courts' resounding rejection of the *Lackey* claim as a means of challenging a death sentence on Eighth Amendment grounds, the Supreme Court should 'consider the experiment concluded'.[128] What this fails to reveal, however, is that, despite consistently rejecting *Lackey* claims, state and federal court judgments had been divided in their approaches, and the judges of those courts divided over whether the *Lackey* claim, in general, has merit.

Myers identifies five classes of case in the lower courts where *Lackey* claims have arisen and been dismissed. Four classes of case may be dealt with in short order in that, firstly, the claim was rejected out of hand; secondly, disposed of on grounds of procedural defect; thirdly, dismissed for want of a factual basis or, fourthly, denied due to lack of precedential support (Myers 2002, 647). The remaining class of case – where the lower courts proceeded to discuss the merits – warrants closer inspection. Where the merits have been addressed, Myers further identifies three forms of reasoning that inevitably led to the claim being rejected. First he notes that courts may find compelling reasons for the delay. Second, they may find that delays caused by way of satisfying the demands of the Eighth Amendment simply cannot violate it. Third, they may find that the delay was not attributable to the state and, as such, was not actionable (Myers 2002, 647). These three reasons form the core of the time served issue as it might be determined domestically. They make it difficult to resolve but, constitutionally, are firmly anchored in home-grown jurisprudence and practice such that, if resolution could be achieved, it would be achieved with the attendant stamp of legitimacy that the mechanical reception of foreign norms so lacks, even though those foreign norms may have arisen out of the consideration of generally similar, yet jurisdictionally particular, issues.

Myers finds that where courts find compelling reasons for delay, they are taking a 'no stone left unturned' (Myers 2002, 659) approach to the matter of the state executing its death row prisoners. This form of reasoning casts the delay not as torture but as 'added protection for the prisoner's benefit' (Myers 2002, 659)

126 supra, n. 7, 1045. Justice Stevens makes reference to McCray v. New York 461 U.S. 961 (1983) where, at 963, the Supreme Court declared that novel issues would permit state and federal courts to 'serve as laboratories in which the issue receives further study before it is addressed by this Court'.

127 *ibid.*

128 *supra*, n. 42, 993.

because it maximises his chances of obtaining relief, an ideal that is both practically and jurisprudentially grounded. On the one hand, it see the courts fulfilling their function by minimising error and, on the other, identifies the courts abiding by *Trop's* evolving standards test which supplies death row petitioners with plenty of opportunities to test their convictions and sentences.

The second form of reasoning – that the delay was caused by the demands of the Eighth Amendment – cuts to the heart of the Constitution. Justice Thomas takes the view that it is 'incongruous to arm capital defendants with an arsenal of constitutional claims with which they may delay their executions, and simultaneously to complain when executions are invariably delayed'[129] and sees the emergence of the *Lackey* claim as a consequence of the delays caused by the Supreme Court's own 'Byzantine death penalty jurisprudence'.[130] That view has been echoed in the lower courts, with the Fourth Circuit declaring that it made a:

> mockery of our system of justice ... for a convicted murderer, who, through his own interminable efforts of delay and systemic abuse has secured the almost-indefinite postponement of his sentence, to then claim that the almost-indefinite postponement renders his sentence unconstitutional. This is the crowning argument on behalf of those who have politicized capital punishment even within the judiciary. With this argument, we have indeed entered the theater of the absurd, where politics disguised as 'intellectualism' occupies center stage, no argument is acknowledged to be frivolous, and common sense and judgment play no role. And while this predictable plot unfolds with our acquiescence, if not our participation, we lament the continuing decline in respect for the courts and for the law.[131]

What is highlighted via the *Lackey* claim, therefore, is not only the direct tension within the Constitution, the location of which is the Eighth Amendment, but the parents of which are the due process clauses of the Fifth and Fourteenth Amendments, but also the politically and legally charged nature of capital punishment. Neither the Fifth nor the Fourteenth Amendment precludes the death penalty[132] but their demands in relation to due process emerge in the jurisprudence

129 *supra*, n42, 992.

130 *ibid*, 991.

131 *Turner v. Jabe* 58 F3d 924 (4th Cir 1995) *per* Judge Littig.

132 The Fifth Amendment states 'No person shall be held to answer for a capital, or otherwise infamous crime, unless on a presentment or indictment of a Grand Jury, except in cases arising in the land or naval forces, or in the Militia, when in actual service in time of War or public danger; nor shall any person be subject for the same offense to be twice put in jeopardy of life or limb; nor shall be compelled in any criminal case to be a witness against himself, nor be deprived of life, liberty, or property, without due process of law; nor shall private property be taken for public use, without just compensation'. The Fourteenth Amendment states 'All persons born or naturalized in the United States, and subject to the jurisdiction thereof, are citizens of the United States and of the State wherein they reside. No State shall make or enforce any law which shall abridge the privileges or immunities

of the Eighth Amendment and, in the case of time served, the possibility arises of the Supreme Court being hoisted by its own procedural petard. As Hedges notes, there is something of a dilemma here in that many years spent on death row prior to execution might well constitute cruel and unusual punishment, yet 'executing prisoners at optimum levels of "efficiency" is at best an infringement upon their due process rights and at worst an arbitrary infliction of a punishment that cannot be undone' (Hedges 2001, 21). Moreover, it is not within the gift of the courts to force a choice of one sacred constitutional guarantee over another (Feldman 1999, 218) since 'the right to pursue due process of law must not be set off against the right to be free of inhuman treatment'.[133] On the face of it, therefore, there is seemingly little that can be done to effect a resolution of the constitutional tension but the third form of reasoning may provide the means by which to do so. That third form of reasoning, when employed in the lower courts, sees *Lackey* claims being rejected because the state did not intentionally or negligently cause the delay (Myers 2002, 660). Myers notes that this is a 'reoccurring theme' in district and circuit court cases and is, essentially, 'an exercise in fault attribution' (Myers 2002, 660) which arises out of a means of approaching the time served issue proposed by Justice Stevens in *Lackey*.

The Stevens 'calculus'[134] requires a court to examine what the petitioner is claiming is an inordinate delay between sentencing and execution from three different perspectives. First, the court must assess whether the delay has occurred as a consequence of abuse by the prisoner resulting from the exploitation of the judicial system or by 'repetitive and frivolous filings'.[135] Second, the court must distinguish the foregoing from the prisoner's 'legitimate exercise of his right to review'.[136] Third, the court must examine the extent to which delay may be attributed to 'negligence or deliberate action by the State'.[137] Clearly, the first two elements of the calculus might circumvent the problems arising out of petitioners perversely prolonging their time on death row in order to substantiate a *Lackey* claim, as well as providing a degree of resolution to the internal constitutional tension alluded to above. The results of applying tests one and two of the Stevens calculus would, therefore, suggest that a *Lackey* claim could only succeed where the state is responsible for inordinate delay between sentencing and execution.

On the face of it, the calculus seems to provide a reasonable basis on which to found a time served doctrine that is sufficiently robust to raise a constitutional bar to the execution of a small number of petitioners. Justice Breyer's dissent in *Foster*

---

of citizens of the United States; nor shall any State deprive any person of life, liberty, or property, without due process of law; nor deny to any person within its jurisdiction the equal protection of the laws'.

133 *District Attorney for Suffolk Dist v. Watson* (1980) 411 NE 2d 1274, 1283.

134 *supra*, n. 7, 1045.

135 *ibid.*

136 *ibid.*

137 *ibid.*

reveals that, at the millennium, 'there were only eight prisoners in the United States who had been under sentence of death for 24 years or more, and none who had been on death row for 27 years. Now we know there is at least one'.[138] This is not suggestive of the floodgates being opened as a result of time served being given Eighth Amendment status but, in reality, matters are not so straightforward. Where the calculus, to all intents and purposes, appears to be aimed at providing an avenue of relief to a few death row inmates who have suffered inordinate delay at the hands of the state, Aarons believes that, in most cases, the lapse between sentencing and execution is almost wholly attributable to the state for, *inter alia*, want of facilities, difficulties in securing the assistance of competent counsel, foot-dragging by counsel, uncertainties regarding the substance of criminal and constitutional law and the failure of courts to address thoroughly the claims raised by capital defendants, which result in further litigation and increased delay (Aarons 1998, 48). In all likelihood, therefore, there is a potentially large number of *Lackey* claims but, providing petitioners with 'yet another ground on which to challenge and delay execution',[139] may serve to create further problems. It is, of course, an obvious point that if *Lackey* claims are available then an incentive may be said to have been provided to petitioners to prolong their death row incarceration. Ostensibly, the Stevens calculus can deal with this but if Aarons is correct, that the state is usually at fault in the case of delay, then state courts might themselves be provided with a perverse incentive 'to give short shrift to a capital defendant's legitimate claims in order to avoid potential violation of the Eighth Amendment' on grounds of inordinate delay (Hedges 2001, 579). In that sense, therefore, the *Lackey* claim undoes itself and, potentially, much of the procedural substance of the Fifth, Fourteenth and Eighth Amendments. Paradoxically, perhaps, were the courts to expedite both mandatory and collateral post-sentencing review, the *Lackey* claim might never arise since inmates would be denied the opportunity to accrue sufficient time on death row for the claim to ripen. Expedited procedures might therefore be deemed to be the answer to the *Lackey* conundrum but would place at increased risk, through the courts' use of *Lackey*-dodging streamlined procedures, many more death row inmates than those who have merely experienced a long delay between sentencing and execution:

> One could argue that procedural reliability does not require a system that allows multiple direct, postconviction and habeas appeals. Yet courts overturn more than two-thirds of all death sentences on appeal because of serious reversible error; a full one-third of these errors surface only on federal habeas appeal, after the defendant has exhausted the lengthy state appellate process. This dramatic error rate indicates that the extensive appellate process is necessary to achieve the accuracy and procedural reliability that the Constitution requires (Anon 2000, 651).

138 *supra*, n. 60, 992.
139 *supra*, n. 42, 992.

In this sense, the *Lackey* claim might, ultimately, cause more harm, and a more 'wantonly and ... freakishly imposed'[140] death penalty, than it avoids.

Conclusion

On the face of it, the *Lackey* claim has much to commend it as a means of further limiting the reach of the death penalty in the United States based on *Gregg v Georgia's* law of diminishing returns in relation to the deterrent and retributive functions of capital punishment, the intentions of the Framers of the Constitution and *Trop v Dulles* evolving standards test. Such an approach has gained currency in the international arena but deep divisions on the Supreme Court bench and a prevailing hostility to extra-jurisdictional norms in Eighth Amendment jurisprudence, indicate that the approach of the international community seems unlikely to be adopted, at least in the short-term. That is not to say, however, that time served will be jettisoned merely as a result of the prevailing stand-off between the Court's abolitionists and its death penalty hawks since the reception of international norms is, in this instance, complicated by the instability, incoherence and lack of unanimity that is apparent in the foreign precedents to which Justices Stevens and Breyer have chosen to refer in support of a time served doctrine. There is also an overriding need to maintain constitutional and democratic integrity. It has been argued here that, ultimately, time served as a barrier to execution must reflect specific jurisdictional procedural guarantees but that, in the case of the United States, those guarantees could not, without diluting the totality of constitutional protection afforded to death row inmates, survive in their current form. In order for the *Lackey* claim to be given life therefore, the Supreme Court would be required to divest the Fifth and Fourteenth Amendments, and much of the Eighth, of both substance and significance and would run the risk of placing the administration of the death penalty in its pre-*Furman* state. As Justice O'Connor pointed out in *Roper*, the Supreme Court's increasingly 'frequent and disruptive reassessments'[141] of Eighth Amendment precedent threaten to subvert the very notion of 'clear, predictable and uniform constitutional standards'.[142] Where these reassessments are based on equivocal evolving standards of the international community, Loveland's argument, that the Supreme Court engages in 'institutional' and 'deliberative disenfranchisement' (Loveland 2003, 56) because it legislates and does so in a democratic vacuum, through a process utterly denuded of the symbols and signs of representative law-making, becomes all the more pertinent.

140 *supra*, n. 16, 310.

141 *supra*, n. 103, 8 (O'Connor's dissent).

142 *ibid.*

Bibliography

Aarons, D. (1998), 'Getting Out of This Mess: Steps Toward Addressing and Avoiding Inordinate Delay in Capital Cases', 89 *J Crim L & Criminology* 1.

Amman, D. (2004), 'Raise the Flag and Let it Talk: On the Use of External Norms in Constitutional Decision-Making', 2(4) *IJCL* 597.

Anon (2000), 'Recent Cases: People v Simms', 114 *Harvard Law Review* 648.

Bell, A. (1996), 'McKenzie v Day: Is Twenty Years on Death Row Curel and Unusual Punishment?', 26 *Golden Gate U L Rev* 41.

Brennan, W. (1986), 'Constitutional Adjudication and The Death Penalty: A View from the Court', 100 *Harvard Law Review* 313.

Brossart, J. (2003), 'Death is Different: An Essay Considering the Propriety of Utilizing Foreign Case Law in Eighth Amendment Jurisprudence', 29 *U Drayton L Rev* 345.

Connolly, M. (1997), 'Better Never Than Late: Prolonged Stays on Death Row Violate the Eighth Amendment', 23 *Criminal and Civil Confinement* 101.

Crocker, D. (1998), 'Extended Stays: Does Lengthy Imprisonment on Death Row Undermine the Goals of Capital Punishment', 1 *Journal of Gender, Race and Justice* 555.

Feldman, J. (1999), 'A Death Row Incarceration Calculus: When Prolonged Death Row Imprisonment Becomes Unconstitutional', 40 *Santa Clara L Rev* 187.

Flynn, K. (1997), 'The "Agony of Suspense": How Protracted Death Row Confinement Gives Rise to an Eighth Amendment Claim of Cruel and Unusual Punishment', 54 *Wash & Lee L Rev* 291.

Greenberg, M. and Litman, H. (1997), 'The Meaning of Original Meaning', 86 *Geo L J* 571.

Hatchard, J. (1993), 'Delay and the Death Sentence: The Zimbabwean Approach', 37(2) *Journal of African Law* 185.

Hedges, R. (2001), 'Justices Blind: How the Rehnquist Court's Refusal to Hear a Claim for Inordinate Delay of Execution Undermines Its Death Penalty Jurisprudence', 74 *S Cal L Rev* 577.

Helfer, L. (2002), 'Overlegalizing Human Rights: International Relations Theory and the Commonwealth Caribbean Backlash against Human Rights Regimes', 102(7) *Columbia Law Review* 1932.

Highet, K., Kahale, G. and Phillips, B. (1994), 'Pratt & Morgan v Attorney General for Jamaica', 88(4) *American Journal of International Law* 775.

Hudson, B. (2000), 'Does the Death Row Phenomenon Violate a Prisoner's Human Rights Under International Law?', 11 *EJIL* 831.

Koh, H. (2002), 'Paying "Decent Respect" to World Opinion on the Death Penalty', 35 *UC Davis L Rev* 1085.

Kozinski, A. and Gallagher, S. (1995), 'Death: The Ultimate Run-on Sentence', 46 *Case W Res L Rev* 1.

Latzer, B. and Cauthen, J. (2000), 'Capital Appeals Revisited', 84 *Judicature* 64.

Lee, Y. (2005), 'The Constitutional Right Against Excessive Punishment', 91 *Virginia Law Review* 677.

Lillich, R. (1996), 'Harmonizing Human Rights Law Nationally and Internationally: The Death Row Phenomenon as a Case Study', 40 *St Louis U L J* 699.

Lillich, R. (1991), 'The Soering Case', 85(1) *American Journal of International Law* 128.

Lillich, R. and Hannum, H. (1985), 'Linkages between International Human Rights and US Constitutional Law', 79(1) *American Journal of International Law* 158.

Loveland, I. [2003], 'Execution of Mentally Retarded Criminals in the United States', Spring *PL* 52.

Myers, K. (2002), 'Practical Lackey: The Impact of Holding Execution After a Long Stay on Death Row Unconstitutional Under Lackey v Texas', 106(3) *Dickinson Law Review* 647.

NAACP (2007), 'Death Row USA', Winter.

Padova, A. (2000), 'Recent Decisions: Thomas Knight v Florida; Carey Dean Moore v Nebraska', 14(2) *Temple Int'l & Comp LJ* 445.

Snell (2006), 'Capital Punishment 2005', Bureau of Justice Statistics Bulletin, December.

Yin (2005), 'Can Death Row Phenomenon be Confined to Death Row Inmates?', University of Iowa Legal Studies Research Paper, No.05–11, February.

Chapter 8

A Crisis of Confidence: Americans' Doubts about the Death Penalty

Richard C. Dieter

Introduction

According to a national public opinion poll (National Omnibus Poll) conducted in 2007 for the Death Penalty Information Center, in Washington D.C., the public is losing confidence in the death penalty.[1] People are deeply concerned about the risk of executing the innocent, about the fairness of the process, and about the inability of capital punishment to accomplish its basic purposes. Most Americans believe that innocent people have already been executed, that the death penalty is not a deterrent to crime, and that a moratorium should be placed on all executions.

Many in America also believe they would be disqualified from serving on a jury in a capital case because of their moral objections. Among women and Catholics, nearly half believe they would be excluded. Two-thirds of black people believe they would be disqualified. Even among those who support the death penalty and believe they would be qualified to serve on a capital jury, the risk of convicting or executing the innocent would make them less likely to vote for a death sentence.

While a majority still support the death penalty in theory, it is becoming irrelevant to many Americans because it is rarely applied, and not always to the worst offenders. Life without parole sentences are becoming more attractive to many Americans, and it is the preferable choice over the death penalty for major subgroups of the population. Two-thirds of Americans do not believe that reforms of the death penalty system will eliminate its problems.

The public's lack of confidence in the death penalty is being echoed by representatives of victims' groups, by former supporters of the death penalty, and in the editorial pages of the nation's newspapers. Although the dissatisfaction with capital punishment has many roots, the common and principal concern heard throughout the country is the risk that innocent people may be caught up with the guilty.

1 Poll Specifications – RT Strategies of Washington, D.C., conducted this National Omnibus Poll on March 8–11, 2007 for the Death Penalty Information Center. The sample was 1,000 adults nationwide, and the margin of error was ±3.1%. DPIC is a non-profit organisation specialising in research and information on capital punishment in the United States.

Poll Results

The Supreme Court has said that the death penalty should reflect the 'conscience of the community',[2] and that its application should be measured against society's 'evolving standards of decency'.[3] In all states, a defendant is entitled to have a jury determine whether he or she is eligible for a death sentence.[4] In almost all states, the jury also makes the crucial decision on the actual sentence. But a recent National Omnibus Poll conducted by RT Strategies for the Death Penalty Information Center in early 2007 indicates that there is a deep divide in the community that is called upon to make such decisions.

Nearly 40% of the public believes that they would be disqualified from serving on a jury in a death penalty case because of their moral beliefs. Over two-thirds (68%) of African-Americans in this survey believe they would be excluded as capital jurors; 48% of women reached the same conclusion, and 47% of Catholics. While these latter numbers are based on sub-samples with a larger margin of error than the whole poll, they point to a problem of unrepresentative capital juries that do not reflect the country's true diversity.

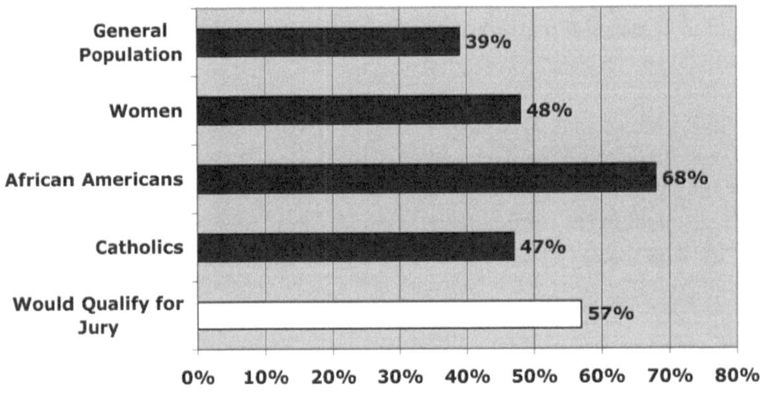

Figure 8.1 Americans' belief that they would be disqualified from capital juries

Jurors in capital cases must be interrogated about their positions on the death penalty. If they are opposed to it in all cases, they will not be permitted to serve. The resultant juries look different than society at large because they will have less minority members, less women, and none of those who represent one side on this divisive issue. If the percentage of those who would be excluded for their views

2 *Witherspoon v. Illinois* 391 U.S. 510, 519 (1968).
3 *Trop v. Dulles* 356 U.S. 86, 101 (1958).
4 *Ring v. Arizona* 536 U.S. 584 (2002).

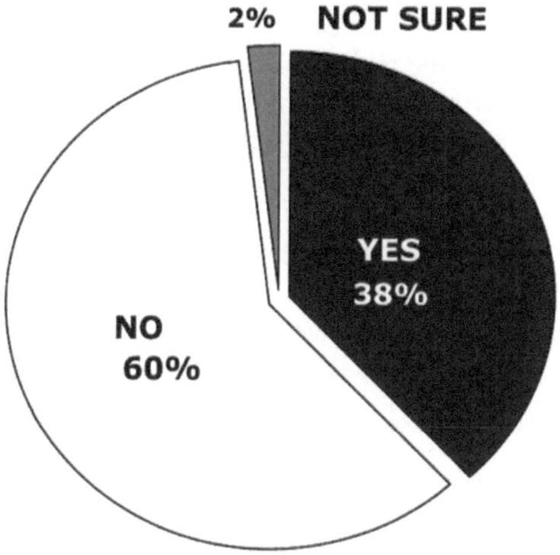

Figure 8.2 Is the death penalty a deterrant to murder?

were miniscule, it might not pose a serious problem. But when the numbers grow to represent nearly half, or even a majority, of significant groups in society, the system runs the danger of being undemocratic.

An Erosion of Confidence

Americans have endorsed the death penalty for generations because they believed it might contribute to saving lives. For a long time, deterrence was the principal reason that Americans gave for their support of capital punishment (Banner 2002). But today, few citizens believe that the death penalty serves as a deterrent. Only 38% of respondents in this recent poll believe that the death penalty is a deterrent; 60% said it was not.

But a larger problem has emerged to challenge the notion that the death penalty saves lives. By a wide margin, the American public believes that the most significant development in the death penalty in recent years has been the advent of DNA testing and the proof that many who were sentenced to death were innocent. The availability of life-without-parole sentences and the exclusion of juveniles from execution were much less significant to the public.

Over 120 people have been freed from death row since 1973 after their convictions were overturned (DPIC's Exoneration List 2007). Many came close to execution before being cleared of all the charges that sent them to death row. In some cases, it was the fortuitous advance of DNA science that led to their exoneration. In other cases, it was the work of journalism students or others outside the legal system who re-investigated what appeared to be closed cases.

In addition to those freed from death row, many have recently been exonerated of non-capital crimes, putting the judicial system further on the defensive. Two hundred people have had their convictions dismissed because of DNA testing since 1989 (Fears 2007, A3). Frequently, the justice system resisted acknowledging the new evidence that was uncovered, even though it pointed to the innocence of the original defendant.

Seeing these repeated mistakes in determining the underlying guilt of those facing execution has sharply eroded the public's confidence in the death penalty. Particularly in this area, the public wants much more assurance that the system works reliably. For many Americans, their patience with the death penalty is wearing thin. Only 39% of the public expressed either complete or 'quite a bit' of confidence that the justice system sentences only the guilty to death.

A strong majority of 75% of those polled believe that we need a higher standard of proof for guilt in death penalty cases. The standard of 'proof beyond a reasonable doubt' may be sufficient when an inmate will still be alive if new evidence overturns his conviction. But before the state should be allowed to execute an individual, a higher degree of confidence that it has charged the right person is required.

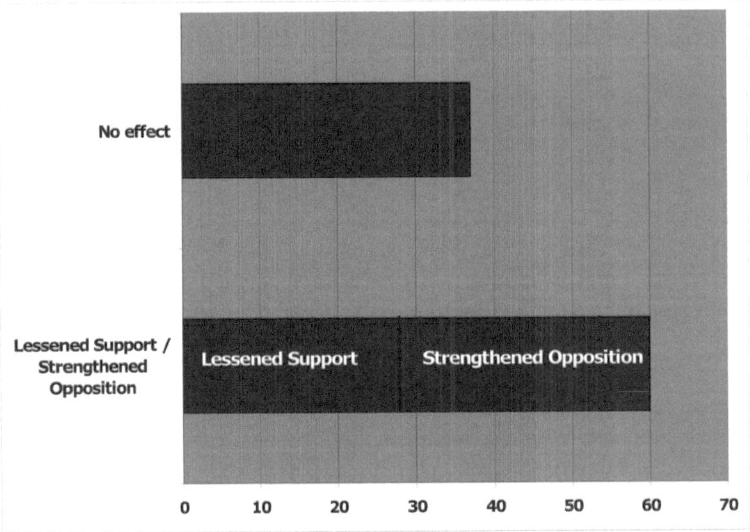

Figure 8.3 Effect of hearing about exonerations on death penalty views

Unfortunately, the search for truth in death penalty cases is obscured by the fact that jurors are chosen from only certain segments of society. Research indicates that those who support the death penalty are also more likely to support the government's case, more likely to believe police testimony and witnesses for the prosecution (Haney and Logan 1994, 75–101). While such sources are often credible, the errors that have occurred in capital cases where innocent people have been wrongly convicted often stem from erroneous identifications and other testimony offered by the state (Morgan 2004, 9). In capital cases it is especially important that people with a wide range of viewpoints critically examine the evidence, but the exclusion of the citizens most likely to be skeptical of the state's evidence makes this goal harder to achieve.

Most Americans have been affected by the news of so many exonerations in death penalty cases. Only 37% said that such news had no effect on their position on the death penalty. Sixty percent of Americans said that these wrongful convictions had either lessened their support for the death penalty or strengthened their already existing opposition.

The Ultimate Error: Executing the Innocent

A similar question regarding the *execution* of possibly innocent defendants also indicated that such information lessens support for the death penalty. And the overwhelming majority of Americans (87%) already believes that the final tragedy has occurred: that innocent people have been executed in recent years.

Figure 8.4 Carlos de Luna

Because courts do not typically provide a forum for determining the innocence of someone who has already been executed, and because states do not pay attorneys to pursue such claims, it is difficult to know how many innocent people have been put to death. Four cases in the past few years that were thoroughly re-investigated after execution indicated a strong likelihood that such mistakes have been made (National Coalition to Abolish the Death Penalty 2006). Larry Griffin was executed in Missouri, Ruben Cantu, Cameron Willingham, and Carlos de Luna (pictured) were executed in Texas. In all four cases, new evidence has emerged that has thrown considerable doubt on their original convictions.

In Griffin's case, the first police officer on the scene has now given a new account of the evidence. Willingham's case was exposed through an investigation by the *Chicago Tribune*. He had been convicted of murder by arson, but now new scientific analysis has questioned whether any arson (and hence any crime) ever occurred.

In de Luna's case, also investigated by the *Chicago Tribune,* another repeat offender now appears to be the likely killer. Ruben Cantu's case, the third of the cases from Texas, was investigated by the *Houston Chronicle*. The former District Attorney who oversaw the prosecution now believes that Cantu was probably innocent and he has apologised for what happened (Pew Forum on Religion and Public Life 2006). An investigation was opened by the new District Attorney in San Antonio. However, this D.A. had served as a judge on Cantu's appeal and signed his death warrant (Houston Chronicle Editorial 2006, 10). This conflict of interest has clouded the investigation.

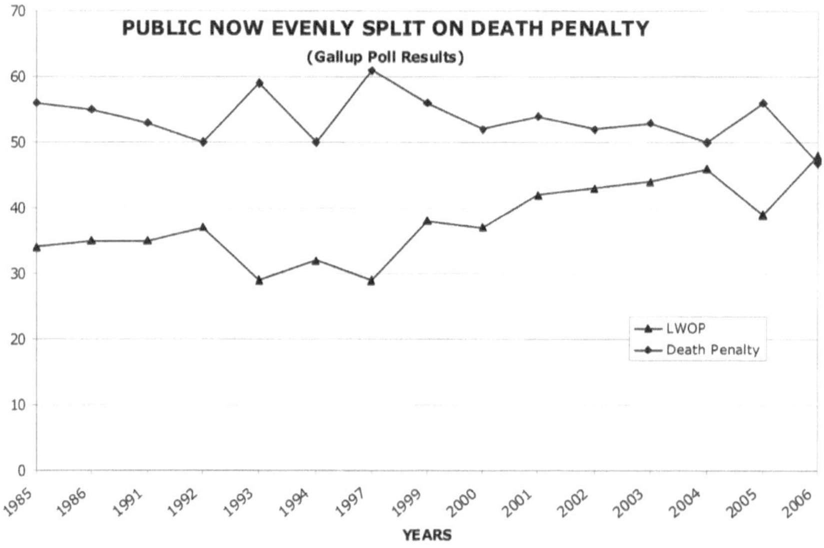

Figure 8.5 Percent of public support for the death penalty for murder

Of those who believe that an innocent person has already been executed, 55% say that has affected their opinion of the death penalty, either making them more skeptical of capital punishment or more opposed to it entirely. Less than a third (31%) of the respondents said that knowing an innocent person may have been executed has had no effect on their death penalty views.

Declining Use of the Death Penalty

One of the apparent results of the declining confidence in the death penalty has been a dramatic drop in death sentences over the past six years. This poll indicates that part of the decline in sentences may be due to less willingness to impose the death penalty because of the innocence issue. Although those chosen to serve on a death penalty jury are more conservative voters, even this group has been affected by the news of exonerations. Of those who believed they qualified for capital jury service, nearly 40% said they would be less likely to vote for a death sentence given what they have heard about exonerations.

Death sentences averaged close to 300 per year during the 1990s. Since then, the number of death sentences per year has dropped about 60%. According to the Bureau of Justice Statistics, there were 128 death sentences in the country in 2005 (Bureau of Justice Statistics 2006), and DPIC has determined that the number of death sentences in 2006 was lower again, approximately 102, the lowest number of sentences since the death penalty was reinstated over 30 years ago.

Other indicators are consistent with the decline in death sentences. There were 98 executions in the country in 1999. In 2006, there were 53 executions – 47% fewer (DPIC, The Death Penalty in 2006). That number will likely decline further in 2007, with executions dropping into the 40s for the first time in over a decade. The recent number of executions has been directly affected by the controversy surrounding the lethal injection process. But even if that problem should be resolved and executions resume in greater numbers, the decline in death sentences will eventually mean that the number of executions will likely stay below that of the late 1990s.

The size of death row increased every year from the reinstatement of the death penalty in 1976 until 1999. Since then, the size of death row has decreased every year, despite the fact that fewer people are being executed. In many states, the death penalty has reached a virtual stalemate. Few people are sentenced to death and even fewer, if any, are executed. Some cases are overturned or inmates die of other causes, leaving death row about the same size. (The costs of maintaining this stagnant system, however, continue to mount.)

Life Without Parole

Americans are nearly evenly split when the death penalty is compared with life without parole (LWOP) as a punishment for murder. In the most recent Gallup Poll in 2006, 48% of the general population chose LWOP and 47% chose a death sentence, marking the first time in 20 years of posing this question that the Gallup Poll showed the death penalty in second place (Jones 2006). In the poll for this report, 47% would choose the death penalty and 43% life without parole (LWOP) as the proper sentence for first degree murder. Many subgroups, such as Democrats, women, African Americans, Hispanics, college graduates, and Catholics preferred LWOP over the death penalty.

However, those who believe they would be qualified as capital jurors were less moved by having the option of a life-without-parole sentence than they were by the innocence issue. Only 37% said having this choice would make them less likely to vote for death.

Life without parole is a relatively new alternative in American criminal sentencing. When the death penalty was overturned by the Supreme Court in 1972, there were about 600 people on death row. All of their sentences were reduced to life sentences and almost all of them became eligible for parole at some point (Marquart and Sorenson 1989, 5–28). Today, 37 of the 38 death penalty states have a sentence of life without parole for at least some defendants (DPIC.com 2007). Texas, the leading execution state, was the most recent state to adopt this option for jurors, having done so in 2005 (Governor Perry's Office 2006). If the death penalty were removed as a sentence today, many of the defendants would still have to serve the rest of their life in prison with no chance of parole. And for future defendants, that sentence would be available for virtually all cases.

Pragmatic Problems Cited by Those Who Support the Death Penalty

Besides the possibility of executing innocent people, what other problems raise doubts in the minds of those who favor the death penalty? What factors might weaken their support? Respondents who favoured the death penalty were given a list of factors and asked which ones (if proven true) would reduce their support. Policy issues such as the rarity of executions and high costs ranked not far behind the possibility of executing the innocent.

While 27% said that the execution of innocent people would lessen their support for the death penalty, 26% would be similarly affected by the fact that 'it takes too long to go through the whole appeals process in death penalty cases and only a few of those sentenced to death are actually executed'. The high costs of the death penalty were cited by 22% as lessening their support. A similar 22% cited the fact that receiving the death penalty often depended on race, economics and geography. Only 11% indicated that statements from leaders in their religious denomination would have a similar effect on their views.

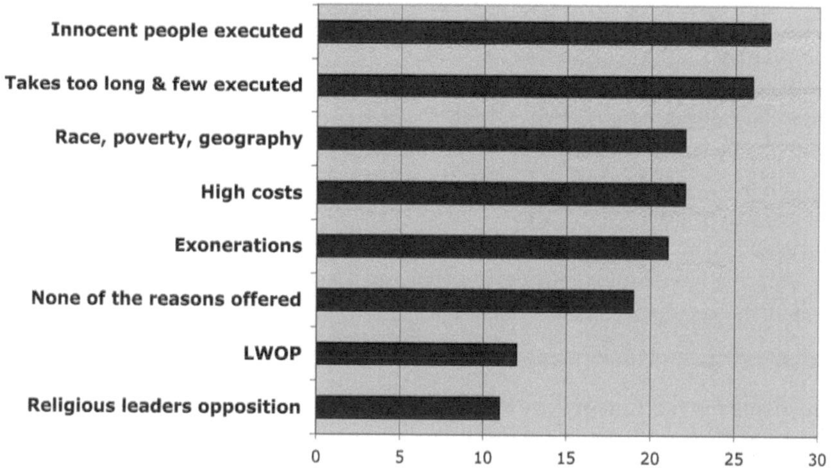

Figure 8.6 Pecentage saying it would lessen their support of death penalty

The Costs of Innocence

The problem of innocence has had a cascading effect on all aspects of the death penalty. After studying the risks of sentencing innocent people to death, many states have introduced reforms. Although the quality of capital representation is still grossly inadequate in many areas, and some states are requiring defence counsel to meet higher standards for capital representation and other states have raised the fees available for such representation. Many states now allow DNA evidence to be tested and introduced on appeal, despite barriers to late-filed challenges in death penalty cases. A few states are requiring that pre-trial interrogations of suspects be recorded to avoid abuses (The Justice Campaign 2007).

Many of these changes are long overdue, but one result could be that the costs of the death penalty will increase compared to what they were when standards were more lax. As executions decline and the costs for each prosecution go up, the cost per execution (including all the legal and custodial costs of all the cases in the death penalty system) has become a concern in many states. In Florida, a 1988 study by the *Miami Herald* concluded that the extra costs associated with the death penalty amounted to $3.2 million per execution (von Drehle 1988). Since then, costs have increased and executions have slowed down. A similar study by the *Palm Beach Post* in 2000 found that the cost per execution was now costing taxpayers $24 million (Date 2000).

Likewise in California, the *Sacramento Bee* had estimated that the state was spending an extra $90 million per year on the death penalty, with no executions to show for it (Maganini 1988, 1). A more recent study by the *Los Angeles Times* indicated that the costs were now more like $124 million per year. With an average of less than one execution every two years, that meant the state was paying *$250 million* per execution (Tempest 2005, 1).

States like New York and New Jersey, where the death penalty is in suspension, spent enormous sums of money with no executions resulting. Hearings in New York cited costs of over $160 million over 7 years with no death sentences carried out and no cases affirmed on appeal (Wise 2003, 1). In New Jersey, the costs were about $250 million over 22 years with no executions (Death penalty cost $253M and executed no one in NJ 2005). In both states, such economic concerns were cited in votes that have brought the death penalty to a halt (reaction to recommendation to abolish New Jersey death penalty 2007).

Prospects for the Future

With the use of the death penalty declining and becoming more isolated in a few states, and with the costs of cases increasing and the time between sentencing and execution not getting any shorter, it is not surprising that the majority of the public is convinced that this government program needs to be halted and studied to see if it is worth continuing. A significant majority of 58% responding in this poll believed it was time for a moratorium on the death penalty while the process undergoes a careful review.

Support for a moratorium was widespread among subgroups: 59% of southerners, 75% of African Americans, 68% of Hispanics, and 66% of Catholics supported such a halt to executions. This support reflects the reality that in practice such a moratorium already exists in much of the country. Most states with the death penalty carried out no executions in 2006 or the first 5 months of 2007. This

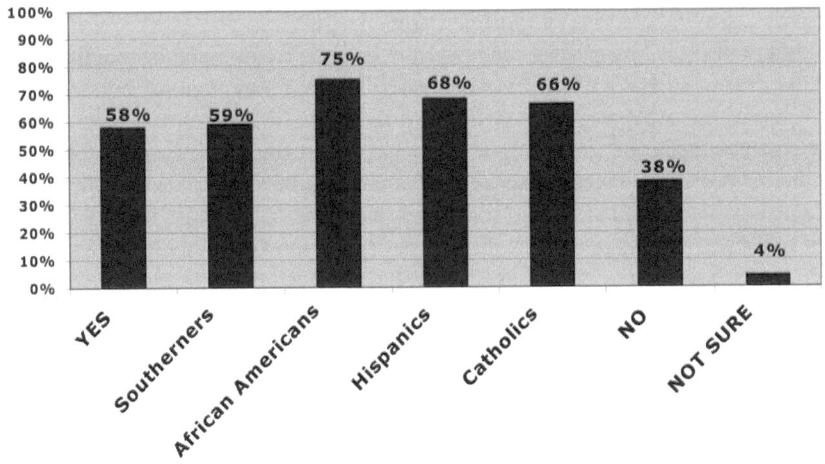

Figure 8.7 Support for a halt to executions: generally and subgroups

year only a handful of states have carried out an execution, and Texas, alone, has been responsible for two-thirds of all executions.

Even in the most active years of the death penalty, about 80% of the executions in the country have been in just one geographical area, the South. A national suspension of executions would hardly change the reality in most of the country.

Executions this year have been impeded by the challenges to the lethal injection process. In eleven states, stays of executions were in place for many months, and the controversy over lethal injection is far from being resolved. Although this debate was not the result of a public outcry, a number of states appear resigned to letting it run its course. North Carolina, which temporarily arrived at a compromise that allowed some executions to go forward, has returned to a stand down position and the governor has said the courts should decide the issue (Weigl 2007).

In other states like California, Maryland and Missouri, it also appears that executions will remain on hold for a considerable period while solutions are explored. Florida, which previously had resisted any challenges to both its faulty electric chair and its lethal injection process, voluntarily halted all executions late last year. Angel Diaz's execution in December 2006 took over 30 minutes, with the drugs being at first injected into his muscles rather than his veins. A complete second series of lethal drugs was administered after he writhed and spoke while on the gurney. Governor Jeb Bush immediately declared a moratorium and appointed a study commission. The new governor, Charlie Crist, has continued the process (Davis 2007).

Weariness with the Death Penalty

The lethal injection issue is not likely to end the death penalty. By itself, it remains probably a temporary hurdle to more executions. But this issue has not arisen in a vacuum. In the past six years, the American public has seen the U.S. Supreme Court place further restrictions on the use of the death penalty.[5] Some state courts have also made the execution of a defendant unpredictable, with stays due to lethal injection challenges and sentences overturned because of inadequate representation. Many family members of homicide victims are realising that accepting a life sentence for a defendant gives them a far greater chance of achieving a resolution to the legal case than holding out for a tenuous death sentence.

A weariness about the death penalty has emerged among some former supporters of the death penalty. If it is not going to be carried out in a short period of time, if many cases are overturned and then receive a life sentence anyhow, and if the costs of the whole process are getting out of hand, then some have concluded that it may not be worth the effort. In this poll, such sentiments ranked as high as innocence in lessening support of the death penalty among its proponents.

5 *Atkins v. Virginia* 536 U.S. 304 (2002); *Wiggins v. Smith* 539 U.S. 510 (2003); and *Roper v. Simmons* 543 U.S. 551 (2005).

In 2006, New Jersey appointed a blue-ribbon commission to study the state's death penalty. The commission concluded by a vote of 12–1 that the death penalty should be abolished. But it was not simply that the members were morally opposed to capital punishment. Rather, their report examined statements from victims' advocates, such as Richard Pompelio, founder of the New Jersey Crime Victims' Law Center and father of a murder victim. According to the commission's report:

> He (Mr. Pompelio) testified that the death penalty is the greatest failing of the justice system in the State and that it re-victimizes victims. He stated that the death penalty should be abolished in favor of life in prison without parole, and that the funds spent on the death penalty be used for services for homicide victims and funding for law enforcement. 'I have absolutely no doubt that there will never be an execution in the State of New Jersey … We are just sitting here playing with words and playing with taxpayers' dollars' (New Jersey Death Penalty Study Commission 2007).

Some prosecutors have echoed these sentiments. Samuel Milsap, former District Attorney of Bexar County, Texas, said:

> I've come to the conclusion … that the system as it relates to capital murder is simply broken. It's my view in fact that because it's driven by human beings and decisions that are made by human beings, it can't be fixed, and that as a result what has to happen is that the option to put people to death has to end (Pew Forum on Religion and Public Life 2007).

His words were similar to those of Justice Blackmun before retiring from the Supreme Court in 1994. Blackmun had voted to uphold the death penalty when it was struck down in 1972, and he voted in favour of its constitutionality when it was reinstated in 1976. But years of exposure to the way the death penalty worked in practice led him to withdraw even his legal judgment that it should be allowed to continue. Justice Blackmun stated

> In recent years, I have grown increasingly skeptical that 'the death penalty really can be imposed fairly and in accordance with the requirements of the Eighth Amendment', given the now limited ability of the federal courts to remedy constitutional errors … I am more optimistic, though, that this Court eventually will conclude that the effort to eliminate arbitrariness while preserving fairness in the infliction of [death] is so plainly doomed to failure that it – and the death penalty – must be abandoned altogether (*Callins v. Collins* (1994), dissenting opinion)).

For Some, A Conclusion That It Cannot Be Fixed

One reason that Americans believe a moratorium may be needed is that they lack confidence that the problems of the death penalty have been fixed. An overwhelming 69% of the public believes that the reforms will not eliminate all wrongful convictions and executions. This sentiment is also reflected by major national newspapers which formerly supported the death penalty for decades, but have now changed their positions.

The *Chicago Tribune* recently pronounced that the revelations about innocence and other problems had shaken 'the foundation of support for capital punishment':

> One of the core tenets of this newspaper since its founding has been that the extraordinary power of government must be wielded carefully and sparingly – particularly when that power weighs on the life and liberty of citizens.
>
> It has, as well, long been the position of this editorial page that the government should have the legal right to impose capital punishment – the death penalty.
>
> ....
>
> We have learned much, particularly with advances in DNA technology, about the criminal justice system's capacity to make terrible mistakes. These revelations – many stemming from investigations by this newspaper – shake the foundation of support for capital punishment.
>
> ....
>
> The evidence of mistakes, the evidence of arbitrary decisions, the sobering knowledge that government can't provide certainty that the innocent will not be put to death – all that prompts this call for an end to capital punishment. It is time to stop killing in the people's name (Chicago Tribune Editorial 2007).

Around the same time, the *Dallas Morning News* shifted from its long-term support for the death penalty because it had 'lost confidence that the state of Texas can guarantee that every inmate it executes is truly guilty of murder'. The editorial board wrote:

> That is why we believe the state of Texas should abandon the death penalty – because we cannot reconcile the fact that it is both imperfect and irreversible.
>
> This board has lost confidence that the state of Texas can guarantee that every inmate it executes is truly guilty of murder. We do not believe that any legal system devised by inherently flawed human beings can determine with moral certainty the guilt of every defendant convicted of murder.
>
> ...
>
> The state holds in its hands the power of life and death. It is an awesome power, one that citizens of a democracy must approach in fear and trembling, and in full knowledge that the state's justice system, like everything humanity touches, is fated to fall short of perfection. If we are doomed to err in matters of life and death, it is far better to err on the side of caution. It is far better to err on the side of life. The state cannot impose death – an irrevocable sentence – with absolute certainty in all cases. Therefore the state should not impose it at all (Dallas Morning News Editorial 2007).

Other papers, such as *The Sentinel* of Pennsylvania, were more succinct, simply calling the death penalty 'useless' (The Sentinel Editorial 2007). The *Rocky Mountain News* of Colorado said that, in their state, 'for all practical purposes the penalty no longer exists in any meaningful sense at all', and hence it should be taken off the books (Editorial Rocky Mountain News 2007). The *Los Angeles Times* called on the state study commission to make a death penalty moratorium its first order of business. The *Houston Chronicle* likewise advocated for a Texas moratorium. National papers such as the *New York Times*, the *Washington Post*, and *USA Today* have had long term editorial positions against the death penalty (DPIC – Editorials 2007).

An Emerging Trend

The death penalty is deeply ingrained in American history and politics. In this poll, 62% supported the death penalty for persons convicted of murder. Even with all that has been revealed about this practice in recent years, the majority of respondents said that their position had not changed in the past ten years. But among those who had shifted their position, more people became opponents of the death penalty than proponents, by a margin of 3 to 2. And the overwhelming reason given by those who have changed from supporters to opponents of the death penalty was the issue of innocence: 62% of those who changed to opposing the death penalty did so because of the risk that innocent people could be sentenced to death.

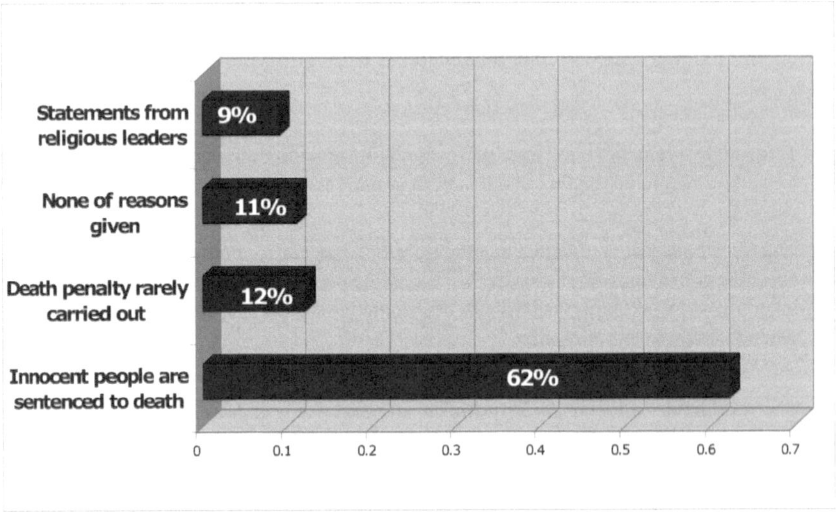

Figure 8.8 Why did you change from being a supporter of the death penalty?

The problem of innocence can be lessened but never completely eliminated. The chance of human error will be present in the investigation of the crime, the testing of evidence, in expert testimony, and in the opinions of jurors and judges passing judgment. When the former governor of Massachusetts, Mitt Romney, claimed to have devised a mistake-proof death penalty, the state legislature strongly rejected his proposal as unrealistic (Helman 2005).

The implications of the realisation that the 'innocence problem' cannot be fixed are profound: there is less talk now of eliminating appeals or cutting back on defence services. The death penalty for the foreseeable future will be time consuming, more expensive, and still unpredictable.

The public is very aware of these developments and many are becoming resigned to the fact that, in the long run, the death penalty is unsustainable. Support for the death penalty drops to less than 50% when compared with the sentence of life-without-parole. Capital punishment is seen as an outmoded government policy that no longer meets its intended uses.

Politicians may still continue to offer a patched-up death penalty as a panacea to the public's fear of crime. But rather than there being some light at the end of the tunnel after thirty years of experiment, the prospects for a 'successful' death penalty seem to be rapidly receding.

Bibliography

'Abolish the Death Penalty' (2007), *Chicago Tribune*, 25 March, [Online] Available at: <http://www.chicagotribune.com/>.

'A Divergent Path: A Death Penalty Slowdown, but not in Texas' (2007), *Dallas Morning News, 15 April*, [Online] Available at: <http://www.dallasnews.com>.

'A Mythical Penalty' (2007), *Rocky Mountain News*, 12 Feb., [Online] Available at: <http://www.rockymountainnews.com>.

The Assembly Speaker (2005), Office of Assembly Releases Death Penalty Report, 4 April, [Online] Available at: <http://www.assembly.state.ny.us/Press/20050404/>.

Associated Press Newswire (2005), 'Death penalty cost $253M and executed no one in NJ', 21 Nov., [Online] Available at: <www.ap.org>.

Banner, S. (2002), *The Death Penalty: An American History*, Harvard University Press, Cambridge.

Bureau of Justice Statistics (2005), 'Capital Punishment,' U.S. Department of Justice, [Online] Available at: <http://www.ojp.usdoj.gov/bjs/>.

Date, S. V. (2000), 'The High Price of Killing Killers', *Palm Beach Post*, 4 Jan.

Davis, P. (2007), 'Panel: Crist should review death drugs', 2007, *Associated Press*, 1 March, [Online] Available at: <www.ap.org>.

DPIC (2006), The Death Penalty in 2006: Year End Report, 2006, Death Penalty Information Center, [Online] Available at: <www.deathpenaltyinfo.org/2006yearend.pdf>.

DPIC (2007), Editorials, 2007, *Death Penalty Information Center*, Available at: <http://www.deathpenaltyinfo.org>.

DPIC (2007), *Innocence*: 'List of Those Freed From Death Row', Death Penalty Information Center, Available at <http://www.deathpenaltyinfo.org/article.php?scid=6&did=110>.

DPIC (2007), *'Life Without Parole'*, Death Penalty Information Center, Available at: <http://www.deathpenaltyinfo.org>.

Drehle, D. V. (1988), 'Bottom Line: Life in Prison One-sixth as Expensive', *The Miami Herald*, 10 July.

Fears, D. (2007), 'Exonerations Change How Justice System Builds a Prosecution: DNA Tests Have Cleared 200 Convicts', *Washington Post*, 3 May, 2007, p. A3.

Forum Transcript (2006), Pew Forum on Religion and Public Life, Transcript, July 21, Available at: <http://pewforum.org/events/index.php?EventID=122>

Governor's Office (2005), Governor Perry Signs Life Without Parole Bill, Austin, Texas [Online] Available at:<http://www.governor.state.tx.us/divisions/press/pressreleases/PressRelease.2005-06-17.2331/view>.

Haney, C. and Logan, D. (1994), 'Broken Promise: The Supreme Court's Response to Social Science Research on Capital Punishment', 50 *Journal of Social Issues*, pp. 75–101.

Helman, S. (2005), 'Death Penalty Bill Fails in House: Romney Initiative Roundly Defeated', *Boston Globe*, 16 Nov. [Online] Available at: <http://www.boston.com>.

Houston Chronicle (2006), Editorial, 'Mistrust: Court's Decision to Leave a Wrongful Execution Inquiry with a Tainted DA Clouds Texas Justice', *Houston Chronicle* 5 September.

'Innocent and Executed: Four Chapters in the Life of America's Death Penalty' (2006) *National Coalition to Abolish the Death Penalty.*

Jones, J. (2006), 'Two in Three Favor Death Penalty for Convicted Murderers', *The Gallup Poll,* 30 June.

Judicature (2002), Journal of the American Judicature Society, September-October.

Maganini, S. (1988), 'Closing Death Row Would Save State $90 Million a Year', *Sacramento Bee*, 28 March.

Marquart, J. and Sorenson, J. (1989), A National Study of the Furman-Commuted Inmates Assessing the Threat to Society from Capital Offenders, 23 *Loyola of Los Angeles Law Review* 5.

Morgan, C. A. (2004), 'Eyewitness Accounts Flawed', Fall/Winter *Yale Medicine.*

2007 New Jersey Death Penalty Report, 2007, New Jersey Death Penalty Study Commission, Jan., [Online] Available at: <http://www.njleg.state.nj.us/committees/njdeath_penalty.asp>.

'Reaction to Recommendation to Abolish New Jersey Death Penalty' (2007), *Associated Press Newswire*, 2 Jan. [Online] Available at: <www.ap.org>.

State Legislation Search (2007), *The Justice Campaign.* [Online] Available at: <http://www.thejusticeproject.org/state/legislation.html>.

Tempest, R. (2005), 'Death Row Often Means a Long Life', *Los Angeles Times*, 6 March.

'The Death Penalty has Served its Time' (2007), *The Sentinel of Pennsylvania*, 3 April [Online] Available at: <http://www.cumberlink.com/>.

Wise, D. (2003), 'Costly Price of Capital Punishment – Case Shows Effort Expended Before the State takes a Life', *Albany Times-Union*, 22 Sept.

Weigl, A. (2007), 'Execution Impasse Unlikely to End Soon', *News & Observer of North Carolina*, 6 April, [Online] Available at: <http://www.newsobserver.com/1509/story/561433.html>.

Chapter 9

The Death Penalty in China: Towards the Rule of Law

Nicola Macbean

Introduction

In the run up to the 2008 Olympics in Beijing, international criticism of China's human rights record has highlighted the use of the death penalty (Amnesty International 2007). While calls for a worldwide moratorium on executions have become louder, capital punishment for a large number of offences remains an integral part of Chinese criminal justice and the state executes more people than the rest of the world put together. Although global activists may try to internationalise China's use of the death penalty, capital punishment is a domestic issue.

At the March 2007 meeting of the United Nations Human Rights Council, China's representative, La Yifan, summed up the official position on the death penalty. He claimed that China was a country with a rule of law where the death penalty was only applied to the worst offences in compliance with the International Covenant on Civil and Political Rights.[1] Responding to criticism of China's use of the death penalty, Mr La explained that the scope of the application of the death penalty was shortly to be reviewed and that this was expected to be reduced 'with the final aim of abolishment' (UN Human Rights Council 2007). The Chinese representative, echoing views presented by Singapore, rejected suggestions that an international consensus on abolition existed and criticised international pressure on governments regarding the death penalty, in particular, the politicisation of the death penalty in relation to China's hosting of the Olympics.

In the Second Five Year Reform Programme for the People's Courts (2004–2008), the Supreme People's Court stated its intention to reform the death penalty system. Since then, measures have been introduced to require appeals, in cases involving the death penalty with immediate execution, to be held in open court and to restore the power of the Supreme People's Court to review all death penalty cases. Despite such moves to 'kill fewer and kill carefully', the death penalty remains central to the expression of state power. The recent execution of the disgraced head of the State Food and Drug Administration, Zheng Xiaoyu, was

1 (1976) 999 UNTS 171.

presented as a warning to top officials. In a commentary the party's official paper, the People's Daily, stated that:

> As a case study of a party member and leading official breaking the law and committing crime, the Zheng Xiaoyu case offers profound lessons that all public servants, especially leading officials at every level, should take to heart (China Daily 2007a).

The international trend towards abolition of the death penalty is framed globally within a discourse of human rights. Although the number of abolitionist countries has increased rapidly in recent years, the globalisation of the abolitionist movement has not yet resulted in establishing a 'stable and universal standard' (Asad 1997) regarding the use of the death penalty. Europe has been keen to promote abolition as a diplomatic objective (European Union 1998, Council of Europe 2004) with the result that for many poorer countries, keen to access European funding and support, abolition is a pragmatic policy and may not necessarily reflect a significant shift in normative values. The introduction of democracy, the end of civil war and the rejection of previous regimes have also been factors in states' decisions to abolish the death penalty (Hood 2002). That two of the world's major democracies, and its largest one, retain capital punishment indicates, however, no obvious correlation between democracy and abolition (Boulanger and Sarat 2005). Despite the international abolitionist trend and the progressive development of legal norms, abolition of the death penalty has not yet become a customary norm in international law (Schabas 2002).

Although many countries are resisting international pressure for a moratorium on executions and abolition, international human rights standards are influencing domestic debates on the death penalty (Schabas 2004). This chapter explores the application of the death penalty within the Chinese criminal justice system and how the emerging domestic debate is framed within overlapping, and sometimes competing, narratives of retribution and rule of law. Traditional support for the death penalty is expressed in terms of the popular *talionic* maxim, 'a life for a life', but critical voices within the legal community – reformist scholars and officials and *weiquan* 'rights-protecting' lawyers – are challenging the status quo and advocating for the death penalty to be more strongly rooted in the rule of law and international standards.

Commitment to the rule of law has become an important legitimising strategy for the current post-Deng leadership. This officially sanctioned discourse also allows critics to frame their resistance with reference to an ideology conferred by policy makers (O'Brien and Li 2006). Growing rights consciousness and the development of a legal ideology are enabling a number of actors within China's expanding legal community to criticise the state's use of capital punishment and exert domestic pressure for reform. Although there are lone voices calling for immediate abolition, there is no evidence of widespread support for this position among lawyers and academics. Instead, legal reformers and the government, alike, declare a shared commitment to eventual abolition when China's 'national conditions allow'. The terms of China's death penalty debate, such as it exists, are about the pace of abolition and the due process protections safeguarding those facing the risk of capital punishment.

A Historical Perspective

The legitimacy of the death penalty in China draws on a long history. It was one of the 'Five Punishments' in imperial China with harsh and precise measures listed for different offences (Scobell 1990). By the time of the Yuan Dynasty there were three officially prescribed methods of execution: decapitation, strangulation and 'death by slicing' (Bodde and Morris 1967). Some flexibility existed, however, in the way punishments could be carried out, including clemency and commutation for cash (Spence 1999). By the nineteenth century, Western governments were demanding that a weakened China grant them separate powers to try and punish their own nationals. Although the resultant concession of extraterritoriality was deeply resented by Chinese mandarins, it was an impetus for reform. In treaties marking the end of the Boxer Rebellion, Britain, the United States and Japan called for the abolition of corporal punishment and the setting up of modern prisons. The introduction of a modern prison system, at the end of the nineteenth century, led to greater emphasis on the possibility of moral rehabilitation of criminals, an approach which chimed both with Confucian ideas of self-cultivation and modern Western penology (Dikötter 2001). Capital punishment, however, continued to be applicable for the most serious offences and it remained part of the Criminal Code of the Republican government which came to power with the collapse of the Qing dynasty in 1911.

A belief in the deterrent effect of the death penalty has deep roots in China; 'kill the chicken to scare the monkeys' is a popular traditional saying. The Legalists placed a strong emphasis on the importance of laws and rights and the deterrence value of punishment. Executions in dynastic China were public events reflecting traditional beliefs that parading evil will lead to a decrease in crime (Bakken 1993). Although public executions were made illegal in the 1979 Criminal Law, public arrest and sentencing rallies have continued to be a feature of police campaigns. A recent directive, jointly issued by the Court, Procuratorate and Ministries of Justice and Public Security, banning the 'parading of convicts and other inhumane treatment of prisoners' (China Daily 2007b) is indicative of changing attitudes.

Maoist China

On coming to power in 1949, Mao Zedong abolished all laws of the Republican period, and the fitful construction of a socialist legal system began. Early efforts to draft a comprehensive criminal code, however, floundered in the political climate of the 1950s and the Anti-Rightists campaign. In a brief period of reform, a criminal procedure code with 200 articles was drafted in 1963, but then suspended in the Cultural Revolution. Criminal justice in the Maoist era was dominated by the political context and punishments were influenced by the offender's class status, his attitude to his offence and the prevailing political line (Leng and Chiu 1985). The severest punishments, including execution, were reserved for those, defined by Mao, in his 1957 speech, 'On the Correct Handling of Contradictions among the People', as 'the enemy'. These included, 'reactionaries, exploiters, counterrevolutionaries, landlords, bureaucrat-capitalists, robbers, swindlers, murderers, arsonists, hooligans and other scoundrels who seriously disrupt social order'. Applying the death penalty to such criminals would, Mao argued, 'assuage the people's anger'.

Chinese official policy on the death penalty was similar to that put forward by the Soviet Union. While capital punishment was, in principle, incompatible with socialist ideals, it was justified, they argued, as an 'exceptional measure of punishment which is temporarily applied pending its complete abolition' (Hood 2002). A 1957 Chinese legal textbook explained, 'We are retaining the death penalty while in the process of gradually abolishing it, and we are reducing the scope of the application of the death penalty to a minimum'. In the early years of the People's Republic the government argued that the death penalty should be 'applied to those counterrevolutionaries whose crimes were persistently hostile to the people, and who adamantly refused to repent and reform' (Cohen 1968).

Trial and punishment in the Chinese criminal justice system remain a 'dramatisation for the masses of the ancient theme of retribution and repentance' (Bakken 1993). Nowhere is this expressed more forcefully than in the targeting of drug dealing in the annual campaigns coinciding with International Drug Awareness Day. For years, around the 26th June, death sentences and executions for drugs offences have been publicised to ensure maximum impact and promote anti-drugs awareness (Amnesty International 2007). Retribution must, however, always be tempered by necessity. Although under Mao, China increased its use of the death penalty (Lu and Miethe 2007), scholars critical of excesses in the 1980s and 1990s, still quote approvingly his admonition to use the measure sparingly in that, '[w]e should only kill a few, and in all cases in which there is a choice whether or not to execute, we should not execute' (Howie 1996).

1979 Criminal Justice Reforms

The Cultural Revolution left a legacy of arbitrary arrests, detention and torture, extrajudicial executions and the abolition of most legal institutions (Chu 2000). The modernising programme, launched by Deng Xiaoping at the 3rd Plenary of the 11th Central Committee in 1979, envisioned 'rule by law' as a central pillar and was a marked shift in policy from the chaos of the Cultural Revolution. Legal scholars acquired new prominence. Many had trained overseas pre-1949 and some had suffered considerably during the previous decade of political upheaval.

Drawing on drafts from the early 1950s and the short-lived Code of 1963, one of the first laws to be passed, following the death of Mao, was the Criminal

Procedure Law. The purpose of legislators was to signal an end to the arbitrary punishments and widespread abuse which marked the earlier period. The law drew on the European civil law inquisitorial system which had influenced earlier Republican lawmaking. The promise of more rigorous procedural protection was soon undermined, however, by the lack of legal professionals. Time constraints for detention and charging were immediately challenged and relaxed in subsequent amendments (Chu 2000).

Defence lawyers historically played a marginal role in Chinese criminal justice. Criminal laws were a tool of class struggle and there was nothing heroic in representing a client who had been labelled a class enemy. The introduction in the 1979 Criminal Law (Article 3) of the statement, that the criminal law is applicable to everyone signalled an end to this policy. The 1979 Criminal Procedure Law, however, failed to give defence lawyers the rights and protections they needed to effectively defend their client. In this very minimalist interpretation of the role of defence counsel, Chinese lawyers could only consult the case files and interview the defendant (Article 29). The defendant was only informed of his right to appoint counsel seven days before the court session (Article 110) and there was no requirement for a lawyer in death penalty cases. The new law set out the procedures in which the court should sentence, allow appeals and approve the death penalty. The suspended death sentence, a traditional feature of capital punishment in China, is introduced as an alternative sentence to immediate execution. Prisoners sentenced to the death penalty with a two year suspension normally have their sentences commuted to fixed term sentences of 15 to 20 years provided that they have demonstrated 'sufficient remorse' and not re-offended while in prison.

In spite of the modernising agenda, the political nature of many offences remained in the new Criminal Law. Of the 28 capital crimes listed in the 1979 Law, 15 were defined as counter-revolutionary offences, a further eight were crimes endangering public security, three were offences against the security of the person and two were property offences, including robbery and corruption. Despite the prominence of counter-revolutionary crimes in the text, government statistics showed that such crimes were insignificant in number (Clarke and Feinerman 1995). More significantly, the 1982 Decision of the Standing Committee of the National People's Congress 'Regarding the Severe Punishment of Criminals who Seriously Undermine the Economy' illustrated the growing severity with which China was prepared to deal with economic crimes. This Decision made heavier sentences available in cases of theft: 'when the circumstances are particularly serious, the sentence is to be not less than ten years of fixed-term imprisonment, life imprisonment or death'. Serious circumstances generally implied particularly large sums of money. In a 1984 explanation, published by the Supreme People's Court and the Supreme People's Procuratorate, the death penalty was recommended for theft of money or articles with a value exceeding 30,000 RMB.

Strike Hard

It was not long before the political agenda of modernisation came into conflict with the Party's overriding imperative to ensure stability. The first 'Strike Hard' (*Yanda*) campaign was launched in September 1983 and lasted until January 1987. The campaign reintroduced the tactics of popular mobilisation and was a significant setback for legal reformers who had been promoting greater legal restraint. In an effort to restore what Tanner calls the 'balance of awe', in response to a perception of growing social disorder and public anxiety about a string of high profile crimes, a nationwide crackdown on crime was announced (Tanner 2000).

Throughout the 1980s the number of capital crimes increased, reflecting public anxieties at rising crime and the incidence of specific offences, including the trafficking of women and children (Tanner 2000), with mandatory death sentences introduced for kidnapping and trafficking. Although the 1979 reforms no longer allowed for the immediate execution of juveniles, anxiety at rising youth crime and fear of gangs led to considerable use, during the first Strike Hard, of the suspended death sentence for those aged below eighteen (Bakken 1993).

The Strike Hard campaign undermined efforts to reinstate the authority of the courts and the law. The National People's Congress was called on to approve measures to relax procedural protections for those facing the death penalty. In its decision, '[r]egarding the Rapid Adjudication of Cases Involving Criminal Elements Who Seriously Endanger Public Security' the Standing Committee of the National People's Congress called for the speedy adjudication of capital cases where 'the main criminal facts are clear and the evidence irrefutable and the people's indignation is very great'. In dealing with such cases, the Decision released courts from various provisions regarding the delivery of court notices and the time limit for lodging an appeal. The time limit for dealing with criminal cases became a criterion for success during Strike Hard campaigns, with the death sentence often being carried out on the same day as the court judgement.

Judicial oversight was reduced with the lowest tier of China's courts given the authority to hear first instance capital cases. This measure was rescinded three months later as the extent of judicial incompetence in the lower level people's courts became apparent (Trevaskes 2002). In a parallel move, the Supreme People's Court was also required to delegate its authority to give the final approval for execution in all violent capital cases to the Higher Courts based at the provincial level. This measure was only rescinded in January 2007 when the Supreme People's Court took back this power.

Major national Strike Hard campaigns took place in 1996 and 2001 and local campaigns continued until an end to the policy was announced in work reports to the 2007 meeting of the National People's Congress (Xinhua 2007). The frequent resort to campaign policing, since the beginning of the reform period, illustrates the extent to which the rational, procedural discourse of the rule of law has been so easily undermined by the imperative to maintain public order. Although in 2001 greater emphasis was placed on 'handling cases according to the law', the campaign agenda of 'severity and swiftness' (*congzhong congkuai*) placed the courts and the police in an impossible position of balancing their growing professionalism with the political demands of the Party-state (Trevaskes 2000). The new slogan, in the current period, of 'balancing severe punishment with leniency' (*kuanyan xiangji*) reflects the same tensions, but signals an attempt to find a new balance and a style of policing that is more appropriate to the construction of Premier Wen Jiabao's 'harmonious society'.

The summary justice of the Strike Hard campaign reportedly resulted in a huge use of the death penalty although the lack of official data has made it impossible to provide a definitive picture. While one scholar estimated that 10,000 executions took place over the three and a half year period of the first Strike Hard (Tanner 2000), estimates for later periods have exceeded this. Although Amnesty International monitors public reports of executions, others, drawing on information provided by contacts, have published claims of annual rates as high as 15,000 executions (Bruce and Gilley 2002). Over the last couple of years a number of reports have claimed the current rate is about 7,500–8,000 (Dui Hua Foundation and personal communications) a year.

Engagement with the International Community

In May and June 1989 demonstrations by students, workers and ordinary citizens took place, first, in the heart of Beijing on Tiananmen Square and, subsequently, in hundreds of other cities across China. Deng Xiaoping labelled the demonstrations 'counter-revolutionary' and gave orders to the army to bring the protests to a close. The massacre brought condemnation from around the world and set back China's international relations.

Prior to Tiananmen, as early as 1985, Chinese leaders had begun to recognise the deficiencies of the newly instated legal system (Chu 2000). The events of 1989, however, provided an impetus in China to the study of human rights and public debate on the 'rights and interests' of citizens. In the 1990s, scholars were given official encouragement to study international human rights law and history and to engage with the international scholarly community (Zhou 1995). Diplomatically, China was under pressure to demonstrate human rights progress to maintain its *most favoured nation* trading status with the United States. The politicisation of human rights in the 1990s coincided with the articulation of a distinct set of Asian values, in the run up to the UN Conference on Human Rights in Vienna. This provided Chinese diplomats with a regionally legitimated language in which to respond to criticism of its human rights record by the international community. Bilateral monitoring of human rights, even by a country as powerful as the US, provided at most 'temporary, superficial and instrumental change' and did not lead to deep-rooted internalisation of human rights norms evidenced by 'continued excessive use of the death penalty' and other human rights violations (Kent 2001).

An outcome of this official attention was the publication of China's first White Paper on Human Rights in 1991 (State Council). Directed at an international rather than domestic audience, the paper emphasises the centrality of the right to subsistence and the government's priority to maintain 'national stability'. In a section on the justice system emphasis is placed on the need to protect the legal rights and interests of 'the whole people' and punish the 'small number of criminals'. With reference to the death penalty China acknowledges that, 'like most countries in the world', it maintains capital punishment, but claims that the death penalty is only applied to those 'guilty of the most heinous crimes'. The paper highlights the use of the two year suspended death sentence as 'an original creation' and an 'effective system by which strict control is exercised over the use of capital punishment'. Subsequent White Papers on Human Rights, published every couple of years and most recently in 2004, provide no further justification on the use of the death penalty. Since that first White Paper, the number of capital offences in China has increased while the international trend on the death penalty has moved in the opposite direction.

1996 Criminal Justice Reforms

The criminal justice institutions have always been an important tool for the Chinese Communist Party to justify theories of social order and disorder. Traditionally, the law was strongly associated with punishment (Clarke and Feinerman 1995), but, following the death of Mao, the new Party leadership had begun to recognise the rights of criminal suspects against the interests of the state. By the mid 1990s, further reforms of the criminal justice system were being proposed. A scholarly draft of a revised Criminal Procedure Law was circulated with strengthened provisions to protect the rights of defendants (Lawyers Committee for Human Rights 1996). Revision to the law was a lengthy and contentious process involving consultations with a number of powerful state organs, but the need for reform had become essential if the Party were to respond to growing dissatisfaction among the general public, the scholarly community and even officials (Chu 2000).

The revised Criminal Procedure Law was approved in March 1996. The new legislation provided defendants with a number of improved procedural safeguards, including the right of defence counsel to participate earlier in the criminal proceedings, and measures to strengthen the trial stage and move away from the practice of 'decision first, trial later'. A requirement for a defence lawyer to be appointed in all death penalty cases was introduced. The same year the Lawyers' Law was adopted, providing a clearer statement of the lawyer's professional status, but failing to further the lawyer's ability to defend the rights and interests of their clients (Lawyers Committee for Human Rights 1998).

While growing rights awareness can be seen in the revised criminal procedures, further changes to the substantive law took place against the backdrop of the second Strike Hard campaign (Zhao 2005). During the drafting stage of the revised

Criminal Law, several prominent scholars argued for a reduction in capital crimes and, in particular, for ending the death penalty for non-violent offences. The impact of market-based reforms in the 1980s had, however, led to growing public concern at the increase not only of violent crime, but also corruption and fraud. In the end, the revised legislation reflected current use of the death penalty, codifying the ad hoc introduction of new capital offences that had occurred throughout the 1980s and early 1990s, during which the number of capital crimes increased from 28 to some sixty eight. A number of offences were re-categorised: many counter-revolutionary crimes became the new offence of 'endangering national security', while others became public order crimes. Probably the most notable change in the revised legislation was the removal of theft from the list of capital crimes.

Critical Voices

While the criminal procedure law revisions were welcomed by the legal community, critical voices were soon raised, questioning both the extent of legal reform and the implementation of the revised laws. It was not long before scholars and lawyers were talking openly again of the need for further reform.

Criticism over the past decade, of both the law and practice, reflects greater international awareness resulting from increased overseas study, contacts and professional exchanges. Signature of the ICCPR in 1998 gave reformers an added impetus. In contrast, however, to the speed with which China has ratified other conventions following signature, ratification of the ICCPR has still not been approved by the National People's Congress. Although in bilateral human rights dialogues the Chinese government has argued that domestic law largely complies with the ICCPR, some lawyers and legal scholars have been vocal in linking their calls for further reform to the obligations of international human rights law.

China's compliance with article 6 of the ICCPR, that the death penalty be restricted to 'the most serious crimes', has been questioned by several scholars. The less inflammatory language of the revised Criminal Law in which the death penalty can only be applied for 'exceptionally serious crimes,' has been welcomed by some as proof of a more 'scientific' or rational approach to criminal justice. Others argue, however, that the wording is less restrictive than the 1979 language which limited the death penalty to the 'most heinous crimes' (Xia 2000). The use of the death penalty for economic crimes has also come under criticism with scholars highlighting both international trends and the view of the United Nations, to argue that economic crimes should no longer attract the death penalty (Zhao 2005). While a revised Criminal Law is not currently on the legislative agenda, legal scholars have argued that ratification of the ICCPR will require China to reduce its number of capital crimes, provide clearer sentencing guidelines and a definition of what constitutes 'exceptionally serious crimes'.

While scholars and lawyers demonstrate growing awareness of international human rights standards, the government remains sensitive to any perception of weakness in the face of international pressure on China. Most scholars and lawyers, therefore, frame their calls for legal reform in the context of a domestic agenda for reform. Although traditionally substantive, rather than procedural, claims have taken priority in Chinese conceptions of justice, the experience of Chinese defence lawyers with the law in practice has drawn attention to the procedural deficiencies in the legal system. The failure of the Criminal Procedure Law to protect the rights of suspects and prevent miscarriages of justice has been highlighted by some high profile cases of torture which have recently come to light, in several of which the defendant had been given the death penalty (Kahn 2005). One of the most widely discussed cases concerned She Xianglin. She was serving a prison sentence in Hubei for the murder of his wife, but, some 11 years after her disappearance, she reappeared having married someone in another province. On his release from prison She Xianglin accused the police of torturing him into confessing to a crime that had not taken place (China Daily 2005b). Concern at the prevalence of forced confessions (*xingxunbigong*) and incidents of torture has now become the overriding justification for further revisions to the Criminal Procedure Law (Chen 2005).

Official recognition of the problem of torture has led to training initiatives and support for a number of pilot projects to reduce the opportunities for the police to abuse their power. The notoriety of the She Xianglin case prompted Hubei province to issue provisional regulations requiring the video and tape recording of all potential death penalty cases. The Chinese government's willingness to acknowledge publicly that torture is a problem paved the way for the invitation of the UN Special Rapporteur on Torture to visit China in November 2005 (UN Human Rights Commission 2006). Although China was displeased with the final report's inclusion of a large number of cases alleging torture against members of the Falun Gong and the conclusion that torture 'remains widespread', the government has continued to allow international cooperation in this area (Great Britain China Centre).

The problem of forced confessions and the use of torture, reveals deep underlying problems within the Chinese criminal justice system. Although the revised Criminal Procedure Law made convictions on confession evidence alone inadmissible, unrealistic targets for 100% clear-up rates in homicide cases, and the lack of skills and resources within the police, have continued to make confessions an important tool for securing forensic evidence. The confession is also critical in validating the state's role in maintaining public security and the reintegrative functions of the criminal justice system (Rojek 2001). In the words of one defence lawyer, 'they (the police) pay a much higher price for failing to maintain the appearance of social order than for torturing suspects' (Kahn 2005). Although suspects have the right not to answer 'irrelevant' questions during interrogation, some local jurisdictions, at the instigation of legal scholars, have recently been experimenting with a more general right to silence or the absence of confession.

For the Chinese government, emerging popular rights awareness and public unease at official complicity in torture and ill-treatment of fellow citizens cannot be as easily ignored as the reports of international NGOs. The centrality of criminal justice to Party-State power, however, makes the government a cautious reformer and reluctant to sanction the wide-ranging changes which critics urge. For some years lawyers have been arguing for the right to be allowed to attend police interrogations of suspects and the All China Lawyers' Association has made this an important campaigning issue in its submission on further criminal procedure reform. Despite successful pilot projects and overwhelming international evidence of the effectiveness of the measure in preventing police abuse, the government remains reluctant to force through reform in the face of opposition from the Ministry of Public Security. To bolster their position, the police have been quick, in today's more 'rights' conscious environment, to voice their concern for the victim's rights in opposing increased protection for the suspects. Long-awaited revisions to the Criminal Procedure Law, may reveal how far the government is prepared to go to enable a stronger role for defence counsel and to challenge the supremacy of the prosecution.

Legal Assistance

Despite the rule of law rhetoric and growing awareness of international standards, Chinese criminal cases are skewed heavily in favour of the prosecution. The reforms of the late 1990s introduced elements of the adversarial Anglo-American model, but, with its foundations in the continental inquisitorial system, the trial still plays a minimal role and there is little official traction for the notion of equality of arms. The procedural focus is on the pre-trial investigation carried out by the police and the procuratorate, and by the time a case reaches the courts it is widely assumed that 'the facts are clear' and there is very little scope for these to be challenged by defence counsel. Trials are often little more than sentencing hearings with lawyers seeing their best hope in influencing the sentence with a plea of mitigating circumstances. For lawyers in capital cases, success is more often than not securing for their clients a fixed term prison sentence or, at worst, a suspended death sentence.

The supply of qualified lawyers across the country has become a litmus test for the development of a legal culture in China. Despite impressive figures for people taking the Bar exams, the number of qualified lawyers is still low for the size of the population. The shortage of lawyers is most acute in the poorer central and western regions as qualified lawyers flock to the cities in the east for well paid jobs in commercial law. The Chinese Communist Party's intolerance for autonomous entities has hampered the development of a professional Bar association which can promote the independence, professionalism and autonomy of the legal profession with the result that the competence and 'professional responsibility' of many Chinese lawyers has been called into question (Alford 1995). With the profession in China still in its infancy, many lawyers struggle to represent a client whose interests are distinct from those of the state.

Traditional hostility to the law and the politicisation of criminality under Mao have meant, in practice, many defence lawyers still face prejudice for defending a client accused of serious crimes, such as murder or rape. This suspicion towards the defence lawyer finds expression in article 306 of China's Criminal Law which makes it a criminal offence for a lawyer to forge evidence or entice or coerce a witness into 'changing his testimony in defiance of the facts or give false testimony'. Article 306, with its exclusive focus on perjury by lawyers, is often cited as indicative of the challenges facing the profession. Clearly the threat of prosecution has cast a chill over the legal profession (Congressional-Executive Commission on China 2006). But, following a detailed study of cases and interviews with all parties, Fu (2006) suggests that the real reason the police and procuratorate pursue prosecutions under article 306 is that the position and role of defence lawyers in China is now beginning to matter and is frustrating the prosecution's traditional reliance on confessions.

Legal aid for defendants in criminal cases is the poor relation in a profession dominated by the well-paid commercial lawyers in China's business centres (Smith and Gompers 2007). The 1996 Lawyers Law led to the setting up of a legal aid system requiring all practising lawyers to provide free legal assistance for up to two cases a year. While some legal aid is discretionary, and reflects local availability of resources, legal assistance is now mandatory for all defendants facing the death penalty. The provision of legal aid is the responsibility of the provincial and county level legal aid offices which will either appoint one of their own lawyers, or require a local firm to provide *pro bono* services. The financing of legal aid, like most social services in China, is the responsibility of local government and central government subsidy for the poorest counties is minimal. Legal aid centres in poorer regions lack sufficient funds to reimburse case-related expenditure and lawyers complain that they must finance their own travel and photocopying of case documents. There are no public funds to pay for expert witnesses for the defence or the defence's own investigation expenses.

Ten days before trial in a death penalty case the court must provide legal aid for any defendant who has not privately appointed defence counsel. Since legal aid centres, however, are given three days to appoint someone, the lawyer usually has just a week to prepare the defence. While the 2003 Legal Aid Rules allow suspects, without financial means, to apply for legal aid following the first interrogation by the police or the beginning of 'compulsory measures', the application process can be slow and approval will reflect the local ability to fund legal assistance. Despite the serious shortcomings in the legal aid available for those facing the death penalty, there has been little serious public attention of this topic. Most domestic and international attention has focused on the appeals and approval process for the death penalty.

Appeals and Approval of the Death Penalty

Despite efforts to modernise and build confidence in the legal system, the educative and propaganda functions of the criminal trial, 'directed at the citizens, to condemn vice and praise justice', remain important (Clarke and Feinerman 1995). China's trial adjudication committees (*shenpan weiyuanhui*) bring together the most senior members of the court to ensure quality control and decide major or complicated cases, including most involving the death penalty. Although the independence of individual judges is not an accepted principle, the collective independence of the judiciary as a whole is, even though, in practice, there are many shortcomings with respect to any form of judicial independence in China (Peerenboom 2002). Local political influence is articulated by the Political-Legal Committee, which is instrumental in promoting Strike Hard targets and local party priorities, and the local People's Congress. Lawyers, police, prosecutors and judges all openly admit the pressure of satisfying local political and public opinion.

In China's two-trial system, a judgement in the court of first instance can be appealed within ten days to the next higher level court. Since the court considering the appeal can review both the facts and the law relating to the initial judgement, death penalty cases face frequent appeals. Appeals are considered by a collegial panel which will review the case file, but could decide not to hear the case in court. If the court had concluded that 'the facts are clear' then no court hearing was required and, in practice, most appeals were no more than a review of the files and interviews with the relevant parties. Policy changes at the end of 2005 now require appeals in cases involving the death penalty, with immediate execution, to be considered in an open court (China Daily 2005c).

Research reveals that the outcome of a successful appeal is rarely a verdict of not guilty or dismissal of the case. The most common result, where miscarriages of justice are alleged, is a retrial at the lower court level, often involving the same panel of judges. Cases have been reported involving as many as four retrials until the Higher Court finally ordered a verdict of not guilty (Lu and Miethe 2007). The value of the appeals process is undermined by the fact that it is normal practice with serious cases, such as capital crimes, for the Intermediate Court to discuss the case with the Higher Court and seek their approval of the lower court judgement. Under the 'erroneous cases investigation system' lower level court judges are reluctant to make independent decisions and later be held responsible for a wrongful conviction. As a result, it is rare for the Higher Court to overturn an Intermediate Court judgement on which it has already been consulted.

Managerial measures introduced to improve accountability in the judicial system have had a number of unfortunate, apparently unintended, consequences on the appeals process. The introduction of the 'responsibility' system in the courts and other parts of the judicial system has resulted in disciplinary measures, including fines, against judges and procurators where cases have been successfully appealed. Under the State Compensation Law, individuals may also be compensated for unlawful detention in the event of a verdict of not guilty, with the costs of compensation borne by the responsible units rather than the state.

The 1979 Criminal Law, article 43, and Criminal Procedure Law, article 144, both provided that death sentences should be verified and approved by the Supreme People's Court. Approval by the Supreme People's Court was also stipulated in the Organic Law of the Courts under article 13. However, not long after the promulgation of this legislation, the National People's Congress Standing Committee ruled that, during 1980, the Supreme People's Court would delegate the approval of death sentences in cases of murder, rape, robbery and arson to Higher Courts in the provinces, municipalities and autonomous regions. In 1981 this measure was extended for a further two years, and then formalised in a revision to the Court Organisation Law approved by the National People's Congress Standing Committee at the outset of the first Strike Hard campaign.

Revision of the criminal laws in the late 1990s maintained the power of the Supreme People's Court to give final approval before execution. A Notice from the Supreme People's Court, from the same period, however, continued to refer to the legal delegation of authority to approve certain death sentences to the Higher Courts. Chinese legal experts have long highlighted the fact that the delegation of authority was a temporary policy, introduced in response to an increase in serious crime and a lack of sufficient personnel in the Special People's Court to review death penalty decisions. The continuation of the policy was, they argued, in violation of Chinese legislative procedures (Congressional-Executive Commission on China 2003).

Delegating the approval of most death sentences to the Higher Courts had resulted in both the appeal and the approval taking place in the same court with the risk that the two procedures became a single process. This risk was compounded by a Supreme People's Court decision, in a move to improve Higher Court efficiency, that there was no need to separately approve a death sentence where the court had already rejected an appeal against the judgement of the Intermediate Court. Concern over the potential lack of rigour in the approvals process also highlighted the shortcomings in China's appeals proceedings.

The restoration of the Supreme People's Court authority over the execution of death sentences became a campaigning issue for both domestic reformers and international human rights organisations. The issue was uncontroversial and had clear legal, procedural and traditional legitimacy. Some Chinese scholars even emphasised its historical roots, arguing that in imperial times even the emperor had been required to approve execution of the death sentence. It was also assumed, if not publicly argued, that the restoration of the Special People's Court's power over approval would reduce the number of executions and address the alleged inconsistencies in provincial death penalty sentencing patterns.

Despite the force of the arguments it was nevertheless not until December 2006 that the Government announced the change of policy. Post-Deng decision-making has become more consensual and negotiated, requiring the support of all influential parties. Opposition from provincial Higher Courts and a shortage of qualified personnel in Beijing were some of the justifications given for the slow pace of reform. Re-establishing the approval of the death penalty as a formal procedure is likely to result in the provincial courts enforcing higher standards on the first and second instance courts to avoid the ramifications of having their decisions overturned. Locating the decision-making in Beijing should also result in more consistent use of the death penalty, and should help defuse the political pressure on Higher Courts, particularly during anti-crime campaigns and in high profile cases. Recent official reports already claim a reduction in the number of executions (China Daily 2007c).

Such government claims cannot be challenged. Anyone who wants to examine the government's position that 'strict control' is applied to the use of the death penalty or recent claims of a decline in the number of executions is hindered by the lack of official data at either the local or national level. In response to international demands for greater transparency, the government has prevaricated on the grounds that the data would be impractical to collect although it does publish a composite figure for the number of people sentenced to prison terms of five years and more. A report from Human Rights in China, however, confirms that national and provincial statistics on the numbers of executions are classified as highly secret (Human Rights in China 2007). Some Chinese scholars have called for publication of the data and acknowledge the secrecy is because there 'are too many death sentences and making the number available to the public would undermine the international image of China' (Chen 2002).

The Death Penalty Debate

Claiming cultural exceptionalism, East Asian countries have been among the most vocal at the United Nations in opposing resolutions against the use of the death penalty. In reality, cultural arguments for and against the death penalty are more complex. Not only is the Asian values thesis undermined by the pro-abolitionist position of the Asian Charter on Human Rights, but Confucianism is no longer a living tradition in China; its influence can only be understood in a concrete institutional context (Chan 1999). With the decline in influence of Marxism and Maoism, the rising tide of nationalism provides considerable scope for state officials to manipulate Confucian traditions for political purposes.

A study of Chinese views on capital punishment reveals public reluctance to express an opinion and a general willingness to concur with an image of the state that is 'caring, careful, impartial and restrained' in its use of the death penalty (Ho 2005). Through its control of information, China continues to present the death penalty as an unfortunate necessity. Reports in the media, highlighting the most extreme examples of cold-blooded killers, serve to endorse capital punishment and promote the view that only the deserving die (Liebman 2005).

The government continues to closely monitor and repress dissent, but it remains vulnerable domestically to revelations of serious rights violations. While Chinese journalists enjoy little freedom of expression, some stories, such as recent reports of slave labour in Shanxi brick kilns, become too big to ignore. The case of Sun Zhigang, a student killed in police detention, led to swift and sweeping changes to the old 'shelter and investigation' system under which migrants had regularly been detained (China Digital Times 2005). Revelations about the torture and wrongful conviction of innocent suspects have undoubtedly contributed to the current high level concern at coerced confessions and wrongful executions (Lu and Miethe 2007) and may help account for some of the recent reforms. Traditional attitudes and the constraints on public debate, however, mean that, in the short term, concerns of miscarriages of justice are unlikely to result in a groundswell of popular opinion supporting abolition. China's 'iron fist' policy has been a popular response to the fear of rising crime and instability as the country rapidly modernises.

China's growing engagement with the international human rights regime reflects a diplomatic objective to be perceived as a constructive member of the international community (Foot 2000). But, international pressure on an ascendant China arguably has limited impact. The main impetus for improved protection of human rights lies within the domestic arena (Harris 2002). Nationalism is a potent force. Any perception that Chinese sovereignty is undermined by foreign governments and international organisations risks a populist backlash. In the aftermath of the 'colour' revolutions in the former Soviet Union, there has been increased suspicion on the part of the authorities of international NGO activity and the role of foreign governments, particularly that of the United States. Although civil society and non-governmental organisations in China continue to grow in number, no independent national human rights organisations are registered. In the absence of an organised human rights community in China, legal scholars and *weiquan* lawyers provide the only significant alternative perspective on the protection of a citizen's right to a fair trial and safeguards when facing the death penalty.

Known as 'rights-protecting' or *weiquan* lawyers, a small number of activist lawyers have been using their position as independent professionals, not only to provide a quality defence to their clients, but also, to speak out for improved implementation of the law in practice and to draw attention to its shortcomings. Much of the work of *weiquan* lawyers has been in relation to land rights and ensuring adequate levels of compensation for the appropriation of farmers' land, bringing them into frequent conflict with local officials. But, a number of criminal defence lawyers have also been drawing attention publicly to the conduct of death penalty cases and highlighting failings in safeguarding the defendant's rights (Teng 2007). But, with activist lawyers under attack and all lawyers facing restrictions from local regulations on handling 'important, difficult or sensitive' cases (Human Rights in China 2006), the pressures on the legal profession undermine the emergence of a collective voice to challenge the more gross violations of fair trial rights.

Chinese academics believe that, in the long term, given international trends, China will abolish the death penalty. Qiu Xinglong, Dean of the Law School at Hunan Xiangtan University, which hosted a seminal conference on the death penalty in 2002, has been one of the most prominent scholars to propose complete abolition of the death penalty in China. He has also been critical of the timidity of most Chinese academics in challenging the dominant view that the death penalty is needed because of the current political-social conditions (Lu and Miethe 2007).

The majority scholarly view supports a step-by-step process of reducing the numbers of capital crimes and restricting the conditions in which the death sentence would be given. It has been suggested that in taking the long view on abolition some academics are thinking in terms of at least a hundred years, referring to the several centuries it took before eventual abolition in Europe (Nowak and Xin 2000). Many scholars subscribe to the opinion, articulated by Professor Chen Xingliang of Beijing University, that the relatively low level of economic development in China provides support for capital punishment since the relative value placed on human life is low. With limited economic resources, the death penalty appears for many people to be a cheap and effective way of responding to growing levels of crime (Lu and Miethe 2007). Arguments supporting such a correlation between wealth and human rights are persuasive in China and some scholars have suggested that abolition could be achieved by 2020, by which time China would be a middle income country. Nevertheless, comparative data reveals that China, like many other countries with a Confucian heritage, still scores low relative to income with respect to the protection of civil and political rights (Peerenboom 2007).

Conclusion

In developing its distinctive discourse on human rights China has drawn on a traditional cultural repertoire which values social relationships and respect for authority. The Confucian overtones provide cultural legitimacy and in the asymmetries of power relations the government perspective on human rights has a hegemonic status. The majority of Chinese reformists operate within this framework drawing on culturally acceptable patterns of behaviour and the language of law to advance human rights understanding. The rule of law has become the principal trope for reformers as they seek to develop a new narrative of a just and modern society. In contrast with the earlier reformist narrative of democracy and political reform, this is a discourse that is state sanctioned (Wang 2006); both government and reformers agree that the rule of law is a desirable alternative to its opposite, a state of lawlessness or *luan* (chaos). To the state's 'thin' concept of law as scientific and rational, lawyers and legal scholars have been adding layers of meaning building a richer, more moral and ethical framework for judging state actions. It is difficult for the government to openly contest this 'thicker' rule of law concept without undermining its own rhetorical commitment to law and the development of a 'harmonious' society.

Working within this framework of ideas, and traditional values of hierarchy, the importance of personal relationships and giving face (usually reinforced by a ritual of banquets and drinking) Chinese reformers participate in a dialogue with the state on the death penalty through conferences and seminars rather than through conflictual discourse and action. Calls for abolition and criticism of current practice can be tolerated politically as individual acts of resistance so long as there is no organised attempt to challenge the dominant party line.

For the time being, reformers are focusing their efforts on revising the Criminal Procedure Law to bring it more closely in line with China's obligations under international law. Since the end of the Cultural Revolution China has come a long way in developing a rule-based criminal justice system and international attention, including pressure in relation to extradition requests, has helped to put the death penalty on the domestic agenda. The recent decision to restore the power of the Supreme People's Court to give final approval of death sentences and the requirement that appeals are held in open court strengthen the state approved discourse of law and provide improved safeguards for those accused of capital offences. But these steps are not a move towards abolition. As Vice Minister of Justice Zhang Jun is quoted saying with respect to sentencing, 'The focus of reforming the punishment system is not to abolish the death penalty, but to set up more long-term prison sentences – for example, 20- or 30-year sentences – to reduce the use of the death penalty' (China Daily 2005a).

As an advocate for abolition in China, Europe's potential moral influence has been strengthened by its vocal condemnation of the death penalty in the United States (European Union 2007). But China is just too powerful to be bullied into abolishing the death penalty and in the long term it is the moral arguments for abolition which will need to be persuasive: already there is an influential view that abolition is a mark of a civilised country. However, while challenging international use of the death penalty has become a defining project for the European Union (Girling 2005), for the Chinese government pursuing abolition promises few perceived benefits to the current Party-State.

The salience of the death penalty lies in its symbolic importance as an expression of sovereign power (Sarat 2001). While in the United States this may, as Sarat suggests, lie in local democracy; in China power resides with the Communist Party. In staking its claim to legitimacy, to both an international and domestic audience, the Chinese government can no longer ignore the dominant discourse of human rights. Operating within a broad internationally shared normative framework, China still presents a culturally relativist perspective which appeals to nationalist aspirations at home and associates it with an anti neo-colonialist policy abroad (Tang 1995). Presenting the image of a state that kills only when absolutely necessary, permits China to endorse a language of law while acquiring legitimacy from carrying out a punishment which is still very widely supported by the public (Lu and Miethe 2007). Growing use of the suspended death sentence may, in the years ahead, pave the way for introducing a moratorium on executions while further delaying the politically sensitive decision to abolish the death penalty. A recent Supreme People's Court document said that, 'All criminals that can be sentenced without the need for immediate execution should be given a death sentence with a two-year reprieve' (China Daily 2007c). The experience with abolition of the death penalty for juveniles has suggested just such a way ahead for reformers (Yao forthcoming).

References

Alford, W. (1995), 'Tasselled Loafers for Barefoot Lawyers: Transformation and Tension in the World of Chinese Legal Workers', *China Quarterly* 141.

Amnesty International (2007), 'The Olympics Countdown: Repression of Activists Overshadows Death Penalty and Media Reforms' (30 April 2007) <http://web.amnesty.org/library/Index/ENGASA170152007>, AI Index: ASA 17/015/2007.

Asad, T. (1997), 'On Torture, or Cruel, Inhuman and Degrading Treatment', in Wilson (ed.).

Bakken, B. (1993), 'Crime, Juvenile Delinquency and Deterrence Policy in China', *The Australian Journal of Chinese Affairs* 30.

Bauer, J. and Bell, D. (eds.) (1999), *The East Asian Challenge for Human Rights* (Cambridge: Cambridge University Press).

Bodde, D. and Morris, C. (1967), *Law in Imperial China: Exemplified by 190 Ch'ing Dynasty Cases* (Cambridge, Mass: Harvard University Press).

Boulanger, C. and Sarat, A. (2005), 'Putting Culture into the Picture: Toward a Comparative Analysis of State Killings', in Sarat and Boulanger (eds.).

Chan, J. (1999), 'A Confucian Perspective on Human Rights for Contemporary China', in Bauer and Bell (eds.).

Chen, W. (2005), 'Prevention of Coerced Confessions will be Key Issue in Next Year's Expected NPC Revisions to Criminal Procedure Law' (originally published 13 July 2005 *Xin Jing Bao*) <http://news.xinhuanet.com/legal/2005-07/13/content_3212099_3.htm>, accessed 5 October 2007.

Chen, Z. (2002), 'Restrictions on the Imposition of the Death Penalty' (published on website of Institute of Law) <http://www.iolaw.org.cn/shownews.asp?id=922>, accessed 5 October 2007.

China Daily (2005a), 'China Questions Death Penalty' (online publication 27 January 2005) <http://www.chinadaily.com.cn/english/doc/2005-01/27/content_412758.htm>.

———(2005b), 'Wronged Man Demands Compensation' (online publication 12 May 2005) <http://www.chinadaily.com.cn/english/doc/2005-05/12/content_441385.htm>.

———(2005c), 'Death Penalty Appeals to be Heard in Open Court' (published online 8 December 2005) <http://www.chinadaily.com.cn/english/doc/2005-12/08/content_501671.htm>.

———(2007a), 'Procedures Detailed for Death Penalties' (Originally published China Daily 12 March 2007, published online 12 March 2007) <http://english.peopledaily.com.cn/200703/12/eng20070312_356528.html>.

———(2007b), 'Official's death sentence a warning – paper' (online publication 31 May 2007) <http://www.chinadaily.com.cn/china/2007-05/31/content_884392.htm>.

———(2007c), 'Capital punishment decreases nationwide' (online publication 5 September 2007) <http://www.chinadaily.com.cn/china/2007-09/05/content_6080916.htm>.

———(2007d), 'SPC relaxes death sentence rules' (online publication 14 September 2007) <http://www.chinadaily.com.cn/china/2007-09/14/content_6106056.htm>.

China Digital Times, Sophie Beach (2005), 'The Rise of Rights?' <http://chinadigitaltimes.net/2005/05/rise_of_rights.php>, accessed 5 October 2007.

Cho, B. (2004), 'The Death Penalty in South Korea and Japan: "Asian Values" and the debate about capital punishment?', in Hodgkinson and Schabas (eds.).

Chu, M. (2000), 'Criminal Procedure Law in the People's Republic of China: The Dilemma of Crime Control and Regime Legitimacy' *UCLA Pacific Basin Legal Journal* 18.

Clarke, D. and Feinerman, J. (1995), 'Antagonistic Contradictions: Criminal Law and Human Rights in China', *The China Quarterly* 141.

Cohen, J. (1968), *The Criminal Process in the People's Republic of China, 1949–1963: An Introduction* (Cambridge, Mass: Harvard University Press).

Congressional-Executive Commission on China (2003), 'The Execution of Lobsang Dondrub and the Case against Tenzin Deleg, the Law, the Courts and the Debate on Legality' (published online 10 February 2003) <http://www.cecc.gov/pages/news/lobsang.php>.

———(2006), *2006 Annual Report* (published online 20 September 2006) <http://www.cecc.gov/pages/annualRpt/annualRpt06/index.php>.

Council of Europe (2004), *The Death Penalty: Beyond Abolition* (Strasbourg: Council of Europe).

Dikötter, F. (2001), *Crime, Punishment and the Prison in Modern China* (London: Hurst & Company).

Dui Hua Foundation (2007), 'Death Penalty Reform Brings Fewer Executions in China' (published online 8 June 2007) <http://www.duihua.org/2007/06/death-penalty-reform-brings-fewer.html>.

European Union (1998), 'Guidelines EU Policy Towards Third Countries on the Death Penalty' (published online 29 June 1998) <http://ec.europa.eu/external_relations/human_rights/adp/guide_en.htm>.

EuropeAid /1165448/C/SV, *European Initiative on Democracy and Human Rights Evaluation on the Abolition of Death Penalty Projects* (published 4 April 2007) <http://ec.europa.eu/europeaid/where/worldwide/eidhr/documents/eidhr_evaluation_death_penalty_final_report_4april07_en.pdf>.

Foot, R. (2000), *Rights Beyond Borders: The Global Community and the Struggle over Human Rights in China* (Oxford: Oxford University Press).

Fu, H. (2006), 'When Lawyers are Prosecuted: the struggle of a profession in transition' (May 2006). Available at SSRN: http://ssrn.com/abstract=956500. unpublished manuscript.

Girling, E. (2005), 'European Identity and the Mission Against the Death Penalty in the United States' in Sarat and Boulanger (eds.).

Great Britain-China Centre, 'Project Updates: Combating Torture Project (2006-8 EU-funded)' <http://www.gbcc.org.uk/project.htm>, accessed 5 October 2007.

Harris, P. (2002), 'Review: Putting China to Rights' *The China Journal* 48.

Ho, V. (2005), 'Capital Punishment in China' in Boulanger and Sarat (eds.).

Hodgkinson, P. and Schabas, W. (2004), *Capital Punishment: Strategies for Abolition* (Cambridge: Cambridge University Press).

Hood, R. (2002), *The Death Penalty: A Worldwide Perspective* (Oxford: Oxford University Press).

Howie, C. (1996), 'Chinese Critiques of the Ultimate Penalty', *China Rights Forum* Fall 1996. <http://hrichina.org/public/contents/article?revision%5fid=2620&item%5fid=2619>, accessed online 5 October 2007.

Human Rights in China (2006), 'Setback for the Rule of Law: Lawyers under Attack in China', *Trends Bulletin* (published 28 August 2006) <http://www.hrichina.org/public/contents/article?revision%5fid=36024&item%5fid=30425>, accessed 5 October 2007.

———(2007), *State Secrets: China's Legal Labyrinth* (published online 11 June 2007) <http://hrichina.org/public/contents/article?revision%5fid=41506&item%5fid=41421#TOC>.

Human Rights Watch, 'Beijing 2008: China's Olympian Human Rights Challenges' <http://china.hrw.org/agenda_for_reform>, accessed 5 October 2007.

Kahn, J. (2005), 'Torture's Role in Chinese Justice', *International Herald Tribune* (1 November 2005).

Kent, A. (2001), 'States Monitoring States: The United States, Australia, and China's Human Rights, 1990–2001', *China Quarterly* 23.

Lawyers Committee for Human Rights (1996), *Opening to Reform? An Analysis of China's Revised Criminal Procedure Law* (New York: Lawyers Committee for Human Rights).

Lawyers Committee for Human Rights (1998), *Lawyers in China: Obstacles to Independence and the Defense of Rights* (New York: Lawyers Committee for Human Rights).

Leng, S. and Chiu, H. (1985), *Criminal Justice in Post-Mao China: Analysis and Documents* (Albany, State University of New York Press).

Liebman, B. (2005), 'Watchdog or demagogue? The Media in the Chinese Legal System', 105 *Columbia Law Review* 1.

Liu, J., Zhang, L. and Messner, S. (eds.) (2001), *Crime and Social Control in a Changing China* (Westport, Connecticut: Greenwood Press).

Lu, H. and Miethe, T. (2007), *China's Death Penalty: History, Law and Contemporary Practices* (New York: Routledge).

Nathan, A. and Gilley, B. (eds.) (2002), *China's New Rulers: the Secret Files* (London: Granta).

Nowak, M. and Xin, C. (eds.) (2000), *EU-China Human Rights Dialogue: Proceedings of the Second EU-China Legal Experts Seminar Held in Beijing on 19 and 20 October 1998* (Vienna: Studienreihe des Ludwig Boltzman Instituts fur Menschenrichte) IV.

O'Brien, K. and Li, L. (2006), *Rightful Resistance in China* (Cambridge: Cambridge University Press).

Peerenboom, R. (2002), *China's Long March toward Rule of Law* (Cambridge: Cambridge University Press).

(2007), *China Modernizes: Threat to the West or Model for the Rest?* (Oxford: Oxford University Press).

Rojek, D. (2001), 'Chinese Social Control: From Shaming and Reintegration to "Getting Rich is Glorious"' in Liu, Zhang and Messner (eds.).

Sarat, A. (2001), *When the State Kills: Capital Punishment and the American Condition* (Princeton: Princeton University Press).

Sarat, A. and Boulanger, C. (eds.) (2005), *The Cultural Lives of Capital Punishment* (Stanford: Stanford University Press).

Schabas, W. (2002), *The Abolition of the Death Penalty in International Law* (Cambridge: Cambridge University Press).

(2004), 'International Law and the Death Penalty: Reflecting or Promoting Change?' in Hodgkinson and Schabas (eds.).

Scobell, A. (1990), 'The Death Penalty in Post Mao China', *China Quarterly* 123.

Smith, J. and Gompers, M. (2007), 'Realizing Justice: The Development of Fair Trial Rights in China', *Chinese Law and Policy Review* 10.

Spence, J. (1999), *The Search for Modern China* (New York: W.W. Norton & Company Inc.) 125.

State Council Information Office, 'Human Rights in China' (published November 1991) <http://www.china.org.cn/e-white/7/index.htm>, accessed 5 October 2007.

Tang, J. (1995), 'Human Rights in the Asia-Pacific Region: Competing Perspectives' in Tang (ed.).

Tang, J. (ed.) (1995), *Human Rights and International Relations in the Asia Pacific* (London: Pinter).

Tanner, M. (2000), 'State Coercion and the Balance of Awe: the 1983–1986 "Stern Blows" Anti-Crime Campaign', *The China Journal* 44.

Teng, B. (2007), Paper presented at *Third World Congress Against the Death Penalty*, Paris 1–3 February 2007.

Trevaskes, S. (2002), 'Courts on the Campaign Path in China: Criminal Court Work in the "Yanda 2001" Anti-Crime Campaign', *Asian Survey* 42:5.

United Nations Commission on Human Rights (2006) (published 10 March 2006) *Report of the Special Rapporteur on torture and other cruel, inhuman or degrading treatment or punishment, Manfred Nowak, Mission to China* E/CN.4/2006/

Add.6. <http://www.ohchr.org/english/bodies/chr/special/countryvisitsa-e.htm>, accessed 5 October 2007.

Human Rights Council, 'Human Rights Council Opens Fourth Session Press Release' (published online 12 March 2007) <http://www.unhchr.ch/huricane/huricane.nsf/0/1DAA6AE8F3FE1970C125729C005CF20F?opendocument>, accessed 5 October 2007.

Wang, Y. (2006), 'Human Rights Lawyers and the Rule-of-Law Camp', *China Rights Forum* 3.

Wilson, R. (ed.) (1997), *Human Rights, Culture and Context: Anthropological Perspectives* (London: Pluto Press).

Xia, Y. (2000), 'Death Penalty and "The Most Serious Crimes": A Critical Review of Article 6(1) of the International Covenant on Civil and Political Rights' in Xia (ed.).

Xia, Y. (ed.) (2000), *Public Law Review in China Vol.2* (Beijing: Law Publishing House).

Xinhua (2007), 'China Rejects "Strike Hard" Anti-crime Policy for More Balanced Approach' (published online 14 March 2007) <http://english.people.com.cn/200703/14/eng20070314_357516.html>.

Yao, J. (forthcoming) 'A Way to Abolish the Death Penalty' Paper presented at the 2nd International Forum on Contemporary Criminal Law (2007) at Renmin University.

Zhao, B. (2005) 'The Gradual Abolition of the Death Penalty for Non-violent Crimes in China', *Journal of China University of Political Sciences and Law* 23.

Zhou, W. (1995) 'The Study of Human Rights in the People's Republic of China' in Tang (ed).

Chapter 10

The Abolitionist Movement in Death Penalty-Friendly Asia: The Cases of South Korea and Taiwan

Sangmin Bae

At the 1993 Asian regional preparatory meeting for the Vienna World Conference on Human Rights, the representatives of some Asian governments asserted that human rights must be understood in the context of 'significance of national and regional particularities and various historical, cultural and religious backgrounds' (Bangkok Declaration 1993). In this, the so-called 'Bangkok Declaration on Human Rights', participating governments stressed that the universalist perspective of human rights does not properly acknowledge and respect cultural variations. Emphasising the incomparability of 'Asian values' and the universal conceptions of democracy and human rights, they contended that Asia has different definitions and standards of human rights that are appropriate to its own cultural legacies. Proponents of Asian values, including politicians and (often politically well-connected) intellectuals denounced the universal application of international human rights standards: 'Imposing the human rights standard of one's own country or region on other countries or regions is an infringement upon other countries' sovereignty and interference into other countries' internal affairs' (Xie and Niu 1994, 1), '[we are] reaffirming the principles of respect for national sovereignty, territorial integrity and non-interference in the internal affairs of States' (Bangkok Declaration 1993). The Asian discourse on human rights has been growing since the 1993 Bangkok meeting, but key components of its arguments already appeared a few years prior in some Asian countries' official governmental documents and statements. For instance, China's 1991 White Paper on human rights stated that, '[o]wing to tremendous differences in historical background, social system, cultural tradition and economic development, countries differ in their understanding and practice of human rights' (Government of China 1991).[1]

The principal component of the Asian values thesis, that is, government's restrictions on human rights are a matter of cultural differences, has been extended to the 'Asian approach' to the death penalty. Malaysia's former Prime Minister

1 Since 1991, the Chinese government has issued the White Paper on a variety of issues of human rights mostly in response to international criticism of the Tiananmen Square incident.

Mahathir Mohamad has argued that policy regarding the death penalty is purely a domestic issue of criminal justice, which is largely determined by Malaysia's internal value system. According to Lee Kuan Yew, the former Prime Minister of Singapore, '[t]he basic difference in our approach springs from our traditional Asian value system, which places the interests of the community over and above that of the individual. In criminal law legislation, our priority is the security and well being of law-abiding citizens rather than the rights of the criminal to be protected from incriminating evidence' (Tan 2002). Like the ongoing debates over the compatibility of the universality of human rights and respect for individual culture, the issue of the death penalty centers on whether it should be considered as a prerogative of the national legal system or simply a violation of the 'right to life', a right to which everyone, including the worst criminal, is entitled.

East Asia, where the Asian values argument has been most developed, is the region leading the world in frequency and scope of capital punishment. According to Amnesty International, many Asian countries are included in the list of twenty-five countries that carried out executions in 2006, including China, Singapore, Vietnam, Indonesia, Malaysia, and Mongolia (Amnesty International 2007). Unlike countries such as Ukraine or Poland, which abolished the death penalty to meet one of the conditions for admission to the Council of Europe and the European Union, East Asian countries are subject to no binding multilateral checks on their domestic policies. With no outside pressure and surrounded by those who equally support capital punishment, Asian countries have little incentive to abolish the death penalty, which may explain why Asia leads the world in its use. In the Asian context, it is easy for those who favour the death penalty to argue that the abolition of capital punishment is an imported idea that does not accord with their domestic norms.

Given that in Asia almost all countries retain and use the death penalty, recent efforts of South Korea and Taiwan in death penalty reform signal an important change. Although neither county has yet to abolish the death penalty, they certainly have taken steps in the direction of abolition. In both countries, the number of crimes which carry a mandatory death sentence has been greatly reduced. The South Korean government has not carried out a single execution since December 1997 and, in Taiwan, the rates of executions have drastically declined over the past ten years culminating in zero executions in 2006 (see table below). The growing abolitionist movement in these two countries stands in marked contrast not only to their death-penalty friendly neighbours but also to their own authoritarian past, during which the death penalty was regularly imposed on political dissidents as well as common criminals.

The purpose of this chapter is to identify similarities and differences in the political and social climate surrounding the abolitionist movement of South Korea and Taiwan. I begin by briefly touching on public opinion in both countries. This section asks about the extent to which domestic public support for the death penalty has an impact on the abolitionist movement. Following this, I move on to

Table 10.1 Number of Executions in South Korea and Taiwan, 1990–2006

Year	90	91	92	93	94	95	96	97	98	99	00	01	02	03	04	05	06
S. Korea	14	9	9	0	15	19	0	23	0	0	0	0	0	0	0	0	0
Taiwan	78	59	35	18	17	16	22	38	32	24	17	10	9	7	3	3	0

Source: Korea National Statistical Office (KNSO); Ministry of Justice of Taiwan, 2007.

an analysis of the abolitionist movement in South Korea and Taiwan focusing on both the grassroots level and the level of political leadership.

Public Opinion on the Death Penalty in South Korea and Taiwan

Public opinion in South Korea is consistently in support of the death penalty. When the most recent abolition bill was presented to the Legislation and Judicial Committee of the National Assembly in February 2005, former Justice Minister Kim Seung-gyu, who favours the death penalty, stated that a majority of the public supported capital punishment. He presented statistics from polls conducted by the National Human Rights Commission (NHRC) and the Korea Society Opinion Institute showing support for the death penalty at 69.5 percent and 66.3 percent, respectively. In June of 2005, the Ministry of Justice, in criticising abolition legislation, noted that two-thirds of the Korean public supported the death penalty (*JoongAng Ilbo*, 22 February 2006).

In Taiwan also, opinion polls have shown that a majority of the population greatly favour retention of the death penalty. According to a survey conducted in the United Daily News in May 2000, 75 percent of respondents said they support the death penalty (Hsu 2000). In the survey carried out by Professor Ben Chang Shia of Fu Jen University in 2001, 79.7 percent of respondents support the death penalty (Ben 2001, 69). In a poll conducted by the Academia Sinica in June 2006, 76 percent of the people oppose the abolition of the death penalty. This number, however, drops to 44 percent when people are asked if the death penalty could be replaced with life imprisonment without parole. Furthermore, 62 percent of respondents said that if a death row inmate has behaved well, his or her sentence could be commuted from death to life in jail or long-term imprisonment, while 35 percent opposed the idea (*Taipei Times*, 13 October 2006).

A broad problem facing abolition of the death penalty in East Asian countries (or anywhere else) relates to the public's common perception on the death penalty as a deterrent and retribution for crime. Strong public support appears to be the main reason for retaining capital punishment (Ellsworth and Ross 1983; Gross and Donald R. Kinder 2000; Warr 1995). However, public sentiment on criminal policy in general has always been conservative everywhere. Public opinion in favour of the death penalty is similar across countries, regardless of political and social backgrounds (Bae 2007, 117–120; Haines 1996, 164; Marshall 2000, 12–14). It means that many countries have abolished the death penalty despite majority public support for its continued use. Their successful and sustained abolition of the death penalty has never been a result of great popular demand.

The Abolitionist Movement in South Korea

While keeping the death penalty in law, South Korea has imposed a moratorium on the practice since December 1997, which has drawn much international attention. In October 2006 the UN Human Rights Committee, which monitors commitment to the provisions of the *International Covenant on Civil and Political Rights* (ICCPR), addressed South Korea's report on the death penalty. In line with the UN's declared goal to provide for the abolition of the death penalty in law, the UN Human Rights Committee called upon South Korea to sign the *Second Optional Protocol* to the ICCPR and to abolish the death penalty.[2] Amnesty International, noting this decade long moratorium, is also urging formal abolition in South Korea. Already engaged in a worldwide campaign to promote abolition, Amnesty International has singled out South Korea for a pro-abolition campaign – the first time this influential human rights organisation has focused on a single nation. Justice Minister Chun Jung-bae stated that the Ministry was 'deeply aware that Amnesty International has selected Korea as a target country for its campaign to abolish death sentences' at the occasion of announcing the Justice Ministry's study on ending the death penalty (*JoongAng Ilbo*, 22 February 2006). In October 2006, Amnesty International teamed up with individual activists and non-governmental organisations across Asia to form the Anti-Death Penalty Asia Network (ADPAN), with the objective of pressing the National Assembly of the Republic of Korea to pass the current abolition bill (*Korea Times*, 10 October 2006). A discussion on how Korea got to this point should start with a description of the grassroots human rights and religious organisations and their anti-death penalty activism.

Movements from Below

At the grassroots level, several human rights and religious groups have been campaigning for abolition in South Korea. One such group is the Lawyers for Democratic Society, also called Minbyun, organised by lawyers who defended victims of the military government. Members of this group have continued their efforts to persuade political and judicial leaders as well as the general public to support the abolitionist cause. The religious community, traditionally a key opinion leader in Korean society, has been active in the abolitionist movement for decades. Their history as a 'resistance group' reveals that for many years before Korea's democratisation, the churches took the initiative in the largely unpopular movement

2 The U.N. General Assembly adopted the *Second Optional Protocol to the International Covenant Aiming at the Abolition of the Death Penalty* on December 15, 1989. The protocol declared that '[n]o one within the jurisdiction of a State Party to the present Protocol shall be executed' (Article 1.1) and that '[e]ach State Party shall take all necessary measures to abolish the death penalty within its jurisdiction' (Article 1.2). The only reservations permitted under the protocol are those that would provide 'for the application of the death penalty in time of war pursuant to a conviction for a most serious crime of a military nature committed during wartime' (Article 2.1).

against the death penalty. Catholic leaders have frequently visited politicians and asked them to introduce appropriate legislation for abolition. Catholic groups in South Korea have long advocated abolition, especially the Catholic Bishops' Conference of Korea, which has been conducting an independent campaign against the death penalty. In addition, the Pan-Religion Union for Abolition of the Death Penalty was formed in 2001 to unite members of varied religious groups, from Catholicism, Protestantism, and Buddhism, to Korean folk religion, in the common cause of abolition. Their religious faith, as an important source of the abolitionist cause, put them on the frontline of the anti-death penalty movement. Leaders from different religions issued a common statement that, '[a]ll life is sacred, including the lives of criminals who have committed heinous crimes. The campaign is inevitable as capital punishment undermines human dignity by taking state revenge on someone for ... past mistakes' (*Chosun Ilbo*, 26 January 2001).

The anti-death penalty movement at the grassroots level shows that Korea is ahead of its neighbours. In the case of Japan, despite a large number of active human rights organisations, the anti-death penalty movement has not been mobilised effectively. When abolishing the death penalty does not appear to be 'the will of the people,' it is considered risky for civil groups, let alone the political leadership, to promote it. Some have argued that grassroots support does not seem to be a necessary condition for abolition (Hood 2004; Zimring 2003). It did not seem so in Europe, where pro-capital punishment sentiment remained relatively high at the time of abolition. However, general public support for capital punishment does not necessarily mean that the anti-capital punishment movement will be likely to remain underdeveloped. South Africa, where robust anti-capital punishment organisations played a decisive role in expediting progress toward abolition, is a good example. Even when a majority of the public backed the retention of capital punishment, invoking the unprecedented growth of violent crime in the post-apartheid era, the South African human rights organisations relentlessly promoted the legitimacy of abolition (Bae 2005, 49–68; Holt 1989, 273–318, Mihalik 1991, 118–42).

Movements from Above

With a newly amended constitution and the first democratic elections being held in 1987, South Korea has successfully made a transition to democracy. The election of President Kim Dae-jung in December 1997, in particular, meant that this country, for the first time in over fifty years, has accomplished the transfer of power from an entrenched ruling camp to an opposition leader. Kim's 'sunshine policy' or active engagement with North Korea, and protection and promotion of human rights became the two most important policy objectives. Upon Kim's election, many national security offenders were released and currently no long term national security offenders remain in Korean prisons.

President Kim Dae-jung's anti-death penalty stance is formed by his personal background as a death row survivor himself and Roman Catholic, which strengthened his belief in the abolitionist cause. He refused to sign death warrants during his entire term as president and pardoned death row inmates on several occations. In his public appeal in 2006, supporting Amnesty International's campaign to abolish South Korea's death penalty, Kim wrote, '[t]he reason [I opposed the death penalty] is because capital punishment cannot be the true solution and it also goes against democracy and human rights. I dearly hope that capital punishment can be abolished to see the true completion of democracy not only in Korea but in the whole world' (Kim 2006). Kim's successor, President Roh Moo-hyun, who assumed office in February 2003, has not signed any death warrants either, making South Korea *de facto* abolitionist.[3]

At the legislative level, resolutions calling for the abolition of the death penalty have also repeatedly been brought up. The Special Bill on Abolishing the Death Penalty (Special Bill) was presented three times to the National Assembly – in 1999, 2001 and 2004. The major premise of the Special Bill is to remove the provision of the death penalty from the Criminal Code and the Special Act, and to make life imprisonment the maximum punishment. The first of its kind in Korea, the Special Bill that was submitted in 1999 to the 15th Session of the National Assembly received the assent from 91 of the 299 members. This first attempts, however, went nowhere as the Bill could not pass the Legislative and Judiciary Committee (LJC) of the National Assembly. In South Korea, Bills are voted on once in the National Assembly and are then passed to an appropriate Committee for discussion and approval before being returned to the National Assembly for a second and decisive vote. In November 2001, 155 members of the 16th National Assembly, then consisting of 273 members, voted for the Special Bill. Despite the majority of the members supporting the Special Bill in November 2001, it failed to be discussed again by the LJC and the Bill lapsed when the National Assembly finished its term in April 2004. Nonetheless, as the same Bill has been repeatedly presented, more and more lawmakers have joined the cause and put their names to it. They share the view that it is a contradiction to take the life of a criminal in the name of justice, that doing so is at odds with the idea of human dignity and the right to life guaranteed by the Constitution. In December 2004, 175 members of the 17th National Assembly, consisting of 299 members, again introduced the Special Bill to abolish the death penalty leading to the re-introduction of the Bill to the LJC in February 2005. The LJC, which has sixteen members and is divided into two sub-committees, discussed the Special Bill for the first time in February 2006 and a public hearing was held at the National Assembly in April 2006. At the hearing, it appeared that only a small majority of the LJC supported the Special Bill, but this was not unexpected given that the Committee was mostly composed of former prosecutors who have strongly supported the death penalty. The LJC itself was reconstituted in July 2006 and it has not been clear how many among

3 *de facto* abolitionist refers to ccountries and territories which retain the death penalty for ordinary crimes but have not conducted executions for at least ten years (Schabas 1997, 32).

the newly reconstituted LJC support the Special Bill. If the LJC votes in favour of the Bill, it is passed on for a final vote in the National Assembly.

Other governmental bodies have given significant support to the value of abolition, notably the recently created National Human Rights Commission (NHRC). Formed in 2001, the NHRC is an independent, government-mandated body with the stated mission of preserving and promoting human rights. In 2003, the commission first raised capital punishment as an issue, and the government included abolition as one of its '[t]op 10 Human Rights Tasks'. This list was drawn up at the urging of the United Nations Human Rights Commission. In March 2005, the NHRC met to discuss the question of abolition. Its members largely supported abolition but had widely divergent opinions of what abolition would entail, opting to convene again in April to decide whether to send the government a formal recommendation to abolish the punishment. Following a decision to recommend abolition, in early 2006 the NHRC drafted a National Action Plan (NAP) that includes various steps to improve the South Korean human rights regime. This plan was fostered by greater participation in the United Nations World Conference on Human Rights and drawn up as part of the Vienna Declaration and Program of Action. The National Action Plan was presented to the UN as required in June, and consequently implemented in 2007. The plan includes a series of reports and recommendations, designed as a blueprint for five years of progress in South Korea's human rights conditions. Among the provisions of the NAP is a recommendation that South Korea abolish the death penalty. The then ruling Uri Party and the minor opposition parties, the Democratic Party and the Democratic Labour Party, support the NAP, but the chief opposition party, the Grand National Party, opposes it on the grounds that 'the recommendations will destroy the basic order of the democracy and shake the basis of the country' (*Korea Times*, 10 January 2006).

Different Justice Ministers have different ideas about the death penalty. About the Special Bill to abolish the death penalty, Justice Minister Kim Seung Kew, whose term lasted for eleven months from July 2004, commented that the death penalty must be maintained for social peace and safety. Referring to cases of serial murder, he asked: 'Should the life of those committing such crimes be respected at the risk of jeopardising the safety of so many innocent citizens?' He urged respect for the fact that two-thirds of the public is opposed to the abolition of the death penalty (*Hangyereh*, 18 February 2005; 29 March 2005).

Kim's successor Justice Minister Chun Jung Bae took a different stance. As part of a larger effort to improve human rights in the criminal justice system, in February 2006, Chun ordered a review of capital punishment to determine whether abolition was desirable (*JoongAng Daily*, 22 February 2006). In addition, the Ministry of Justice conducted a public hearing on the death penalty. The results of the hearing were intended to guide the Ministry in deciding whether or not to endorse the abolition bill. Despite its previous support for capital punishment, and in contrast to its previous stance that talk of abolition was 'premature', the Ministry of Justice signalled its intent to eventually drop the death penalty in favour of life imprisonment without parole. The subsequent Justice Minister, Kim Seong-ho, took a similar stance on the death penalty when announcing that his ministry was considering revising some provisions on capital punishment, '[b]efore making a decision on whether to abolish the death penalty, we are considering whether there are some provisions that need to be scrapped'. His Ministry studied a provision which allows a judge to order the death penalty against soldiers who injure themselves to avoid battle (*Yonhap News, 22 April 2007).*

Changing attitudes toward capital punishment are also apparent in the courts. Although judges still sentence some convicted offenders to death, they are reluctant to hand down such sentences. Thus the judiciary continues to affirm the status of capital punishment as the most extreme punishment, reserved for correspondingly extreme circumstances. An example of the opposition to the overuse of capital punishment occurred in a case from April 2006. A Seoul court rejected the death penalty for a man convicted of sexually assaulting and murdering a schoolgirl, despite the strong objections of the public. The court stated that capital punishment had been ruled out because the crime was not premeditated, '[t]he death penalty is a very exceptional punishment which takes human life, and it should be handed down only when there is evident and objective reason' (*Korea Times*, 13 April 2006). The court here appears to recognise that capital punishment is a potential violation of the human right to life, though it is suitable in exceptional cases. Such reluctance to impose the death penalty provides hope for an easier transition toward abolition, as people already recognise the severity of the death penalty in contrast to other methods of punishment. A recent appointee to the Supreme Court, Justice Chon Soo-an, also expressed her support for abolition during her hearing confirmation in June 2006, strengthening the stance of the abolitionist camp in the highest court (*Korea Times*, 29 June 2006).

The abolitionist movement in South Korea has stimulated public debate on the death penalty, which until recently had been almost entirely absent. As the debate has continued, public support for the death penalty has lessened. According to a 2001 poll conducted by the Korean newspaper *Chosun Ilbo* and the mobile research institute *Mbizon*, 36 percent of 838 respondents over the age of twenty opposed the death penalty, compared with 34 percent in 1999 and 20 percent in 1994 (*Korea Herald*, 4 December 2001). Other polls have yielded similar findings. The Korea Survey Research Organisation poll in 2002 found that 54 percent favoured the death penalty and 45 percent were against it. When the same questions were asked in 1992, 67 percent were in favour of the death penalty, while only 20 percent opposed it (Chyung 2002, 11). Gallup Korea's survey confirmed that opponents of capital punishment have significantly increased over the years; 20 percent opposed it in 1994, 31 percent in 2001, and 40 percent in 2003. In 1994, 70 percent of Koreans reportedly supported the death penalty; this had dropped to 55 percent by 2001, and to 52 percent by 2003 (Gallup Korea, 27 September 2003). Certainly the majority of the Korean population still supports capital punishment, yet a growing number favour its abolition. The efforts of abolitionists during the past decade to make the death penalty a social and political issue have contributed to the drop in public support.[4]

More importantly, people who advocate the abolition of capital punishment state that legal and policy changes that address fundamental human rights cannot be dependent on popular opinion and cannot wait for change from the 'bottom up'. It is true that in all successful cases of abolition, political elites, including the executives, legislators, and judges, were active in shaping public opinion. It is often up to the authorities to challenge public beliefs that are contrary to fundamental human rights, particularly in cases that determine life and death.

The Abolitionist Movement in Taiwan

Until the late 1990s, Taiwan had been one of the top ten executioners worldwide; thirty-eight executions were performed in 1997, thirty-two in 1998, and twenty-four in 1999, which amounts to more executions per capita than in the United States. However, the nation's annual number of executions has rapidly declined in recent years. Seventeen prisoners were executed in 2002, and that number shrank to ten in 2001, nine in 2002, seven in 2003, and three each in 2004 and 2005, while 2006 marked the first year in Taiwan's recent history with no executions. A series of amendments to laws have also been made in the pursuit of reducing the use of the death penalty. With the repeal in 2000 of the controversial Act for the Control and Punishment of Banditry, most crimes carrying a mandatory death sentence have been redefined as crimes for which the death penalty is an option but not a requirement. In January 2005, the Taiwanese legislative Yuan passed amendments to the Criminal Code that prohibit capital punishment for those under the age of eighteen or over the age of eighty. Most recently, in December 2006, another round of amendments to several laws has made the death penalty no longer mandatory. Judges can decide whether to mete out capital punishment or life sentences to convicts who have committed such crimes as serious currency counterfeiting and to members of the military who disobey orders on the front line with formidable negative military consequences (*China Post*, 23 December 2006).

Movements from Below

Over the past decade several non-governmental groups in Taiwan have campaigned for the abolition of the death penalty. The Taiwan Alliance to End the Death Penalty

4 Public support for the death penalty understandably waxes and wanes in response to arbitrary events. When serial murder suspect Yoo Young-chul confessed in July 2004 that he killed at least twenty-one innocent people, countless internet articles called for immediate executions of death row prisoners. It happens worldwide that opinion polls taken at the time of well-publicised violent crimes show a peak in support for the death penalty, perhaps distorting the true figures.

(TAEDP), formed in 2003, encompasses such groups as Amnesty International Taiwan Chapter, the Taiwan Association for Human Rights, religious organisations, and the Judicial Reform Foundation. In particular Amnesty International's Taiwan chapter, working closely with the Taiwan Association for Human Rights, has pressured successive Taiwanese governments to end executions and abolish the death penalty.

As in South Korea, the Catholic Church in Taiwan has had a leading moral role in the drive for abolition. A number of Christian organisations have been involved in the campaign for the abolition of the death penalty and participated in prison visiting programs with prisoners on death row. Wu Chung-yuan, secretary-general of the Catholic Diocese of Kaohsiung stated, '[t]he death penalty is barbaric and primitive ... If we believe that one human being should not take the life of another, then the same should hold true that the government must not be allowed to kill ... The death penalty only kills the convicted. It does not solve the real problems in society which led to the crime' (Hsu 2000). Fr. John Chen Kun-chen, secretary general of the Taipei-based Chinese Regional Bishops' Conference, welcomed the recent amendment to Taiwan's criminal code as a step toward abolition of the death penalty by stating that '[it's] proof of Taiwan's increased regard for human rights' (Coday 2005). On the Protestant side, the Taiwan Presbyterian Church, which has long worked on a range of human rights issues, has also campaigned vigorously against the death penalty. The Chi-nan Presbyterian Church in Taipei, located right next to the Legislative Yuan, has been the site of many candlelight vigils against the death penalty, and some Presbyterian elders have been vocal in calling for an end to the death penalty.

The Judicial Reform Association has drawn attention to the legal issues of Taiwan's death penalty. This group widely publicised a number of death penalty cases where serious legal errors went unresolved by the courts, yet the defendants were executed nonetheless. Working together, these different groups within the Taiwanese NGO community have made the death penalty an issue that has caught the attention of government officials and the general public alike.

Movements from Above

At present, a significant change is occurring in Taiwan. In spite of public opinion polls that consistently show 70 percent of Taiwanese in favour the death penalty, President Chen Shui-bian has repeatedly remarked that capital punishment will be phased out in Taiwan once and for all and he has stated, '[s]ince I became president in 2000, Taiwan launched the campaign to abolish the death penalty by reducing the handing down and execution of capital punishment ... My goal is to achieve zero executions within the shortest time and eventually abolish the death penalty' (*Taiwan Times*, 8 September 2005). The Taiwanese presidential office and the cabinet have jointly drafted legislation to abolish the death penalty, resulting in the Criminal Code amendment on 7 January 2005. A major amendment to the entire death penalty section of the Criminal Code took effect on July 1, 2006 (*Taipei Times*, 8 September 2003, 3 October 2003, 8 January 2005).

The Ministry of Justice has initiated a program that seeks to educate the public about abolition of the death penalty. The ministry hopes that its long-range program will eventually create a more fertile ground for public acceptance of abolition. According to the ministry's policy paper, this program includes enlisting the assistance of the Government Information Office in making public service announcements, holding education classes for police and prosecutors, and asking scholars to write articles on abolition, as well as conducting public hearings and seminars in order to publicise the idea of abolition (*China Post*, 11 January 2007). In addition to this long-term educational approach, the Ministry of Justice also takes immediate short-term steps to ensure that all death penalty verdicts receive the most thorough review. Prosecutors at the High Court and Supreme Court levels review death penalty cases to see if any extraordinary appeals should be filed. Extraordinary appeals are appeals filed by prosecutors calling for 'extra' rounds of appellate court review. Once the normal and 'extraordinary' appellate process is completed, the case returns to the Ministry of Justice for a final review before the minister signs the execution warrant.

In spite of such meaningful efforts recently taken by governmental leadership, prompt action does not seem to be forthcoming. Individual ministers, in particular, take a different view on the death penalty. Minister of Justice Morley Shih, for instance, suggested in October 2006 that 'Taiwan might not be able to abolish the death penalty soon, because the vast majority of the public is consistently opposed to abolition' (*Taipei Times*, 12 October 2006). Many working prosecutors and judges are strongly in favour of the death penalty. According to surveys by the Ministry of Justice, between 80 and 90 percent of Taiwan's judges believe that capital punishment is an appropriate measure (Hsu 2000). It is not uncommon for judges to view capital punishment as a deterrent to crime and to see discussion of abolition as 'mostly for foreign dignitaries, scholars, and the media' (Lin 2002). This widely held view among the judiciary certainly makes the death penalty a highly controversial issue at the leadership level, especially given its conflict with the President's aspirations toward abolition. According to a survey released by the Huang Judicial Reform Foundation in 2005, the debate over capital punishment ranked third out of the top ten most controversial legal issues. This report points out the rift in the positions of the different branches in government – the administration's vowing to reform the death penalty and prosecutors and judges who continue to recommend and grant death sentences (*Taiwan Headlines*, 18 April 2005).

In Taiwan's prosecutorial system, the Minister of Justice has no authority to dictate what position of each individual prosecutor should be on the appropriateness of the death penalty in certain cases. This allows the prosecutors to have a large affect on whether or not the death penalty will be pursued since there is no official oversight as to when capital punishment is put on the table for various crimes. The difference between Taiwan and South Korea in their progress toward abolition is partly explained by who the final decision maker is. In Taiwan's case, the Minister of Justice signs the execution order – the final step before execution. Not all ministers fulfill this duty easily, and some even refuse to sign. Whether a minister signs or not can depend on her or his character and personal attitude. Yet most of them consider signing it a duty, regardless of their personal views. After all, a Justice Minister is merely the top of a bureaucratic organisation, and the bureaucracy demands continuity. In South Korea, it is the president who authorises executions. The autonomy and prerogative of the president's political leadership allow Korea to take a stronger stance in favour of the abolitionist cause.

Arguments and Motivations in Pursuit of Abolition

Historically the death penalty was abolished more quickly in countries that experienced radical political transition. Those countries could precipitate legal reforms that might have taken much longer to accomplish in times of political stability (Bae 2007, 121–122). In Taiwan and South Korea a strong political willingness among elites exists to implement the international human rights standards in domestic law. Political leaders in these countries are more motivated to enact reforms, especially because their recent path to democratic transition and consolidation provides a favourable climate for rapid change in the human rights area. Both Taiwan and South Korea have achieved concrete progress in strengthening civil society and cultivating open political debate, through which political leaders seek opportunities to implement the standards set by international human rights law.

In the abolitionist movement in both South Korea and Taiwan, two rationales rest primarily on the principle of the 'right to life' and the state's effort, driven by both moral and political considerations, to comply with international human rights standards. According to the former, all human beings have a fundamental right to life, and capital punishment obviously violates this right. Commemorating the World Day Against the Death Penalty, Former President Kim Dae-jung said that 'to end a person's life even in the name of the law clearly runs counter to the basic principle of human rights' (*Hankyoreh*, 10 October 2007). Although the strong statement against the death penalty came after he had already left office, it is notable that no executions occurred during his time in the presidency. Korea's National Human Rights Commission also cited the right to life as the primary grounds for its recommendation of abolition. The NHRC contends that capital punishment violates not only the right to life but also provisions against disproportionate punishment and cruel and unusual punishment (National Human Rights Commission of Korea 2003). At the February 2005 presentation of his abolition bill for consultation, Representative Yoo Ihn-tae stated, 'it is contrary to the spirit of the Constitution that the government wields the power to take the life of a human being' (*Donga Ilbo*, 18 February 2005).

Outside the philosophical arguments of human rights and the intricacies of constitutional law, objections to capital punishment arise in other ways. Some people are motivated by the government's willingness to comply with international human rights norms and standards. The government of South Korea is itself motivated in this fashion, having voluntarily participated in programs like the UN World Conference on Human Rights. By actively seeking to participate in international human rights campaigns and considering the recommendations of multinational human rights bodies, South Korea and Taiwan indicate an interest in becoming part of the trend toward stronger human rights initiatives on a global scale. As citizens of a relatively recent industrialised nation of increasing global importance, domestic actors may feel that the country should support human rights initiatives for purposes of prestige. Chang Chu-young, Secretary General of Minbyun, has linked Korean development to abolition, '[t]o become an advanced country in terms of human rights, it is desirable for the nation to abolish the death penalty' (*Korea Times*, 22 February 2006). In a similar fashion, Peter Huang, leader of the Taiwan Alliance to End of the Death Penalty, states that, 'Taiwan's level of [democratic] development is high, and so international expectations are naturally higher for Taiwan than for other countries conducting executions, like Iran or Saudi Arabia' (*Taipei Times*, 28 December 2006). In Taiwan's case, in particular, the abolition of capital punishment relates to the nation's wish to gain diplomatic recognition from major external powers:

> Taiwan's move toward abolishing capital punishment has been closely followed by the EU and international human rights organisations ... Given Taiwan's diplomatic predicament, it is very important to promote substantial relations with powerful nations. The government's declaration that it would abolish the death penalty raised hopes that this could be a factor in strengthening diplomatic relations with the EU (Chiu 2007).

According to South Korea Representative Chyung Dai-chul, who took the lead in drafting the 2001 abolition bill, state executions should be prohibited as soon as possible not only because they contradict the spirit of the Constitution, which stipulates human dignity and respect for life, but because abolition is also a global trend: over a hundred nations have so far pursued abolition in their legal systems (Chyung 2002, 4–5). To abolish capital punishment, he implied, is to join an international human rights project. Each step the nation takes in the field of human rights narrows the long-standing gap between the world's leading nations and South Korea, which seeks to earn respect on the global stage. The death penalty is a topic that transcends national debate; it entails a significant international dimension.

Conclusion

Korea's possible passing of the bill to abolish the death penalty would be historic, as it is the first abolitionist bill in East Asia. International human rights organisations note that South Korea's decision would be an example to other countries in the region that are beginning to see the retention of the death penalty as a violation of international human rights norms rather than the state's prerogative. Such move would also provide South Korea with an opportunity to exercise regional leadership in the defence of human rights. Taiwan's President Chen Shui-bian said that he felt that a strong stance on the abolition of the death penalty could assist its neighbours, particularly mainland China, in dealing with human rights issues. In both countries, advocates for abolition believe that momentum has already gathered for abolition and reform of the criminal justice system. They consider abolition as elevation of human rights standards, through which the countries can establish themselves as 'a beacon of human rights' throughout the region.

Within Asia, three most outspoken and influential critics of the Asian values argument have been the two former Presidents of Taiwan, Lee Teng-hui and Chen Shui-bian, and the former President of South Korea, Kim Dae-jung, whose countries have much stronger abolitionist movements, involving both state and private actors, than do neighbouring nations. Although it remains uncertain whether South Korea and Taiwan will take legal action to abolish the death penalty, pending legislation presents the strongest opportunity yet. Long-standing attitudes among those in the government that capital punishment is necessary are steadily wearing away. Time will tell whether these two countries can make the transition and become the first nations in East Asia to abolish capital punishment, thus weakening the 'cultural variations' argument in relation to a principal human rights issue. Until then, human rights advocates must be satisfied with keeping the moratorium in place.

References

Amnesty International, 'Death Penalty Statistics 2006' (published online April 2007) <http://web.amnesty.org/library/Index/ENGACT500122007> accessed 9 September 2007.

Bangkok Declaration, 'Final Declaration of the Regional Meeting for Asia of the World Conference on Human Rights' (adopted on 2 April 1993) <http://www.unhchr.ch/html/menu5/wcbangk.htm> accessed 9 September 2007.

Bae, S. (2005), 'The Right to Life vs. the State's Ultimate Sanction: Abolition of Capital Punishment in Post-Apartheid South Africa', 9:1 *International Journal of Human Rights* 49–68.

Bae, S. (2007), *When the State No Longer Kills: International Human Rights Norms and Abolition of Capital Punishment* (Albany: State University of New York Press).

Ben, C. (2001), 'Survey on Abolition of the Death Penalty', in Ryden S.J. (ed.).

Chyung, D. (2002), 'Capital Punishment Abolition Campaign in Korea and Its Prospect', paper presented at a seminar entitled 'Justice and Human Rights in Council of Europe Observer States: The Abolition of the Death Penalty', Tokyo, May 27–28.

Coday, D. (2005), 'Taiwan in Death Penalty Debate', *National Catholic Reporter* (January 28).

Council of Europe (ed.) (2004), *Death Penalty: Beyond Abolition*, edited by the Council of Europe (Strasbourg: Council of Europe).

Ellsworth, P.C. and Ross, L. (1983), 'Public Opinion and Capital Punishment: A Close Examination of the Views of Abolitionists and Retentionists', *Crime and Delinquency* 29, 116–169.

Government of China (1991), 'White Paper on Human Rights in China', <http://library.thinkquest.org/26639/newpage22.htm> accessed 9 August 2007.

Gross, K. and Kinder, D.R. (2000), 'Ethnocentrism Revisited: Explaining American Opinion on Crime and Punishment', paper presented at the Annual Meeting of the American Political Science Association, Washington D.C.

Haines, H.H. (1996), *Against Capital Punishment: the Anti-Death Penalty Movement in America, 1972–1994* (New York: Oxford University Press).

Hall, P.A. and Taylor, R.C.R. (1996), 'Political Science and the Three New Institutionalism', 44 *Political Studies* 936–957.

Holt, N.V. Jr. (1989), 'Human Rights and Capital Punishment: The Case of South Africa', 30: 1 *Virginia Journal of International Law* 273–318.

Hood, R. (2004), 'Introduction – The Importance of Abolishing the Death Penalty', in the Council of Europe (ed.).

Hsu, J. (2000), 'Debate over Death Penalty', *Taiwan Journal* (June 16) <http://taiwanjournal.nat.gov.tw/site/Tj/ct.asp?xItem=18035&CtNode=122>accessed 9 September 2007.

Kim, D. (2006), 'A Contribution to the Campaign of Amnesty International for the Abolition of Capital Punishment', Asia Death Penalty [website] <http://asiadeathpenalty.blogspot.com/2006/03/south-korea-kim-dae-jungs-call-for.html> accessed 9 August 2007.

Larkin, J. (2000), 'Death, Be Not Proud', 26:7 *Asiaweek* (February 25).

Lin, F. (2002), 'Experts Meet at Human Rights Symposium', *Taiwan Journal* (October 25) <http://taiwanjournal.nat.gov.tw/site/Tj/ct.asp?xItem=19665&CtNode=118> accessed 9 August 2007.

Marshall, J.M. (2000), 'Death in Venice: Europe's Death-penalty Elitism', 223:5 *The New Republic* 12–14.

Mihalik, J. (1991), 'The Moratorium on Executions: Its Background and Implication', 108 *The South African Law Journal* 118–142.

National Human Rights Commission of Korea, 'Mandate & Jurisdiction / About the Commission' (published online 2001) <http://humanrights.go.kr/english/about_nhrck/mandate_01.jsp> accessed 9 September 2007.

National Human Rights Commission of Korea, *'Sahyŏngjedoe taehan kungminŭisikchosa'* [Survey of Public Opinion on the Death Penalty] (published online 2003) <http://library.humanrights.go.kr/global/docs/s_detail.html?mastid=20242> accessed 9 September 2007.

Ryden E.S.J. (ed.) (2001), *Taiwan Opposes the Death Penalty* (Taipei: John Paul II Peace Institute).

Schabas, W. (ed.) (1997). *The International Sourcebook on Capital Punishment* (Boston: Northeastern University Press).

Tan, A. (2002) 'Singapore Death Penalty Shrouded in Silence', *Reuters*, April 12.

Thelen, K. (1999) 'Historical Institutionalisms in Comparative Politics', 2 *Annual Review of Political Science* 369–404.

Warr, M. (1995) 'Poll Trends: Public Opinion on Crime and Punishment', 59:2 *Public Opinion Quarterly* 296–310.

Xie, Bohua and Niu, L. (1994) 'Review and Comments on the Issue of Human Rights', paper presented at JUST International Conference, 'Rethinking Human Rights', Kuala Lumpur, Malaysia.

Zimring, F.E. (2003), *The Contradictions of American Capital Punishment* (New York: Oxford University Press).

PART III
OVERVIEW OF ABOLITION STRATEGIES AND ALTERNATIVES TO THE DEATH PENALTY

Chapter 11

Capital Punishment: A Review and Critique of Abolition Strategies

Peter Hodgkinson, Seema Kandelia and Lina Gyllensten

This chapter engages with the various strategies adopted in pursuit of the abolition of capital punishment and proffers a model that is both evidence based and holistic in preparing for abolition and its aftermath. In our opinion it is essential to such an approach that attention and resources are dedicated to improving legal services, prison and police practices, crime victims' services, humane and proportionate alternatives to the death sentence, the public and elites' knowledge about the death penalty and finally promoting a political philosophy that avoids reinforcing the myths of the benefits of capital punishment. The replacement of capital punishment and all its trappings should be addressed as a penal policy issue informed by reference to the wealth of available evidence. Paradoxically, abolition of the death penalty itself rarely leads to improvements to the administration of justice that such a radical step would indicate. Reliance by many abolitionists on the moral high ground can be counter-productive, though that is not to deny that there is a moral and an emotional dimension. In this brief overview, we will address some of the most frequently cited justifications for the death penalty including the theories of deterrence, retribution and incapacitation, as well as looking at the concept of abolitionism itself. Issues relating to the law, victims, public opinion, moratoria and alternatives to the death sentence will also be explored.

The Usual Suspects

Deterrence

Deterrence claims for the death penalty make occasional appearances in the academic literature and more often in the rhetoric of activists and politicians who favour capital punishment. On many occasions this has prompted equally ill-informed rebuttals from the anti-capital punishment lobby. Most informed commentators have now put the deterrence justification aside because it usually generates more heat than light, and it is essentially a politically motivated distraction deployed to reassure an electorate fearful of crime who are receptive to any purported solution on offer. Roger Hood notes, 'the issue is not whether the death penalty deters some – if only a few – people but whether, when all the circumstances surrounding the use of capital punishment are taken into account, it is associated with a marginally lower rate of the kind of murders for which it has been appointed' (Hood 2002, 208). The reliance on deterrence assumes that a person who is about to commit a crime, most likely murder, would take into account what the likely punishment will be, once detected and convicted.

Even so, the deterrence argument continues to be relied on by governments to justify the use of the punishment. The evidence most commonly relied on is based on Isaac Ehrlich's (1975) econometric analysis, though usually without any reference to the many authoritative refutations of his findings and methodology. Ehrlich set out to refute earlier studies by criminologist Thorsten Sellin (1959) who had argued that his research showed that the death penalty is no better a deterrent to murder than life imprisonment. Ehrlich used sophisticated economic statistical analysis when looking at the relation between the death penalty and murder and came to the conclusion that from 1933 to 1965, 'an additional execution per year ... may have resulted on average in seven or eight fewer murders'. However, he did concede that this alone was not necessarily sufficient justification to use the death penalty over other punishments. There are several recent studies, currently being analysed by legal scholars and economists, which claim that each execution reduces homicides by between three and eighteen. These include the work of Dezhbakhsh *et al* (2002) who claim that capital punishment has a strong deterrent effect, and that each execution contributes on average to eighteen fewer murders. In fact, as recognised in the same study, an increase in any of three probabilities – arrest, sentencing or execution – tends also to reduce the murder rate. On the other hand, Sorenson *et al* (1999) examined executions in Texas between 1984 and 1997 and speculated that if a deterrent effect were to exist, it would be found in Texas because of the high number of death sentences and executions. Using patterns of executions across the study period and the relatively steady rate of murders in Texas, the authors found no evidence of a deterrent effect. The study concluded that the number of executions was unrelated to murder rates in general, and that the number of executions was unrelated to felony rates.

However, any lingering doubts about deterrent effects should be dispelled when introduced to the evidence. Multiple flaws in the administration of the death penalty are revealed annually by US research. A deeper appreciation of the issues and the research generated by the deterrence debate is provided by Bailey and Peterson (1997), Hood (2002) and Bowers and Pierce (1975) who used Ehrlich's model and did not find any deterrent effect.

A recent and very telling contribution to this debate was made by Jeffrey Fagan of Columbia Law School in his testimony to the hearings on the future of capital punishment in the State of New York. Fagan noted that there appears to have been a resurgence in studies examining execution rates and linking capital punishment with a reduced number of murders; the alleged deterrent effect is then used as a foundation for the argument of increasing the use of capital punishment. It is not unexpected that these studies should receive acclaim as they give a highly emotive and political issue a scientific twist. However, as Fagan points out:

> These new studies are fraught with technical and conceptual errors: inappropriate methods of statistical analysis, failures to consider all the relevant factors that drive murder rates, missing data on key variables in key states, the tyranny of a few outlier states and years, and the absence of any direct test of deterrence (Fagan 2005, 2).

Assertions of 'strong causal effects' are not uncommon even in the legal sphere and as such, most claims of 'new deterrence' disintegrate once examined in greater detail (Fagan 2005). Nevertheless, a recent New York Times article surveyed the current spate of analyses and concludes from the research and the comments of several of its authors, many of whom are abolitionists, that the deterrent justification warrants re-visiting (Liptak 2007). Finally, it is worth noting that whilst there is no clear evidence that the death penalty is a more effective deterrent than the usual alternative of long-term imprisonment, it would be incorrect and grossly misleading to characterise the death penalty as having no deterrent effect.

Retribution

In any survey of popular opinion about the death penalty, retribution and deterrence are the principal justifications given for approval of the punishment. In fact, since the demise of support for deterrence, retribution has become the key reason for supporting the death penalty. It is best summarised by the scriptural invocation to take 'an eye for an eye, a tooth for a tooth', and in the case of the death penalty, a 'life for a life'.[1] As a consequence of public and political pressure, retribution is all too frequently confused with revenge; confused because retribution differs from revenge as legal constraints are placed upon its severity in the interests of justice and proportionality. Retribution unlike deterrence does not need to meet any statistically measurable outcomes in terms of its effectiveness; it is an entirely subjective measure of people's feelings, which is what makes it difficult to distinguish from the popularly expressed need for revenge. As Justice Chaskalson in *The State v Makwanyane* (1995) said:

> The righteous anger of family and friends of the murder victim, reinforced by the public abhorrence of vile crimes, is easily translated into a call for vengeance. But capital punishment is not the only way that society has of expressing its moral outrage at the crime that has been committed. We have long outgrown the literal application of the biblical injunction of "an eye for an eye, and a tooth for a tooth". Punishment must to some extent be commensurate with the offence, but there is no requirement that it be equivalent or identical to it (paragraph 129).

---

1 Indeed, a number of passages in the Bible codify notions of justice and retribution: 'Eye for eye, tooth for tooth' (Leviticus 24:20 and Exodus 21:24), '[h]e that smiteth a man, so that he die, shall be surely put to death' (Exodus 21:12), and '[w]hoever sheds the blood of man, by man shall his blood be shed, for God made man in his own image' (Genesis 9:6).

Incapacitation

Finally, in the diet of punishment philosophies, putting aside rehabilitation, we come to incapacitation; a purpose of punishment that is generally associated with an outcome of imprisonment. In the context of the death penalty, incapacitation is frequently confused with individual deterrence. Inherent to deterrence policy, is the intention to influence future behaviour and whilst the execution of offenders certainly 'incapacitates' them, thus bringing an end to their criminal careers, it is not deterrence. However, it is surely unacceptable for any society to descend to such actions in the name of effective penal policy? Incapacitation in the imprisonment context is favoured by some to support calls for whole of life imprisonment as the alternative to the death sentence, which itself raises profound questions, which we will address later, not least because preventative claims applied to either imprisonment or the death sentence are complex and controversial.[2]

Core Issues and Strategies

Abolitionism: A Flag of Convenience?

As an objective of this paper is to critique the received wisdom of abolition strategies, an appropriate starting point is to try to tease out the motivation of individuals and groups that consider themselves death penalty abolitionists – they are a mixed bunch. On the one hand, there are those who oppose capital punishment based on the offence, and others, based on the characteristics of the defendant or on the death penalty process itself. Some individuals and countries restrict their support to murder; others for crimes including rape, child sexual abuse, drug trafficking, kidnapping, bribery, corruption, adultery, apostasy and arson. There is neither clarity, agreement, nor consistency worldwide about which crimes should attract the death sentence, nor, as to why a particular crime should be distinguished as deserving death. 'Abolitionists' influenced by this approach remain so only until the 'unacceptable' crimes have been removed from the purview of capital punishment.

Further opposition to capital punishment is based on specific characteristics of the defendant, for example, they oppose sentencing to death those under the age of eighteen at the time of the offence, those with mental impairment or mental illness, women, pregnant women, or those over a certain age (e.g. 65 years). Some oppose its mandatory imposition, possibility of wrongful convictions, mode of execution, or policies with their roots in religious beliefs (Islam, Mormonism and some schools of Christianity).

Examples of dissonance within the abolitionist camp are provided by such occasions as the trial and execution of Timothy McVeigh, the Oklahoma City

---

2 See Dieter (1997).

bomber. A poll conducted shortly before Timothy McVeigh's execution showed that 20% out of the 80% that supported his execution were ordinarily opposed to capital punishment (Sundby 2006). In another report, Richard Dieter, Director of the Death Penalty Information Center, is reported as saying, '[w]ith McVeigh, you don't have the questions of innocence or lack of counsel or some of the others things that have particularly troubled folks about (other recent) executions. It's nothing like the typical death-penalty case' (Willing 2001).

Another example of this 'exceptionalism' is demonstrated by Australia's policy regarding the death penalty and the case of the Bali bombers. In an ABC News broadcast in 2006, Philip Alston, Professor of Law at New York University and the UN spokesman on the death penalty describes the stance taken by the Federal Government of Australia over the execution of the Bali bombers as 'Australian exceptionalism strategy', as it appears to support a position inconsistent with its apparent opposition to the death penalty in cases involving Australian citizens (ABC News 2006). Perhaps we can look forward to a less ambiguous position from the recently elected Australian Labour Party and therefore an opportunity in Australasia to develop a coalition of countries opposed to capital punishment.

The execution of Saddam Hussein in Iraq led to the unseemly spectacle of governments and individuals worldwide falling over themselves to avoid making unequivocal statements opposing it. Some disguised their obvious approval by restricting their criticism to the process not the principle. In the UK, then Foreign Secretary, Margaret Beckett, was reported as saying that she welcomed the fact that Saddam Hussein 'has been tried by an Iraqi court for at least some of the appalling crimes he committed against the Iraqi people' and that his execution meant that he had been 'held to account'. In the same statement, she did, however, confirm that the British government remained opposed to the death penalty (BBC News 2006). Another example of exceptionalism?

Capital Punishment and the Law

It does not help the credibility of the debate or the authority of the abolitionist industry when claims continue to be made that capital punishment is unlawful. On the contrary, most international and regional human rights instruments expressly provide for it as an exception to the right to life.[3] It only becomes unlawful when

3 Article 6 of the *International Covenant on Civil and Political Rights* (1976) 999 UNTS 171; Article 2 of the *European Convention on Human Rights* (1955) 213 UNTS 221; Article 4 of the *American Convention on Human Rights* (1978) 1144 UNTS. 123; and Articles 10–12 of the *Arab Charter of Human Rights*, 15 September 1994, Council of the League of Arab States, 102nd Session, Res. 5437 (unofficial translations) in (1996) 56 Review of the International Commission of Jurists 57 and (1997) 4 International Human Rights Reports 850, revised May 2004. The Arab Charter reiterates the limitations on capital punishment in the other international instruments, but it is not in force and has found little support. Article

states decide to subject themselves to the aspirations, restrictions and protections that underpin international law. Absent from these instruments is any form of legal sanction for those who breach them. What limited sanctions there are take other forms, for example, censure by the UN Committee on Human Rights or the International Court of Justice and any subsequent negative press that might cause embarrassment.

Four instruments aimed at abolishing the death penalty are currently in force. The *Second Optional Protocol to the International Covenant to Civil and Political Rights*[4] has a worldwide scope and provides for the total abolition of the death penalty except in times of war. To date, 64 countries are state parties to the protocol. A further eight countries have signed, but not yet ratified it.

Protocol No. 6 of the European Convention on Human Rights[5] places restrictions on the use of the death penalty in peace-time, an undertaking ratified thus far by 46 of the 47 member states of the Council of Europe with Russia being the exception. The only piece of legislation to be found in regional or international human rights treaties which outlaws the death penalty under all circumstances is *Protocol No. 13 to the European Convention on Human Rights*.[6] *Protocol No.13*, a long time aspiration of the Parliamentary Assembly of the Council of Europe (PACE), was eventually opened for signatory on 3rd May 2002 entering into force 1st July 2003. To date, 40 member states of the Council have ratified it, with five signature states.[7]

The *Protocol to the American Convention on Human Rights to Abolish the Death Penalty*[8] provides for the total abolition of the death penalty, but allows

---

4 of the *African Charter on Human and Peoples' Rights*, O.A.U. Doc. CAB/LEG/67/3 Rev. 5 recognises the right to life, but is silent on the subject of the death penalty although the African Commission did passed a resolution in 1999 urging states to consider a moratorium which indicates that the death penalty is permissible under the Charter.

4 *Second Optional Protocol to the International Covenant on Civil and Political Rights, aiming at the abolition of the death penalty*, General Assembly resolution 44/128 of 15 December 1989.

5 *Protocol No. 6 to the Convention for the Protection of Human Rights and Fundamental Freedoms Concerning the Abolition of the Death Penalty*, ETS no. 114.

6 *Protocol No.13 to the Convention for the protection of Human Rights and Fundamental Freedoms, concerning the abolition of the death penalty in all circumstances*, CETS No. 187.

7 Albania, Andorra, Austria, Belgium, Bosnia- Herzegovina, Bulgaria, Croatia, Cyprus, Czech Republic, Denmark, Estonia, Finland, France, Georgia, Germany, Greece, Hungary, Iceland, Ireland, Liechtenstein, Lithuania, Luxembourg, Macedonia, Malta, Moldova, Monaco, Montenegro, Netherlands, Norway, Portugal, Romania, San Marino, Serbia, Slovakia, Slovenia, Sweden, Switzerland, Turkey, Ukraine, United Kingdom (40); signed but not ratified: Armenia, Italy, Latvia, Poland, Spain (5); not signed: Azerbaijan, Russia.

8 *Protocol to the American Convention on Human Rights to Abolish the Death Penalty*, adopted by the General Assembly of the Organization of American States in 1990, OASTS 73.

state parties to retain the punishment in wartime if a reservation is made to that effect. Currently there are nine state parties to the protocol, with a further two that have signed, but not yet ratified it.

There have been a number of legal challenges brought in relation to certain aspects of the death penalty. The issue of delay in carrying out executions, for example, was addressed by the Zimbabwean case of *Catholic Commission for Justice and Peace in Zimbabwe v. The Attorney General and Others* (1993). It was held that delay in implementation of death sentences of up to 72 months was contrary to article 15(1) of the Zimbabwean Constitution, which provides that no person shall be subjected to 'torture or to inhuman or degrading punishment or other such treatment'. The decision relied on several US court[9] decisions as well as the opinions of Indian judges[10] and those of the Judicial Committee of the Privy Council[11] describing the effects of incarceration on death row. More recently, the Constitutional Court of Uganda in *Kigula & Other v The Attorney General* (2005) held that persons on death row for three or more years, after all appeals have been exhausted, were entitled to have their death sentences commuted to life imprisonment. The Supreme Court is yet to rule on the issue. There have been other challenges brought to the courts on issues such as the mandatory nature of

9 *People v Anderson* 493 P.2d. 8880 (1972) Wright CJ stresses the tortuousness of delay involved in the death penalty, at 892. *District Attorney for Suffolk District v Watson* Mass. 411 N.E. 2d 1274 (1980) held the death penalty to be a violation of the cruel punishment clause in the state's constitution.

10 *Francis Coralie Mullin v The Administrator, Union Territory of Delhi* AIR 1983 SC 746, held the right to live with basic human dignity implicit in the right guaranteed under Article 21 of the Constitution, included the right not to be subjected to torture or cruel, inhuman or degrading treatment. *Triveniben and Others v State of Gujarat and Others* (1989) 1 S.C.J. 383 held only the delay since the end of the judicial process was relevant. In *Madhu Mehta v Union of India* [1989] 3 S.C.R. 775 it was held that an eight-year wait for the outcome of a mercy petition to the President was too long and the sentence was commuted to life imprisonment.

11 *Riley and others v Attorney-General of Jamaica* [1982] 3 All ER 469 (PC). Although there was found to be no breach of the Jamaican Constitution in carrying out a death sentence it was stated: "Sentence of death is one thing: sentence of death followed by lengthy imprisonment prior to execution is another".

the death penalty,[12] method of execution[13] and particular offences that attract the death penalty.[14] In all of these cases, however, the death penalty *per se* has been upheld.

Progress Through the Constitutional Courts

An approach favoured by some politicians nervous of the repercussions of abolition is to actively encourage and support their supreme courts in reviewing the constitutional 'right to life' provision. This is an approach taken most notably by the provisional Constitutional Court in South Africa (*The State v. Makwanyane* 1995) and by courts in Lithuania (1999), Albania (1999), Hungary (1990) and Belarus (2004) among others.

Litigation and Capital Punishment

It is arguable that a strategy to remove the death penalty by relying *solely* on litigation is as much part of the problem as of the solution (Hodgkinson 2005). The unintended, though entirely foreseeable, consequences of legal victories can be illustrated by reference to the experiences of the USA and in the British Commonwealth Caribbean where reliance solely on litigation strategies has arguably had the effect of entrenching capital punishment as each legal 'victory' sets off a chain of further litigation and counter-litigation. In the USA, the effectiveness of the federally funded capital defence resource centres in stalling executions can be said to have led to an increase in capital punishment legislation, an increase in the number of capital crimes, severe restrictions to the appeal process and the removal

12 In *Lennox Ricardo Boyce and Jeffrey Joseph v. The Queen* (Appeal No. 99 of 2002) and *Charles Matthews v. The State* (Appeal No. 12 of 2004), 7 July 2004, the Privy Council upheld the constitutionality of mandatory death penalty in Barbados and Trinidad & Tobago respectively (overturning its decision in *Balkissoon Roodal v The State* (Appeal No. 18 of 2003), 20 November 2003). The death penalty in no longer mandatory in Jamaica (*Lambert Watson v. The Queen* (Appeal No. 36 of 2003), 7 July 2004), St. Christopher and Nevis (*Berthill Fox v R* (Appeal No. 66 of 2000), 11 March 2002), Belize (*Patrick Reyes v R*) (Appeal No. 64 of 2001), 11 March 2002) and St. Lucia (*R v Peter Hughes* (Appeal No. 91 of 2001), 11 March 2002).

13 The method of lethal injection was recently upheld by the US Supreme Court in the case of *Baze v. Rees*, 553 U.S. (2008), while the method of hanging in Uganda was upheld in *Kigula & Other v The Attorney General* (2005).

14 In *Coker v. Georgia* (1977), the US Supreme Court barred the death penalty for the crime of rape, and by implication, for any offence which did not result in the death of another person. A challenge to death penalty for drug related offences was recently turned down by the Indonesian Constitutional Court. See Nathalia (2007).

of federal funding.[15] The damage that this could have caused was in great measure mitigated by the presence of an otherwise richly resourced activist infrastructure available in the USA, but not in other parts of the world.

For several decades, lawyers from the UK have been actively involved in capital litigation in the British Commonwealth Caribbean through representation in the Judicial Committee of the Privy Council and supporting local lawyers with challenges in the domestic courts. A consequence of these 'victories', which laudably had secured fundamental protections for their clients, has been to attract considerable hostility from all sectors of Caribbean society. Against this background and in a climate of endless litigation, it was only a matter of time before the region raised the stakes, which is precisely what happened in Belize, Barbados, Trinidad & Tobago and Jamaica. All of these countries began the process of amending their Constitutions in such a way as to overturn the fundamental protections secured by the domestic and UK legal communities. The 'retaliatory' nature of their responses even found their way into the discussions about the recently established Caribbean Court of Justice, which was characterised as a 'hanging' court, one of whose purposes was to restore 'justice' and the 'will of the people' to the region, though the framers refuted this.[16] To date, Belize and Barbados have amended their Constitutions though it is only Barbados that has enacted the amendments. The Jamaican debate has taken place against a backdrop of an alarming number of homicides and other violent crimes, pressing the political imperative of being seen to do something – anything. Jamaica, with a population of 2.7 million recorded 1,671 homicides in 2005, 1,300 in 2006 and up until September 2007 1,400 (Gayle and Glenory 2007; Gomez 2007).

Jamaica has not carried out an execution for over 15 years and thus sits very comfortably in the *de facto* abolition statistics. Leading up to the elections in 2007, both main parties focussed attention on the high homicide rate and the party then in opposition, the Jamaica Labour Party, chided the governing Peoples' National Party for failing to reinstitute executions. The Jamaica Labour Party were returned to government after a lengthy period in opposition and have decided to hold a referendum on the death penalty and to hold a free vote in parliament. The concerns are that these votes will support the resumption of executions and that a cross-party motion to amend the Constitution as in Barbados, could now attract the necessary two-thirds majority. This possibility is of even greater concern in Trinidad & Tobago, which is a friend of the death penalty.[17]

Other derogations from international human rights standards have occurred, for instance, through removal of the protections afforded by the *First Optional Protocol of the* ICCPR in Jamaica in January 1998, Trinidad & Tobago in May

15 For example, the 1996 Antiterrorism and Effective Death Penalty Act, signed into law on 24 April 1996.

16 For a summary of some of the discussions, see Anthony (2003).

17 Trinidad and Tobago, with a population of 1million recorded 386 homicides in 2005 (Seelal 2006) and 269 in 2006 (Ramnarine 2007).

1998, and Guyana in December 1998. This has the effect of denying to all citizens of these countries the right to individual petition to the United Nations Human Rights Committee. Both Guyana and Trinidad & Tobago attempted to re-accede to the First Optional Protocol on the day of withdrawing but with a reservation attempting to exclude all those on death row from taking up the right to individual petition. The Human Rights Committee concluded that to exclude a whole group of persons from this right was so discriminatory and contrary to the object and purpose of the ICCPR that the reservation was invalid.[18] Therefore, in the latter states, all citizens, not just those on death row, continue to be denied the right to individually petition the Human Rights Committee. Thus a strong argument could be advanced that the 'victories' of the defence and the pique of the vanquished have led to an entrenchment of the death penalty, as well as the far reaching consequences of denying every citizen protection against violations of other human rights. It is difficult to know quite how this impasse can be negotiated without recourse to further resource-sapping litigation.[19]

The Moratorium Movement

A focus of abolitionist activity in recent years has been the push for a moratorium on executions. The idea of a moratorium as a campaign dates to the initial activity in the United Nations in the late 1960s. Treaty bodies like the Human Rights Committee have frequently recommended that states still using the death penalty consider a moratorium in an attempt to further the goal of abolition set out in Article 6(6) of the ICCPR. The moratorium demand was revived in 1994, in the doomed United Nations General Assembly resolution, and again in 1999.

In December 2007, a resolution calling for a global moratorium on executions with a view to total abolition was passed by the UN General Assembly. The resolution which asks member states to progressively restrict the use of the death penalty and ensure that international standards on the death penalty are met was adopted with 104 votes in favour, 54 against and 29 abstentions. Even though the resolution has been passed by the full Assembly, its impact is difficult to judge. The General Assembly is only empowered to make non-binding recommendations so, although adoption of the moratorium resolution conveys a strong political message to retentionists, there is no legal obligation stopping states handing down death sentences or carrying out executions. During the debate on the resolution, many states that voted against it reiterated the fact that capital punishment is not against international law and that they retained the right to set their own criminal and penal policies (UN Department of Public Information 2007).

18 *Rawle Kennedy* (Communication 845, 1999).

19 For a counter argument, see Mendes and Delzin 2005, 18–21.

Similarly, the African Commission on Human and Peoples' Rights passed a resolution in 1999 urging state parties to adopt a moratorium on the death penalty.[20] The resolution calls upon member states to limit the imposition of the death penalty only to the most serious crimes, to consider establishing a moratorium on executions and to reflect on the possibility of abolishing the punishment.

Retentionists, on the other hand, use the opportunity of a moratorium period to 'fix' capital punishment's flaws. In the USA, religious fundamentalist supporters of the death penalty, like Pat Robertson, Jerry Falwell and members of the Christian Coalition, were aligned to the Moratorium 2000 movement solely for the purpose of tidying up capital punishment's worst excesses, and to make it more palatable for both domestic and international audiences. That the two sides found some common ground presents those who seek the replacement of the death penalty with both opportunity and danger (Hodgkinson 2004b, 5–8).

Is there any evidence for the claim that abolition will follow a period of review? In the 1960s, executions in the United States were halted *de facto* and between 1972 and 1976 there was a *de jure* halt to executions.[21] Although the ruling in *Furman v Georgia* (1972) had the effect of rendering forty death penalty statutes unconstitutional, the success of the legal argument was not matched with a political will to abolish capital punishment. In response to the *Furman* ruling, states drew up new regulations to ensure that the death penalty was not applied arbitrarily. So despite the numerous calls for moratoriums at the national, regional and international level, little attention has thus far been paid to states' experiences of death penalty moratoria. The effect a suspension of executions has had and what can be learned from these experiences to evaluate the role of moratoria has still to be quantified. Some abolitionists believe that a period without capital punishment will show its folly or that it is unnecessary, and that it bears unnecessary political and financial costs thus eventually leading to abolition. The American Bar Association (ABA) has called for a nationwide moratorium on executions for the purpose of studying the inherent flaws in the USA's death penalty system. Although the ABA clearly states that it takes no position on the question of the death penalty itself, some scholars have suggested that there are underlying abolitionist notions in the ABA's call (Sarat 2001: 255).

Perhaps the most cited moratorium recently is that implemented in January 2000, by Governor George Ryan of Illinois, who suspended executions until a thorough review of the administration of the death penalty had been conducted. His decision was based on his realisation that over a ten year period, thirteen wrongfully convicted inmates had been released from death row, which was more than the number of those executed. Governor Ryan's Commission, presented its findings in April 2002, making eighty-five recommendations, all with the objective of correcting the flaws and weaknesses identified in the Illinois system. While not

20 ACHPR / Res.42(XXVI)99: Resolution Urging the State to Envisage a Moratorium on Death Penalty (1999).

21 For further discussion of the moratorium approach in this era, see Haines (1996).

in the Commission's brief, a narrow majority of its members were inclined to state that the death penalty should be replaced believing that the system was incapable of correction. Those who favour the death penalty in Illinois and elsewhere view the experience not as a weakness but as a measure of the rigour of the present capital punishment process in identifying such flaws. Two days before he left his office, Governor Ryan commuted the death sentences of 157 people on death row (Ryan 2003). To this extent, the suspension of executions has been beneficial but, and it is a big but, the future in Illinois seems to be concerned with improving the death penalty, not removing it.

The moratorium remains in place in Illinois, but recent calls to halt executions have centred on the use of lethal injection as an execution method. As of 17 November 2007, twenty jurisdictions have suspended executions following claims that the combination of drugs used in the execution process can leave the condemned in excruciating pain, thereby violating the constitutional prohibition on cruel and unusual punishment. Executions are also on hold in Nebraska because of a challenge to executions by electrocution (Death Penalty Information Centre 2007a).

While the recent enthusiasm for moratoria may be welcomed by death penalty opponents as it indicates fewer executions, for the time being at least, it should be noted that if the lethal injection method of execution is found to be unconstitutional, there is nothing to prevent states searching for a different method of execution. On 25 September 2007, the US Supreme Court agreed to hear a challenge on the constitutionality of lethal injection, with oral arguments scheduled for 7 January 2008. The last execution in the USA took place on 25 September 2007 with no more expected until the Supreme Court rules mid-2008.[22] Whether the temporary suspension of executions will encourage states to re-examine the use of capital punishment *per se* remains to be seen, but it is the first time in 30 years that they will have the opportunity to assess the effect that no executions have on crime rates and public attitudes.

Many countries do, of course, go through periods of *de facto* abolition before they proceed to eliminate it from their statute books. However, to describe the status of such countries as *de facto* abolitionist, as some do, is misleading. It would be more correct to describe their status as having suspended executions as, in general, the rest of the panoply of death penalty legislation continues. For example, although there had been no declaration of a moratorium in India, between April 1995 and July 2004 no executions had taken place. According to the criteria applied by some groups to *de facto* abolition status, India had almost made the list.

---

22 On 16 April 2008, the Supreme Court upheld lethal injection as a method of execution in Kentucky. However, the question of whether a similar three-drug protocol can be used in other States remains open. Lethal injection will be deemed unconstitutional if litigants can show that there is a 'substantial or objectively intolerable risk of serious harm' and that there is an alternative procedure which is 'feasible, readily implemented, and in fact significantly reduces a substantial risk of severe pain' (*Baze v. Rees*, 553 U.S. (2008)).

However, during this period, death sentences continued to be handed down and in August 2004 Dhananjoy Chatterjee was executed for the rape and murder of a 16-year-old girl.

Similarly, in February 2004, President Levy Mwanawasa of Zambia declared that he would not sign any death warrants for those convicted of capital crimes as long as he was in office. The last execution in Zambia was in 1997 and following his re-election in 2006, the *de facto* moratorium will continue until 2011. President Levy Mwanawasa died in August 2008. Vice-President Rupiah Banda is currently acting President, until the elections on 30 October 2008. In December 2005, the Constitutional Review Commission recommended that Zambia retain the death penalty on its statute books and last year, the Supreme Court rejected a challenge to the death penalty on the grounds that it did not have the power to strike it down. On both occasions, the government remained silent (Sibanda 2007).

The Zambian experience and the resumption of hangings in India highlights the importance of special scrutiny on *de facto* abolition countries as their status is entirely quixotic and vulnerable to swift changes in personnel. This observation highlights a shortcoming in the reliance on a moratorium as a tool for abolition. The important lesson to be learned from these examples is that the moratorium should never become a goal in itself, and that it be continually presented, by abolitionists at any rate, as a step towards total and permanent replacement of capital punishment. Even more desirable, would be to obtain a complete suspension of the death penalty process (no prosecutions, no sentences and no executions) while the raft of essential changes to legislation and infrastructure to prepare society for a life without capital punishment, are put in place. The period of this suspension is one that should be agreed at the outset with a timetable for action.

The Council of Europe model of requiring suspension of executions immediately on accession followed by an agreed timetable to the signing and ratification of the *Protocol No. 6 to the European Convention on Human Rights* comes closest to this model. However, it falls short in not requiring a suspension of the total apparatus of capital punishment or providing sufficient support (technical and financial) for the necessary infrastructure changes in areas such as prisons, probation, victims, alternatives and public reassurance.

Public Opinion

Overwhelmingly, public opinion supports the death penalty – a position not to be lightly dismissed – in that politicians, many of whom mesmerised by such polls, are reluctant to question them or to encourage a more authoritative evaluation. The concern that in the absence of the death penalty personal security will be eroded with a resurgence of disorder, is understandable and the reason for this fear is quite simple; the public have been assured by governments for generations that the solution to serious violent crime is capital punishment. Compared to the number of people who are in fact executed each year worldwide,[23] the death penalty has arguably attained an unhealthy prominence in politics as well as in the popular press. Consequently, appeals to the populist support for capital punishment will in many countries be politically beneficial.

Few countries would have abolished the death penalty if they had waited for public approval, although support for it is rarely tested after abolition.[24] A number do claim to have removed capital punishment with the public's support, for example, after the downfall of the totalitarian regime, the Parliament of the former Czechoslovakia voted in 1990 to abolish capital punishment in response to public opinion and in the same year, as a result of the collapse of the communist dictatorship and in response to public opinion, Romania abolished the death penalty by decree (Economic and Social Council 1995). Nevertheless, the death penalty maintains its popularity in most countries so the argument goes, abolishing it without public support is undemocratic. Naturally, legislators should reflect public opinion to some degree. However, it is imperative that governments lead and inform the debate, not hide behind the views of an ill-informed majority. Nobody suggests, for example, that fiscal policy should be lead by popular opinion (Schabas 2004).

As noted above, it is not uncommon for decisions about capital punishment to be transferred from elected representatives to the judiciary, as the courts may also refer to opinion polls for an indication of public support (Schabas 2004). Rulings on the constitutionality of capital punishment may involve conceptual terms such as 'cruel', 'inhuman' or 'degrading', are all subjectively interpreted, varying between different societies and evolving over time with public opinion being taken into account in this process (Schabas 2004). However, it should not be relied upon too heavily as the purpose of human rights is to protect the individual, regardless of the views of the majority. In *The State v Makwanyane* (1995), the Constitutional Court of South Africa, commenting on the significance of public opinion, held that the purpose of the system was to protect minorities and the marginalised in the democratic process and 'if public opinion were to be decisive there would be no need for constitutional adjudication' (paragraph 88). Practices which are now found to be deplorable once had widespread support and part of a mature democracy is a properly functioning judicial system where the legitimacy of law can be tested.

Regular polls have been undertaken on the death penalty in the US since the 1930s with 1966 standing out as the only year when the opposition to the death penalty was greater than the support (Newport 2007). Notably, this was just a few years before *Furman v Georgia* (1972) where the US Supreme Court Justice, Thurgood Marshall, stated that, 'the question with which we must deal is not

23 Amnesty International estimate that at least 1,591 people were executed in 25 countries in 2006.

24 In the referendum in Ireland in 2001, 62% voted for an amendment abolishing the death penalty.

whether a substantial proportion of American citizens would today, if polled, opine that capital punishment is barbarously cruel, but whether they would find it to be so in the light of all information presently available' (paragraph 362). This hypothesis has to some extent been tested. In studies undertaken in the US, respondents were presented with various issues in relation to the death penalty, such as the mental condition of the offender, disproportionate sentencing based on race or financial status, innocent people being sentenced to death and the availability of life without parole. With each example, as the awareness of the issues increased the support for the death penalty dwindled (Vollum *et al* 2004).

Public support for the death penalty fluctuates and whilst exposure to the academic research that refutes the myths surrounding capital punishment may not in itself be sufficient, some programme of reassurance and information will help. Even though it may not change the views of many who support the death penalty, what it will do if responsibly conducted, is to provide an authoritative basis on which governments can explain their reasons for moving in this direction. The Centre for Capital Punishment Studies (CCPS) has developed a protocol to address this which has been piloted in Malawi, Nigeria, the Philippines and Trinidad & Tobago. Drawing on the available literature, this activity sets out to design a model of information dissemination and awareness raising that could be adapted by different cultures and jurisdictions in confronting the issue of public opinion. Earlier models that influenced our thinking are provided by the consultations undertaken by the Commissions on capital punishment in the UK (RCCP 1953) and Sri Lanka (then Ceylon) (RCICP 1959). Eliciting people's 'belief' in the death penalty does little to inform the debate and majority opinion in support of the death penalty is by and large predictable. However, establishing how important the death penalty is in the 'fight' against serious violent crime reveals altogether different responses with the majority of respondents placing the death penalty low on the list of effective remedies to crime. Another way to approach this issue of 'beliefs' and the death penalty is to ascertain what measures 'the public' considers necessary in the battle against serious crime. An example of this is a recent analysis undertaken by Market and Opinion Research International (MORI) of four social surveys conducted in 1994, 1996, 2000 and 2001. Subjects were asked: 'Which two or three of the following [measures] do you think would do most to reduce crime in Britain?' In the first three surveys, the police were ranked as the most important (51%, 58%, 54%). In 2001, 'better parenting' was considered the most important measure with 55% support. Capital punishment for murder was rated third with 38% support in 1994 and third with 35% support in 1996. By 2000, capital punishment was tied in fourth place with tougher institutions for young offenders, at 25%, and in 2001 it had fallen to seventh place with 20%.[25]

25 MORI Crime and Punishment Polls of 1994, 1996, 2000 and 2001. In the 2001 poll in rank order: better parenting (55%), more police (53%), better discipline in schools (49%), more constructive activities for young people (40%), introduction of a national identity card (29%) and in 6th place more effective programmes to change behaviour (21%).

The CCPS project addresses a number of priorities by targeting the public and key opinion makers regarding the principal arguments on the death penalty and alternative punishments, and helping to establish a dialogue with policy makers on these issues. This in turn lends support to the arguments of those seeking policy options for reforms to limit or abolish the death penalty.

Victims and the Death Penalty

Crime victims are invariably ignored and when remembered, too often exploited in the interest of political imperatives rather than victims' needs. They are a constituency almost universally overlooked by the traditional abolitionist movement, which has proved a significant obstacle to the process of replacing the death penalty. Politicians the world over justify the retention of the death penalty, in part, because of their concerns about crime victims though frequently little or no provision for them has been made by the state.[26]

The victims' needs and rights issue is increasingly having an influence on the shape and direction of legal and penal policy and we see evidence for this in all our current country activities. For example, victims' rights are enshrined in Sha'ria law, which provides for the homicide victims' family to accept financial compensation from the defendant in lieu of execution. In some Islamic countries, the victim's family are entitled to perform the execution. There is some evidence from research in the USA that certain victims lobbies are enjoying a number of procedural gains such as being consulted about prosecution policy, victim impact statements, intervention at parole and clemency hearings and witnessing executions. The most vociferous of these are based in the United States where such groups have made considerable inroads into influencing legal and penal policy. Groups such as Justice for All[27] and Parents of Murdered Children[28] characterise the pro-punishment victim movement in the US and both enjoy considerable political support. The justification politically for these significant procedural rights is that they are responses to the spoken needs of victim groups and that the right to witness the execution provides the final 'closure' to a very painful episode despite the wealth of anecdotal evidence to suggest that any benefit or 'closure'

26 This section draws from Hodgkinson (2004c, 332–358). By 'victims' the author includes the primary victim as well as secondary victims, i.e. close friends and family of the victim and the condemned.

27 Justice for All announces on its website that it is a criminal justice reform organisation that 'shall act as an advocate for change in a criminal justice system that is inadequate in protecting the lives and property of law-abiding citizens'. See <www.jfa.net>. Other sites supported by Justice for All, <www.prodeathpenalty.com> and <www.murdervictims.com>.

28 National Organisation of Parents of Murdered Children, Incorporated <www.pomc.com>.

is illusory. It is crucial to ensure that the victim services model that is adopted is one that addresses the identified needs and not one that is punishment focused or uses victims as part of the prosecution process – the latter is characteristic of the approach in the USA.

There has been an exponential growth in victim research and services over the past two to three decades with international and regional bodies such as the United Nations[29] and the European Commission[30] dedicating research and resources to improved guidelines and practice. These have developed largely through the work of International Victimology,[31] the World Society of Victimology[32] and the European Forum for Victims Services.[33] We would refer you to the excellent text by Paul Rock (1998), which provides a wealth of information in a very sympathetic format about how homicide affects individuals and the range of responses that have been developed to address the pain and suffering experienced by the families and friends of homicide victims.

The victim issue, rather like the offence issue, receives too little attention in both the scholarship and the debate, given that both have developed to a great extent around the paradigm offence of murder, its victims and their families. We need to remind ourselves when considering victims' needs that for many crimes that attract the death penalty there is some difficulty in identifying just exactly who has been victimised, as in most countries where the death penalty is available, it is not reserved for the offence of murder alone.

A case could be made for saying that there is no place for a separate victim service as the state prosecutes not on behalf of individuals but society as a whole, and the 'victim' loss or suffering is already factored into the decision to prosecute and the final sentence. Whilst this is a good argument for not including the victim's perspective into the trial process, it should not replace the development of services

29 United Nations Victim Charter, <www.odccp.org/crime_cicp_sitemap.html>.

30 Commission of the European Communities, 'Crime victims in the European: reflections on standards and action', European Commission, Brussels, 1999. COM (1999) 349 Final.

31 The International Victimology website (IVW) was launched in June 1999 as a resource for all those interested in improving justice for victims of crime and abuse of power. Through IVW, the UN Centre for International Crime Prevention, the Research and Documentation Centre of the Netherlands Ministry of Justice and the World Society of Victimology aim to promote the UN Declaration of Basic Principles of Justice for Victims of Crime and Abuse of Power. <www.victimology.nl>.

32 World Society of Victimology (WSV). The purposes of the WSV are to promote research on victims and victim assistance; advocacy of their interests throughout the world; to encourage interdisciplinary and comparative research in victimology; to advance the co-operation of international, regional, and local agencies, groups, and individuals concerned with the problems of victims. <www.world-society-victimology.de/frameset.html>.

33 European Forum for Victim Services, 'Statement of victims' rights in the process of criminal justice'. Victim Support, London (1996). <www.victimology.nl/onlpub/eurforvicrts96a.html>.

to meet the material and psychological needs of individuals who are primary or secondary victims of crime.

In Trinidad and Tobago, the Caribbean Centre for Human Rights (CCHR), founded and funded by the CCPS in 2006, has established a Victim Support Programme (VSP). The VSP started in November 2006 and has already shown tremendous progress with counsellors identified, volunteers recruited and trained, and a sample of homicide victims' families contacted and surveyed with the CCPS instrument. To date, it has trained over 75 volunteers and there is a waiting list of 30 who will undergo the training soon. The VSP provides on-going training and counselling support to all its volunteers. The victims initiative in Trinidad & Tobago is an example of a traditional needs based service, which is able to offer emotional support, supermarket hampers and refer victims to counselling where appropriate.

The survey used by the CCHR to identify victims' needs can be readily adapted to evaluate the experiences and needs of the families of the condemned as well. Though meeting the needs of the families of the condemned is much more politically contentious, it is nonetheless important and the success of a victims' initiative is enhanced by addressing both groups in parallel. The CCHR focuses on these 'secondary' victims with the aim of establishing a protocol with its roots in restorative justice principles and practice.

Alternative Punishments

An Overview of Life Sentences

A significant flaw in many abolitionist campaigns is the lack of attention given to the issue of an alternative sanction to the death penalty. Demands to abolish the death penalty are all very well, but without an informed discussion about alternative punishments, it is inevitable that governments will opt for the nearest hard line penalties that they believe will placate a public hostile to abolition.

In those countries which have abolished the death penalty, the most common alternative has been a form of life imprisonment, although the term life imprisonment itself is a source of much confusion. In the USA, life without parole[34] is generally taken to mean exactly that. Forth-eight states have the option of life without parole, the exceptions being New Mexico, a death penalty state, and Alaska, a non-death penalty state (Death Penalty Information Centre, 2007b). For certain crimes, particularly first-degree murder, life without parole is the only

34 Other jurisdictions may use different terminology such as 'life without the possibility of parole', 'life without the possibility of release', 'whole life tariff' and 'natural life'. For the purposes of this chapter, all terms are treated as being synonymous, unless otherwise stated.

sentence available in states that have abolished the death penalty.[35] What is more, forty-one states and the federal government, apply life without parole provisions to juvenile offenders despite international consensus against such practice.[36] The result is that there are now over 2,200 juvenile offenders who will spend the rest of their lives in prison (Human Rights Watch 2005; Pilkington 2007). Of these, seventy-three were 13 or 14 years old when they committed their crimes (Equal Justice Initiative 2007).

The prison population in the USA has increased dramatically in the last few decades, as has the lifer population. A comprehensive study carried out by The Sentencing Project in 2004 reveals that the number of lifers in prison rose by 83% from 69,845 in 1992 to 127,677 in 2003. One in every eleven (9.4%) offenders in state/federal prison, that is 127,677 persons, is now serving a life sentence. Of these, one in four (26.3%) is serving a sentence of life without parole, having increased from one in six (17.8%) in 1992 (Mauer *et al* 2004).

By comparison, Europe is almost entirely a death penalty free zone.[37] The Council of Europe requires all member states to impose a moratorium on the death penalty with a view to abolition. Similarly, all member states of the European Union are required to abolish the death penalty before their accession. Most member states have adopted a form of life imprisonment as the alternative sanction, though few anticipate that those sentenced to life will in fact remain in prison for the rest of their natural lives. However, the process of selecting the alternative penalty appears not to have been the subject of much discussion and lacks consistency. Life sentences vary considerably in terms of their length[38] and their use across Europe. The UK makes the greatest use of life sentences, followed by Luxembourg. The countries that tend to use it the least include Bulgaria, Estonia, Latvia, Lithuania, Moldova, the Netherlands, Romania, Slovakia and the Former Yugoslav Republic of Macedonia (Newcomen 2005, 32).

Currently, only a handful of countries in the Council of Europe have provisions for whole life imprisonment including Bulgaria, Sweden, Ukraine, the Netherlands,

---

35 In Illinois, Iowa, Louisiana, Maine, Pennsylvania, and South Dakota, all life sentences are imposed without the possibility of parole. See Marc Mauer *et al* (2004) and Appleton and Grøver (2007).

36 See Article 6(5) of the *International Convention on Civil and Political Rights*; Article 37a of the *UN Convention on the Rights of the Child*; and paragraph 31(a) of UN General Assembly resolution on the rights of the child, A/RES/61/146, passed by 185 votes to 1. The USA has not signed up to these provisions.

37 Belarus is an exception. Although a reference to the temporary nature of the death penalty has been incorporated into law, the death penalty is currently in use for cases of premeditated murder with aggravating circumstances. See OSCE Office for Democratic Institutions and Human Rights (2006, 54–7). Other European and Central Asian states have imposed a moratorium on executions even though the death penalty may still exist *de jure*.

38 See Hodgkinson (2004a, 160).

Estonia and Turkey.[39] Although normally a whole life tariff will only be imposed under special circumstances, such as multiple murders or prior convictions, in some cases, it is possible to petition the president for a pardon (e.g. Bulgaria[40] and Estonia[41]) or the court for a determinate tariff (e.g. Sweden[42]) after a certain period of time has passed.

England and Wales recently joined the list of those countries with whole life tariffs. Stricter penalties brought in under the 2003 Criminal Justice Act mean that for the first time courts have the possibility of handing down a whole life sentence.[43] After abolition of the death penalty in 1965, the tariff introduced for all murders was a mandatory life sentence, although at that time, life did not mean life. When sentencing a person convicted of murder, the judge would set a period of imprisonment that should be served to meet the needs of retribution and deterrence (punishment phase) prior to consideration for release (risk phase). In the 1950s and 60s, the average time a person would spend in prison was nine years. Since then, the average time a person spends in prison has increased to around fifteen years (Blom-Cooper and Morris 2004, 177).

Under the new guidelines, persons convicted of murder after December 2003 are sentenced in accordance with the four starting points set out in the Criminal Justice Act. The starting points depend on the seriousness of the crime and the age of the offender. For offenders under the age of 18, the starting point is twelve years imprisonment. For adult offenders the entry points are fifteen years, thirty years or in the case of offenders over the age of 21, whole of life imprisonment. Mitigating and aggravating factors will then come into consideration, which could increase or decrease the tariff.

The new provisions will place a huge burden on the prison services in England and Wales. A worrying fact is that prior to the new provision coming into force, at the end of 2002, England and Wales had a higher lifer population (5,268) than the other twenty-four members of the European Union combined (5,046) (Prison Reform Trust 2004) and just short of the total of the forty-six member states of

---

39 Article 38.a. (New, SG 50/95) (1) of the 1968 Penal Code of Bulgaria, amended 13 September 2002; Chapter 3, Section 1 of the 1962 Swedish Penal Code, Ds 1999:36, published 1999; see Articles 51, 64 and 115 of the Criminal Code of Ukraine, entered into force 1 September 2001; Article 31 of the Dutch Penal Code, adopted 3 March 1881, updated by amendments up to 1994; Article 45 of the Penal Code of Estonia, RT I 2001, 61, 364; consolidated text RT I 2002, 86, 504, Passed 6 June 2001, entered into force 1 September 2002; Articles 47(1) and 48(1) of the Criminal Code of Turkey, Law Nr. 5237, passed on 26 September 2004. Whilst every effort has been made to ensure that the correct articles and dates have been cited in this note, due to translation issues, some errors might remain undetected.

40 Article 74 of the 1968 Penal Code of Bulgaria, amended 13 September 2002.

41 Article 77 of the Penal Code of Estonia, RT I 2001, 61, 364; consolidated text RT I 2002, 86, 504, passed 6 June 2001, entered into force 1 September 2002.

42 See Kriminalvården (2007a; 2007b).

43 Section 269 (4) and Schedule 21.

the Council of Europe. By the end of 2005, the number of life sentenced inmates rose to 6,431 in England and Wales, a 12% rise on the year before (Prison Reform Trust 2006a).[44] As of 30 September 2007, there were thirty-five prisoners serving a whole life tariff, seventeen of whom had received their sentence after the Criminal Justice Act came into force (Hansard 2007). With the lifer population in England and Wales, and beyond, rising at a considerable rate, it is perhaps useful to consider what the perceived benefits of life without parole are.

The Rationale for Life Meaning Life

The advantages of a life sentence without the possibility of parole are appealing to governments who require a punishment that achieves the same 'benefits' as the death penalty. In particular, a life term without the possibility of release protects the public as it incapacitates an offender for the rest of their life. It also appeals to those members of the public who have become increasingly frustrated at offenders being sentenced to life, but being released early on parole, while at the same time giving the anti-death penalty movement more credibility by showing that they are not soft on crime. Yet, if we consider the public protection element, lifers eligible for parole tend to have very low rates of recidivism after release (see Mauer *et al* 2004, 23–24). Data on reconviction rates in England and Wales reveals that of the 1,719 lifers released between 1 April 2000 and 31 March 2007, 73 were reconvicted of an offence, of which 30 were convicted of a serious offence such as offences against the person or sexual offences (Home Office 2007).

A life sentence with or without the possibility of parole also eliminates the danger of executing innocent people. The irreversibility of the death penalty is a factor that has greatly reduced its support in recent years. A recent survey conducted by the Death Penalty Information Centre highlighted that 87% of Americans believe that an innocent person has been executed in recent years, with 55% saying that this fact has either made them more sceptical of capital punishment or more opposed to it entirely. However 31% said that knowing an innocent person may have been executed has had no effect on their death penalty views (Dieter 2007, 5).

The results reflect a growing discomfort among the American population with the death penalty and may explain in part why Americans are less likely to support the death penalty if there is a suitable alternative. The October 2007 Gallup poll shows that 69% of Americans are in favour of the death penalty for a person convicted of murder. This figure has remained more or less consistent since 1999. However, when presented with an alternative of 'life imprisonment, with absolutely no possibility of parole', support for the death penalty in previous years had dropped to between 47% and 54% (Newport 2007).

---

44 The November 2006 update reveals that at the end of August 2006, there were 7,628 people serving indefinite sentences (life sentenced and indeterminate sentenced prisoners), a rise of 27% on the year before: Prison Reform Trust 2006b).

Life without parole is also attractive because of its strong retributive element. Keeping someone locked up for the rest of his or her life is as harsh a punishment as the death penalty, if not harsher. In fact, Hugo Bedau, arguably the most influential thinker and activist in the abolitionist debate in the US, has questioned abolitionists who favour this alternative, stating that it too is an 'unreasonably severe' punishment: 'The dilemma of the opponent of the death penalty, if current research survey is a reliable guide, is that at present the public is prepared to accept the abolition of capital punishment only if the alternative to it is itself a morally unacceptable deprivation of liberty' (Bedau 1997).

Even in nineteenth century England, the severity of whole life imprisonment was considered by some to be a worse punishment than the death penalty. In an 1868 parliamentary speech, John Stuart Mill, argued unequivocally for the retention of the death penalty, as the alternative – natural life imprisonment with hard labour – subjected offenders to a 'living tomb' and was therefore 'far more cruel in reality' (Mill 1868). Mill's speech apparently rocked the abolitionist movement to such an extent that it did not recover for many years (Radzinowicz and Hood 1986, 685).

In Trinidad and Tobago, as a result of several Privy Council decisions,[45] a number of death row inmates have had their death sentences commuted to a prison term of seventy-five years or natural life with hard labour.[46] It has frequently been reported that many inmates would, however, prefer the death penalty given that the alternative is spending the rest of their life in prison, often in harsh conditions (Ní Ghrálaigh 2005, 47; Black 2005, 127; Choudhury 2005, 166; West 2006, 52). Some have argued that the severity of a natural life sentence and the quality of life in prison has as strong a deterrent effect as the death penalty, if not stronger (Katz *et al* 2003).

The severity of life without parole is perhaps recognised in the decisions of some states not to extradite offenders to countries where they might be subjected to a whole life tariff. Uruguay refused to extradite a suspected terrorist following his part in the 1997 attack at a temple in Luxor unless Egypt guaranteed that he would not receive the death penalty or a natural life sentence (US Department of State 2004). Mexico too has in the past refused to extradite suspects to the USA without

---

45 For example, *Earl Pratt and Evan Morgan v The Attorney General for Jamaica and The Superintendent of Prisons, Saint Catherine's Jamaica* [1993] UKPC 10; *Balkissoon Roodal v The State of Trinidad and Tobago* [2003] UKPC 18; *Charles Mathews v The State of Trinidad and Tobago* [2004] UKPC 12.

46 The actual meaning of a life sentence in Trinidad and Tobago however remains largely undefined in the statute books. See Cook (2004, 59–60). Although it is a discretionary sentence, 75 years or natural life with hard labour has emerged as the norm particularly for those whose death sentence has been commuted to life. There is currently a constitutional motion scheduled to be heard in 2008 on the meaning of a life sentence, following the *Matthews* decision. See Holland and Chidgey (2007, 117) and Charan and Swamber (2007).

securing an undertaking that neither the death penalty nor life imprisonment will be imposed. Regrettably, Mexico's Supreme Court has recently overturned this policy (BBC News 2005).

It will be interesting to see how the practice regarding the principle of whole life imprisonment develops. There already seems to be some trends emerging. Constitutional Courts in Germany (1977), France (1994), Italy (1987) and Namibia (1996) have recognised that life sentenced offenders have a 'fundamental right to be considered for release' (Zyl Smit 2003, 213). Edward Fitzgerald QC, a leading British human rights lawyer, also notes that 'in Europe there is a growing trend to recognise that there must always be a recognition of the capacity for redemption, the capacity for rehabilitation, and that any sentence that effectively closed the door forever would be contrary to Article 3 of the European Convention on Human Rights prohibiting cruel and inhuman treatment or punishment' (Fitzgerald 2005, 53). The UK is currently awaiting a judgment from the European Court of Human Rights in a case which will review the practice of whole life sentences (BBC News 2007).

It is important to note that neither the Council of Europe recommendations on the management of long term prisoners,[47] nor the UN recommendations on life imprisonment,[48] concede the possibility of whole life sentences, although both acknowledge that following regular and rigorous review, some life sentenced prisoners may never be deemed safe for release. One of the reasons is that the guidelines envisage rehabilitation as an integral part of the penal process; sentencing someone to a whole life tariff takes away that possibility. Similarly, Article 10(3) of the ICCPR stipulates that 'the penitentiary system shall comprise treatment of prisoners the essential aim of which shall be their reformation and social rehabilitation'. It is also important to note that under the 1998 Rome Statue of the International Criminal Court, although life imprisonment is the maximum penalty for crimes such as genocide, crimes against humanity and war crimes, an assessment to determine whether the sentence should be reviewed must take place after 25 years (Articles 77 and 110).

One must also consider that locking more people up for life will have an enormous impact on the management of the prison service. Not only will whole life imprisonment result in an increased and ageing prison population, in most jurisdictions, keeping someone in prison for the rest of his or her life clearly costs more. It also creates a dangerous environment for those managing lifers. With no prospect of release, what incentives are available to ensure the co-operation and compliance of prisoners who have neither hope nor anything to lose? There has to be light at the end of the tunnel (Hodgkinson 2004a, 187–188).

---

47 Recommendation Rec(2003)23 on the management by prison administrations of life sentence and other long-term prisoners, adopted by the Committee of Ministers on 9 October 2003 at the 855th meeting of the Ministers' Deputies.

48 United Nations (1996) The Life Sentence, Report of the Criminal Justice Branch of UNOV, UN Publication Geneva.

Despite its flaws, one reason why death penalty opponents might push for or accept life without parole as an alternative sanction is the belief that it will reduce the number of executions. Whilst it is true that the number of death penalty sentences and executions have dropped significantly in the USA in recent times, one must view this in context. Over the last decade or so, the number of violent crimes has also decreased considerably. It follows that lower incidents of crime will result in less people being eligible for the death penalty. Furthermore, declining public support for the death penalty and increased judicial scrutiny of death penalty provisions, particularly for certain groups such as juveniles and the mentally impaired, have also contributed to the decrease in execution (Harvard Law Journal 2006, 1845–1851). A recent state-by-state analysis conducted on this issue concludes that life without parole statutes 'are a relatively minor factor in the reduced number of executions over the past several years. The data demonstrate that life-without-parole statutes do not account for the decreased number of executions, although they may play a part in the reduction of death sentences. Even though the number of death sentences decreases after the passage of life-without-parole statutes, the number of people executed remains unchanged' (*ibid*, 1847).

With this in mind, consideration needs be given to the effect life without parole provisions have had on non-capital defendants. Most life without parole statutes in the USA affect not just those defendants that would have received the death penalty, they also impose permanent incarceration on all those death penalty eligible defendants that would never have received the punishment. As the Harvard Law Journal article notes:

> While a death sentence and a life-without-parole sentence are surely not equivalent, declining to compare their costs is unjust. To refuse to look at the effect of life-without-parole statutes on non-capital defendants is to sanction or encourage a law that holds twenty five men in prison until their natural deaths in order to spare one man the death penalty. That has been the position of many death penalty abolitionists, and it is a troubling one.
>
> The purpose of this Note is not to argue that life-without-parole statutes should be abolished. Rather, it is to argue that such statutes are neither a necessary nor a particularly useful step toward eliminating the death penalty, and that death penalty abolitionists have a responsibility to consider carefully the effects of such laws on non-capital defendants before they engineer or encourage their passage (*ibid*, 1854).

While some death penalty opponents may regard the acceptance of whole life sentences as the only way of getting the death penalty off the statute books, they should consider the fact that they may be trading one disproportionately severe punishment for another.

Concluding Comments

The discourse on capital punishment and activities associated with it, has become very prominent in the past two decades, and this has spawned a host of activists and activities many of which rely on an 'emotional' approach be they 'for' or 'against' capital punishment. Discounting popular opinion which overwhelmingly favours the death penalty, there are a multitude of groups which coalesce around its abolition and compete with one another for funding and for ideology. They offer *ad hoc* 'solutions' which are rarely subjected to rigorous evaluation as to their effectiveness. By contrast there are very few formal groups that lobby for the retention or reinstatement of the death penalty, explained perhaps by the popular and political support that their position already attracts, and most of those that do exist do so by exploiting the crime victim issue. Examples of such movements can be found in the USA (see above), Taiwan and Japan. Abolition of the death penalty and penal reform in general is not to be gained at the expense of the inherent needs and rights of crime victims. The simple analysis provided by some politicians that money spent on offenders is money denied to victim services is a grotesque calumny. Victims' needs and rights should not be met at the expense of humane, effective and proportional responses to offenders and their needs should not be confused with or influence the treatment of offenders.

Hardly a day passes by without an 'abolitionist' conference being staged somewhere in the world though perhaps more pertinent to a global strategy invariably in North America or Western Europe. A question remains about the nature and purpose of such fora, which dominate the calendars of activists. We would suggest that these activities need to be radically rethought and evaluated. For example, did the 3rd World Congress against the death penalty in Paris in 2007 staged by Ensemble Contre la Peine de Mort [ECPM],[49] in the jargon, build capacity and is its agenda [not the inevitability of a 4th World Congress] sustainable? This year's congress did stage a number of fact based panels, which represented an advance on the earlier congresses. Meetings to provide emotional support for battle weary campaigners are understandable, but this function needs to be distinguished from rigorous think tanks that should be concerned with the evaluation of all abolition activities and activists. Perhaps a better use of the energies and resources available to such groups would be to proactively engage with supporters of capital punishment rather than meet in the comfort and safety of their own supporters?

It is difficult to envisage a litigation strategy that could avoid the unintended consequences referred to earlier, especially as the law is a blunt instrument leaving no grey areas; their clients are either found guilty or not. Whilst appreciating the dilemmas of both the prosecution and defence in a capital trial, the research evidence on whole of life imprisonment discussed above is suggestive of avoidable consequences by both parties. This 'win at any cost' approach has had the effect of

49 Ensemble Contre la Peine de Mort (ECPM), see, <www.abolition.fr>.

consigning thousands of defendants worldwide to unacceptably disproportionate determinate sentences thus compounding the damage already caused by the exponential growth in natural life sentences. The 'either / or' justification for this approach is entirely fallacious.

The strength of the research evidence suggests that the death penalty has little or no impact on the reduction of the crimes for which it is traditionally reserved but merely perpetuates the pain and anger experienced by homicide victims' families and those employed to administer the process. Its promotion creates a false sense of security to all those citizens who believe the claims of its effectiveness. Retentionist governments should be reassured by the research evidence and by the experiences of those who have replaced the death penalty without any obvious negative consequences or repercussions, and those in the traditional abolitionist community may want to consider whether undue reliance on an emotional and morality based strategy needs reviewing.

Bibliography

ABC News (2006), 'Council perfect forum for death penalty debate, UN official says', 18 September 2006, available at: <http://www.abc.net.au/am/content/2006/s1743119.htm>, accessed 5 December 2007.

Amnesty International, 'Death Sentences and Executions in 2006', available at: <http://web.amnesty.org/pages/deathpenalty-sentences-eng>, accessed 20 November 2007.

Anthony (2003), 'The Caribbean Court Of Justice: Will It Be A Hanging Court?' Address by Dr. The Honourable Kenny D. Anthony, Prime Minister of Saint Lucia, at the Norman Manley Law School, 28 June 2003, available at: <http://www.stlucia.gov.lc/primeminister/former_prime_ministers/kenny_d_anthony/statements/2003/the_caribbean_court_of_justice_will_it_be_a_hanging_court_june_28_2003.htm>, accessed 5 December 2007.

Appleton, C. and Grøver, B. (2007), 'The Pros and Cons of Life Without Parole', 47:4 *British Journal of Criminology*, 597–615.

Bailey, W. C., Peterson, R. D. (1997), 'Murder, Capital Punishment, and Deterrence: a Review of the Literature' in Bedau, H. A. (ed.) (1997) *The Death Penalty in America. Current Controversies* (Oxford: Oxford University Press).

BBC News (2005), 'Mexico alters extradition rules', 30 November 2005, available at: <http://news.bbc.co.uk/1/hi/world/americas/4483746.stm>, accessed 3 December 2007.

_________ (2006), 'Saddam has been "held to account"', 30 December 2006, available at: <http://news.bbc.co.uk/1/hi/uk/6218533.stm>, accessed 13 December 2006.

_________ (2007), 'Police killer awaits Euro ruling', 21 February 2007, available at: <http://news.bbc.co.uk/1/hi/england/west_yorkshire/6381409.stm>, accessed 3 December 2007.

Bedau, H. (1997), 'The Controversy over Public Support for the Death Penalty: The Death Penalty verses Life Imprisonment' in Bedau, H. (ed.) *The Death Penalty in America: Current Controversies* (Oxford: Oxford University Press).

_________ (1997), *The Death Penalty in America: Current Controversies.* (Oxford: Oxford University Press).

Black, K. (2005), CCPS Internship Reports 2005, published by the Centre for Capital Punishment Studies.

Blom-Cooper, L. and Morris, T. (2004), *With Malice Aforethought. A Study of the Crime and Punishment for Homicide* (Oxford: Hart Publishing).

Bowers, W. J. and Pierce, G. L. (1975), 'The Illusion of Deterrence in Isaac Ehrlich's Research on Capital Punishment', 85 *Yale Law Journal* 187–208.

Charan, R. and Swamber, K. (2007), 'Lawyers Fight for Convicted Killers', *Trinidad and Tobago Express*, 28 November 2007.

Choudhury, N. (2005), CCPS Internship Reports 2005, published by the Centre for Capital Punishment Studies.

Cook, J. (2004), CCPS Internship Reports 2004, published by the Centre for Capital Punishment Studies.

Death Penalty Information Centre (2007a), 'Death Penalty in Flux', updated 17 November 2007, available at: <http://www.deathpenaltyinfo.org/article.php?did=2289>, accessed 3 December 2007.

Death Penalty Information Centre (2007b), 'Life Without Parole', available at: <http://www.deathpenaltyinfo.org/article.php?did=555&scid=59>, accessed 6 November 2007.

Dezhbakhsh, H., Rubin, P. H. and Shepherd, J. M. (2002), 'Does Capital Punishment have a Deterrent Effect? New Evidence from Post-Moratorium Panel Data', 5:2 *American Law and Economics Review* 344–376.

Dieter, R. (1997), 'Sentencing for Life: Americans Embrace Alternatives to the Death Penalty' in Bedau, H. A. (ed.) *The Death Penalty in America. Current Controversies* (Oxford: Oxford University Press).

_________(2007), 'A Crisis of Confidence: Americans' Doubts About the Death Penalty', A Death Penalty Information Centre Report Based on A National Opinion Survey, June 2007.

Ehrlich, I. (1975), 'The Deterrent Effect of Capital Punishment: A Question of Life and Death', 65:3 *The American Economic Review* 397–417.

Equal Justice Initiative (2007), 'Cruel and Unusual: Sentencing 13- and 14-Year-Old Children to Die in Prison', November 2007.

Fagan, J. (2005), 'Deterrence and the Death Penalty: A Critical Review of New Evidence', Testimony to New York hearings on the future of capital punishment in the State of New York, Columbia Law School, New York, 21 January 2005.

Fitzgerald, E. (2005), 'A Review of the Litigation Concerning the UK's Alternative to the Death Penalty – The Mandatory Reviewable Life Sentence and the Contentious Issue of Whole Life Imprisonment', in Browne, N. and Kandelia, S. (eds), 'Managing Effective Alternatives to Capital Punishment. 24th June 2005 – Conference Papers', Occasional Paper Series – Special Edition, Volume Three, Centre for Capital Punishment Studies.

Gayle, B. and Sinclair, G. (2007), '2006 Year in Review: Crime and Justice – Police gain ground but murders still high', *Jamaica Gleaner*, 15 January 2007, available at: <http://www.jamaica-gleaner.com/gleaner/20070115/lead/lead9.html>, accessed 10 December 2007.

Gomes, A. (2007), 'The right to life', *Jamaican Observer*, 5 December 2007, available at: http://www.jamaicaobserver.com/columns/html/20071204T210000-0500_130037_OBS_THE_RIGHT_TO_LIFE.asp, accessed 10 December 2007.

Haines, H. H. (1996), *Against Capital Punishment: The Anti-death Penalty Movement in America, 1972–1994* (New York: Oxford University Press).

Hansard (2007), Written Answers for 24 October 2007, House of Commons Debates, published by the UK Parliament, available at: <http://www.publications.parliament.uk/pa/cm200607/cmhansrd/cm071024/text/71024w0013.htm>, accessed 03 December 2007.

Henry, B. (2007), 'More Death Penalty Delays', *Jamaican Observer*, 17 December 2007, available at: <http://www.jamaicaobserver.com/news/html/20071217T010000-0500_130460_OBS_MORE_DEATH_PENALTY_DELAYS_.asp>, accessed 18 December 2007.

Harvard Law Journal (2007), 'A Matter of Life and Death: The Effect of Life-without-parole Statutes on Capital Punishment', Vol. 119(6), 2006, 1838–1854.

Hodgkinson, P (2004a), 'Alternatives to the Death Penalty – The United Kingdom Experience' in *Death Penalty. Beyond Abolition* (Strasbourg, Council of Europe Publishing).

__________(2004b), 'Capital punishment: improve it or remove it?' in Hodgkinson, P. and Schabas, W. A. (eds), *Capital Punishment – Strategies for Abolition* (Cambridge: Cambridge University Press).

__________ (2004c), 'Capital Punishment – meeting the needs of the families of the homicide victim and the condemned' in: Hodgkinson, P. and Schabas, W. A. (eds), *Capital Punishment – Strategies for Abolition* (Cambridge: Cambridge University Press).

__________ (2005), 'The Unintended, Entirely Foreseeable Though Perhaps Unavoidable Consequences of Litigating the Abolition of Capital Punishment', 13 *Amicus Journal*, 2005.

Holland, R. and Chidgey, K. (2007), CCPS Internship Reports 2007, published by the Centre for Capital Punishment Studies.

Home Office (2007), 'Analysis of True Lifer Reconviction. 1 April 2000 – 31 March 2007', obtained via personal communication between the CCPS and the Home Office, Pre-release Section.

Hood, R. (2002), *The Death Penalty: A worldwide Perspective*, 3rd Edition (Oxford: Oxford University Press).

Human Rights Watch (2005), 'The Rest of Their Lives. Life without Parole for Child Offenders in the United States', October 2005.

Katz, L., Levitt, S. D. and Shustorovich, E. (2003), 'Prison Conditions, Capital Punishment, and Deterrence', 5:2 *American Law and Economics Review* 2003, 318–343.

Kriminalvården (2007a), 'Livstidsstraff – längre och vanligare', available at: <http://www.kriminalvarden.se/templates/KVV_InfopageGeneral____4381.aspx>, accessed 03 December 2007 (in Swedish).

_________ (2007b), 'The Swedish system of Sanctions – Det svenska påföljdssystemet', available at: http://www.kriminalvarden.se/upload/Informationsmaterial/Sanctionssyst.pdf, accessed 03 December 2007 (in English).

Liptak, A. (2007), 'Does Death Penalty Save Lives? A New Debate', *New York Times*, 18 November 2007.

Mauer, M., King, R. S. and Young, M. C. (2004), 'The Meaning of "Life": Long Prison Sentences in Context', The Sentencing Project, May 2004.

Mendes, D. and Delzin, G. (2005), 'Using the Bill of Rights to halt executions: A reply to Peter Hodgkinson', 15 *Amicus Journal*, 18–21.

Mill, J. S. (1868), 'Speech In Favour of Capital Punishment', Parliamentary Debates, House of Commons, Vol. 191, cols. 1047–1055, 21 April 1868.

Nathalia, T. (2007), 'Indonesia Court Rejects Challenge to Death Penalty', *Reuters*, 30 October 2007, available at: <http://www.reuters.com/article/latestCrisis/idUSJAK56440>, accessed 03 December 2007.

Ní Ghrálaigh, B. (2005), CCPS Internship Reports 2005, published by the Centre for Capital Punishment Studies.

Newcomen, N. (2005), 'Managing the Penal Consequences of Replacing the Death Penalty in Europe' in Browne, N. and Kandelia, S. (eds), 'Managing Effective Alternatives to Capital Punishment. 24th June 2005 – Conference Papers', Occasional Paper Series – Special Edition, Volume Three, Centre for Capital Punishment Studies.

Newport, F. (2007), 'Sixty-Nine Percent of Americans Support Death Penalty', *Gallup News Service* [website], published 12 October 2007, available at: <http://www.gallup.com/poll/101863/Sixtynine-Percent-Americans-Support-Death-Penalty.aspx>, accessed 22 November.

OSCE/ODHIR (2006), 'The Death Penalty in the OSCE Area', Background Paper 2006, Human Dimension Implementation Meeting October 2006, OSCE Office for Democratic Institutions and Human Rights.

Pilkington, E. (2007), 'Life Without Hope', *The Guardian*, 4 August 2007.

Prison Reform Trust (2004), 'England and Wales – Europe's Lifer Capital', March 2004.

Prison Reform Trust (2006a), 'Bromley Briefings. Prison Factfile', April 2006.

Prison Reform Trust (2006b), 'Bromley Briefings. Prison Factfile', November 2006.

Radzinowicz, L. and Hood, R. (1986), 'A History of English Criminal Law and its Administration from 1750', Vol. 5 (London: Stevens and Sons) cited in van Zyl Smit, D. (2002), *Taking Life Imprisonment Seriously in National and International Law* (The Hague: Kluwer Law International).

Ramnarine, K. (2007), 'Team effort essential', 7 January 2007, available at: <http://www.trinidadexpress.com/index.pl/article_archive?id=161078155>, accessed 10 December 2007.

Rock, P. (1991), 'The Victim in Court Project at the Crown Court at Wood Green', *Howard Journal*, 30/4, 301–310.

Rock, P. (1998), *After Homicide: Practical and Political Responses to Bereavement* (Oxford, Clarendon Press).

Ryan, G. (2003), 'Gov. George Ryan's Commutation Announcement', announcement in a lecture at the School of Law, Northwestern University, 11 January 2003, available at: <http://www.law.northwestern.edu/news/spring03/ryanspeech.html>, accessed 4 October 2007.

Saad, L. (2001), 'Americans Willing to Wait Longer for McVeigh's Execution', *Gallup News Service* (website), published 3 May 2001, available at: http://www.gallup.com/poll/3652/Americans-Willing-Wait-Longer-McVeighs-Execution.aspx, accessed 22 November 2007.

Sarat, A. (2001), *When the State Kills: Capital Punishment and the American Condition* (New Jersey: Princeton University Press).

Schabas, W. A. (2004), 'Public Opinion and the Death Penalty' in Hodgkinson, P. and Schabas, W. A. (eds), *Capital Punishment – Strategies for Abolition* (Cambridge: Cambridge University Press).

Seelal, N. (2006), '2005 Murder Toll Ends at 386', 2 January 2006, available at: <http://newsday.co.tt/news/0,33329.html>, accessed 10 December 2007.

Sellin, J. T. (1959), *The Death Penalty* (Philadelphia: American Law Institute).

Sibanda, N. (2007), 'DEATH PENALTY: Concerned Zambian Activists Look Beyond Moratorium', *Inter Press Service*, 25 June 2007, available at: <http://ipsnews.net/news.asp?idnews=38311>, accessed 4 October 2007.

Sorenson, J., Wrinkle, R., Brewer, V., and Marquart, J. (1999), 'Capital Punishment and Deterrence: Examining the Effect of Executions on Murder in Texas', 45:4 *Crime and Delinquency* 481–493.

Sundby, S. E. (2006), 'The Death Penalty's Future: Charting the Crosscurrents of Declining Death Sentences and the McVeigh Factor', 84:7 *Texas Law Review*, 1929–1972.

UN Department of Public Information (2007), 'GENERAL ASSEMBLY ADOPTS LANDMARK TEXT CALLING FOR MORATORIUM ON DEATH PENALTY', Sixty-second General Assembly Plenary, 76th & 77th Meetings (AM & PM), GA/10678, 18 December 2007, available at: http://www.un.org/News/Press/docs/2007/ga10678.doc.htm, accessed 11 January 2008.

US Department of State (2004), 'Patterns of Global Terrorism – 2003', Office of the Coordinator for Counterterrorism, 29 April 2004, available at: <http://www.globalsecurity.org/security/library/report/2004/pgt_2003/pgt_2003_31640pf.htm>, accessed 03 December 2007.

Vollum, S., Longmire, D. R. and Buffington-Vollum, J. (2004), 'Confidence in the death penalty and support for its use: Exploring the value-expressive dimension of death penalty attitudes', 21:3 *Justice Quarterly* September 2004, 521–546.

Walton, M. (2005), 'The Death Penalty in Australia and Overseas', Background Paper 2005/3, New South Wales Council for Civil Liberties.

West, F. (2006), CCPS Internship Reports 2006, published by the Centre for Capital Punishment Studies.

Willing, R. (2001), 'Foes of death penalty say McVeigh is an exception', *USA TODAY*, 20 June 2001, available at: <http://www.usatoday.com/news/nation/2001-05-03-mcveigh-cappunish.htm#more>, accessed 03 December 2007.

van Zyl Smit, D. (2002), *Taking Life Imprisonment Seriously in National and International Law* (The Hague: Kluwer Law International).

Chapter 12
A Fate Worse than Death? The Problems with Life Imprisonment as an Alternative to the Death Penalty

Rachael Stokes[1]

> We're supposedly doing them a favour by not executing them but in fact by keeping them in the SIZO, we're killing them slowly.
>
> *Head of the Prison Service, Kyrgyzstan (International Crisis Group 2006, 16).*[2]

> Some prisoners say long prison terms are like drawn out death sentences. I will just say they are futile and excessive acts of vengeance.
>
> *Michael Santos, written in his eighth year of a 45-year prison sentence in a federal correctional institution in Pennsylvania, USA (Santos 1995, 40).*

Introduction

In the past few decades significant progress has been made towards the global abolition of the death penalty. Since 1990 45 countries have abolished the death penalty, bringing the current total of abolitionist countries to 128 (Amnesty International 2007).[3] Of the countries that have yet to abolish the death penalty in law, the introduction of moratoria has resulted in a reduction in the number of prisoners sentenced to death, as well as those being executed. And of those countries that still retain and use the death penalty, signs are emerging of an

---

1 The author would like to thank colleagues at Penal Reform International who have advised on the production of this chapter, notably: Dena Fisher, Mel James, Gulnara Kaliakbarova, Mary Molloy, Mary Murphy, Vika Sergeeva, Jenni Gainsborough and Chian Yew Lim.

2 A SIZO (*sledstvennye izoliatory*) is a pre-trial detention facility.

3 In total, 88 countries have abolished the death penalty for all crimes: 11 countries have abolished the death penalty for all but exceptional crimes; and 30 countries are considered to be abolitionist in practice. Of the 69 countries that retain and use the death penalty, 91 per cent of known executions are thought to take place in just six countries (China, Iraq, Iran, Sudan, Pakistan and the USA). Those remaining on death row and awaiting execution are thought to number between 19,000 and 24,000.

increasing willingness to review its application. In China, for example, legislative amendments introduced in January 2007 now require all death sentences to be reviewed by the Supreme Peoples' Court. State figures indicate that this has resulted in a significant reduction in the number of executions conducted in 2007 compared with figures from previous years (Associated Press 2007; Human Rights in China 2007, 26–39). In Rwanda, the government has recently voted to abolish the death penalty as part of moves to facilitate the extradition of those suspected of involvement in the Rwandan genocide (Death Penalty Information Center, 2007).

The abolition of the death penalty inevitably raises the question of what alternative sanctions are implemented in its place. In the majority of cases, the answer is life imprisonment. But what does 'life' actually mean? And is it, as some cases would seem to suggest, tantamount to or even worse than a death sentence? At the 12th European Conference of the Directors of Prison Administration in 1997, concerns were raised about the marked increased in life- and long-term sentenced prisoner populations within member states in response to the abolition of the death penalty. A Committee of Experts was subsequently established by the European Committee on Crime Problems in 2000, specifically to review the management of life- and long-term prisoners in light of these developments (European Committee on Crime Problems 2000).

This chapter argues that current discourses on the death penalty need to look increasingly beyond abolition to the implementation of alternative sanctions. This demands a closer inspection of the impact of abolition on the use and implementation of life- and long-term sentences. It also requires that greater attention is paid to the conditions of detention and the treatment of life-sentenced prisoners, as well as the effects of long term imprisonment. The chapter will present an overview of the international trends in life imprisonment, including its implementation following abolition of the death penalty. It will then consider the human rights implications of life- and long-term sentences with particular reference to the case of *Léger v. France*.[4]

The meaning of life

With the exception of the death penalty, life imprisonment is usually the maximum punishment for criminal offences and is therefore usually applied to the most serious of crimes. Yet the sanction of life imprisonment has different meanings in different countries. Variations occur, for example, in the types of crimes carrying the sanction of life imprisonment, whether sentences are mandatory or discretionary, the minimum or maximum prison term for life sentence prisoners, and the conditions attached to parole. The result of these variations is that offenders

4 *Léger v. France (application no. 19324/02) Judgement*, Strasbourg, 11 April 2006.

sentenced to life imprisonment can spend anything between 10 years and the rest of their natural lives in prison.

It is important to note that not all countries make provisions for life imprisonment. It is prohibited for example in Brazil, Colombia, Croatia, El Salvador, Nicaragua, Norway, Portugal, Spain, Slovenia, and Venezuela (Mauer *et al.* 2004; Newcomen 2005). However, this does not exempt prisoners from serving long prison sentences in these countries; prisoners may in fact serve prison terms that far exceed the minimum terms served by life-sentenced prisoners elsewhere. In Spain, for example, prisoners can serve determinate sentences of up to 30 years (Coyle 2005); Slovenia similarly provides for a maximum sentence of 30 years; and in Norway, the most severe sanction is a determinate sentence of 21 years (Council of Europe 2003). There are also cases of *de facto* life imprisonment where prisoners convicted of multiple offences are required to serve the sentences consecutively. This is the case in South Africa, where multiple, determinate sentences can amount to the same or even longer prison terms than life imprisonment.[5]

Life imprisonment as an alternative to the death penalty

Life imprisonment is invariably the main alternative sanction to the death penalty available to countries as they move towards abolition. Death row prisoners in Russia, for example, had their sentences commuted to life imprisonment following a presidential decree in 1999. More than 1,600 prisoners are currently serving life sentences which require them to serve a minimum term of 25 years in prison.[6] Following the abolition of the death penalty in the Philippines in 2006, more than 1,200 prisoners on death row had their sentences commuted to life imprisonment (Toms 2005). In Kazakhstan, the sanction of life imprisonment was introduced under legislation passed in January 2004 in preparation for full abolition of the death penalty; life imprisonment in this case equates to a 20-year prison term (Hands off Cain 2007).[7] More recently, legislative amendments signed by President Bakiyev in Kyrgyzstan in June 2007 will result in the substitution of the death penalty for life imprisonment. Under the new law, prisoners will be expected to serve a minimum of 30 years in prison (Shulman 2007).

---

5 Lukas Muntinghe, Civil Society Prison Reform Initiative, through personal communication, December 2006. Life sentences in South Africa under the Correctional Services Act 2004 require prisoners to serve a minimum of 25 years in prison before being considered for parole.

6 Vika Sergeeva, PRI Regional Director (Russia, Ukraine and Belarus), through personal communication, May 2007.

7 In May 2007, President Nursultan Nazarbayev announced proposals for a constitutional amendment which would restrict the use of the death penalty for terror crimes and grave crimes committed in wartime (ibid.).

Elsewhere, current campaigns to abolish the death penalty are explicitly advocating life imprisonment as an alternative. A presidential declaration in Kenya has recently requested that the parliament enact an immediate freeze on all death sentences and that all prisoners on death row have their sentences commuted to life imprisonment (Wafula 2007). Similarly, in Nigeria, the Presidential Commission on the Reform of the Administration of Justice in Nigeria has recommended that prisoners who have spent between 10 and 15 years on death row should have their sentences commuted to life imprisonment (Olori 2007).[8] More recently, in Rwanda, the parliamentary decision to abolish the death penalty has made provisions for the implementation of life without parole as its replacement (Death Penalty Information Center 2007). And in Uzbekistan, legislative amendments passed in June 2007 in preparation for the abolition of the death penalty, which took place in January 2008, have resulted in the introduction of two new sentences of life- and long-term imprisonment. The sentences apply to offences of terrorism and aggravated murder, resulting in minimum prison terms of 25 and 20 years respectively.[9]

However, in cases where abolition or the introduction of a moratorium has not been followed with a review or commutation of existing sentences, prisoners on death row are being subjected to indefinite detention that is equivalent to a lifelong sentence. Guatemala has not carried out any executions since 2000. However, subsequent legislative changes have removed the president's right to pardon condemned prisoners or commute their sentences. As a result, 21 prisoners remain on death row, some of whom have spent up to 11 years in prison (Benitez 2007). In Kyrgyzstan, it is estimated that up to 175 prisoners have been serving indeterminate sentences following the introduction of a moratorium on executions in 1998.[10] In Azerbaijan, the abolition of the death penalty in 1998 created uncertainty as to the legal status of prisoners on death row: whilst the law on abolition automatically replaced capital punishment with life imprisonment, the maximum punishment within the existing criminal code was 15 years. The adoption of a new criminal code in 2000 failed to clarify the situation (International Federation for Human Rights 2007; Council of Europe 2007, 8.9).[11]

8 This was agreed by the Federal Ministry of Justice in a joint meeting held on 28 February 2007. The number of prisoners on death row who could have their sentences commuted to life imprisonment is estimated at 111. Further information, see the commission's website: <www.pcraj.org>.

9 Prisoners will be eligible to apply for a pardon after serving these minimum periods in prison (GFR coalition, Uzbekistan, 30 June 2007, through personal communication). A presidential decree issued in August 2005 announced that Uzbekistan would abolish the death penalty as of 1 January 2008. A moratorium on sentences or executions has not been introduced in the intervening period.

10 Penal Reform International Central Asia office, Kazakhstan, through personal communication, May 2007.

11 The Council of Europe Resolution 1545 (2007) urges the Azerbaijan authorities to, 'ensure a case by case review of life sentences which were the result of the abolition of the

International trends in life imprisonment

Whilst the implementation of life imprisonment as an alternative to the death penalty has had an obvious impact on the growth of life-sentenced prisoner populations in certain countries, it is in reality part of a wider trend in which the number of offenders serving life sentences is steadily increasing. In England and Wales, the prison population serving life sentences increased from 3,192 in 1994 to 5,594 in 2004 – an increase of 75 per cent during the 10-year period. In fact the UK prison population serving life sentences comprises nearly half of the total life-sentenced prison population in Europe (Council of Europe 2005).[12] In the US, the number of life-sentenced prisoners increased by 83 per cent between 1992 and 2003 – an increase from nearly 70,000 prisoners to 128,000 prisoners. As a result, one in every eleven offenders in state and federal prisons is currently serving a life sentence (Mauer *et al.* 2004).[13] In South Africa, the number of life-sentenced prisoners increased from 443 to 5,745 between 1995 and 2005 – an increase of over 1,000 per cent, compared to an overall prison population growth of 60 per cent during the 10-year period (Giffard and Mutinghe 2006).

One explanation for this trend is the rise in the number of offences carrying the sanction of life imprisonment. Although life imprisonment is typically reserved for the most serious offences, such as murder, it is increasingly being used for less serious and non-violent offences. In the US, for example, life sentences are now imposed for drug crimes and non-violent offences resulting from the 'three strikes' rule used in some states.[14] Four percent of people serving life sentences in the US have been convicted of a drug offence. This figure rises to 39 per cent within the federal system (Mauer *et al.* 2004).[15] Under California's 'three strikes' law, 31 per cent of life convictions are for property offences such as theft. Overall, 57.5 per cent of convictions involve a non-violent offence as the 'third strike'. 'Accountability' sentences are also applied in a number of US states. Under these provisions, participants in a crime, such as the getaway driver in a robbery, can

---

death penalty and allow the persons concerned to benefit from the retroactive application of the most favourable criminal law provisions adopted in 2000', para. 8.9.

12 The UK lifer population in 2004 stood at 6,344, comprising 46 per cent of the total lifer population in Europe which numbered 13,699.

13 In some states, the average is significantly higher: in the states of Alabama, California and New York, for example, 17 per cent, 18 per cent and 19 per cent of the prison population respectively are serving life sentences – almost one in five of the prison population (ibid.).

14 The general rule under 'three strikes' legislation is that anyone convicted of a third offence, following two previous convictions for serious or violent crimes, can be sentenced to life imprisonment.

15 In the state of Michigan, for example, 200 people are serving life terms for drug offences under the '650 lifer' law. This law legislates for people convicted of selling 650 grams of cocaine or heroin to be sentenced to life imprisonment.

be held accountable if the crime results in a murder, even if they were not directly responsible for committing the murder (Mauer *et al.* 2004).

These trends are being accompanied by a reduction in the use of parole for life sentence offenders. Recent figures published by the England and Wales Parole Board showed a significant reduction in the proportion of both life- and fixed-sentence prisoners being freed on parole. Between April and September 2006, one in nine life-sentenced prisoners was released on parole, compared to one in five for the same period the previous year (BBC News 2006). Similarly, in South Africa, measures under the Correctional Services Act 2004 have resulted in longer non-parole periods and more stringent requirements for granting parole to life-sentenced prisoners (Giffard and Mutinghe 2006). This necessarily results in an increase in the average prison term for life sentence offenders. In the US, the average length of time served in prison by lifers increased by 37 per cent between 1991 and 1997 – from 21.2 years to 29 years. The average life sentence in the US now results in nearly three decades of incarceration (Mauer *et al.* 2004).

In some cases, hardening sentencing practices have resulted in the complete removal of the possibility for parole. In the US, one in four prisoners currently serving a life sentence is ineligible for parole, representing one in 40 of the entire prison population. In five US states – Illinois, Iowa, Louisiana, Pennsylvania and South Dakota – all life sentences are imposed without the possibility of parole. In Louisiana, one in ten of the entire prison population is serving a sentence of life imprisonment without the possibility of parole.[16] The removal of parole even extends to sentencing of juveniles. Although 14 countries[17] are thought to have laws allowing children to be sentenced to life imprisonment without the possibility of release, nowhere is this as prevalent as in the US. As many as 2,225 children have been given such sentences, the majority of whom are first time offenders (Amnesty International/Human Rights Watch 2005).

In justice systems that practice detention without charge or trial, detainees can spend indefinite periods in detention that are tantamount to a life sentence. In 2003, as many as 58 countries were identified as practising arbitrary arrest and detention without charge or trial (Amnesty International 2004).[18] In Nigeria, for example, a recent presidential commission on justice reform found that more than

16 Only two states in the US – New Mexico and Alaska – do not offer life without parole as a sentencing option.

17 Life sentences without the possibility of release are currently imposed on juveniles in Israel, Kenya, South Africa, and Tanzania. It is also provided for in criminal legislation in Antigua and Barbuda, Australia, Brunei, Dominica, Kenya, St Vincent and the Grenadines, the Solomon Islands, Sri Lanka, Burkina Faso, and Cuba.

18 These were: Afghanistan, Algeria, Bangladesh, Burundi, Brunei Darussalam, Central African Republic, Chad, China, Colombia, Cote d'Ivoire, Cuba, Democratic Republic of Congo, Egypt, Eritrea, Ethiopia, Guinea-Bissau, India, Iran, Israel/OPT, Jamaica, Kenya, Lebanon, Libya, Madagascar, Malawi, Malaysia, Maldives, Mauritania, Morocco/Sahara, Myanmar, Nepal, Niger, Nigeria, North Korea, Palestinian Authority, Pakistan, Papua New Guinea, Rwanda, Saudi Arabia, Senegal, Sierra Leone, Singapore,

half of the prison population of 40,000 had not been tried or sentenced. Some had been waiting more than 10 years for trial (PCRAJ 2006). Similarly in India, 2006 figures revealed that as many as 70 per cent of the country's 320,000 inmates were awaiting trial (Biswas and Tewary 2006). Such practices are increasingly being used as part of anti-terrorism measures. In Malaysia, 700 criminal suspects are being held under Emergency Ordinance legislation passed in 1969 as a 'temporary measure' to curb ethnic riots. Detainees are subject to beating and ill-treatment, and are kept in overcrowded cells with poor hygiene, inadequate light and ventilation, and inedible food (Human Rights Watch 2006).[19]

Treatment and conditions of detention for life-sentenced prisoners

At the 24th Conference of the European Ministers of Justice in 2001, concern was expressed over the rise in number and length of life and long term sentences following the abolition of the death penalty in a number of European states, notably in terms of the implications for prison overcrowding and the effective and humane management of prisoners. Yet the conditions of detention and treatment of life-sentenced prisoners are not explained entirely by prison overcrowding: they can additionally experience differential treatment and worse conditions of detention as a direct result of the prison regulations associated with their sentence. Information on life-sentenced prisoner populations and their conditions of detention is generally difficult, if not impossible, to obtain. However, the 11th General Report of the European Council for the Prevention of Torture and Inhuman or Degrading Treatment or Punishment indicated situations in which prisoners in member states were found to be subject to 'special restrictions likely to exacerbate the deleterious effects inherent in long-term imprisonment' (ECPTIDT 2001, 17). Examples included separation from the rest of the prison population, handcuffing when they were taken out of their cells, prohibition of communication with other prisoners, and limited visit entitlements.

Punitive conditions of detention and less favourable treatment are thought to be particularly prevalent for reprieved death row prisoners:

> Singling long-term prisoners out for harsh treatment is a particular problem in countries that are in the process of adjusting their penal policy to deal with those prisoners who would have previously been executed (Coyle 2005, 44).

Somalia, Sri Lanka, Sudan, Swaziland, Syria, Tanzania, Togo, Uganda, UAE, UK, USA, Vietnam, Yemen, and Zimbabwe.

19 In addition to the provisions within Emergency Ordinance, the police can also detain individuals under the Internal Security Act (1960), which allows for detention without charge for up to sixty days without warrant, trial or access to legal counsel. The Minister of Internal Security is able to extend the period of detention through renewable two-year detention orders.

In Russia, the majority of life-sentenced prisoners are detained in specially designated high security colonies where prisoners are subject to high levels of surveillance and strict conditions of detention. Contact with other prisoners is prohibited and they are allowed only two short term visits each year. Each prisoner is allocated cell space of just two square metres, which is where they are obliged to both eat and wash so as to avoid contact with other prisoners. Daily exercise is limited to 1.5 hours a day and prisoners are let out of their cells in rotation. The experience of life imprisonment has led some to question whether life is indeed preferable to a death sentence:

> When punishment for criminals is being discussed … it is difficult to say what would be worse punishment for them – life imprisonment in a Russian prison or instant death (Fr. Mikhail Dudko cited in Hands off Cain 2005).

In Kyrgyzstan, the conditions of detention of the prisoners subject to the moratorium have come under criticism from the human rights ombudsman, who has described living conditions as inhumane. Prisoners are detained in pre-trial detention centres in underground cells with no light, limited ventilation, poor sanitary conditions and a lack of fresh water supply. Overcrowding means that cells designed for two in fact hold three, with one prisoner having to sleep on the floor. The prisoners receive smaller food rations than the other categories of prisoner. They are also subject to mandatory handcuffing when taken out of their cells, irrespective of the individual risk they may pose. Exercise is restricted to one hour a day and poor conditions of detention mean that health problems, particularly TB, are widespread. In 2006, the former head of the prison system confirmed that more than 70 inmates had died since the introduction of the moratorium, the majority from TB, other illnesses associated with harsh prison conditions and suicide (Abdymen 2007; Amnesty International 2006; International Crisis Group 2006). The lack of adequate medical care in prison facilities has led Akin Toktaliev, Chairman of the Committee for the Protection of the Dignity and Honour of the Kyrgyz Nation to conclude that 'instead of keeping them [prisoners] in such unacceptable conditions, it would be more humane if they were sent to death' (Abdymen 2007, 1).

The effects of long-term imprisonment

Life imprisonment and long-term sentences can have a profound social and psychological impact on prisoners, as the United Nations Crime Prevention and Criminal Justice Branch has noted: 'Prisoners sentenced to life imprisonment may suffer from psychological and sociological problems that may cause de-socialisation and dependence, which are harmful to the health of the individual prisoner' (UNCPCJB 1994, 20).[20] It adds that these problems are particularly compounded by the indeterminate nature of some life and long-term sentences, as the uncertainty of release makes it difficult for prisoners to envision a future outside the prison environment:

> The lifer, though he may know the average sentence, can never count on release until it is actually granted. This uncertainty weighs heavily on lifers, for in some cases the whole of their future lives are at risk from moment to moment; they can never know that they have not condemned themselves to a vastly extended term in prison because of one momentary aberration (UNCPCJB 1994, 20, citing Sapsford, R).

The prolonged deprivation of liberty and curtailment of basic rights can lead to numerous ill-effects, including increased social isolation, de-socialisation, the loss of personal responsibility, an identity crisis and an increased dependency on the penal institution. Stress and anxiety is caused by the removal of normal patterns of social interaction and prisoners' powerlessness to provide support to others. They are not only deprived of access to their families and bringing up their children, but also the opportunity of having children. The loss of responsibility and the increased dependence that results from prolonged detention can hamper efforts at rehabilitation and reintegration into society. Negative coping mechanisms can result in emotional or situational withdrawal (UNCPCJB 1994).

The long term effects of imprisonment recently led hundreds of prisoners serving life sentences in Italy to call for the re-introduction of the death penalty. In May 2007, more than 300 life sentence prisoners signed a letter to the President requesting that their sentences be changed to death sentences on the grounds that they are 'tired of dying a little every day' (Fraser 2007).[21] In Azerbaijan, life-sentenced prisoners in Qobustan prison launched a hunger strike in June 2007 following the failure of the authorities to review their sentences and improve conditions of detention. This is the fifth hunger strike organised in Qobustan prison since 1999 (International Federation for Human Rights 2007). In extreme cases, prolonged and indefinite imprisonment has been attributed as a cause of prison suicide. A review conducted by the Chief Inspector of Prisons in England and Wales found that life-sentenced prisoners were disproportionately represented among cases of prison suicides: although accounting for six per cent of the prison population, they accounted for 20 per cent of suicides (Prison Reform Trust 2004). The Prison Reform Trust found that the risk of suicide in England and Wales was

---

20 The United Nations Crime Prevention and Criminal Justice Branch (UNCPCJB) has since become the United Nations Office for Drugs and Crime (UNODC).

21 Italy currently has a lifer population of approximately 1300, more than 200 of whom have served sentences of more than 20 years. Under Italian legislation they can obtain the right to brief periods of release after serving 10 years and conditional release after serving 26 years of good conduct (Ibid.).

twice as high as the average prisoner population: between 1998 and 2001, 80 life-sentence prisoners took their own lives (Prison Reform Trust 2004).

The increased length of prison sentences, in particular life imprisonment without parole, is contributing to an ageing prison population. In 2002, US state and federal prisons held 121,000 prisoners aged 50 or over, more than double the figure a decade earlier. In the state of Texas alone it is estimated that by 2008 there will be more than 10,000 prisoners over the age of 55 (Mauer *et al.* 2004). Although this is a relatively recent trend, an ageing prison population poses significant challenges for the care and treatment of offenders, particularly for those who require specialist medical treatment on a long-term basis.

International standards relating to life imprisonment

The only human rights treaty standards that refer specifically to life imprisonment concern the use of life imprisonment without the possibility of release. Article 37 of the *UN Convention of the Rights of the Child* prohibits life imprisonment without the possibility of parole for offences committed by people below the age of 18 as it states '[n]either capital punishment nor life imprisonment without possibility of release shall be imposed for offences committed by persons below eighteen years of age'.[22] Although there are no universal provisions to prohibit the sentencing of life imprisonment without the possibility of parole to adult offenders, measures contained in the *Rome Statute of the International Criminal Court* ensure that life imprisonment without parole is not available to the court as a punishment for the gravest crimes: war crimes, crimes against humanity and genocide. Article 110(3) of the statute provides that sentences of life imprisonment, which is the maximum sentence available to the court, must be reviewed after 25 years:

> When the person has served two-thirds of the sentence, or 25 years in the case of life imprisonment, the Court shall review the sentence to determine whether it should be reduced. Such a review shall not be conducted before that time.

Other treaty standards related to life imprisonment concern the extent to which life imprisonment constitutes a loss of dignity or amounts to inhuman or degrading treatment. Article 10(1) of the *International Covenant on Civil and Political Rights* states, '[a]ll deprived of their liberty shall be treated with humanity and with respect for the inherent dignity of the human person'. National courts, such as the Mexican Supreme Court and the German Federal Constitutional Court, have ruled, for instance, that sentencing without the possibility of release is an affront to human dignity.[23] Similarly, the European Court of Human Rights has

---

22 The Convention has been ratified by all but two countries: Somalia and the US.

23 The German Federal Constitutional Court held in 1977 that life imprisonment could only be compatible with human dignity if there was a concrete and realisable expectation of

considered whether lifelong sentences could amount to a violation of the *European Convention on Human Rights*, article 3 (prohibiting cruel and inhuman treatment or punishment). In the case of *Einhorn v. France*[24] the Court's judgement of 16 October 2001 stated that it, 'does not rule out the possibility that the imposition of an irreducible life sentence may raise an issue under Article 3 of the Convention'. It additionally stated:

> It is not to be excluded that the extradition of an individual to a State in which he runs the risk of being sentenced to life without the possibility of early release may raise an issue under Article 3 of the Convention (para. 27).

In 1976, a report produced by a Council of Europe sub-committee on the treatment of long-term prisoners concluded:

> It is inhuman to imprison a person for life without any hope of release. A crime prevention policy which accepts keeping a prisoner for life even if he is no longer a danger to society would be compatible neither with modern principles on the treatment of prisoners during the execution of their sentence now with the idea of the reintegration of offenders into society (Council of Europe 1977, 22).

The extent to which life imprisonment, particularly life imprisonment without the possibility of release, undermines the rehabilitative purpose of imprisonment is also subject to debate. Article 10(3) of the *International Covenant on Civil and Political Rights* states: 'The penitentiary system shall comprise treatment of prisoners the essential aim of which shall be their reformation and social rehabilitation'. However, the removal of the possibility of release necessarily removes the recognition of the potential for rehabilitation or reform, resulting in efforts directed towards such an end being largely fruitless.

The case of *Léger v. France*

One of the most prominent test cases on the application of human rights law to the execution of life sentences is that of *Léger v. France,* which was admitted to the European Court of Human Rights in 2004.[25] The case concerns the continued detention of the applicant, Lucien Léger, who was sentenced to life imprisonment in May 1966 following his conviction for the abduction and murder of 11-year-

---

being released. 'The essence of human dignity is attacked if the prisoner, notwithstanding his personal development, must abandon any hope of ever regaining his freedom' (van Zyl Smit 2005, 20).

24 *Einhorn v. France* (application 71555/01) 16 October 2001.

25 *Léger v. France (application no. 19324/02) Judgement*, Strasbourg, 11 April 2006.

old Luc Taron in July 1964. In spite of numerous applications for release, Léger was not granted release on licence until 2005, at which point he had served more than 40 years in prison. The applicant alleged that his continued detention as a result of his life sentence was arbitrary, in breach of article 5 1(a) of the *European Convention of Human Rights*, and constituted inhuman and degrading treatment, a breach of article 3.

Léger became eligible for release in July 1979, after serving 15 years in prison, and subsequently made several applications for release including nine applications for release on licence.[26] He also made several applications for release on presidential pardon, the last being in 1998. All the applications were refused. In 1999, Léger made a further application for release on licence, which received a positive response from the sentencing board. An expert report produced on the request of the board concluded that 'there do not currently seem to be any formal obstacles to his release' (para. 22). In 2000, the judge responsible for the execution of sentences gave the following opinion:

> After almost 35 years in prison it is appropriate to review his situation and thus assess the purpose of his sentence. Releasing him on licence would enable him to undergo compulsory medical and psychological treatment and to regain his liberty within a clearly defined framework, unlike an individual pardon (para. 23).

In spite of this, the Minister of Justice refused the application. Subsequent reforms to the post-sentencing system resulted in the case being referred to the newly created parole courts.[27] In 2001, the sentence enforcement board issued a unanimous opinion in favour of Léger's release. However, the regional parole court denied the application on the grounds that Léger continued to deny his responsibility for the crime and was not making serious efforts to readjust to society.[28] The decision was upheld by the national parole court following an appeal in the same year. In 2004, an application for the commutation of Léger's sentence was refused on the grounds that a fresh psychiatric report could not conclude 'with absolute certainty' that he would not pose a significant danger to the community.

The final application for Léger's release was made in 2005. A judgement made in July the same year supported his release on licence with effect from October 2005 until October 2015. The court concluded that 'Refusing his application for release on licence would amount to his virtually permanent exclusion from society,

26 Léger's applications for release on licence were made in 1985, 1988, 1990, 1991, 1992, 1993, 1994, 1995 and 1997 (paragraph 19).

27 Reforms to the post-sentencing system as part of Law no. 2000-516 of 15 June 2000 included removing the Minister of Justice's powers and replacing them with an adversarial judicial procedure, and broadening the conditions for release on licence.

28 Although Léger confessed to the abduction and murder within his first month in police custody, he retracted the confession 10 months later and has protested his innocence ever since.

which does not seem justified in view of his resettlement plan and the limited nature of the risk of his re-offending'.

The applicant's submission to the Court contended that whilst his initial detention was lawful, it had become arbitrary over time and no longer had a sufficient link with his initial conviction. He referred in particular to the refusal by the courts to release him on licence in 2001 on the grounds that he would not confess to the crime. The applicant asserted that his continued detention was no longer based on considerations of dangerousness but rather on political expediency – a move that had resulted in him serving a sentence that was unparalleled in France.

In 2006 the European Court of Human Rights concluded that the detention of Léger had not resulted in the violation of either article 5 1(a) or article 3 of the Convention.[29] In response to the alleged violation of article 5, the Court observed that although no minimum term had been set within the applicant's sentence, the continued detention of the applicant had been based on factors relating to risk and dangerousness. It therefore concluded that the detention remained lawful since it never lost its connection with the initial purpose of imprisonment. In response to the alleged violation of article 3, the Court took the view that the applicant had not been serving an irreducible life sentence, either *de jure* or *de facto*, since he had been given the opportunity to apply for release at regular intervals since 1979. On this basis, the Court was unable to conclude that the continued detention of the applicant amounted to inhuman or degrading treatment.

The case of *Léger v. France* raises some interesting questions about the application of international human rights standards to life- and long-term imprisonment, notably in relation to arbitrary detention and inhuman and degrading treatment. As the Court pointed out in its assessment, once the punitive element of a sentence has been carried out, the grounds for continued detention must be based upon considerations of risk and dangerousness; any other grounds for continued detention would necessarily carry the risk of arbitrariness. However, it should equally follow that an uncritical appraisal of how risk and dangerousness are precisely defined and assessed can similarly open the door to indefinite and arbitrary detention. In the case of Léger, for example, the grounds on which his release was refused in 2001 were based on an expert report which stated that it could not conclude 'with absolute certainty' that the applicant would not pose a significant danger in the community. The presence of 'zero risk' set an almost unachievable, nigh impossible, precondition for his release. As one of the dissenting judges, Judge Mularoni, noted, 'Making the application of measures to adjust sentences on a zero risk of reoffending would in practice mean almost never granting parole'. Similarly, Judge Costa concluded, 'In my opinion there is unfortunately no such thing as zero risk, but if we take that approach, then we should never release prisoners on licence: life sentences would always be served

29 The Court held by five votes to two that there had been no violation of article 5 1(a) of the Convention, and five votes to two that there had been no violation of article 3 of the Convention.

for a whole life term and determinate sentences would always be served in full' (paragraph 13).

In the same 2001 court ruling, it was also noted that the applicant continued to deny the crime and refused to undergo counselling. From this it was determined that the applicant was not making 'serious efforts to readjust to society', thereby failing to meet the criteria for parole as defined by article 729 of the *Criminal Procedural Code*. This was in spite of the fact that the prison reports described the applicant as a 'model prisoner' and that evidence of a social resettlement plan in the form of accommodation and employment had been repeatedly provided to the courts. The alleged failure of the applicant to make serious efforts to readjust to society not only raises questions about what standards of proof are required, but also how such efforts have a bearing on the potential risk and danger they may pose within the community on release. In contesting the decision of the Court, Judge Fura-Sandström argued that the acknowledgment of the offence as a pre-condition for social rehabilitation was problematic and should not be a major consideration once the punitive element of a sentence has been satisfied; the lack of employment prospects similarly did not provide sufficient grounds to refuse release on licence.[30]

The argument that the applicant's detention became arbitrary over time is strengthened further when taking into account that the rulings made in 2001 and 2005 were made by the same court with the same evidence, yet reached such diametrically opposed views. It illustrates that whilst a discretionary system of parole allows an individualised and flexible approach to be applied to each case, the lack of formal assessment criteria can engender a highly subjective – and indeed political – process. One potential outcome of this is the excessive and arbitrary use of detention. The issue of subjectivity in turn raises fundamental questions about the authority of expert assessments – not only in terms of how they conducted and how experts are selected, but also in terms of how the assessments are analysed and interpreted by the authorities.

In relation to life and long-term sentences amounting to inhuman or degrading treatment, the Court noted that circumstances in which a sentence might raise an issue under article 3 would include not being given hope of entitlement to a measure such as parole. However, it can be equally argued that the length of incarceration itself can amount to inhuman or degrading treatment. As Judge Fura-Sandström notes, whilst the purpose of imprisonment is two-fold – the exclusion

30 All the applications for release over the 17-year period were supported by the Bernhard family's repeated offers of accommodation and employment in their family bakery. In 2001, the National Parole Court upheld the decision of the Regional Parole court to refuse conditional release because it was concerned that Leger's social resettlement plan had been brought into doubt because Mr Bernhard had since made a file of bankruptcy. (The bakery had in fact been sold to a private company founded by his children and continued to be registered at the same address. The offers of accommodation and employment still remained in place and the family had attested to this during the proceedings.)

of offenders and their reintegration into society – 'these factors are not sufficient, however, to persuade me that continued detention beyond a certain period does not raise an issue in terms of fundamental rights' (para. 14). The judge cites in particular a UK parliamentary debate on the death penalty dating back to 1964 during which the following was stated:

> Generally speaking, experience shows that nine years, ten years, or thereabouts is the maximum period of confinement that normal human beings can undergo without their personality decaying, their will going, and their becoming progressively less able to re-enter society and look after themselves and become useful citizens (same paragraph).

In the case of *Léger v. France,* the right to conditional release was not in question. However, what has been brought into doubt is the manner of its implementation: notably, the lack of clear and objective criteria with which to assess risk and dangerousness, as well as whether the applicant was eligible for release. As a result, the applicant was mercy to political judgements and the unattainable expectation of zero risk. It will be interesting to see how the Grand Chamber reaches its decision when the case comes to appeal and whether consideration will be given to the dissenting opinions of judges Costa, Mularoni and Fura-Sandström, along with previous judgements such as *Einhorn v. France.*

Implementing life imprisonment as an alternative to the death penalty

Although any sanction of imprisonment necessarily carries a punitive element, the ultimate purpose and justification of depriving an individual of their liberty is to protect society. In some cases, the crimes committed are so heinous that long periods of incarceration are necessary to ensure this purpose is fulfilled. Yet, at all times, the total length of incarceration should be determined in the end by the threat that the individual poses to society. This is reiterated by the Council of Europe's *Resolution (76)2 on the treatment of long-term prisoners* (adopted by the Committee of Ministers on 17 February 1976), which recommends that member states 'pursue a criminal policy under which long-term sentences are imposed *only if they are necessary for the protection of society*' (Council of Europe 1976, 1, emphasis added).

When a state deprives an individual of their liberty they have a positive obligation to ensure that their rights are protected; their humanity and inherent dignity must always be recognised. Although international human rights standards provide the framework through which *all* prisoners should be treated – irrespective of the sentence they are serving – special measures are required that recognise the unique experience of life and long term imprisonment. This is not only to counteract the negative impact of long, and often indeterminate, periods of detention, but also to address the diversity of problems that are at the root of an individual's criminal behaviour. The Council of Europe's *Recommendations*

(2003)23 on the management by prison administrations of life-sentence and other long-term prisoners (adopted by the Committee of Ministers on 9 October 2003) place particular emphasis, for example, on ensuring that those serving long prison terms are given opportunities to maintain contact with the outside world. Measures can involve ensuring prisoners are allocated to prisons as close as possible to their families or close relatives through to maximising contact by letter, telephone and visits. Taken further, this can involve encouraging prisoners to work outside the prison environment or being granted periods of leave from prison.[31] The recommendations also emphasise the need for prison life to be organised as closely as possible to the realities of life in the community, and for prisoners to be given opportunities to exercise responsibility in daily prison life. Combined, these measures could help ensure that prisoners are able to lead a law abiding and self-supporting life on their return to society.

Central to the management of life sentence prisoners should be the assurance they do not receive discriminatory treatment. This is of particular relevance concerning their security classification and conditions of detention. The Council of Europe Resolution (76)2 for instance recommends that member states should, '[a]pply stringent measures of security only in those places where genuinely dangerous prisoners are detained' (Council of Europe 1976, 1). Not all life sentence prisoners, however, are dangerous or pose a threat to other prisoners, staff or indeed themselves. As such, stringent security measures should not be applied automatically to life sentence prisoners, but be based on individual assessments of risk. In the same way, life sentence prisoners do not need to be separated from other categories of prisoner. One of the core principles endorsed in the Council of Europe Recommendations 2003(23) states 'Consideration should be given to not segregating life-sentence and other long-term prisoners on the sole ground of their sentence' (Council of Europe 2003a, 5).

Prison administrations should at all times recognise the diverse profile of offenders serving life sentences. This not only requires an individualised approach to sentence planning and rehabilitation, but also recognising the needs of special categories of prisoner, such as the elderly, the terminally ill, mothers and children, as well as those being required to spend the rest of their natural life in prison.[32]

If a prisoner continues to serve a prison term while no longer posing a threat to society, their continued detention can become arbitrary and amount to inhuman and degrading treatment. As such, all prisoners should have the right to have their sentences reviewed with the aim of implementing conditional release.[33] This should be regardless of the offence they have committed. Principle 4(a) of the

31 See, for example, articles 7 and 8 of the *Council of Europe Resolution (76)2 on the treatment of long-term prisoners.*

32 For discussion of the needs of special categories of life-sentence and long-terms prisoners (see Council of Europe 2003a, 34–37).

33 Conditional release is defined here as the early release of sentenced prisoners under individualised post-release conditions. This does not include amnesties or pardons.

Council of Europe *Recommendations 2003(22) on conditional release* (adopted by the Committee of Ministers on 24 September 2003) supports this view:

> In order to reduce the harmful effects of imprisonment and to promote the resettlement of prisoners under conditions that seek to guarantee safety of the outside community, the law should make conditional release available to all sentenced prisoners, *including life-sentence prisoners* (Council of Europe 2003b, 2, emphasis added).

Principle 6 additionally states, 'The minimum or fixed period should not be so long that the purpose of conditional release cannot be achieved' (Council of Europe 2003b, 2). As with their initial detention, the criteria for assessing conditional release of a prisoner should be based on considerations of the risk and dangerousness: the Council of Europe *Resolution (76)2*, for example, states that 'considerations of general crime prevention alone should not justify refusal of conditional release'. Adherence to these recommendations will not only militate against the practice of arbitrary detention, but will also ensure that the essential aim of imprisonment – that of reformation and social rehabilitation – is respected and remains the central focus of the implementation of a life or long-term sentence.[34] To support the implementation of conditional release, life sentence prisoners should have their sentences reviewed after a specified period and then repeated at regular intervals. Articles 9 and 12 of Council of Europe Resolution (76)2, specifically recommend the following:

> 9. Ensure that the cases of all prisoners will be examined as early as possible to determine whether or not conditional release can be granted;
>
> ...
>
> 12. Ensure that a review, as referred to in 9, of the life sentence should take place, if not done before, after eight to fourteen years of detention and be repeated at regular intervals.

It should be noted that in determining the period after which sentences should be reviewed, the *Rome Statute*, which determines sentencing practices for the gravest crimes, requires that life sentences are reviewed after 25 years.

Additionally, prisoners should be informed at the start of their sentence when they will become eligible for release and the criteria that will be applied to determine their release (within discretionary release systems) or when they become entitled for release by virtue of having served a fixed period or proportion of a sentence (within mandatory release systems).

---

34 This supports article 10(3) of the *International Covenant on Civil and Political Rights*, which states, 'the penitentiary system shall comprise the treatment of prisoners the essential aim of which shall be their reformation and social rehabilitation'.

Penal Reform International's work on life imprisonment and the death penalty

Penal Reform International (PRI) is an international non-governmental organisation promoting penal reform worldwide. Working in partnership with governments and civil society, PRI advocates for and supports the practical implementation of prison and penal reform in accordance with international human rights standards. A cornerstone of this work is advocating for the abolition of the death penalty and the introduction of humane alternative sanctions.

In Central Asia PRI has developed recommendations for the governments of Kazakhstan and Kyrgyzstan on the introduction of life (and fixed long-term imprisonment as alternative sanctions to the death penalty) legislation which was passed in 2004 and 2007 respectively. It has also undertaken public information campaigns to raise awareness and support for the abolition of the death penalty and has lobbied governments to make the constitutional and legislative amendments required for full abolition. In Kyrgyzstan, PRI has organised study visits for justice officials to see the implementation of life imprisonment in the UK. It has also produced guidance on the management of life- and long-term prisoners in Kazakhstan (Penal Reform International 2000). These activities are part and parcel of a wider programme of work that supports the promotion of humane conditions of detention, the prevention of torture and ill-treatment, and an increase in the role of independent public monitoring – all of which provide a strong basis for the sustainability of penal reform in the region.

In 2007 PRI launched a cross-regional death penalty and life imprisonment programme in the Middle East and North Africa, Eastern Europe, South Caucasus and Central Asia with support from the European Commission.[35] The project aims to support governments and other stakeholders in progressing towards the abolition of the death penalty and challenging the validity of life imprisonment as an alternative sanction to the death penalty. Programmes of research, advocacy, public awareness, training and technical assistance are being coordinated across the four regions. A briefing paper on implementing life imprisonment as an alternative to the death penalty has already been produced as part of the project (Penal Reform International 2007).

In July 2007 PRI organised a regional conference in Amman, Jordan, in conjunction with the Amman Centre for Human Rights. The purpose of the conference was to raise awareness about the death penalty and its alternatives, and to develop plans for research and campaigning on the issue, taking into consideration the area's cultural, historic and religious particularities. Representatives of national coalitions against the death penalty and other civil society members from Algeria, Egypt, Jordan, Lebanon, Morocco, the Occupied Palestinian Territories, Tunisia and Yemen attended the event, which resulted in the creation of a regional coalition against the death penalty. Key objectives were established for

35 The title of the EC project is 'Global Action to Abolish the Death Penalty'.

the regional coalition, including: facilitating the exchange of expertise and good practice between the national coalitions; establishing an Arab observatory for the death penalty; developing a programme of events within the region to mark the World Day Against the Death Penalty; and extending membership of the regional coalition.[36]

PRI also worked with the World Coalition Against the Death Penalty to generate support for the draft resolution on a worldwide moratorium on executions, which was presented at the Sixty-second session of the UN General Assembly.[37] The 'Moratorium on the use of the death penalty'[38] which was passed represents an important milestone in the progress towards the worldwide abolition of the death penalty. It is within this context that work to develop appropriate alternatives to the death penalty, particularly the use of life imprisonment, will become critical.

Conclusion

Current trends in life imprisonment are part of a wider process that is resulting in the global overuse of imprisonment. As governments adopt increasingly punitive criminal justice policies using the justification of tackling heightened threats to public safety and security, more people are going to prison and staying there for longer periods. The abolition of the death penalty provides a unique opportunity for reformers to attempt to buck this trend and instigate a human rights culture within penal systems that extends beyond the recognition of the right to life, to the recognition of the inherent dignity of the person and the right to humane treatment. It provides an in-road to reinforcing the rehabilitative element of imprisonment and granting prisoners the prospect of leading a law-abiding and self-supporting life on their return to society. This is no small task. In fact, it requires a huge cultural leap for penal systems that have long been founded on the belief that taking someone's life is a justifiable form of punishment. And of course, this does not happen within a political vacuum; governments are under pressure to demonstrate that by removing the death penalty they are replacing it with an equitable form of punishment that delivers meaningful justice.

It is important to note that the question of alternatives to the death penalty – and indeed of penal reform more widely – is not just a question of human rights; it is also a question of resources. The imposition of longer prison terms, greater restrictions on the use of parole and an increase in indeterminate sentencing will not only contribute to the growth and ageing profile of prison populations, they will also, by consequence, lead to a rise in the proportion of prisoners with ongoing health and personal care needs. The financial and human resource implications of

36 For an overview of the death penalty in the Arab world and the key issues emerging from the conference see (PRI forthcoming).

37 The EU Council of Foreign Ministers agreed in June 2007 to table the resolution.

38 Moratorium on the use of the death penalty, A/C.3/62/L.29 1 November 2007.

such policies should not be underestimated. In fact, they should be integral to any review of alternative sanctions.

PRI believes that the immediate challenge is to ensure that international human rights standards provide the bedrock on which alternative sanctions to the death penalty are implemented. This approach demands the adoption of some fundamental principles within the penal system: that the ultimate purpose and justification of imprisonment is to protect society; that all prisoners should have the right to conditional release; that conditions of detention and treatment should not provide additional punishment to the deprivation of liberty; and that prisoners should not be discriminated against on the grounds of their sentence. Progress towards these ends will help ensure that those reprieved from death row are not fated to an alternative that is equivalent to or worse than their original sentence.

Bibliography

Abdymen, K. (2007), 'Central Asia: abolition close, but sceptre of death remains', *IPS News*, 24 September.

Amnesty International (AI) (2004), *Amnesty International Report 2004* (London: AI).

Amnesty International (AI) (2007), *Death Penalty: Stop the State Killings* (London: AI).

Amnesty International (AI) & Human Rights Watch (HRW) (2005), *The rest of their lives: life without parole for child offenders in the United States* (USA: AI/HRW).

Associated Press News (AP) (2007), 'Report: Less Capital Punishment in China', 8 June.

BBC News (2006), 'Drop in Lifers released on parole', 6 November.

Benitez, I. (2007), 'Inmates in limbo', *IPS News*, 18 May.

Biswas, S. and Tewary, A. (2006), 'Hope for India's Remand Prisoners', *BBC News online*, 29 June.

Brown, N. and Kandelia, S. (eds.) (2005), *Managing effective alternatives to capital punishment*, *Centre for Capital Punishment Studies Occasional Paper 3* (London: Centre for Capital Punishment Studies).

Council of Europe (1977), *Treatment of long-term prisoners* (Strasbourg: Council of Europe).

Council of Europe (ed.) (2004), *Death Penalty: beyond abolition* (Strasbourg: Council of Europe).

Council of Europe (2005), *SPACE 1: Annual penal statistics of the Council of Europe, 2004 enquiry* (Strasbourg: Council of Europe).

Council of Europe Committee of Ministers (1976) *Resolution (76)2 on the treatment of long-term prisoners* (Strasbourg: Council of Europe).

Council of Europe Committee of Ministers (2003a), *Management by prison administrations of life-sentence and other long-term prisoners: Recommendation Rec (2003) 23 and Report* (Strasbourg: Council of Europe).

Council of Europe Committee of Ministers (2003b), *Recommendations Rec (2003) 22 of the Committee of Ministers to member states on conditional release (parole)* (Strasbourg: Council of Europe).

Council of Europe Parliamentary Assembly (2007), *Honouring of obligation and commitments by Azerbaijan, Resolution 1545* (Strasbourg: Council of Europe).

Coyle, A. (2005), 'Management of long-term and life-sentenced prisoners internationally in the context of a human rights strategy' in Browne and Kandelia (eds.).

Death Penalty Information Center (2007), 'Rwanda Votes to Abolish the Death Penalty', 10 June.

European Committee on Crime Problems (2000), *Committee of experts on the management of life-sentenced and other long term prisoners: summary report* (Strasbourg: Council of Europe).

European Council of Prevention of Torture and inhuman or Degrading Treatment (2001), *11th General Report on the CPT's activities* (Strasbourg: Council of Europe).

Flanagan, T. (ed.) (1995), *Long-term Imprisonment: policy, science and correctional practice* (California: SAGE publications).

Fraser, C. (2007), 'Italy inmates seek the death penalty', *BBC News online*, 31 May.

Giffard, C. and Muntingh, L. (2006), *The effect of sentencing on the size of the South African prison population* (South Africa: Open Society Foundation).

Hands off Cain (2005), 'Russia – life imprisonment may be worse than death – church official', 25 October <http://www.handsoffcain.info/archivio_news/200510.php?iddocumento=7403088&mover=1>.

Hands off Cain (2007), 'Kazakhstan set to "virtually" abolish the death penalty', 16 May.

Human Rights in China (HRIC) (2007), 'China's death penalty reforms' in *China Rights Forum No. 2: Legal Reform and Accountability* (New York: HRIC).

Human Rights Watch (2006), *Convicted before Trial: indefinite detention under Malaysia's Emergency Ordinance* (USA: Human Rights Watch).

International Crisis Group (2006), *Kyrgyzstan's Prison System Nightmare, Asia report No. 118* (:International Crisis Group).

International Federation for Human Rights (FIDH) (2007), 'The hunger strike in Azerbaijani prison', 28 June.

International Federation for Human Rights (FIDH) & the Human Rights Center of Azerbaijan (2007), *Après l'abolition de la peine capitale, les condamnés à perpétuité en danger de mort: torture et mauvais traitement dans les prisons d'Azerbaïdjan* (Paris: FIDH).

Mauer, M. et al. (2004), *The Meaning of 'Life': long prison sentences in context* (USA: The Sentencing Project).

Newcomen, N. (2005), 'Managing the penal consequences of replacing the death penalty in Europe' in Browne, N. and Kandelia, S. (eds.).

Olori, T. (2007), 'Hope held out for death row inmates', *IPS News*, 16 April.

Penal Reform International (PRI) (2000), *Long-term and life sentence prisoners: a briefing paper prepared by the International Centre for Prison Studies, UK, on behalf of Penal Reform International, for the Government of the Republic of Kazakhstan* (London: PRI).

Penal Reform International (PRI) (2007) *Alternatives to the Death Penalty: the problems with life imprisonment, Penal Reform Briefing No.1* (London: PRI).

Penal Reform International (PRI) (forthcoming) *Studies on the Death Penalty and the Right to Life in the Arab World* (Amman: PRI).

Presidential Commission on the Reform of the Administration of Justice in Nigeria (PCRAJ) (2006), *Proposals for reform of the Administration of Justice in Nigeria* (Abuja: PCRAJ).

Prison Reform Trust (2004), 'England and Wales – Europe's Lifer Capital', March 2004.

Santos, M. (1995), 'Facing Long-term Imprisonment', in Flanagan, T. (ed.).

Schulman, L. (2007), 'Kyrgyzstan president signs legislation ending capital punishment', *Jurist Legal News and Research*, 27 June.

Toms, S. (2006), 'Philippines stops death penalty', *BBC News Online*, 24 June.

United Nations Crime Prevention and Criminal Justice Branch (1994), *Life Imprisonment* (Vienna: UNCPCJB).

Van Zyl Smit, D. (2005), 'Life Imprisonment issues in national and international law' in N Browne and S Kandelia (eds.).

Wafula, C. (2007), 'Will fate of death sentences hang in the balance again?', *The Nation*, Nairobi, 18 April.

Index